Introduction

Trager is a grill and smoker-manufacturing company that is based in Oregon and reputed for using all-natural flavored wood pellets. As far as its origins, Joe Pit boss wanted to cook a scrumptious meal for his family when he discovered that his gas grill was burned down. Therefore, the famous brand came to be after Joe built a grill with his sons.

A Pit boss grill is an outdoor charcoal grill and smoker that uses flavored wood pellets as fuel source. This makes it an eco-friendly option for cooking because it does not need gas or electricity. With this setup, you can enjoy fresh outdoor cooking using your own ingredients. It is therefore a healthier alternative because you get to control the amount of nicotine and preservatives that will go into your meal.

The company has built a good reputation by using premium-grade materials and manufacturing the product with high brewing capacity. A Pit boss grill makes it easy to smoke any type of food. The company offers options for different levels of smoking temperature, including low, medium, and high temperatures. You can find different models for smoking with different wood pellets or smoking methods. These are ideal for beginners who need to warm up before starting a meal or even experienced professionals who want to experiment with various flavors of meat.

This Pit boss Pellet Grill Review will allow you to get a clear understanding of the main features of the grill. You will know it comes with a sophisticated design and a stylish exterior that makes it look good and useful. It is portable as well. As mentioned, you can operate this grill using electricity or wood pellets, and with its high-quality construction, you are assured of its durability.

You will also be able to appreciate every feature since this smoker uses professional grade materials for construction which ensures durability in use. It can support all types of food including delicate items like fish, meat. This grill can meet any taste while ensuring that the food remains healthy.

A Pit boss grill review should also include a clear explanation of the controls and operation of the product to ensure that you understand how to use it well. You will be able to learn about its versatility and features. The choice of various settings has helped many people save money since they can control cooking times and heat levels according to their preferences. If you want your food cooked exactly right inside and out, this may be a good option for you since it comes with very high-quality design standards. Other useful features include a viewing window and temperature gauge.

This is an open-air smoker which means that food will need adequate space for smoking when cooking on lower temperatures. You can get the desired results because of the temperature control. You will always be able to keep your food safe since you do not have direct contact with the fire. There is no risk of spilling or steaming food which makes it safe to use. The smoke is unique because of its flavor and moisture content.

Traeger's patented smoker technology, called "velocity cooking", creates delicious food without burning wood chips or charcoal. As such, there is no need for chimney or charcoal starter kits when using this grill. The pellets are lit with a push-button controller which is simple to use and helps maintain your desired cooking temperature for longer than traditional grills.

Chapter 1.   <u>Grill Beef</u>

1. Bacon-Swiss Cheesesteak Meatloaf

Preparation Time: 15 minutes
Cooking Time: 2 hours
Servings: 8-10
Ingredients:

- 1 tablespoon canola oil
- 2 garlic cloves finely chopped.
- 1 medium onion finely chopped.
- 1 poblano chile, stemmed, seeded, and finely chopped.
- 2 pounds extra-lean ground beef
- 2 tablespoons Montreal steak seasoning
- 1 tablespoon A.1. Steak Sauce
- ½ pound bacon, cooked and crumbled.
- 2 cups shredded Swiss cheese.
- 1 egg, beaten.
- 2 cups breadcrumbs
- ½ cup Tiger Sauce

Directions:

1. On your stove top, heat the canola oil in a medium sauté pan over medium-high heat. Add the garlic, onion, and poblano, and sauté for 3 to 5 minutes, or until the onion is just barely translucent.
2. Supply your smoker with wood pellets and follow the manufacturer's specific start-up procedure. Preheat, with the lid closed to 225°F.
3. In a large bowl, combine the sautéed vegetables, ground beef, steak seasoning, steak sauce, bacon, Swiss cheese, egg, and breadcrumbs. Mix with your hands until well incorporated, then shape into a loaf.
4. Put the meatloaf in a cast iron skillet and place it on the grill. Insert meat thermometer inserted in the loaf reads 165°F.
5. Top with the meatloaf with the Tiger Sauce, remove from the grill, and let rest for about 10 minutes before serving.

Nutrition:
Calories: 120 Cal
Fat: 2 g
Carbohydrates: 0 g

Protein: 23 g
Fiber: 0 g

2. London Broil

Preparation Time: 20 minutes
Cooking Time: 12-16 minutes
Servings: 3-4
Ingredients:

- 1 (1½- to 2-pound) London broil or top round steak
- ¼ cup soy sauce
- 2 tablespoons white wine
- 2 tablespoons extra-virgin olive oil
- ¼ cup chopped scallions.
- 2 tablespoons packed brown sugar.
- 2 garlic cloves, minced.
- 2 teaspoons red pepper flakes
- 1 teaspoon freshly ground black pepper.

Directions:

1. Using a meat mallet, pound the steak lightly all over on both sides to break down its fibers and tenderize. You are not trying to pound down the thickness.
2. In a medium bowl, make the marinade by combining the soy sauce, white wine, olive oil, scallions, brown sugar, garlic, red pepper flakes, and black pepper.
3. Put the steak in a shallow plastic container with a lid and pour the marinade over the meat. Cover and refrigerate for 4 hours.
4. Supply your smoker with wood pellets and follow the manufacturer's specific start-up procedure. Preheat, with the lid closed to 350°F.
5. Place the steak directly on the grill, close the lid, and smoke for 6 minutes. Flip, then smoke with the lid closed for 6 to 10 minutes more, or until a meat thermometer inserted in the meat reads 130°F for medium-rare.
6. The meat's temperature will rise by about 5 degrees while it rests.

Nutrition:
Calories: 316 Cal
Fat: 3 g
Carbohydrates: 0 g

Protein: 54 g
Fiber: 0 g

3. French Onion Burgers

Preparation Time: 35 minutes
Cooking Time: 20-25 minutes
Servings: 4
Ingredients:

- 1-pound lean ground beef
- 1 tablespoon minced garlic
- 1 teaspoon Better Than Bouillon Beef Base
- 1 teaspoon dried chives
- 1 teaspoon freshly ground black pepper.
- 8 slices Gruyere cheese, divided.
- ½ cup soy sauce
- 1 tablespoon extra-virgin olive oil
- 1 teaspoon liquid smoke
- 3 medium onions, cut into thick slices (do not separate the rings)
- 1 loaf French bread cut into 8 slices.
- 4 slices provolone cheese

Directions:

1. In a large bowl, mix the ground beef, minced garlic, beef base, chives, and pepper until well blended.
2. Divide the meat mixture and shape into 8 thin burger patties.
3. Top each of 4 patties with one slice of Gruyere, then top with the remaining 4 patties to create 4 stuffed burgers.
4. Supply your smoker with wood pellets and follow the manufacturer's specific start-up procedure. Preheat, with the lid closed to 425°F.
5. Arrange the burgers directly on one side of the grill, close the lid, and smoke for 10 minutes. Flip and smoke with the lid closed for 10 to 15 minutes more, or until a meat thermometer inserted in the burgers reads 160°F. Add another Gruyere slice to the burgers during the last 5 minutes of smoking to melt.
6. Meanwhile, in a small bowl, combine the soy sauce, olive oil, and liquid smoke.
7. Arrange the onion slices on the grill and paste on both sides with the soy sauce mixture. Smoke with the lid closed for 20 minutes, flipping halfway through.
8. Lightly toast the French bread slices on the grill. Layer each of 4 slices with a burger patty, a slice of provolone cheese, and some of the smoked onions. Top each with another slice of toasted French bread. Serve immediately.

Nutrition:

Calories: 704 Cal
Fat: 43 g
Carbohydrates: 28 g

Protein: 49 g
Fiber: 2 g

4. Beef Shoulder Clod

Preparation Time: 10 minutes
Cooking Time: 12-16 hours
Servings: 16-20
Ingredients:

- ½ cup sea salt
- ½ cup freshly ground black pepper.
- 1 tablespoon red pepper flakes
- 1 tablespoon minced garlic
- 1 tablespoon cayenne pepper
- 1 tablespoon smoked paprika.
- 1 (13- to 15-pound) beef shoulder clod

Directions:

1. Combine spices.
2. Generously apply it to the beef shoulder.
3. Supply your smoker with wood pellets and follow the manufacturer's specific start-up procedure. Preheat, with the lid closed to 250°F.
4. Put the meat on the grill grate, close the lid, and smoke for 12 to 16 hours, or until a meat thermometer inserted deeply into the beef reads 195°F. You may need to cover the clod with aluminum foil toward the end of smoking to prevent overbrowning.
5. Let the meat rest and serve.

Nutrition:

Calories: 290 Cal
Fat: 22 g
Carbohydrates: 0 g

Protein: 20 g
Fiber: 0 g

5. Corned Beef and Cabbage

Preparation Time: 30 minutes
Cooking Time: 4-5 hours
Servings: 6-8
Ingredients:

- 1-gallon water
- 1 (3- to 4-pound) point cut corned beef brisket with pickling spice packet.
- 1 tablespoon freshly ground black pepper.
- 1 tablespoon garlic powder
- ½ cup molasses
- 1 teaspoon ground mustard
- 1 head green cabbage
- 4 tablespoons (½ stick) butter
- 2 tablespoons rendered bacon fat.
- 1 chicken bouillon cube, crushed.

Directions:

1. Refrigerate overnight, changing the water as often as you remember to do so—ideally, every 3 hours while you are awake—to soak out some of the curing salt initially added.
2. Supply your smoker with wood pellets and follow the manufacturer's specific start-up procedure. Preheat, with the lid closed to 275°F.
3. Remove the meat from the brining liquid, pat it dry, and generously rub with the black pepper and garlic powder.
4. Put the seasoned corned beef directly on the grill, fat-side up, close the lid, and grill for 2 hours. Remove from the grill when done.
5. In a small bowl, combine the molasses and ground mustard and pour half of this mixture into the bottom of a disposable aluminum pan.
6. Transfer the meat to the pan, fat-side up, and pour the remaining molasses mixture on top, spreading it evenly over the meat. Cover tightly with aluminum foil.
7. Transfer the pan to the grill, close the lid, and continue smoking the corned beef for 2 to 3 hours, or until a meat thermometer inserted in the thickest part reads 185°F.
8. Rest meat
9. Serve.

Nutrition:
Calories: 295 Cal
Fat: 17 g
Carbohydrates: 19 g
Protein: 18 g
Fiber: 6 g

6. Cheeseburger Hand Pies

Preparation Time: 35 minutes
Cooking Time: 10 minutes
Servings: 6
Ingredients:

- ½ pound lean ground beef
- 1 tablespoon minced onion
- 1 tablespoon steak seasoning
- 1 cup cheese
- 8 slices white American cheese, divided.
- 2 (14-ounce) refrigerated prepared pizza dough sheets, divided.
- 2 eggs
- 24 hamburger dill pickle chips
- 2 tablespoons sesame seeds
- 6 slices tomato, for garnish
- Ketchup and mustard, for serving.

Directions:

1. Supply your smoker with wood pellets and follow the manufacturer's specific start-up procedure. Preheat, with the lid closed to 325°F.
2. On your stove top, in a medium sauté pan over medium-high heat, brown the ground beef for 4 to 5 minutes, or until cooked through. Add the minced onion and steak seasoning.
3. Toss in the shredded cheese blend and 2 slices of American cheese and stir until melted and fully incorporated.
4. Remove the cheeseburger mixture from the heat and set aside.
5. Make sure the dough is well chilled for easier handling. Working quickly, roll out one prepared pizza crust on parchment paper and brush with half of the egg wash.
6. Arrange the remaining 6 slices of American cheese on the dough to outline 6 hand pies.

Nutrition:
Calories: 325 Cal
Fat: 21 g
Carbohydrates: 11 g
Protein: 23 g
Fiber: 0 g

7. Pastrami

Preparation Time: 10 minutes
Cooking Time: 4-5 hours
Servings: 12
Ingredients:

- 1-gallon water, plus ½ cup
- ½ cup packed light brown sugar.
- 1 (3- to 4-pound) point cut corned beef brisket with brine mix packet.
- 2 tablespoons freshly ground black pepper.
- ¼ cup ground coriander

Directions:

1. Cover and refrigerate overnight, changing the water as often as you remember to do so—ideally, every 3 hours while you are awake—to soak out some of the curing salt originally added.
2. Supply your smoker with wood pellets and follow the manufacturer's specific start-up procedure. Preheat, with the lid closed to 275°F.
3. In a small bowl, combine the black pepper and ground coriander to form a rub.
4. Drain the meat, pat it dry, and generously coat on all sides with the rub.
5. Place the corned beef directly on the grill, fat-side up, close the lid, and smoke for 3 hours to 3 hours 30 minutes, or until a meat thermometer inserted in the thickest part reads 175°F to 185°F.
6. Add the corned beef, cover tightly with aluminum foil, and smoke on the grill with the lid closed for an additional 30 minutes to 1 hour.
7. Remove the meat.
8. Refrigerate

Nutrition:

Calories: 123 Cal
Fat: 4 g
Carbohydrates: 3 g

Protein: 16 g
Fiber: 0 g

8. Smoked and Pulled Beef

Preparation Time: 10 Minutes
Cooking Time: 6 Hours
Servings: 6
Ingredients:

- 4 lb. beef sirloin tip roast
- 1/2 cup BBQ rub
- Two bottles of amber beer
- One bottle barbecues sauce

Directions:

1. Turn your wood pellet grill onto smoke setting, then trim excess fat from the steak.
2. Coat the steak with BBQ rub and let it smoke on the grill for 1 hour.
3. Continue cooking and flipping the steak for the next 3 hours. Transfer the steak to a braising vessel. Add the beers.
4. Braise the beef until tender, then transfer to a platter reserving 2 cups of cooking liquid.
5. Use a pair of forks to shred the beef and return it to the pan. Add the reserved liquid and barbecue sauce. Stir well and keep warm before serving.
6. Enjoy.

Nutrition:

Calories 829
Total fat 46g
Total carbs 4g

Protein 86g
Sodium: 181mg

9. Wood Pellet Smoked Beef Jerky

Preparation Time: 15 Minutes
Cooking Time: 5 Hours
Servings: 10
Ingredients:

- 3 lb. sirloin steaks sliced into 1/4-inch thickness.
- 2 cups soy sauce
- 1/2 cup brown sugar
- 1 cup pineapple juice
- 2 tbsp. sriracha
- 2 tbsp. red pepper flake
- 2 tbsp. hoisin
- 2 tbsp. onion powder
- 2 tbsp. rice wine vinegar
- 2 tbsp. garlic, minced.

Directions:
1. Mix all the fixings in a Ziplock bag.
2. Seal the bag and mix until the beef is well coated.
3. Put the bag in the fridge overnight to let marinate. Remove the bag from the fridge 1 hour before cooking.
4. Startup your wood pallet grill and set it to smoke setting. You need to layout the meat on the grill with a half-inch space between them.
5. Let them cook for 5 hours while turning after every 2-1/2 hours.
6. Transfer from the grill and let cool for 30 minutes before serving.
7. Enjoy.

Nutrition:

Calories 80

Total fat 1g

Total carbs 5g

Protein 14g

Sugar 5g

Sodium: 650mg

10. Reverse Seared Flank Steak

Preparation Time: 10 Minutes
Cooking Time: 10 Minutes
Servings: 2
Ingredients:

- 1.5 lb. Flank's steak
- 1 tbsp. salt
- 1/2 onion powder
- 1/4 tbsp. garlic powder
- 1/2 black pepper coarsely ground.

Directions:
1. Preheat your wood pellet grill to 225°F.
2. In a mixing bowl, mix salt, onion powder, garlic powder, and pepper. Generously rub the steak with the mixture.
3. Place the steaks on the preheated grill, close the lid, and let the steak cook.
4. Crank up the grill to high, then let it heat. The steak should be off the grill and tented with foil to keep it warm.
5. Once the grill is heated up to 450°F, place the steak back and grill for 3 minutes per side.
6. Remove from heat, pat with butter, and serve. Enjoy.

Nutrition:

Calories 112

Total fat 5g

Total carbs 1g

Protein 16g

Sodium: 737mg

11. Smoked Midnight Brisket

Preparation Time: 15 Minutes
Cooking Time: 12 Minutes
Servings: 6
Ingredients:

- 1 tbsp. Worcestershire sauce
- 1 tbsp. Pit boss beef Rub
- 1 tbsp. Pit boss Chicken rub
- 1 tbsp. Pit boss Blackened Saskatchewan rub
- 5 lb. flat cut brisket
- 1 cup beef broth

Directions:
1. Rub the sauce and rubs in a mixing bowl, then rub the mixture on the meat.
2. Preheat your grill to 180°F with the lid closed for 15 minutes. You can use super smoke if you desire.
3. Place the meat on the grill and grill for 6 hours or until the internal temperature reaches 160°F.
4. Remove the meat from the grill and double wrap it with foil.
5. Add beef broth and return to grill, with the temperature increased to 225°F. Cook for 4 hours or until the internal temperature reaches 204°F.
6. Remove from grill and let rest for 30 minutes. Serve and enjoy with your favorite BBQ sauce.

Nutrition:

Calories 200

Total fat 14g

Total carbs 3g

Protein 14g

Sodium: 680mg

12. Cocoa Crusted Grilled Flank Steak

Preparation Time: 15 Minutes
Cooking Time: 6 Minutes
Servings: 7
Ingredients:

- 1 tbsp. cocoa powder
- 2 tbsp. chili powder
- 1 tbsp. chipotle chili powder
- 1/2 tbsp. garlic powder
- 1/2 tbsp. onion powder
- 1-1/2 tbsp. brown sugar
- 1 tbsp. cumin
- 1 tbsp. smoked paprika.
- 1 tbsp. kosher salt
- 1/2 tbsp. black pepper
- Olive oil
- 4 lb. Flank steak

Directions:

1. Whisk together cocoa, chili powder, garlic powder, onion powder, sugar, cumin, paprika, salt, and pepper in a mixing bowl.
2. Drizzle the steak with oil, then rub with the cocoa mixture on both sides.
3. Preheat your wood pellet grill for 15 minutes with the lid closed.
4. Cook the meat on the grill grate for 5 minutes or until the internal temperature reaches 135°F.
5. Remove the meat from the grill and cool for 15 minutes to allow the juices to redistribute.
6. Slice the meat against the grain and on a sharp diagonal.
7. Serve and enjoy.

Nutrition:

Calories 420
Total fat 26g
Total carbs 21g
Protein 3g

Sugar 7g,
Fiber 8g
Sodium: 2410mg

13. Wood Pellet Grill Prime Rib Roast

Preparation Time: 5 Minutes
Cooking Time: 4 Hours
Servings: 10
Ingredients:

- 7 lb. bone prime rib roast
- Pit boss prime rib rub

Directions:

1. Coat the roast generously with the rub, then wrap in a plastic wrap. Let sit in the fridge for 24 hours to marinate.
2. Set the temperatures to 500°F.to to preheat with the lid closed for 15 minutes.
3. Place the rib directly on the grill fat side up and cook for 30 minutes.
4. Decrease the temperature to 300°F and cook for 4 hours or until the internal temperature is 120°F- rare, 130°F-medium rare, 140°F-medium and 150°F-well done.
5. Remove from the grill and let rest for 30 minutes, then serve and enjoy.

Nutrition:

Calories 290
Total fat 23g
Total carbs 0g

Protein 19g
Sodium: 54mg
Potassium 275mg

14. Smoked Longhorn Cowboy Tri-Tip

Preparation Time: 15 Minutes
Cooking Time: 4 Hours
Servings: 7
Ingredients:

- 3 lb. tri-tip roast
- 1/8 cup coffee, ground
- 1/4 cup Pit boss beef rub

Directions:

1. Preheat the grill to 180°F with the lid closed for 15 minutes.
2. Meanwhile, rub the roast with coffee and beef rub. Place the roast on the grill grate and smoke for 3 hours.
3. Remove the roast from the grill and double wrap it with foil. Increase the temperature to 275°F.
4. Return the meat to the grill and cook for 90 minutes or until the internal temperature reaches 135°F.
5. Remove from the grill, unwrap it and let rest for 10 minutes before serving.
6. Enjoy.

Nutrition:

Calories 245

Total fat 14g

Total Carbs 0g

Protein 23g

Sodium: 80mg

15. Wood Pellet Grill Teriyaki Beef Jerky

Preparation Time: 15 Minutes

Cooking Time: 5 Hours

Servings: 10

Ingredients:

- 3 cups soy sauce
- 2 cups brown sugar
- Three garlic cloves
- 2-inch ginger knob peeled and chopped.
- 1 tbsp. sesame oil
- 4 lb. beef, skirt steak

Directions:

1. Place all the fixings except the meat in a food processor. Pulse until well mixed.
2. Trim any extra fat from the meat and slice into 1/4-inch slices. Add the steak with the marinade into a zip lock bag and let marinate for 12-24 hours in a fridge.
3. Set the wood pellet grill to smoke and let preheat for 5 minutes.
4. Arrange the steaks on the grill, leaving a space between each. Let smoke for 5 hours.
5. Remove the steak from the grill and serve when warm.

Nutrition:

Calories 80

Total fat 1g

Total Carbs 7g

Protein 11g

Sugar 6g

Sodium: 390mg

16. Grilled Butter Basted Rib-eye

Preparation Time: 20 Minutes

Cooking Time: 20 Minutes

Servings: 4

Ingredients:

- Two rib-eye steaks, bone-in
- Salt to taste
- Pepper to taste
- 4 tbsp. butter, unsalted

Directions:

1. Mix steak, salt, and pepper in a Ziplock bag. Seal the bag and mix until the beef is well coated. Ensure you get as much air as possible from the Ziplock bag.
2. Set the wood pellet grill temperature to high with a closed lid for 15 minutes. Place a cast-iron into the grill.
3. Place the steaks on the grill's hottest spot and cook for 5 minutes with the lid closed.
4. Open the lid and add butter to the skillet. When it is almost melted, place the steak on the skillet with the grilled side up.
5. Cook for 5 minutes while busting the meat with butter. Close the lid and cook until the temperature is 130°**F.**
6. Remove the steak from the skillet and let rest for 10 minutes before enjoying with the reserved butter.

Nutrition:

Calories 745

Total fat 65g

Total Carbs 5g

Net Carbs 5g

Protein 35g

17. Wood Pellet Smoked Ribeye Steaks

Preparation Time: 15 Minutes

Cooking Time: 35 Minutes

Servings: 1

Ingredients:

- 2-inch-thick ribeye steaks
- Steak rub of choice

Directions:

1. Preheat your pellet grill to low smoke.
2. Sprinkle the steak with your favorite steak rub and place it on the grill. Let it smoke for 25 minutes.
3. Remove the steak from the grill and set the temperature to 400°**F.**
4. Return the steak to the grill and sear it for 5 minutes on each side.
5. Cook until the desired temperature is achieved; 125°F-rare, 145°F-Medium, and 165°F.-Well done.
6. Wrap the steak with foil and let rest for 10 minutes before serving. Enjoy.

Nutrition:
Calories 225
Total fat 10.4g
Total Carbs 0.2g

Protein 32.5g
Sodium: 63mg,
Potassium 463mg

18. Smoked Trip Tip with Java Chophouse

Preparation Time: 10 Minutes
Cooking Time: 90 Minutes
Servings: 4
Ingredients:

- 2 tbsp. olive oil
- 2 tbsp. java chophouse seasoning
- 3 lb. trip tip roast, fat cap, and silver skin removed.

Directions:

1. Startup your wood pellet grill and smoker and set the temperature to 225°F.
2. Rub the roast with olive oil and seasoning, then place it on the smoker rack.
3. Smoke until the internal temperature is 140°F.
4. Remove the tri-tip from the smoker and let rest for 10 minutes before serving. Enjoy.

Nutrition:
Calories 270
Total fat 7g
Total Carbs 0g

Protein 23g
Sodium: 47mg
Potassium 289mg

19. Supper Beef Roast

Preparation Time: 5 Minutes
Cooking Time: 3 Hours
Servings: 7
Ingredients:

- 3-1/2 beef top round
- 3 tbsp. vegetable oil
- Prime rib rub
- 2 cups beef broth
- One russet potato peeled and sliced.
- Two carrots peeled and sliced.
- Two celery stalks, chopped.
- One onion, sliced.
- Two thyme sprigs

Directions:

1. Rub the roast with vegetable oil and place it on the roasting fat side up. Season with prime rib rub, then pours the beef broth.
2. Set the temperature to 500°F and preheat the wood pellet grill for 15 minutes with the lid closed.
3. Cook for 30 minutes or until the roast is well seared.
4. Reduce temperature to 225°F. Add the veggies and thyme and cover with foil. Cook for three more hours or until the internal temperature reaches 135°F.
5. Remove from the grill and let rest for 10 minutes. Slice against the grain and serve with vegetables and the pan drippings.
6. Enjoy.

Nutrition:
Calories 697
Total fat 10g
Total Carbs 127g
Protein 34g

Sugar 14g
Fiber 22g
Sodium: 3466mg
Potassium 2329mg

20. Wood Pellet Grill Deli-Style Roast Beef

Preparation Time: 15 Minutes
Cooking Time: 4 Hours
Servings: 2
Ingredients:

- 4lb round-bottomed roast
- 1 tbsp. coconut oil
- 1/4 tbsp. garlic powder
- 1/4 tbsp. onion powder
- 1/4 tbsp. thyme
- 1/4 tbsp. oregano
- 1/2 tbsp. paprika
- 1/2 tbsp. salt
- 1/2 tbsp. black pepper

Directions:

1. Combine all the dry hubs to get a dry rub.
2. Roll the roast in oil, then coat with the rub.
3. Set your grill to 185°F and place the roast on the grill.
4. Smoke for 4 hours or until the internal temperature reaches 140°F.
5. Remove the roast from the grill and let rest for 10 minutes.
6. Slice thinly and serve.

Nutrition:

Calories 90
Total fat 3g
Total Carbs 0g
Protein 14g
Sodium: 420mg

Chapter 2. Pork recipe

21. Maple Baby Backs

Preparation Time: 25 minutes
Cooking Time: 4 hours
Servings: 4-6
Ingredients:

- 2 (2- or 3-pound) racks baby back ribs
- 2 tablespoons yellow mustard
- 1 batch Sweet Brown Sugar Rub
- ½ cup plus 2 tablespoons maple syrup, divided.
- 2 tablespoons light brown sugar
- 1 cup Pepsi or other non-diet cola
- ¼ cup Bill's Best BBQ Sauce

Directions:

1. Supply your smoker with wood pellets and follow the manufacturer's specific start-up procedure. Preheat the grill.
2. Eradicate the membrane. This can be done by cutting just through the membrane in an X pattern and working a paper towel between the membrane and the ribs to pull it off.
3. Coat the ribs on both sides with mustard and season them with the rub. Rub into meat.
4. Grill ribs and smoke for 3 hours.
5. Remove grill and place bone-side up, on enough aluminum foil to wrap the ribs completely. Add maple syrup over the ribs and sprinkle them with 1 tablespoon of brown sugar. Flip the ribs and repeat the maple syrup and brown sugar application on the meat side.
6. Increase the grill's temperature to 300°F.
7. Fold in three sides of the foil around the ribs and add the cola. Fold in the last side, completely enclosing the ribs and liquid. Place ribs back to the grill for 30 to 45 minutes.
8. Remove the ribs from the grill and unwrap them from the foil.
9. In a small bowl, stir together the barbecue sauce and remaining 6 tablespoons of maple syrup. Use this to baste the ribs. Return the ribs to the grill, without the foil, and cook for 15 minutes to caramelize the sauce.
10. Cut into individual ribs and serve immediately.

Nutrition:

Calories: 330 Cal
Fat: 24 g
Carbohydrates: 11 g
Protein: 17 g
Fiber: 0 g

22. Simple Smoked Baby Backs

Preparation Time: 25 minutes
Cooking Time: 4-6 hours
Servings: 4-8
Ingredients:

- 2 (2- or 3-pound) racks baby back ribs
- 2 tablespoons yellow mustard
- 1 batch Not-Just-for-Pork Rub

Directions:

1. Supply your smoker with wood pellets and follow the manufacturer's specific start-up procedure. Preheat grill.
2. Eradicate the membrane from the backside of the ribs. This can be done by cutting just through the membrane in an X pattern and working a paper towel between the membrane and the ribs to pull it off.
3. Coat the ribs on both sides with mustard and season them with the rub. Work rubs onto meat.
4. Smoke until their internal temperature reaches between 190°F and 200°F.
5. Remove the racks from the grill and cut into individual ribs. Serve immediately.

Nutrition:

Calories: 245 Cal
Fat: 12 g
Carbohydrates: 10 g
Protein: 22 g
Fiber: 0 g

23. Sweet Smoked Country Ribs

Preparation Time: 25 minutes
Cooking Time: 4 hours
Servings: 2-4
Ingredients:

- 2 pounds country-style ribs
- 1 batch Sweet Brown Sugar Rub
- 2 tablespoons light brown sugar
- 1 cup Pepsi or other cola
- ¼ cup Bill's Best BBQ Sauce

Directions:

1. Supply your smoker with wood pellets and follow the manufacturer's specific start-up procedure. With the lid closed, preheat the grill until the temperature is 180 degrees.
2. Sprinkle the ribs with the rub and use your hands to work the rub into the meat.
3. Place the ribs directly on the grill grate and smoke for 3 hours.
4. Remove the ribs from the grill and place them on enough aluminum foil to wrap them completely. Dust the brown sugar over the ribs.
5. Increase the grill's temperature to 300°F.
6. Fold in three sides of the foil around the ribs and add the cola. Fold in the last side, completely enclosing the ribs and liquid. Return the ribs to the grill and cook for 45 minutes.
7. Remove the ribs from the foil and place them on the grill grate. Baste all sides of the ribs with barbecue sauce. Cook for 15 minutes more to caramelize the sauce.
8. Remove the ribs from the grill and serve immediately.

Nutrition:
Calories: 230 Cal
Fat: 17 g
Carbohydrates: 0 g
Protein: 20 g
Fiber: 0 g

24. Classic Pulled Pork

Preparation Time: 15 minutes
Cooking Time: 16-20 hours
Servings: 8-12
Ingredients:

- 1 (6- to 8-pound) bone-in pork shoulder
- 2 tablespoons yellow mustard
- 1 batch Not-Just-for-Pork Rub

Directions:

1. Supply your smoker with wood pellets and follow the manufacturer's specific start-up procedure.
2. Coat the pork shoulder all over with mustard and season it with the rub.
3. Place the shoulder on the grill grate and smoke until its internal temperature reaches 195°F.
4. Pull the shoulder from the grill and wrap it completely in aluminum foil or butcher paper. Place it in a cooler, cover the cooler, and let it rest for 1 or 2 hours.
5. Remove the pork shoulder from the cooler and unwrap it. Remove the shoulder bone and pull the pork apart using just your fingers. Serve immediately as desired. Leftovers are encouraged.

Nutrition:
Calories: 414 Cal
Fat: 29 g
Carbohydrates: 1 g
Protein: 38 g
Fiber: 0 g

25. Maple-Smoked Pork Chops

Preparation Time: 10 minutes
Cooking Time: 55 minutes
Servings: 4
Ingredients:

- 4 (8-ounce) pork chops, bone-in or boneless (I use boneless)
- Salt
- Freshly ground black pepper

Directions:

1. Supply your smoker with wood pellets and follow the manufacturer's specific start-up procedure.
2. Drizzle pork chop with salt and pepper to season.
3. Place the chops directly on the grill grate and smoke for 30 minutes.

4. Increase the grill's temperature to 350°F. Continue to cook the chops until their internal temperature reaches 145°F.
5. Remove the pork chops from the grill and let them rest for 5 minutes before serving.

Nutrition:

Calories: 130 Cal

Fat: 12 g

Carbohydrates: 3 g

Protein: 20 g

Fiber: 0 g

26. Apple-Smoked Pork Tenderloin

Preparation Time: 15 minutes
Cooking Time: 4-5 hours
Servings: 4-6
Ingredients:

- 2 (1-pound) pork tenderloins
- 1 batch Not-Just-for-Pork Rub

Directions:
1. Supply your smoker with wood pellets and follow the manufacturer's specific start-up procedure. Preheat the grill.
2. Generously season the tenderloins with the rub. W
3. Put tenderloins on the grill and smoke for 4 or 5 hours, until their internal temperature reaches 145°F.
4. The tenderloins must be put out of the grill and let it rest for 5-10 minutes then begin slicing into thin pieces before serving.

Nutrition:

Calories: 180 Cal

Fat: 8 g

Carbohydrates: 3 g

Protein: 24 g

Fiber: 0 g

27. Barbecued Tenderloin

Preparation Time: 5 minutes
Cooking Time: 30 minutes
Servings: 4-6
Ingredients:

- 2 (1-pound) pork tenderloins
- 1 batch Sweet and Spicy Cinnamon Rub

Directions:
1. Supply your smoker with wood pellets and follow the manufacturer's specific start-up procedure. Preheat the grill.
2. Generously season the tenderloins with the rub. Work rubs onto meat.
3. Place the tenderloins and smoke internal temperature reaches 145°F.
4. As you put out the tenderloins from the grill, let it cool down for 5-10 minutes before slicing it up and serving it.

Nutrition:

Calories: 186 Cal

Fat: 4 g

Carbohydrates: 8 g

Protein: 29 g

Fiber: 1 g

28. Lovable Pork Belly

Preparation Time: 15 Minutes
Cooking Time: 4 Hours and 30 Minutes
Servings: 4
Ingredients:

- 5 pounds of pork belly
- 1 cup dry rub
- Three tablespoons olive oil

For Sauce
- Two tablespoons honey
- Three tablespoons butter
- 1 cup BBQ sauce

Directions:
1. Take your drip pan and add water. Cover with aluminum foil.
2. Pre-heat your smoker to 250 degrees F
3. Add pork cubes, dry rub, olive oil into a bowl and mix well.
4. Use water fill water pan halfway through and place it over drip pan.
5. Add wood chips to the side tray.

6. Transfer pork cubes to your smoker and smoke for 3 hours (covered)
7. Remove pork cubes from the smoker and transfer to foil pan, add honey, butter, BBQ sauce, and stir.
8. Cover the pan with foil and move back to a smoker, smoke for 90 minutes more.
9. Remove foil and smoke for 15 minutes more until the sauce thickens.
10. Serve and enjoy!

Nutrition:

Calories: 1164

Fat: 68g

Carbohydrates: 12g

Protein: 104g

29. County Ribs

Preparation Time: 15 Minutes
Cooking Time: 3 Hours
Servings: 4
Ingredients:

- 4 pounds country-style ribs
- Pork rubs to taste.
- 2 cups apple juice
- ½ stick butter, melted.
- 18 ounces BBQ sauce

Directions:

1. Take your drip pan and add water. Cover with aluminum foil.
2. Pre-heat your smoker to 275 degrees F
3. Season country style ribs from all sides
4. Use water fill water pan halfway through and place it over drip pan.
5. Add wood chips to the side tray.
6. Transfer the ribs to your smoker and smoke for 1 hour and 15 minutes until the internal temperature reaches 160 degrees F.
7. Take foil pan and mix melted butter, apple juice, 15 ounces BBQ sauce and put ribs back in the pan, cover with foil.
8. Transfer back to smoker and smoke for 1 hour 15 minutes more until the internal temperature reaches 195 degrees F.
9. Take ribs out from liquid and place them on racks, glaze ribs with more BBQ sauce, and smoke for 10 minutes more.
10. Take them out and let them rest for 10 minutes, serve, and enjoy!

Nutrition:

Calories: 251

Fat: 25g

Carbohydrates: 35g

Protein: 76g

30. Wow-Pork Tenderloin

Preparation Time: 15 Minutes
Cooking Time: 3 Hours
Servings: 4
Ingredients:

- One pork tenderloin
- ¼ cup BBQ sauce
- Three tablespoons dry rub

Directions:

1. Take your drip pan and add water. Cover with aluminum foil.
2. Pre-heat your smoker to 225 degrees F
3. Rub the spice blend all finished the pork tenderloin.
4. Use water fill water pan halfway through and place it over drip pan.
5. Add wood chips to the side tray.
6. Transfer pork meat to your smoker and smoke for 3 hours until the internal temperature reaches 145 degrees F.
7. Brush the BBQ sauce over pork and let it rest.
8. Serve and enjoy!

Nutrition:

Calories: 405

Fat: 9g

Carbohydrates: 15g

Protein: 59g

31.Awesome Pork Shoulder

Preparation Time: 15 Minutes + 24 Hours
Cooking Time: 12 Hours
Servings: 4
Ingredients:

- 8 pounds of pork shoulder

For Rub

- One teaspoon dry mustard
- One teaspoon black pepper
- One teaspoon cumin
- One teaspoon oregano
- One teaspoon cayenne pepper

- 1/3 cup salt
- ¼ cup garlic powder
- ½ cup paprika
- 1/3 cup brown sugar
- 2/3 cup sugar

Directions:

1. Bring your pork under salted water for 18 hours.
2. Pull the pork out from the brine and let it sit for 1 hour.
3. Rub mustard all over the pork.
4. Take a bowl and mix all rub ingredients. Rub mixture all over the meat.
5. Wrap meat and leave it overnight.
6. Take your drip pan and add water. Cover with aluminum foil. Pre-heat your smoker to 250 degrees F
7. Use water fill water pan halfway through and place it over drip pan. Add wood chips to the side tray.
8. Transfer meat to smoker and smoke for 6 hours
9. Take the pork out and wrap in foil, smoke for 6 hours more at 195 degrees F.
10. Shred and serve.
11. Enjoy!

Nutrition:
Calories: 965
Fat: 65g
Carbohydrates: 19g
Protein: 71g

32.Herbed Prime Rib

Preparation Time: 15 Minutes
Cooking Time: 4 Hours
Servings: 4
Ingredients:

- 5 pounds prime rib
- Two tablespoons black pepper
- ¼ cup olive oil
- Two tablespoons salt

Herb Paste

- ¼ cup olive oil

- One tablespoon fresh sage
- One tablespoon fresh thyme
- One tablespoon fresh rosemary
- Three garlic cloves

Directions:

1. Take a blender and add herbs, blend until thoroughly combined.
2. Take your drip pan and add water. Cover with aluminum foil.
3. Pre-heat your smoker to 225 degrees F
4. Use water fill water pan halfway through and place it over drip pan.
5. Add wood chips to the side tray.
6. Coat rib with olive oil and season it well with salt and pepper
7. Transfer seasoned rib to your smoker and smoke for 4 hours.
8. Remove rib from the smoker and keep it on the side. Let it cool for 30 minutes.
9. Cut into slices and serve.
10. Enjoy!

Nutrition:
Calories: 936
Fat: 81g
Carbohydrates: 2g
Protein: 46g

33. Premium Sausage Hash

Preparation Time: 30 Minutes
Cooking Time: 45 Minutes
Servings: 4
Ingredients:

- Nonstick cooking spray
- Two finely minced garlic cloves
- One teaspoon basil, dried
- One teaspoon oregano, dried
- One teaspoon onion powder
- One teaspoon of salt
- 4-6 cooked smoker Italian Sausage (Sliced)
- One large-sized bell pepper, diced.
- One large onion, diced.
- Three potatoes cut into 1-inch cubes.
- Three tablespoons of olive oil
- French bread for serving.

Directions:

1. Pre-heat your smoker to 225 degrees Fahrenheit using your desired wood chips.
2. Cover the smoker grill rack with foil and coat with cooking spray.
3. Take a small bowl and add garlic, oregano, basil, onion powder, and season the mix with salt and pepper.
4. Take a large bowl and add sausage slices, bell pepper, potatoes, onion, olive oil, and spice mix.
5. Mix well and spread the mixture on your foil-covered rack.
6. Place the rack in your smoker and smoke for 45 minutes.
7. Serve with your French bread.
8. Enjoy!

Nutrition:

Calories: 193

Carbs: 15g

Fats: 10g

Fiber: 2g

34. Explosive Smoky Bacon

Preparation Time: 20 Minutes
Cooking Time: 2 Hours and 10 Minutes
Servings: 10
Ingredients:

- 1-pound thick cut bacon
- One tablespoon BBQ spice rub
- 2 pounds bulk pork sausage
- 1 cup cheddar cheese, shredded.
- Four garlic cloves, minced.
- 18 ounces BBQ sauce

Directions:

1. Take your drip pan and add water, cover with aluminum foil.
2. Pre-heat your smoker to 225 degrees F
3. Use water fill water pan halfway through and place it over drip pan.
4. Add wood chips to the side tray.
5. Reserve about ½ a pound of your bacon for cooking later
6. Lay 2 strips of your remaining bacon on a clean surface in an X formation.
7. Alternate the horizontal and vertical bacon strips by waving them tightly in an over and under to create a lattice-like pattern.
8. Sprinkle one teaspoon of BBQ rub over the woven bacon
9. Arrange ½ a pound of your bacon in a large-sized skillet and cook them for 10 minutes over medium-high heat.
10. Drain the cooked slices on a kitchen towel and crumble them.
11. Place your sausages in a large-sized re-sealable bag.
12. While the sausages are still in the bag, roll them out to a square that has the same sized as the woven bacon.
13. Cut off the bag from the sausage and arrange them sausage over the woven bacon.
14. Toss away the bag.
15. Sprinkle some crumbled bacon, green onions, cheddar cheese, and garlic over the rolled sausages.
16. Pour about ¾ bottle of your BBQ sauce over the sausage and season with some more BBQ rub.
17. Roll up the woven bacon tightly all around the sausage, forming a loaf.
18. Cook the bacon-sausage loaf in your smoker for about one and a ½ hour.
19. Brush up the woven bacon with remaining BBQ sauce and keep smoking for about 30 minutes until the center of the loaf is no longer pink.
20. Use an instant thermometer to check if the internal temperature is at least 165 degrees Fahrenheit.
21. If yes, then take it out and let it rest for 30 minutes.
22. Slice and serve!

Nutrition:

Calories: 507

Fats: 36g

Carbs: 20g

Fiber: 2g

35. Alabama Pulled Pig Pork

Preparation Time: 1 Hour

Cooking Time: 12 Hours

Servings: 8

Ingredients:

- 2 cups of soy sauce
- 1 cup of Worcestershire sauce
- 1 cup of cranberry grape juice
- 1 cup of teriyaki sauce
- One tablespoon of hot pepper sauce
- Two tablespoons of steak sauce
- 1 cup of light brown sugar
- ½ a teaspoon of ground black pepper
- 2 pound of flank steak cut up into ¼ inch slices.

Directions:

1. Take a non-reactive saucepan and add cider, salt, vinegar, brown sugar, cayenne pepper, black pepper, and butter.
2. Bring the mix to a boil over medium-high heat.
3. Add in water and return the mixture to a boil.
4. Carefully rub the pork with the sauce
5. Take your drip pan and add water. Cover with aluminum foil.
6. Pre-heat your smoker to 225 degrees F
7. Use water fill water pan halfway through and place it over drip pan.
8. Add wood chips to the side tray.
9. Smoke meat for about 6-10 hours. Make sure to keep basting it with the sauce every hour or so.
10. After the first smoking is done, take an aluminum foil and wrap up the meat forming a watertight seal.
11. Place the meat in the middle of your foil and bring the edges to the top, cupping up the meat complete.
12. Pour 1 cup of sauce over the beef and tight it up.
13. Place the package back into your smoker and smoke for 2 hours until the meat quickly pulls off from the bone.
14. Once done, remove it from the smoker and pull off the pork, discarding the bone and fat
15. Place the meat chunks in a pan and pour 1 cup of sauce for every4 pound of meat.
16. Heat until simmering and serve immediately!

Nutrition:

Calories: 1098

Fats: 86g

Carbs: 38g

Fiber: 3g

Chapter 3. Grill Lamb Recipes

36. Grilled Lamb Burgers

Preparation Time: 10 minutes
Cooking Time: 15 minutes
Servings: 5
Ingredients:

- 1 1/4 pounds of ground lamb.
- 1 egg.
- 1 teaspoon of dried oregano.
- 1 teaspoon of dry sherry.
- 1 teaspoon of white wine vinegar.
- 4 minced cloves of garlic.
- Red pepper
- 1/2 cup of chopped green onions.
- 1 tablespoon of chopped mint.
- 2 tablespoons of chopped cilantro.
- 2 tablespoons of dry breadcrumbs.
- 1/8 teaspoon of salt to taste.
- 1/4 teaspoon of ground black pepper to taste.
- 5 hamburger buns.

Directions:

1. Preheat a Wood Pellet Smoker or Grill to 350-450 degrees F then grease it grates.
2. Using a large mixing bowl, add in all the ingredients on the list aside from the buns then mix properly to combine with clean hands.
3. Make about five patties out of the mixture then set aside.
4. Place the lamb patties on the preheated grill and cook for about seven to nine minutes turning only once until an inserted thermometer reads 160 degrees F.
5. Serve the lamb burgers on the hamburger, add your favorite toppings, and enjoy.

Nutrition:

Calories: 376 Cal
Fat: 18.5 g
Carbohydrates: 25.4 g

Protein: 25.5 g
Fiber: 1.6 g

37. Grilled Lamb Sandwiches

Preparation Time: 5 minutes
Cooking Time: 50 minutes
Servings: 6
Ingredients:

- 1 (4 pounds) boneless lamb.
- 1 cup of raspberry vinegar.
- 2 tablespoons of olive oil.
- 1 tablespoon of chopped fresh thyme.
- 2 pressed garlic cloves.
- 1/4 teaspoon of salt to taste.
- 1/4 teaspoon of ground pepper.
- Sliced bread.

Directions:

1. Using a large mixing bowl, add in the raspberry vinegar, oil, and thyme then mix properly to combine. Add in the lamb, toss to combine then let it sit in the refrigerator for about eight hours or overnight.
2. Next, discard the marinade the season the lamb with salt and pepper to taste. Preheat a Wood Pellet Smoker and grill to 400-500 degrees F, add in the seasoned lamb and grill for about thirty to forty minutes until it attains a temperature of 150 degrees F.
3. Once cooked, let the lamb cool for a few minutes, slice as desired then serve on the bread with your favorite topping.

Nutrition:

Calories: 407 Cal
Fat: 23 g
Carbohydrates: 26 g

Protein: 72 g
Fiber: 2.3 g

38. Lamb Chops

Preparation Time: 10 minutes
Cooking Time: 12 minutes
Servings: 6
Ingredients:

- 6 (6-ounce) lamb chops
- 3 tablespoons olive oil
- Ground black pepper

Directions:

1. Preheat the pallet grill to 450 degrees F.

2. Coat the lamb chops with oil and then, season with salt and black pepper evenly.
3. Arrange the chops in pallet grill grate and cook for about 4-6 minutes per side.

Nutrition:

Calories: 376 Cal

Fat: 19.5 g

Carbohydrates: 0 g

Protein: 47.8 g

Fiber: 0 g

39. Lamb Ribs Rack

Preparation Time: 10 minutes
Cooking Time: 2 hours
Servings: 2
Ingredients:

- 2 tablespoons fresh sage
- 2 tablespoons fresh rosemary
- 2 tablespoons fresh thyme
- 2 peeled garlic cloves
- 1 tablespoon honey
- Black pepper
- ¼ cup olive oil
- 1 (1½-pound) trimmed rack lamb ribs.

Directions:

1. Combine all ingredients.
2. While motor is running, slowly add oil and pulse till a smooth paste is formed.
3. Coat the rib rack with paste generously and refrigerate for about 2 hours.
4. Preheat the pallet grill to 225 degrees F.
5. Arrange the rib rack in pallet grill and cook for about 2 hours.
6. Remove the rib rack from pallet grill and transfer onto a cutting board for about 10-15 minutes before slicing.
7. With a sharp knife, cut the rib rack into equal sized individual ribs and serve.

Nutrition:

Calories: 826 Cal

Fat: 44.1 g

Carbohydrates: 5.4 g

Protein: 96.3 g

Fiber: 1 g

40. Lamb Shank

Preparation Time: 10 minutes
Cooking Time: 4 hours
Servings: 6
Ingredients:

- 8-ounce red wine
- 2-ounce whiskey
- 2 tablespoons minced fresh rosemary.
- 1 tablespoon minced garlic
- Black pepper
- 6 (1¼-pound) lamb shanks

Directions:

1. In a bowl, add all ingredients except lamb shank and mix till well combined.
2. In a large resealable bag, add marinade and lamb shank.
3. Seal the bag and shake to coat completely.
4. Refrigerate for about 24 hours.
5. Preheat the pallet grill to 225 degrees F.
6. Arrange the leg of lamb in pallet grill and cook for about 4 hours.

Nutrition:

Calories: 1507 Cal

Fat: 62 g

Carbohydrates: 68.7 g

Protein: 163.3 g

Fiber: 6 g

41. Leg of a Lamb

Preparation Time: 10 minutes
Cooking Time: 2 hours and 30 minutes
Servings: 10
Ingredients:

- 1 (8-ounce) package softened cream cheese.
- ¼ cup cooked and crumbled bacon.
- 1 seeded and chopped jalapeño pepper.
- 1 tablespoon crushed dried rosemary.
- 2 teaspoons garlic powder
- 1 teaspoon onion powder
- 1 teaspoon paprika
- 1 teaspoon cayenne pepper
- Salt, to taste
- 1 (4-5-pound) butterflied leg of lamb
- 2-3 tablespoons olive oil

Directions:
1. For filling in a bowl, add all ingredients and mix till well combined.
2. For spice mixture in another small bowl, mix all ingredients.
3. Place the leg of lamb onto a smooth surface. Sprinkle the inside of leg with some spice mixture.
4. Place filling mixture over the inside surface evenly. Roll the leg of lamb tightly and with a butcher's twine, tie the roll to secure the filling.
5. Coat the outer side of roll with olive oil evenly and then sprinkle with spice mixture.
6. Preheat the pallet grill to 225-240 degrees F.
7. Arrange the leg of lamb in pallet grill and cook for about 2-2½ hours. Remove the leg of lamb from pallet grill and transfer onto a cutting board.
8. With a piece of foil, cover leg loosely and transfer onto a cutting board for about 20-25 minutes before slicing.
9. With a sharp knife, cut the leg of lamb in desired sized slices and serve.

Nutrition:
Calories: 715 Cal
Fat: 38.9 g
Carbohydrates: 2.2 g
Protein: 84.6 g
Fiber: 0.1 g

42. Lamb Breast

Preparation Time: 10 minutes
Cooking Time: 2 hours and 40 minutes
Servings: 2
Ingredients:
- 1 (2-pound) trimmed bone-in lamb breast.
- ½ cup white vinegar
- ¼ cup yellow mustard
- ½ cup BBQ rub

Directions:
1. Preheat the pallet grill to 225 degrees F.
2. Rinse the lamb breast with vinegar evenly.
3. Coat lamb breast with mustard and the season with BBQ rub evenly.
4. Arrange lamb breast in pallet grill and cook for about 2-2½ hours.
5. Remove the lamb breast from the pallet grill and transfer onto a cutting board for about 10 minutes before slicing.
6. With a sharp knife, cut the lamb breast in desired sized slices and serve.

Nutrition:
Calories: 877 Cal
Fat: 34.5 g
Carbohydrates: 2.2 g
Protein: 128.7 g
Fiber: 0 g

43. Lamb Shoulder Chops

Preparation Time: 4 hours
Cooking Time: 25-30 minutes
Servings: 4
Ingredients:
- 4 lamb shoulder chops
- 4 cups buttermilk
- 1 cup cold water
- ¼ cup kosher salt
- 2 tablespoons olive oil
- 1 tablespoon Texas style rub

Directions:
1. In a large bowl, add buttermilk, water and salt and stir till salt is dissolved.
2. Add chops and coat with mixture evenly.
3. Refrigerate for at least 4 hours. Remove the chops from bowl and rinse under cold water.
4. Coat the chops with olive oil and then sprinkle with rub evenly. Preheat the pallet grill to 240 degrees F.
5. Arrange the chops in pallet grill grate and cook for about 25-30 minute or till desired doneness.
6. Meanwhile preheat the broiler of oven.
7. Cook the chops under broiler till browned.

Nutrition:
Calories: 328 Cal
Fat: 18.2 g
Carbohydrates: 11.7 g
Protein: 30.1 g
Fiber: 0 g

44. Lamb Skewers

Preparation Time: 5 minutes
Cooking Time: 8-12 minutes
Servings: 6
Ingredients:

- One lemon, juiced.
- Two crushed garlic cloves
- Two chopped red onions
- One t. chopped thyme.
- Pepper
- Salt
- One t. oregano
- 1/3 c. oil
- ½ t. cumin
- Two pounds cubed lamb leg

Directions:

1. Refrigerate the chunked lamb.
2. The remaining ingredients should be mixed. Add in the meat. Refrigerate overnight.
3. Pat the meat dry and thread onto some metal or wooden skewers. Wooden skewers should be soaked in water.
4. Add wood pellets to your smoker and follow your cooker's startup procedure. Preheat your smoker, with your lid closed, until it reaches 450.
5. Grill, covered, for 4-6 minutes on each side.
6. Serve.

Nutrition:
Calories: 201 Cal
Fat: 9 g
Carbohydrates: 3 g
Protein: 24 g
Fiber: 1 g

45. Brown Sugar Lamb Chops

Preparation Time: 2 hours
Cooking Time: 10-15 minutes
Servings: 4
Ingredients:

- Pepper
- One t. garlic powder
- Salt
- Two t. tarragon
- One t. cinnamon
- ¼ c. brown sugar
- 4 lamb chops
- Two t. ginger

Directions:

1. Combine the salt, garlic powder, pepper, cinnamon, tarragon, ginger, and sugar. Coat the lamb chops in the mixture and chill for two hours.
2. Add wood pellets to your smoker and follow your cooker's startup procedure. Preheat your smoker, with your lid closed, until it reaches 450.
3. Place the chops on the grill, cover, and smoke for 10-15 minutes per side.
4. Serve.

Nutrition:
Calories: 210 Cal
Fat: 11 g
Carbohydrates: 3 g
Protein: 25 g
Fiber: 1 g

46. Pit boss Crown Rack of Lamb

Preparation Time: 30 Minutes
Cooking Time: 30 Minutes
Servings: 6
Ingredients:

- Two racks of lamb. Frenched
- 1 tbsp. garlic, crushed.
- 1 tbsp. rosemary
- 1/2 cup olive oil
- Kitchen twine

Directions:

1. Preheat your Pit boss to 450ºF.
2. Rinse the lab with clean cold water, then pat it dry with a paper towel.
3. Lay the lamb even on a chopping board and score a ¼ inch down between the bones. Repeat the process between the bones on each lamb rack. Set aside.

4. In a small mixing bowl, combine garlic, rosemary, and oil. Brush the lamb rack generously with the mixture.
5. Bend the lamb rack into a semicircle, then place the racks together such that the bones will be up and will form a crown shape.
6. Wrap around four times, starting from the base moving upward. Tie tightly to keep the racks together.
7. Place the lambs on a baking sheet and set in the Traeger. Cook on high heat for 10 minutes. Reduce the temperature to 300OF and cook for 20 more minutes or until the internal temperature reaches 130OF.
8. Remove the lamb rack from the Pit boss and let rest while wrapped in a foil for 15 minutes.
9. Serve when hot.

Nutrition:

Calories 390

Total fat 35g

Total carbs 0g

Protein 17g

Sodium 65mg

47.Pit boss Smoked Leg.

Preparation Time: 15 Minutes
Cooking Time: 3 Hours
Servings: 6
Ingredients:
- One leg of lamb, boneless
- 2 tbsp. oil
- Four garlic cloves, minced.
- 2 tbsp. oregano
- 1 tbsp. thyme
- 2 tbsp. salt
- 1 tbsp. black pepper freshly ground.

Directions:
1. Trim excess fat from the lamb, ensuring you keep the meat in an even thickness for even cooking.
2. In a mixing bowl, mix oil, garlic, and all spices. Rub the mixture all over the lamb, then cover with a plastic wrap.
3. Place the lamb in a fridge and let marinate for an hour.
4. Transfer the lamb on a smoker rack and set the Pit boss to smoke at 250OF.
5. Smoke the meat for 4 hours or until the internal temperature reaches 145OF.
6. Remove from the Pit boss and serve immediately.

Nutrition:

Calories 356

Total fat 16g

Total carbs 3g

Protein 49g

Sugars 1g

Fiber 1g

Sodium 2474mg

48.Pit boss Grilled Aussie Leg of Lamb

Preparation Time: 30 Minutes
Cooking Time: 2 Hours
Servings: 8
Ingredients:
- 5 lb. Aussie Boneless Leg of lamb

Smoked Paprika Rub
- 1 tbsp. raw sugar
- 1 tbsp. salt
- 1 tbsp. black pepper
- 1 tbsp. smoked paprika.
- 1 tbsp. garlic powder
- 1 tbsp. rosemary

- 1 tbsp. onion powder
- 1 tbsp. cumin
- 1/2 tbsp. cayenne pepper

Roasted Carrots
- One bunch of rainbow carrots
- Olive oil
- Salt and pepper

Directions:
1. Preheat your Pit boss to 350OF and trim any excess fat from the meat.
2. Combine the paprika rub ingredients and generously rub all over the meat.
3. Place the lamb on the preheated Pit boss over indirect heat and smoke for 2 hours.
4. Meanwhile, toss the carrots in oil, salt, and pepper.
5. Add the carrots to the grill after 1 ½ hour or until the internal temperature has reached 90OF.
6. Cook until the internal meat temperature reaches 135OF.
7. Remove the lamb from the Pit boss and cover it with foil for 30 minutes.
8. Once the carrots are cooked, serve with the meat and enjoy it.

Nutrition:

Calories 257
Total fat 8g
Total carbs 6g
Protein 37g

Sugars 3g
Fiber 1g
Sodium 431mg
Potassium 666mg

49. Simple Pit boss Grilled Lamb Chops

Preparation Time: 10 Minutes
Cooking Time: 20 Minutes
Servings: 6
Ingredients:

- 1/4 cup white vinegar, distilled.
- 2 tbsp. olive oil
- 2 tbsp. salt
- 1/2 tbsp. black pepper
- 1 tbsp. minced garlic
- One onion thinly sliced.
- 2 lb. lamb chops

Directions:

1. In a resealable bag, mix vinegar, oil, salt, black pepper, garlic, and sliced onions until all salt has dissolved.
2. Add the lamb and toss until evenly coated. Place in a fridge to marinate for 2 hours.
3. Preheat your Traeger.
4. Remove the lamb from the resealable bag and leave any onion that is stuck on the meat. Use an aluminum foil to cover any exposed bone ends.
5. Grill until the desired doneness is achieved. Serve and enjoy when hot.

Nutrition:

Calories 519
Total fat 44.8g
Total carbs 2.3g
Protein 25g

Sugars 0.8g
Fiber 0.4g
Sodium 861mg
Potassium 358.6mg

50. Pit boss Grilled Lamb with Sugar Glaze

Preparation Time: 15 Minutes
Cooking Time: 20 Minutes
Servings: 4
Ingredients:

- 1/4 cup sugar
- 2 tbsp. ground ginger
- 2 tbsp. dried tarragon
- 1/2 tbsp. salt
- 1 tbsp. black pepper, ground
- 1 tbsp. ground cinnamon
- 1 tbsp. garlic powder
- Four lamb chops

Directions:

1. In a mixing bowl, mix sugar, ground ginger, tarragon, salt, pepper, cinnamon, and garlic.
2. Rub the lamb chops with the mixture and refrigerate for an hour.
3. Meanwhile, preheat your Traeger.
4. Brush the grill grates with oil and place the marinated lamb chops on it—Cook for 5 minutes on each side.
5. Serve and enjoy.

Nutrition:

Calories 241
Total fat 13.1g
Total carbs 15.8g
Protein 14.6g

Sugars 13.6g
Fiber 0.7g
Sodium 339.2mg
Potassium 256.7mg

51. Pit boss Grilled Leg of Lamb Steak

Preparation Time: 10 Minutes
Cooking Time: 10 Minutes
Servings: 4
Ingredients:

- 4 reaches lamb steaks, bone-in
- 1/4 cup olive oil
- Four garlic cloves, minced.
- 1 tbsp. rosemary freshly chopped.
- Salt and pepper to taste

Directions:

1. Arrange the steak in a dish in a single layer. Cover the meat with oil, garlic, fresh rosemary, salt, and pepper.

2. Flip the meat to coat on all sides and let it marinate for 30 minutes.
3. Preheat your Pit boss and lightly oil the grates. Cook the meat on the grill until well browned on both sides, and the internal temperature reaches 140oF.
4. Serve and enjoy.

Nutrition:

Calories 327.3

Total fat 21.9g

Total carbs 1.7g

Protein 29.6g

Sugars 0.1g

Fiber 0.2g

Sodium 112.1mg

Potassium 409.8mg

52. Pit boss Garlic Rack Lamb

Preparation Time: 45 Minutes
Cooking Time: 3 Hours
Servings: 4
Ingredients:

- Lamb Rack
- Basil – 1 teaspoon
- Oregano – 1 teaspoon
- Peppermill – 10 cranks
- Marsala wine – 3 oz.
- Cram Sherry – 3 oz.
- Olive oil
- Madeira wine – 3 oz.
- Balsamic vinegar – 3 oz.
- Rosemary – 1 teaspoon

Directions:

1. Add all the ingredients into a zip bag the mix well to form an emulsion.
2. Place the rack lamb into the bag the release all the air as you rub the marinade all over the lamb.
3. Let it stay in the bag for about 45 minutes.
4. Get the wood pellet grill preheated to 2500F, then cook the lamb for 3 hours as you turn on both sides.
5. Ensure that the internal temperature is at 1650F before removing from the grill.
6. Allow to cool for a few minutes, then serve and enjoy.

Nutrition:

Calories: 291 Cal

Protein: 26 g

Fat: 21 g

53. Pit boss Braised Lamb Shank

Preparation Time: 20 Minutes
Cooking Time: 4 Hours
Servings: 6
Ingredients:

- Lamb shanks – 4
- Olive oil as required.
- Beef broth – 1 cup
- Red wine – 1 cup
- Fresh thyme and sprigs – 4

Directions:

1. Season lamb shanks with prime rib rub, then allow resting.
2. Get the wood pellet grill temperature set to high, then cook the lamb shanks for about 30 minutes.
3. Place the shanks directly on the grill grate, then cook for another 20 minutes until browned on the outside.
4. Transfer the cooked lamb shanks into a Dutch oven, then pour beef broth, the herbs, and wine. Cover it with a fitting lid, then place it back on the grill grate and allow it to cook at a reduced temperature of 3250F.
5. Brace the lamb shanks for about 3 hours or until the internal temperature gets to 1800F.
6. Remove the lid once ready, then serve on a platter together with the accumulated juices and enjoy.

Nutrition:

Calories: 312 Cal

Protein: 27 g

Fat: 24 g

54. Simple Grilled Lamb Chops

Preparation Time: 10 minutes
Cooking Time: 6 minutes
Servings: 6
Ingredients:

- 1/4 cup distilled white vinegar.
- 2 tbsp. salt
- 1/2 tbsp. black pepper
- 1 tbsp. garlic, minced.
- 1 onion thinly sliced.
- 2 tbsp. olive oil
- 2 lb. lamb chops

Intolerances:
- Gluten-Free
- Egg-Free
- Lactose-Free

Directions:
1. In a resealable bag, mix vinegar, salt, black pepper, garlic, sliced onion, and oil until all salt has dissolved.
2. Add the lamb chops and toss until well coated. Place in the fridge to marinate for 2 hours.
3. Preheat the wood pellet grill to high heat.
4. Remove the lamb from the fridge and discard the marinade. Wrap any exposed bones with foil.
5. Grill the lamb for 3 minutes per side. You can also broil in a broiler for more crispness.
6. Serve and enjoy.

Nutrition:

Calories: 519   Carbs: 2g

Fat: 45g   Protein: 25g

55. Spicy Chinese Cumin Lamb Skewers

Preparation Time: 20 minutes
Cooking Time: 6 minutes
Servings: 10
Ingredients:
- 1 lb. lamb shoulder cut into 1/2-inch pieces.
- 10 skewers
- 2 tbsp. ground cumin

- 2 tbsp. red pepper flakes
- 1 tbsp. salt

Intolerances:
- Gluten-Free
- Egg-Free

- Lactose-Free

Directions:
1. Thread the lamb pieces onto skewers.
2. Preheat the wood pellet grill to medium heat and lightly oil the grill grate.
3. Place the skewers on the grill grate and cook while turning occasionally. Sprinkle cumin, pepper flakes, and salt every time you turn the skewer.
4. Cook for 6 minutes or until nicely browned. Serve and enjoy.

Nutrition: Calories: 77 Fat: 5g Carbs: 2g Protein: 6g

56. Garlic and Rosemary Grilled Lamb Chops

Preparation Time: 10 minutes
Cooking Time: 20 minutes
Servings: 4
Ingredients:
- 2 lb. lamb loin, thick cut
- 4 garlic cloves, minced.
- 1 tbsp. rosemary leaves, fresh chopped
- 1 tbsp. kosher salt

- 1/2 tbsp. black pepper
- 1 lemon zest
- 1/4 cup olive oil

Intolerances:
- Gluten-Free
- Egg-Free

- Lactose-Free

Directions:
1. In a small mixing bowl, mix garlic, lemon zest, oil, salt, and black pepper then pour the mixture over the lamb.
2. Flip the lamb chops to make sure they are evenly coated. Place the chops in the fridge to marinate for an hour.
3. Preheat the wood pellet grill to high heat then sear the lamb for 3 minutes on each side.
4. Reduce the heat and cook the chops for 6 minutes or until the internal temperature reaches 150 F.
5. Remove the lamb from the grill and wrap it in a foil. Let it rest for 5 minutes before serving. Enjoy.

Nutrition:

Calories: 171   Carbs: 1g

Fat: 8g   Protein: 23g

57. Grilled Leg of Lambs Steaks

Preparation Time: 10 minutes
Cooking Time: 10 minutes
Servings: 4
Ingredients:

- 4 lamb steaks, bone-in
- 1/4 cup olive oil
- 4 garlic cloves, minced.
- 1 tbsp. rosemary freshly chopped.
- Salt and black pepper

Intolerances:

- Gluten-Free
- Egg-Free
- Lactose-Free

Directions:

1. Place the lamb in a shallow dish in a single layer. Top with oil, garlic cloves, rosemary, salt, and black pepper then flip the steaks to cover on both sides.
2. Let sit for 30 minutes to marinate.
3. Preheat the wood pellet grill to high and brush the grill grate with oil.
4. Place the lamb steaks on the grill grate and cook until browned and the internal is slightly pink. The internal temperature should be 140 F.
5. Let rest for 5 minutes before serving. Enjoy.

Nutrition:
Calories: 325
Fat: 22g
Carbs: 2g
Protein: 30g

58. Grilled Lamb Loin Chops

Preparation Time: 10 minutes
Cooking Time: 10 minutes
Servings: 6
Ingredients:

- 2 tbsp. herbs de Provence
- 1-1/2 tbsp. olive oil
- 2 garlic cloves, minced.
- 2 tbsp. lemon juice
- 5 oz. lamb loin chops
- Salt and black pepper to taste

Intolerances:

- Gluten-Free
- Egg-Free
- Lactose-Free

Directions:

1. In a small mixing bowl, mix herbs de Provence, oil, garlic, and juice. Rub the mixture on the lamb chops then refrigerate for an hour.
2. Preheat the wood pellet grill to medium-high then lightly oil the grill grate.
3. Season the lamb chops with salt and black pepper.
4. Place the lamb chops on the grill and cook for 4 minutes on each side.
5. Remove the chops from the grill and place them in an aluminum covered plate. Let rest for 5 minutes before serving. Enjoy.

Nutrition:
Calories: 570
Fat: 44g
Carbs: 1g
Protein: 42g

59. Greek-Style Roast Leg of Lamb

Preparation Time: 25 Minutes
Cooking Time: 1 Hour & 35 Minutes
Servings: 12 Persons
Ingredients

- 6 tbsp. extra-virgin olive oil
- 1 Leg of lamb (6 to 7 pounds), bone-in
- Juice of 2 lemons, freshly squeezed.
- Two sprigs of fresh rosemary stem discarded stripped needles.
- One sprig of fresh oregano or 1 tsp. Dried
- Eight garlic cloves
- Freshly ground black pepper & kosher salt (coarse) as required.

Directions

1. Make a series of small slits within the meat using a sharp paring knife.
2. For herb & garlic paste: Finely mince the rosemary with oregano and garlic the use of a chef's knife on a clean, giant reducing board. Alternatively, upload these substances in a meal's processor.
3. Stuff some of the prepared paste into each of the slits on meat; ensure which you upload it into the slit the usage of any of the utensils. Next, upload the coated lamb on a rack, preferably inner a large roasting pan. For easier smooth-up, do not forget to line the pan with aluminum foil.
4. Rub the outside of meat first with the freshly squeezed lemon juice, after which olive oil. Using a plastic wrap, cowl & refrigerate overnight.
5. The next day, dispose of the meat from the refrigerator & allow sit down at room temperature for 1/2 an hour.
6. Get rid of the plastic wrap & season the beef with pepper and salt to taste. When ready, preheat the wooden pellet's grill on Smoke for four to 5 minutes, with the lid open. Set the cooking temperature to four hundred F and near the lid.
7. Roast the lamb for half an hour. Decrease the heat to 350 F & keep cooking for an hour extra until the meat's inner temperature reflects 140 F.
8. Transfer the cooked lamb to a vast, clean slicing board & allow rest for a couple of minutes then, slice diagonally into skinny slices. Serve even as nevertheless hot and enjoy.

Nutrition:

769 Calories
64g Total Fat
618mg Potassium

0.7g Total Carbohydrates
45g Protein

60. Rosemary Lamb

Preparation Time: 20 Minutes
Cooking Time: 3 Hours & 10 Minutes
Servings: 2 Persons
Ingredients

- One rack lamb, rib
- A bunch of fresh asparagus
- Two rosemary springs
- One dozen baby potato
- 2 tbsp. olive oil
- Pepper & salt to taste
- ½ cup butter

Directions

1. Preheat the grill of your wood pellet to 225 F in advance.
2. Get rid of the membrane from the ribs' backside, after which, drizzle on each side with olive oil; finally sprinkle with the rosemary.
3. Combine the butter with potatoes in a deep baking dish.
4. Place the rack of prepared ribs alongside the dish of potatoes on the grates. Smoke till the inner temperature of the meat displays a 145 degrees F for three hours. During the remaining 15 minutes of cooking, do not neglect to add asparagus to the potatoes & hold to cook until turn tender.
5. Slice the lamb into desired portions & serve with cooked asparagus and potatoes.

Nutrition:

668 Calories
57g Total Fat
665mg Potassium

17g Total Carbohydrates
2.3g Dietary Fiber
0.8g Sugars 22g Protein

61. Spice Marinated and Grilled Lamb Chops

Preparation Time: 20 Minutes
Cooking Time: 20 Minutes
Servings: 4 Persons
Ingredients

- ½ tsp. fennel seeds
- One grated Serrano chili
- One 2inch piece of ginger, finely grated.
- Four finely grated garlic cloves
- ¼ cup sour cream

- 2 tbsp. fresh lime juice
- 1 tbsp. mustard oil (optional)
- 1 tsp. dried mango powder
- 1 tsp. dried fenugreek leaves
- 1 tsp. grounded black pepper
- ½ tsp. of finely grated nutmeg
- 1 tsp. Kashmiri chili powder or paprika
- 2 tbsps. vegetable oil and more for the grill
- 12 lamb rib chops (about 2¼ pounds)
- Kosher salt mint leaves, cilantro leaves, and lemon wedges

Special Equipment
A spice mill or mortar and pestle

Directions:
1. Toast the fennel seeds in a dry little skillet over medium warmness, often shaking, for about 45 seconds, and then let it cool. Finely fall apart them with the spice mill or with mortar and pestle. Move into a huge bowl, positioned in the chili, ginger, garlic, the sour cream, lime juice, mustard oil (if utilizing), mango powder (if utilizing), fenugreek leaves, the pepper, nutmeg, 1 tsp. stew powder and 2 tbsp. of vegetable oil and blend nicely. Season the lamb chops with salt and upload to the marinade. Cover and relax for a minimum of one hour.
2. Let the lamb chops take a seat at room temperature for one hour before grilling. Set up the grill for medium heat and oil the grate. Grill the lamb for about three minutes for each side. Move onto a platter and let it rest for five to 10 minutes.
3. Top the lamb with mint, cilantro, and additional chili powder.
4. Serve it with lemon wedges.
5. Do Ahead: The lamb can be marinated 12 hours beforehand. Keep it chilled.

Nutrition:

Energy (calories): 1772 kcal

Protein: 212.17 g

Fat: 88.77 g

Carbohydrates: 21.02 g

62. Rack of Lamb

Preparation Time: 20 Minutes
Cooking Time: 1 Hour & 20 Minutes
Servings: 4 Persons
Ingredients
- A rack of lamb, preferably 4 to 5 pounds
- 1 tsp. each of pepper & salt

For Marinade
- One medium lemon
- Four garlic cloves, minced.
- 1 tsp. thyme
- ¼ cup balsamic vinegar
- 1 tsp. basil

For Glaze
- 2 tbsp. soy sauce
- ¼ cup Dijon mustard
- 2 tbsp. Worcestershire sauce
- ¼ cup dry red wine

Directions
1. Combine the whole marinade components in a gallon-sized zip-lock bag. Once done, trim the silver skin from the lamb racks and then upload the trimmed racks into the gallon bag with the marinade; blend the pieces well & refrigerate overnight.
2. The next day, preheat your wood pellet to three hundred F in advance. In the meantime, combine the entire glaze elements in a large-sized blending bowl.
3. Once the glaze is mixed, and the grill is preheated, place the lamb's rack over the recent grill. Cook them for 12 to 15 minutes and then baste with the organized glaze aggregate; flip & cook the meat until the inner temperature displays somewhere between 135 to 145 degrees F, about for an hour; do not neglect to baste the beef with the glaze after each half of an hour. Once done, eliminate the meat from the grill & let sit down for a few minutes. Once done, cut the beef into favored portions; serve warm & enjoy.

Nutrition:

788 Calories

62g Total Fat

204mg Cholesterol

630mg Sodium

755mg Potassium

49g Protein

63. Grilled Rosemary Lamb with Juicy Tomatoes

Preparation Time: 10 Minutes
Cooking Time: 40 Minutes
Servings: 6
Ingredients

- Lamb and Sauce
- 1 3–4lb of boneless lamb shoulder
- Kosher salt and grounded pepper
- Two chopped red onions
- One bunch of rosemary leaves
- One bunch of oregano leaves
- ¾ cup of red wine vinegar
- ¼ cup of extra virgin olive oil
- 1 cup plain whole-milk Greek yogurt
- ¼ cup of fresh lemon juice
- One grated garlic clove
- Tomatoes and Assembly
- Five beefsteak tomatoes (about 4 lb.)
- sea salt flakes grounded black pepper.
- 3 tbsp. of fresh lemon juice
- One halved red onion thinly sliced.
- extra virgin olive oil

Directions:

Lamb and Sauce
1. Put the lamb shoulder, cut side up, on a slicing board. Use a sharp knife to separate the beef into smaller portions along its herbal seams. You should discover yourself with five or 1/2 dozen pieces of assorted sizes. Put the lamb into a tumbler baking dish and season with salt and grounded pepper.
2. Mix the onions, rosemary leaves, and oregano leaves till finely chopped. Add the vinegar and the oil and blend till rigid purée forms. Season the marinade with salt and pepper, and then pour it over the lamb pieces. Cover and allow it to take a seat for two or three hours.
3. Mix the yogurt, the lemon juice, and garlic in a medium bowl. Put some seasonings in the sauce with salt and pepper, then cowl and relax.
4. Do Ahead: Lamb may be seasoned one day in advance and the sauce-eight hours ahead.

Tomatoes and Assembly
1. Before grilling, slice the tomatoes into ½"thick rounds and put them onto a platter. Season with salt and black pepper, then drizzle with 1/2 of the lemon juice. Add onion, season with salt and pepper, drizzle the ultimate juice over, unfold rosemary sprigs, and then be placed apart.
2. Set up the grill for medium warmness. Put the larger lamb pieces onto the grate and grill till the lowest is well brown, about five minutes. Spoon some remaining marinade over the lamb, flip and keep grilling, turning every five minutes until the lamb is roasted in spots and well browned.
3. After a quarter-hour greater or much less, upload the smaller pieces to the grill and comply with the same instructions. They take less time to cook. The instant-read thermometer inserted into the middle of every part must register a hundred and forty for large portions. Begin checking the smaller ones after 7 to 10 minutes. As every bit finish, circulate onto a platter, spreading on the rosemary. Let it rest for at least 20 or 30 minutes.
4. Move the lamb onto a reducing board and add rosemary sprigs on the perimeters of the platter. Tip the platter just so gathered tomato and lamb juices pool at one cease and spoon over the tomatoes. With a pointy knife, slice the lamb into skinny portions and add onion and tomatoes: season with salt and drizzle with oil.
5. Sprinkle with the yogurt sauce and additional virgin oil and serve.

Nutrition:

Energy (calories): 311 kcal
Protein: 36.21 g

Fat: 15.73 g
Carbohydrates: 5.88 g

64. Lamb Chops (Lollipops)

Preparation Time: 20 Minutes
Cooking Time: 55 Minutes
Servings: 4 Persons
Ingredients

- 2 tbsp. fresh sage
- One rack of lamb
- Two garlic cloves, large, roughly chopped.
- 1 tbsp. fresh thyme
- Three sprigs of fresh rosemary, approximately 2 tbsps.
- ¼ cup olive oil
- 2 tbsp. shallots roughly chopped.
- 1 tbsp. honey
- ½ teaspoon each of course ground pepper & salt

Directions
1. Using a fruitwood, preheat your smoker to 225 F in advance.

2. Trim any silver pores and skin & excess fats from the rack of lamb.
3. Thoroughly combine the leftover ingredients collectively (for the herb paste) in a food processor & liberally practice the paste over the rack of lamb.
4. Place the covered lamb at the preheated smoker & cook until the rack of lamb's internal temperature displays 120 F, for 45 minutes to 55 minutes. Remove the beef & prepare your smoker or grill for direct warmness now.
5. Cook until brown the lamb for a few minutes on every side. Let rest for five minutes, after which, slice into person lollipops; serve warm & enjoy.

Nutrition:

184 Calories

16g Total Fat

12mg of Cholesterol

75mg of Potassium

6g Total Carbohydrates

4.2g Protein

65. Seven Spice Grilled Lamb Chops with Parsley Salad

Preparation Time: 3 hours
Cooking Time: 1 hour
Servings: 6
Ingredients

- 1 cup plain whole-milk yogurt (not Greek)
- 1 tsp. grounded black pepper
- 1 tsp. ground coriander
- 1 tsp. ground cumin
- 1 tsp. paprika
- ½ tsp. ground cardamom
- ½ tsp. ground cinnamon
- ½ tsp. ground nutmeg
- 12 untrimmed lamb rib chops (about three lb.) patted dry.
- Kosher salt
- One thinly sliced small red onion.
- 1 cup coarsely chopped parsley
- 1 tbsp. of fresh lemon juice
- 2 tsp. sumac

Directions:

1. Mix the yogurt, grounded black pepper, coriander, cumin, paprika, cardamom, cinnamon, and nutmeg in a big bowl.
2. Season the two facets of lamb chops with salt and add them to the bowl with marinade. Turn lamb in marinade, cowl, and kick back for at least 3 hours and no greater than 12 hours.
3. Let the lamb sit down at room temperature for one hour earlier than grilling.
4. Set up the grill for medium-high warmness. Grill the lamb, around three minutes for each aspect, and let it rest for five or 10 minutes.
5. In the meantime, blend the onion, parsley, lemon juice, and sumac with a touch of salt in a medium bowl. Serve the lamb chops with parsley salad on top.

Nutrition:

Energy (calories): 284 kcal

Protein: 36.49 g

Fat: 12.84 g

Carbohydrates: 3.76 g

66. Loin Lamb Chops

Preparation Time: 20 Minutes
Cooking Time: 1 Hour & 20 Minutes
Servings: 6 Persons
Ingredients

- 10 to 12 Lamb loin chops
- Jeff's Original rub recipe
- Rosemary finely chopped.
- Olive oil
- Coarse kosher salt

Directions

1. Place the chops on a cookie sheet or cooling rack.
2. To dry brine, generously sprinkle the pinnacle of chops with salt.
3. Place in a refrigerator for an hour or two.
4. Once done, put off the coated meat from the fridge; ensure that you do not rinse the meat.

5. Prepare an infusion of olive oil and rosemary by pouring about ¼ cup of the olive oil on the pinnacle of 1 tablespoon of the chopped rosemary; set the combination apart and let sit for an hour.
6. Brush the organized aggregate on pinnacle & facets of your lamb chops.
7. Generously sprinkle the pinnacle, aspects, and bottom of chops with the rub.
8. Preheat your smoker at 225 F on oblique heat.
9. For outstanding results, ensure which you use a combination of apple and pecan for the smoke.
10. Cook the lined chops for forty to 50 minutes until the chops' internal temperature displays 138 F.
11. Let relaxation on the counter for 5 to 7 minutes, with foil tented.
12. Serve warm and enjoy.

Nutrition:

652 Calories
53g Total Fat
693mg Potassium

0.2g Total Carbohydrates
41g Protein

Chapter 4.   Grill Poultry Recipes

67.Pit boss Chile Lime Chicken

Preparation Time: 2 Minutes
Cooking Time: 15 Minutes
Servings: 1
Ingredients

- 1 chicken breast
- 1 tbsp. oil
- 1 tbsp. spice ology Chile Lime Seasoning

Directions:
1. Preheat your Pit boss to 4000F.
2. Brush the chicken breast with oil then sprinkle the chile-lime seasoning and salt.
3. Place the chicken breast on the grill and cook for 7 minutes on each side or until the internal temperature reaches 1650F.
4. Serve when hot and enjoy.

Nutrition: Calories 131, Total fat 5g, Saturated fat 1g, Total carbs 4g, Net carbs 3g Protein 19g, Sugars 1g, Fiber 1g, Sodium 235mg

68.Pit boss Grilled Buffalo Chicken

Preparation Time: 5 Minutes
Cooking Time: 10 Minutes
Servings: 6
Ingredients

- 5 chicken breasts, boneless and skinless
- 2 tbsp. homemade BBQ rub
- 1 cup homemade Cholula Buffalo sauce

Directions:
1. Preheat the Pit boss to 4000F.
2. Slice the chicken breast lengthwise into strips. Season the slices with BBQ rub.
3. Place the chicken slices on the grill and paint both sides with buffalo sauce.
4. Cook for 4 minutes with the lid closed. Flip the breasts, paint again with sauce, and cook until the internal temperature reaches 1650F.
5. Remove the chicken from the Pit boss and serve when warm.

Nutrition: Calories 176, Total fat 4g, Saturated fat 1g, Total carbs 1g, Net carbs 1g Protein 32g, Sugars 1g, Fiber 0g, Sodium 631mg

69.Pit boss Sheet Pan Chicken Fajitas

Preparation Time: 10 Minutes
Cooking Time: 10 Minutes
Servings: 10
Ingredients

- 2 lb. chicken breast
- 1 onion, sliced.
- 1 red bell pepper seeded and sliced.
- 1 orange-red bell pepper seeded and sliced.
- 1 tbsp. salt
- 1/2 tbsp. onion powder
- 1/2 tbsp. granulated garlic
- 2 tbsp. Spice ologist Chile Margarita Seasoning
- 2 tbsp. oil

Directions:
1. Preheat the Pit boss to 4500F and line a baking sheet with parchment paper.
2. In a mixing bowl, combine seasonings and oil then toss with the peppers and chicken.
3. Place the baking sheet in the Pit boss and let heat for 10 minutes with the lid closed.
4. Open the lid and place the veggies and the chicken in a single layer. Close the lid and cook for 10 minutes or until the chicken is no longer pink.
5. Serve with warm tortillas and top with your favorite toppings.

Nutrition: Calories 211, Total fat 6g, Saturated fat 1g, Total carbs 5g, Net carbs 4g Protein 29g, Sugars 4g, Fiber 1g, Sodium 360mg

70. Pit boss Asian Miso Chicken wings

Preparation Time: 15 Minutes
Cooking Time: 25 Minutes
Servings: 6
Ingredients

- 2 lb. chicken wings
- 3/4 cup soy
- 1/2 cup pineapple juice
- 1 tbsp. sriracha
- 1/8 cup miso
- 1/8 cup gochujang
- 1/2 cup water
- 1/2 cup oil
- Togarashi

Directions:

1. Preheat the Pit boss to 3750F
2. Combine all the ingredients except togarashi in a zip lock bag. Toss until the chicken wings are well coated. Refrigerate for 12 hours.
3. Pace the wings on the grill grates and close the lid. Cook for 25 minutes or until the internal temperature reaches 1650F.
4. Remove the wings from the Pit boss and sprinkle Togarashi.
5. Serve when hot and enjoy.

Nutrition: Calories 703, Total fat 56g, Saturated fat 14g, Total carbs 24g, Net carbs 23g Protein 27g, Sugars 6g, Fiber 1g, Sodium 1156mg

71. Yan's Grilled Quarters

Preparation Time: 20 minutes (additional 2-4 hours marinade)
Cooking Time: 1 to 1.5 hours
Servings: 4
Ingredients:

- 4 fresh or thawed frozen chicken quarters
- 4-6 glasses of extra virgin olive oil
- 4 tablespoons of Yang's original dry lab

Directions:

1. Configure a wood pellet smoker grill for indirect cooking and use the pellets to preheat to 325 ° F.
2. Place chicken on grill and cook at 325 ° F for 1 hour.
3. After one hour, raise the pit temperature to 400 ° F to finish the chicken and crisp the skin.
4. When the inside temperature of the thickest part of the thighs and feet reaches 180 ° F and the juice becomes clear, pull the crispy chicken out of the grill.
5. Let the crispy grilled chicken rest under a loose foil tent for 15 minutes before eating.

Nutrition: Calories 956, Total fat 47g, Saturated fat 13g, Total carbs 1g, Net carbs 1g Protein 124g, Sugars 0g, Fiber 0g, Sodium 1750mg

72. Cajun Patch Cock Chicken

Preparation Time: 30 minutes (additional 3 hours marinade)
Cooking Time: 2.5 hours
Servings: 4
Ingredients:

- 4-5 pounds of fresh or thawed frozen chicken
- 4-6 glasses of extra virgin olive oil
- Cajun Spice Lab 4 tablespoons or Lucile Bloody Mary Mix Cajun Hot Dry Herb Mix Seasoning

Directions:

1. Use hickory, pecan pellets, or blend to configure a wood pellet smoker grill for indirect cooking and preheat to 225 ° F.
2. If the unit has a temperature meat probe input, such as a MAK Grills 2 Star, insert the probe into the thickest part of the breast.
3. Make chicken for 1.5 hours.
4. After one and a half hours at 225 ° F, raise the pit temperature to 375 ° F and roast until the inside temperature of the thickest part of the chest reaches 170 ° F and the thighs are at least 180 ° F.
5. Place the chicken under a loose foil tent for 15 minutes before carving.

Nutrition: Calories 956, Total fat 47g, Saturated fat 13g, Total carbs 1g, Net carbs 1g Protein 124g, Sugars 0g, Fiber 0g, Sodium 1750mg

73. Roasted Tuscan Thighs

Preparation Time: 20 minutes (plus 1-2 hours marinade)
Cooking Time: 40-60 minutes
Servings: 4
Ingredients:

- 8 chicken thighs, with bone, with skin
- 3 extra virgin olive oils with roasted garlic flavor
- 3 cups of Tuscan or Tuscan seasoning per thigh

Directions:

1. Set the wood pellet smoker grill for indirect cooking and use the pellets to preheat to 375 degrees Fahrenheit.
2. Depending on the grill of the wood pellet smoker, roast for 40-60 minutes until the internal temperature of the thick part of the chicken thigh reaches 180 ° F. Place the roasted Tuscan thighs under a loose foil tent for 15 minutes before serving.

Nutrition: Calories 956, Total fat 47g, Saturated fat 13g, Total carbs 1g, Net carbs 1g Protein 124g, Sugars 0g, Fiber 0g, Sodium 1750mg

74. Bone In-Turkey Breast

Preparation Time: 20 minutes
Cooking Time: 3-4 hours
Servings: 6-8
Ingredients:

- 1 (8-10 pounds) boned turkey breast
- 6 tablespoons extra virgin olive oil
- 5 Yang original dry lab or poultry seasonings

Directions:

1. Configure a wood pellet smoker grill for indirect cooking and preheat to 225 ° F using hickory or pecan pellets.
2. Smoke the boned turkey breast directly in a V rack or grill at 225 ° F for 2 hours.
3. After 2 hours of hickory smoke, raise the pit temperature to 325 ° F. Roast until the thickest part of the turkey breast reaches an internal temperature of 170 ° F and the juice is clear.
4. Place the hickory smoked turkey breast under a loose foil tent for 20 minutes, then scrape the grain.

Nutrition: Calories 956, Total fat 47g, Saturated fat 13g, Total carbs 1g, Net carbs 1g Protein 124g, Sugars 0g, Fiber 0g, Sodium 1750mg

75. Teriyaki Smoked Drumstick

Preparation Time: 15 minutes (more marinade overnight)
Cooking Time: 1.5 hours to 2 hours
Servings: 4
Ingredients:

- 3 cup teriyaki marinade and cooking sauce like Yoshida's original gourmet
- Poultry seasoning 3 tsp
- 1 tsp garlic powder
- 10 chicken drumsticks

Directions:

1. Configure a wood pellet smoking grill for indirect cooking.
2. Place the skin on the drumstick and, while the grill is preheating, hang the drumstick on a poultry leg and wing rack to drain the cooking sheet on the counter. If you do not have a poultry leg and feather rack, you can dry the drumstick by tapping it with a paper towel.
3. Preheat wood pellet smoker grill to 180 ° F using hickory or maple pellets.
4. Make marinated chicken leg for 1 hour.
5. After 1 hour, raise the whole temperature to 350 ° F and cook the drumstick for another 30-45 minutes until the thickest part of the stick reaches an internal temperature of 180 ° F.
6. Place the chicken drumstick under the loose foil tent for 15 minutes before serving.

Nutrition: Calories 956, Total fat 47g, Saturated fat 13g, Total carbs 1g, Net carbs 1g Protein 124g, Sugars 0g, Fiber 0g, Sodium 1750mg

76. Hickory Spatchcock Turkey

Preparation Time: 20 minutes
Cooking Time: 3-4 hours
Servings: 8-10
Ingredients:

- 1 (14 lb.) fresh or thawed frozen young turkey
- ¼ extra virgin olive oil with cup roasted garlic flavor
- 6 poultry seasonings or original dry lab in January

Directions:

1. Configure a wood pellet smoking grill for indirect cooking and preheat to 225 ° F using hickory pellets.
2. Place the turkey skin down on a non-stick grill mat made of Teflon-coated fiberglass.
3. Suck the turkey at 225 ° F for 2 hours.
4. After 2 hours, raise the pit temperature to 350 ° F.
5. Roast turkey until the thickest part of the chest reaches an internal temperature of 170 ° F and the juice is clear.
6. Place the Hickory smoked roast turkey under a loose foil tent for 20 minutes before engraving.

Nutrition: Calories 956, Total fat 47g, Saturated fat 13g, Total carbs 1g, Net carbs 1g Protein 124g, Sugars 0g, Fiber 0g, Sodium 1750mg

77. Lemon Cornish Chicken Stuffed with Crab

Preparation Time: 30 minutes (additional 2-3 hours marinade)
Cooking Time: 1 hour 30 minutes
Servings: 2-4
Ingredients:

- 2 Cornish chickens (about 1¾ pound each)
- Half lemon, half
- 4 tbsp. western rub or poultry rub
- 2 cups stuffed with crab meat

Directions:

1. Set wood pellet smoker grill for indirect cooking and preheat to 375 ° F with pellets.
2. Place the stuffed animal on the rack in the baking dish. If you do not have a rack that is small enough to fit, you can also place the chicken directly on the baking dish.
3. Roast the chicken at 375 ° F until the inside temperature of the thickest part of the chicken breast reaches 170 ° F, the thigh reaches 180 ° F, and the juice is clear.
4. Test the crab meat stuffing to see if the temperature has reached 165 ° F.
5. Place the roasted chicken under a loose foil tent for 15 minutes before serving.

Nutrition: Calories 956, Total fat 47g, Saturated fat 13g, Total carbs 1g, Net carbs 1g Protein 124g, Sugars 0g, Fiber 0g, Sodium 1750mg

78. Bacon Cordon Blue

Preparation Time: 30 minutes
Cooking Time: 2 to 2.5 hours
Servings: 6
Ingredients:

- 24 bacon slices
- 3 large boneless, skinless chicken breasts, butterfly
- 3 extra virgin olive oils with roasted garlic flavor
- 3 Yang original dry lab or poultry seasonings
- 12 slice black forest ham
- 12-slice provolone cheese

Directions:

1. Using apple or cherry pellets, configure a wood pellet smoker grill for indirect cooking and preheat (180 ° F to 200 ° F) for smoking.
2. Inhale bacon cordon blue for 1 hour.
3. After smoking for 1 hour, raise the pit temperature to 350 ° F.
4. Bacon cordon blue occurs when the internal temperature reaches 165 ° F and the bacon becomes crispy.
5. Rest for 15 minutes under a loose foil tent before serving.

Nutrition: Calories 956, Total fat 47g, Saturated fat 13g, Total carbs 1g, Net carbs 1g Protein 124g, Sugars 0g, Fiber 0g, Sodium 1750mg

79. Roast Duck à l Orange

Preparation Time: 30 minutes
Cooking Time: 2 to 2.5 hours
Servings: 3-4
Ingredients:

- 1 (5-6 lb.) Frozen Long Island, Beijing, or Canadian ducks
- 3 tbsp. west or 3 tbsp.
- 1 large orange, cut into wedges
- Three celery stems chopped into large chunks
- Half a small red onion, a quarter
- Orange sauce:
- 2 orange cups
- 2 tablespoons soy sauce
- 2 tablespoons orange marmalade
- 2 tablespoons honey
- 3g tsp grated raw

Directions:

1. Set the wood pellet smoker grill for indirect cooking and use the pellets to preheat to 350 ° F.
2. Roast the ducks at 350 ° F for 2 hours.
3. After 2 hours, brush the duck freely with orange sauce.
4. Roast the orange glass duck for another 30 minutes, making sure that the inside temperature of the thickest part of the leg reaches 165 ° F.
5. Place duck under loose foil tent for 20 minutes before serving.
6. Discard the orange wedge, celery, and onion. Serve with a quarter of duck with poultry scissors.

Nutrition: Calories 956, Total fat 47g, Saturated fat 13g, Total carbs 1g, Net carbs 1g Protein 124g, Sugars 0g, Fiber 0g, Sodium 1750mg

80. Herb Roasted Turkey

Preparation Time: 30 minutes (additional 2-3 hours marinade)
Cooking Time: 1 hour 30 minutes
Servings: 2-4
Ingredients:

- 8 Tbsp. Butter, Room Temperature
- 2 Tbsp. Mixed Herbs Such as Parsley, Sage, Rosemary, And Marjoram, Chopped
- 1/4 Tsp. Black Pepper, Freshly Ground
- 1 (12-14 Lbs.) Turkey, Thawed If pre-frozen.
- 3 Tbsp. Butter

Directions:

1. In a small mixing bowl, combine the 8 tablespoons of softened butter, mixed herbs, and black pepper and beat until fluffy with a wooden spoon.
2. Remove any giblets from the turkey cavity and save them for gravy making, if desired. Wash the turkey, inside and out, under cold running water. Dry with paper towels.
3. Using your fingers or the handle of a wooden spoon, gently push some of the herbed butter underneath the turkey skin onto the breast halves, being careful not to tear the skin.
4. Rub the outside of the turkey with the melted butter and sprinkle with the Pit boss Pork and Poultry Rub. Pour the chicken broth in the bottom of the roasting pan.
5. When ready to cook, set temperature to 325 F and preheat, lid closed for 15 minutes.

Nutrition: Calories 956, Total fat 47g, Saturated fat 13g, Total carbs 1g, Net carbs 1g Protein 124g, Sugars 0g, Fiber 0g, Sodium 1750mg

81. Bourbon & Orange Brined Turkey

Preparation Time: 30 minutes
Cooking Time: 1 hour 30 minutes
Servings: 2-4
Ingredients:

- Pit boss Orange Brine (From Kit)
- Pit boss Turkey Rub (From Kit)
- 1.25-2.5 Gallons Cold Water
- 1 Cup Bourbon
- 1 Tbsp. Butter, Melted

Directions:

1. Mix Pit boss Orange Brine seasoning (from Orange Brine & Turkey Rub Kit) with one quart of water. Boil for 5 minutes. Remove from heat, add 1 gallon of cold water and bourbon.
2. Place turkey breast side down in a large container. Pour cooled brine mix over bird. Add cold water until bird is submerged. Refrigerate for 24 hours.

3. Remove turkey and disregard brine. Blot turkeys dry with paper towels. Combine butter and Grand Marnier and coat outside of turkey.
4. Season outside of turkey with Pit boss Turkey Rub (from Orange Brine & Turkey Rub Kit).
5. When ready to cook, set temperature to 225 F and preheat, lid closed for 15 minutes.

Nutrition: Calories 956, Total fat 47g, Saturated fat 13g, Total carbs 1g, Net carbs 1g Protein 124g, Sugars 0g, Fiber 0g, Sodium 1750mg

82. Pit boss Leftover Turkey Soup

Preparation Time: 30 minutes
Cooking Time: 1 hour 30 minutes
Servings: 2-4
Ingredients:

- 1 Turkey Carcass
- 16 Cups Cold Water
- 2 Large Celery Ribs, Sliced
- 2 Large Carrots, Scraped and Sliced
- 2 Red Onions, Quartered

Directions:
1. Strip a turkey carcass of all meat; set aside in a container.
2. Break up the bones of the turkey carcass and place them in a large pot. Add any turkey skin or other assorted "bits" that are not edible meat.
3. Once the stock has come to a boil, add all remaining Ingredients, and turn heat down until the bubbles barely break the surface. Let simmer for 3 to 4 hours, stirring occasionally.
4. When the stock is ready, strain it through a fine-meshed sieve into a large bowl; if your sieve is not fine, and line it first with cheesecloth.
5. Refrigerate stock, covered, for several hours or preferably overnight. You can either make soup the then day or freeze the stock.

Nutrition: Calories 956, Total fat 47g, Saturated fat 13g, Total carbs 1g, Net carbs 1g Protein 124g, Sugars 0g, Fiber 0g, Sodium 1750mg

83. Turkey by Rob's cooks

Preparation Time: 30 minutes
Cooking Time: 1 hour 30 minutes
Servings: 2-4
Ingredients:

- Smoked Turkey by Rob's cooks
- 1 (12-14 Lb.) Turkey, Fresh or Thawed
- 3/4 Lb. (3 Sticks) Unsalted Butter
- 1 (5 Gal) Bucket or Stock Pot
- Foil Pan, Large Enough for Turkey

Directions:
1. This method requires an overnight brining so collect everything the day before your meal.
2. The afternoon before, prepare your brine by adding the kosher salt and sugar to a medium saucepan. Cover with water and bring to a boil. Stir to dissolve the salt and sugar.
3. Prepare your turkey by removing the neck, gizzards, and truss, if pre-trussed. Trim off excess skin and fat near the cavity and neck. Place the turkey in bucket with the brine.
4. When ready to cook, set temperature to 180 F and preheat, lid closed for 15 minutes.
5. Remove your turkey from the brine. Remember there is a cavity full of water so make sure to do this over the sink, otherwise you will have brine all over the place.

Nutrition: Calories 956, Total fat 47g, Saturated fat 13g, Total carbs 1g, Net carbs 1g Protein 124g, Sugars 0g, Fiber 0g, Sodium 1750mg

84. Traditional Thanksgiving Turkey

Preparation Time: 30 minutes
Cooking Time: 1 hour 30 minutes
Servings: 2-4
Ingredients:

- 1 (18-20lb) Turkey
- 1/2 Lb. Butter, Softened
- 8 Sprigs Thyme
- 6 Cloves Garlic, Minced
- 1 Sprig Rosemary, Rough Chop

Directions:

1. In a small bowl, combine butter with the minced garlic, thyme leaves, chopped rosemary, black pepper and kosher salt.
2. Prepare the turkey by separating the skin from the breast creating a pocket to stuff the butter-herb mixture in.
3. Cover the entire breast with 1/4" thickness of butter mixture.
4. Season the whole turkey with kosher salt and black pepper. As an option, you can also stuff the turkey cavity with Traditional Stuffing.
5. When ready to cook, set the temperature to 300 F and preheat, lid closed for 15 minutes.

Nutrition: Calories 956, Total fat 47g, Saturated fat 13g, Total carbs 1g, Net carbs 1g Protein 124g, Sugars 0g, Fiber 0g, Sodium 1750mg

85. Turkey Jalapeno Meatballs

Preparation Time: 30 minutes
Cooking Time: 1 hour 30 minutes
Servings: 2-4
Ingredients:

- Turkey Jalapeño Meatballs
- 1 1/4 Lbs. Ground Turkey
- 1 Jalapeño Pepper, Deseeded and Finely Diced
- 1/2 Tsp Garlic Salt
- 1 Tsp Onion Powder

Directions:

1. In a separate small bowl, combine the milk and breadcrumbs.
2. In a large bowl, mix turkey, garlic salt, onion powder, salt, pepper, Worcestershire sauce, cayenne pepper, egg, and jalapeños.
3. Add the bread crumb milk mixture to the bowl and combine. Cover with plastic and refrigerate for up to 1 hour.
4. When ready to cook, set the temperature to 350°F and preheat, lid closed for 15 minutes.
5. Roll the turkey mixture into balls, about one tablespoon each and place the meatballs in a single layer on a parchment lined baking sheet.

Nutrition: Calories 956, Total fat 47g, Saturated fat 13g, Total carbs 1g, Net carbs 1g Protein 124g, Sugars 0g, Fiber 0g, Sodium 2750mg

86. Wild Turkey Southwest Egg Rolls

Preparation Time: 30 minutes
Cooking Time: 1 hour 30 minutes
Servings: 2-4
Ingredients:

- 2 Cups Leftover Wild Turkey Meat
- 1/2 Cup Corn
- 1/2 Cup Black Beans
- 3 Tbsp. Taco Seasoning
- 1/2 Cup White Onion, Chopped

Directions:

1. Add olive oil to a large skillet and heat on the stove over medium heat. Add onions and peppers and sauté 2-3 minutes until soft. Add garlic, cook 30 seconds, then Rote and black beans.
2. Pour taco seasoning over meat and add 1/3 cup of water and mix to coat well. Add to veggie mixture and stir to mix well. If it seems dry, add 2 tbsp. water. Cook until heated all the way through.
3. Remove from the heat and transfer the mixture to the fridge. The mixture should be completely cooled prior to stuffing the egg rolls or the wrappers will break.
4. Place spoonful of the mixture in each wrapper and wrap tightly. Repeat with remaining wrappers. When ready to cook, set temperature to High and preheat, lid closed for 15 minutes.
5. Brush each egg roll with oil or butter and place directly on the Pit boss grill grate. Cook until the exterior is crispy, about 20 min per side.

Nutrition: Calories 456, Total fat 37g, Saturated fat 13g, Total carbs 1g, Net carbs 1g Protein 124g, Sugars 0g, Fiber 0g, Sodium 1750mg

87. Grilled Wild Turkey Orange Cashew Salad

Preparation Time: 30 minutes
Cooking Time: 1 hour 30 minutes
Servings: 2-4
Ingredients:

- Turkey Breast
- 2 Wild Turkey Breast Halves, Without Skin
- 1/4 Cup Teriyaki Sauce
- 1 Tsp Fresh Ginger
- 1 (12 Oz) Can Blood Orange Kill Cliff or Similar Citrus Soda
- 2 Tbsp. Pit boss Chicken Rub
- Cashew Salad
- 4 Cups Romaine Lettuce, Chopped
- 1/2 Head Red or White Cabbage, Chopped
- 1/2 Cup Shredded Carrots
- 1/2 Cup Edamame, Shelled
- 1 Smoked Yellow Bell Pepper, Sliced into Circles
- 1 Smoked Red Bell Pepper, Sliced into Circles
- 3 Chive Tips, Chopped
- 1/2 Cup Smoked Cashews
- Blood Orange Vinaigrette
- 1 Tsp Orange Zest
- Juice From 1/2 Large Orange
- 1 Tsp Finely Grated Fresh Ginger
- 2 Tbsp. Seasoned Rice Vinegar
- 1 Tsp Honey
- Sea Salt, To Taste
- 1/4 Cup Light Vegetable Oil

Directions:

1. For the Marinade: Combine teriyaki sauce, Kill Cliff soda and fresh ginger. Pour marinade over turkey breasts in a Ziplock bag or dish and seal.
2. When ready to cook, set temperature to 375 F and preheat, lid closed for 15 minutes.
3. Remove turkey from the refrigerator, drain the marinade and pat turkey dry with paper towels.
4. Place turkey into a shallow oven proof dish and season with Pit boss Chicken Rub.
5. Place dish in the Pit boss and cook for 30-45 minutes or until the breast reaches an internal temperature of 160 F.
6. Remove the breast from the grill and wrap in Pit boss Butcher Paper. Let turkey rest for 10 minutes. While turkey is resting, prepare salad.
7. Assemble salad Ingredients in a bowl and toss to mix. Combine all Ingredients in list for vinaigrette.
8. After resting for 10 minutes, slice turkey and serve with cashew salad and blood orange vinaigrette. Enjoy!

Nutrition: Calories 956, Total fat 47g, Saturated fat 13g, Total carbs 1g, Net carbs 1g Protein 124g, Sugars 0g, Fiber 0g, Sodium 1750mg

88. Baked Cornbread Turkey Tamale Pie

Preparation Time: 30 minutes
Cooking Time: 1 hour 30 minutes
Servings: 2-4
Ingredients:

- Filling
- 2 Cups Shredded Turkey
- 2 Cobs of Corn
- 1 (15 Oz) Can Black Beans, Rinsed and Drained
- 1 Yellow Bell Pepper
- 1 Orange Bell Pepper
- 2 Jalapeños
- 2 Tbsp. Cilantro
- 1 Bunch Green Onions
- 1/2 Tsp Cumin
- 1/2 Tsp Paprika
- 1 (7 Oz) Can Chipotle Sauce
- 1 (15 Oz) Can Enchilada Sauce
- 1/2 Cup Shredded Cheddar Cheese
- Cornbread Topping
- 1 Cup All-Purpose Flour
- 1 Cup Yellow or White Cornmeal
- 1 Tbsp. Sugar
- 2 Tsp Baking Powder
- 1/2 Tsp Salt
- 3 Tbsp. Butter
- 1 Cup Buttermilk
- 1 Large Egg, Lightly Beaten

Directions:

1. For the filling: Mix to combine filling Ingredients Place in the bottom of a butter greased 10-inch pan.
2. For the cornbread topping: In a mixing bowl, combine the flour, cornmeal, sugar, baking powder, and salt. Melt the butter in a small saucepan.
3. Add the milk-egg mixture to the dry Ingredients and stir to combine. Do not over mix.

4. To assemble Tamale Pie: Fill the bottom of a butter greased 10-inch pan with the shredded turkey filling. Top with the cornbread topping and smooth to the edges of pan.
5. When ready to cook, set the temperature to 375 F and preheat, lid closed for 15 minutes.
6. Place directly on the grill grate and cook for 45-50 minutes or until the cornbread is lightly browned and cooked through. Enjoy!

Nutrition: Calories 956, Total fat 47g, Saturated fat 13g, Total carbs 1g, Net carbs 1g Protein 124g, Sugars 0g, Fiber 0g, Sodium 1750mg

89. Pit boss BBQ simple Turkey Sandwiches

Preparation Time: 30 minutes
Cooking Time: 45 minutes
Servings: 10
Ingredients:
- 6 Turkey Thighs, Skin-On
- 1 1/2 Cups Chicken or Turkey Broth
- Pork & Poultry Rub
- 1 Cup barbeque Sauce, Or More as Needed
- 6 Buns or Kaiser Rolls, Split and Buttered

Directions:
1. Season turkey thighs on both sides with the Pork & Poultry rub.
2. When ready to cook, turn temperature to 180 degrees F and preheat, lid closed for 15 minutes.
3. Arrange the turkey thighs exactly on the grill grate and smoke for 30 minutes.
4. Transfer the thighs to sturdy disposable aluminum foil or baking tray. Pour the broth around the thighs and then cover the pan with foil or a lid.
5. Increase temperature to 325 degrees F and preheat, lid closed. Roast the thighs until it reaches an internal temperature of 180 degrees F.
6. Remove pan from the grill but leave the grill on. Let the turkey thighs cool slightly up to they can be handled comfortably.
7. Let the drops drip off and keep. Remove skin and discard.
8. Pull out the shredded turkey meat with your fingers and return it to the roasting pan.
9. Add a cup or more of your favorite BBQ Sauce along with some of the drippings.
10. Recover the pan with foil and reheat the BBQ turkey on the grill for 20 to 30 minutes.
11. Serve with toasted buns if desired. Enjoy!

Nutrition:
Energy (calories): 25 kcal
Protein: 0.7 g
Fat: 1.53 g
Carbohydrates: 2.59 g

90. Roasted Spatchcock Turkey

Preparation Time: 30 minutes
Cooking Time: 3-4 hours
Servings: 4
Ingredients:
- 1 (18-20 Lb.) Whole Turkey
- 4 tbsps. Turkey Rub
- 1 tbsp. Jacobsen Sea Salt
- 4 Cloves Garlic, Minced
- 3 tbsps. Parsley, Chopped.
- 1 tbsp. Rosemary, Chopped.
- 2 tbsps. Thyme Leaves, Chopped
- 2 Scallions, Chopped.
- 3 tbsps. Olive Oil

Directions:
1. When ready to cook, turn temperature to High and preheat, lid closed for 15 minutes.
2. On a cutting board, mix the garlic, parsley, thyme, rosemary, and green onions. Chop the mixture until it turns into a paste. Set aside.
3. Spatchcock the turkey: With a large knife or shears, cut the bird open along the backbone on both sides, through the ribs, and remove the backbone.
4. Once the bird is open, split the breastbone to spread the bird flat, allowing it to roast evenly.
5. With the bird's breast facing up, season the outside with half of the Turkey Rub, then follow 2/3 of the herb mixture by rubbing it into the bird. Drizzle with olive oil.
6. Roll over the bird and then season generously with the remaining Turkey Rub.
7. Place the turkey exactly on the grill grate and cook for 30 minutes.
8. Turn to low temperature on the grill to 300 degrees F and continue to cook for 3-4 hours or until the internal temperature reaches 160 degrees F in the breast.

9. The finished inside temperature should reach 165 degrees F, but it will continue to rise after the bird is totally removed it from the grill.
10. Prepare the bird and let it rest 20-25 minutes before carving. Enjoy!

91. Spatchcocked Maple Brined Turkey

Preparation Time: 40 minutes
Cooking Time: 2-3 hours
Servings: 6
Ingredients:

- 1 (12-14 Lbs.) Turkey, Thawed If Frozen
- 5 Qtrs. Hot Water
- 1 1/2 Cups Kosher Salt
- 3/4 cup of Bourbon
- 1 cup of Pure Maple Syrup
- 1/2 Cup of Brown Sugar
- 1 Onion
- 3-4 Strips Orange Peel
- 3 Bay Leaves, Broken into Pieces
- 2 tbsps. Black Peppercorns
- 1 tbsp. Whole Cloves
- 3 Qtrs. Ice
- 1 cup Butter, Melted.
- Pork & Poultry Rub, As Needed
- Sprigs of Fresh Sage and Thyme, To Garnish
- Orange Wedges, Lady Apples, Or Kumquats, To Serve

Directions:
Note: Do not use kosher turkey or basting turkey for this recipe as they have already been fortified with saline.
For the Brine:
1. In a large stockpot or container, combine the hot water, kosher salt, bourbon, 3/4 cup of the maple syrup, brown sugar, onion, bay leaves, orange peel, peppercorns, and cloves and stir until well mixed. Add the ice.
2. Rinse or drain the turkey, inside and out, under cold running water. Remove giblets and discard or save for another use. Some turkeys come with a gravy packet as well; remove it before roasting the bird.
3. Add the turkey to the brine and refrigerate 8 to 12 hours, or overnight—weight with an ice pack to keep the bird immerse.
4. Rinse and pat dry it with paper towels; discard the brine.
5. Spatchcock the turkey: Using a knife or shears, cut the bird open along the spine on both sides, then through the ribs and removes the backbone.
6. Once the bird is open, split the breastbone to spread the bird flat, allowing it to roast evenly.
7. Mix the melted butter and the remaining 1/4 cup of maple syrup and divide in half. Brush half of the blend on the bird and then sprinkle with Pork and Poultry Rub or the salt and black pepper.
8. Set aside the other half of the blend mixture until ready to use.
9. Prepare and ready to cook, set the temperature to 350 degrees F and preheat, lid closed for 15 minutes.
10. Roast or cook the turkey until the internal temperature in the thickest part of the breast reaches 165 degrees F, about 2-3 hours.
11. Brush with the remaining butter-maple syrup glaze while having the last 30 minutes of cooking the meat.
12. Let the turkey remain rest for 15 to 20 minutes and then garnish, if desired, with fresh herbs and or kumquats. Enjoy!

Nutrition:
Energy (calories): 748 kcal
Protein: 18.11 g
Fat: 50.92 g
Carbohydrates: 55.01 g

92. Home Turkey Gravy

Preparation Time: 30 minutes
Cooking Time: 3-4 hours
Servings: 8
Ingredients:

- 4 cups Homemade Chicken Stock
- 2 Large Onions Cut Into 8th
- 4 Carrots, Rough Chop
- 4 Celery Stalks
- 8 Sprigs Thyme
- 8 Cloves Garlic, Peeled and Smashed
- 1 Turkey Neck
- 1 cup Flour
- 1 Stick Butter, Cut into About 8 Pieces
- 1 tsp. Kosher Salt
- 1 tsp. Cracked Black Pepper

Directions:
1. When all are prepared ready to cook, set the temperature to 350 degrees and preheat with the lid closed for 15 minutes.
2. In a large pan, place turkey neck, plus onion, celery, also carrot, garlic, and thyme. Please add 4 cups of chicken stock and then sprinkle with salt and pepper.

3. Put the prepped turkey on the rack into the roasting pan and place it in the wood pellet grill.
4. Cook for 3-4 hours or until the breast reaches 160 degrees F. When you remove from the grill, the turkey will continue to cook and reach a finished internal temperature of 165degrees F.
5. Rinse the drippings into a saucepan and simmer on low.
6. In a larger saucepan, combine butter and flour with a whisk stirring until golden tan. It takes about 8 minutes, stirring constantly.
7. Next, whisk the drippings into the roux and cook until it comes to a boil. Season with salt and pepper and serve hot. Enjoy!

Nutrition:

Energy (calories): 621 kcal

Protein: 99.57 g

182%

Fat: 13.18 g

Carbohydrates: 19.82 g

93. Roasted Honey Bourbon Glazed Turkey

Preparation Time: 40 minutes
Cooking Time: 3-4 hours
Servings: 8
Ingredients:

- Turkey
- 1 (16-18 Lbs.) Turkey
- 1/4 Cup of Fin and Feather Rub
- Whiskey Glaze
- 1/2 cup Bourbon
- 1/2 Cup Honey
- 1/4 Cup Brown Sugar
- 3 tbsps. Apple Cider Vinegar
- 1 tbsp. Dijon Mustard
- Salt and Pepper, To Taste

Directions:

1. Prepare and ready to cook, set the temperature to 375 degrees F and preheat, lid closed for 15 minutes.
2. Truss the turkey legs together and then season the exterior of the bird and the cavity with Fin and Feather Rub.
3. Place the turkey exactly on the grill grate and cook for 20-30 minutes at 375 degrees F or until the skin begins to brown.
4. After 30 minutes, turn down the temperature to 325 degrees F and continue to cook until the inside temperature registers 165 degrees F when an instant-read thermometer is inserted into the thickest part of the breast, about 3-4 hours.

For the Whiskey Glaze:

1. Blend or mix all ingredients in a small saucepan and bring to a boil. Turn down the heat and simmer for 15-20 minutes or until thick enough to cover the back of a spoon. Remove from heat and set aside.
2. Meanwhile the last ten minutes of cooking, brush the turkey's glaze while on the grill and cook until it is set, 10 minutes.
3. Remove from grill and let it rest 10-15 minutes before carving. Enjoy!

Nutrition:

Energy (calories): 333 kcal

Protein: 9.77 g

Fat: 22 g

Carbohydrates: 25.13 g

94. Roasted Autumn Brined Turkey Breast

Preparation Time: 40 minutes
Cooking Time: 3-4 hours
Servings: 6
Ingredients:

- 6 Cups Apple Cider
- 2 Cloves Garlic, Smashed
- 1/3 Cup Brown Sugar
- 1 tbsp. Allspice
- 1/3 cup Kosher Salt
- 3 Bay Leaves
- 4 Cups Ice Water
- 1 Turkey Breast
- 1/2 Cup Plus Two Tbsps. Unsalted Butter, Softened
- Pork and Poultry Rub

Directions:

For the Brine:

1. In a large pot or saucepan, Mix 4 cups of apple cider, the garlic cloves, brown sugar, allspice, salt, and bay leaves. Simmer on the stovetop for 5 minutes, stirring often.
2. Take off the stovetop and add in the ice water.
3. Put turkey in the brine and add water as needed until the turkey is fully submerged. Cover and refrigerate overnight.

For the Cider Glaze:
1. Let the remaining 2 cups of apple cider in a saucepan until reduced to 1/4 cup, about 30-45 minutes. Whisk in butter and cool completely.
2. After the turkey has brined overnight, drain the turkey and rinse.
3. Using your fingers, take two tablespoons of the softened butter and smear it under the breast's skin. Season the breast of the turkey with Pork & Poultry Rub.
4. When ready to cook, turn the temperature to 325 degrees F and preheat, lid closed for 15 minutes.
5. Cook turkey until it reaches an inside temperature of 160 degrees F, about 3-4 hrs. After the first 20 minutes of cooking, rub turkey with the cider glaze.
6. When the breast starts to get too dark you should cover it with foil. Let stand 30 minutes before carving. Enjoy!

Nutrition:

Energy (calories): 680 kcal

Fat: 32.92 g

Protein: 62.27 g

Carbohydrates: 30.71 g

95. BBQ Chicken Breasts

Preparation Time: 40 minutes
Cooking Time: 15 minutes
Servings: 6
Ingredients:
- 4-6 Boneless and skinless Chicken Breast
- 1 half Cup of Sweet & Heat BBQ Sauce
- Salt and Pepper
- 1 tbsp. Chopped Parsley, To Garnish

Directions:
1. Put the chicken breasts and a cup of Sweet & Heat BBQ sauce in a Ziploc bag and marinate overnight.
2. Turn temperature to High and preheat, lid closed for 15 minutes.
3. Remove chicken from marinade and season with salt and pepper.
4. Place directly on the grill grate and cook for 10 minutes on each side, flipping once or until the internal temperature reaches 150 degrees F.
5. Brush remaining sauce on chicken while on the grill and continue to cook 5-10 minutes longer or until a finished internal temperature of 165 degrees F.
6. Move away from grill and let rest 5 minutes before serving. Sprinkle with chopped parsley. Enjoy!

Nutrition:

Energy (calories): 183 kcal

Fat: 3.48 g

Protein: 29.82 g

Carbohydrates: 7.73 g

Chapter 5. Turkey, Rabbit and Veal

96. Wild Turkey Egg Rolls

Preparation Time: 10 minutes
Cooking Time: 55 minutes
Servings: 1
Ingredients:

- Corn - ½ cup
- Leftover wild turkey meat - 2 cups
- Black beans - ½ cup
- Taco seasoning - 3 tablespoon
- Water ½ cup
- Rote chilies and tomatoes - 1 can
- Egg roll wrappers- 12
- Cloves of minced garlic- 4
- 1 chopped Poblano pepper or 2 jalapeno peppers
- Chopped white onion - ½ cup.

Directions:

1. Add some olive oil to a large skillet. Heat it over medium heat on a stove.
2. Add peppers and onions. Sauté the mixture for 2-3 minutes until it turns soft.
3. Add some garlic and sauté for another 30 seconds. Add the Rote chilies and beans to the mixture. Keeping mixing the content gently. Reduce the heat and then simmer.
4. After about 4-5 minutes, pour in the taco seasoning and 1/3 cup of water over the meat. Mix everything and coat the meat well. If you feel that it is a bit dry, you can add 2 tablespoons of water. Keep cooking until everything is heated all the way through.
5. Remove the content from the heat and box it to store in a refrigerator. Before you stuff the mixture into the egg wrappers, it should be completely cool to avoid breaking the rolls.
6. Place a spoonful of the cooked mixture in each wrapper and then wrap it securely and tightly. Do the same with all the wrappers.
7. Preheat the Pit boss grill and brush it with some oil. Cook the egg rolls for 15 minutes on both sides, until the exterior is nice and crispy.
8. Remove them from the grill and enjoy with your favorite salsa!

Nutrition:

Carbohydrates: 26.1 g
Protein: 9.2 g
Fat: 4.2 g

Sodium: 373.4 mg
Cholesterol: 19.8 mg

97. BBQ Pulled Turkey Sandwiches

Preparation Time: 30 minutes
Cooking Time: 4 Hours
Servings: 1
Ingredients:

- 6 skin-on turkey thighs
- 6 split and buttered buns
- 1 ½ cups of chicken broth
- 1 cup of BBQ sauce
- Poultry rub

Directions:

1. Season the turkey thighs on both the sides with poultry rub.
2. Set the grill to preheat by pushing the temperature to 180 degrees F.
3. Arrange the turkey thighs on the grate of the grill and smoke it for 30 minutes.
4. Now transfer the thighs to an aluminum foil which is disposable and then pour the brine right around the thighs.
5. Cover it with a lid.
6. Now increase the grill, temperature to 325 degrees F and roast the thigh till the internal temperature reaches 180 degrees F.
7. Remove the foil from the grill but do not turn off the grill.
8. Let the turkey thighs cool down a little
9. Now pour the dripping and serve.
10. Remove the skin and discard it.
11. Pull the meat into shreds and return it to the foil.
12. Add 1 more cup of BBQ sauce and some more dripping.
13. Now cover the foil with lid and re-heat the turkey on the smoker for half an hour
14. Serve and enjoy.

Nutrition:

Carbohydrates: 39 g

Protein: 29 g

Sodium: 15 mg

Cholesterol: 19 mg

98. Tempting Tarragon Turkey Breasts

Preparation Time: 20 Minutes (Marinating Time: Overnight)

Cooking Time: 3½ to 4 hours

Servings: 4 to 5

Ingredients:

For the marinade

- ¾ cup heavy (whipping) cream
- ¼ cup Dijon mustard
- ¼ cup dry white wine
- 2 tablespoons olive oil
- ½ cup chopped scallions, both white and green parts, divided.
- 3 tablespoons fresh tarragon finely chopped.
- 6 garlic cloves coarsely chopped.
- 1 teaspoon salt
- 1 teaspoon freshly ground black pepper.

For the turkey:

- (6- to 7-pound) bone-in turkey breast
- ¼ cup (½ stick) unsalted butter, melted.

Directions:

1. To make the marinade
2. In a large bowl, whisk together the cream, mustard, wine, and olive oil until blended.
3. Stir in ¼ cup of scallions and the tarragon, garlic, salt, and pepper.
4. Rub the marinade all over the turkey breast and under the skin. Cover and refrigerate overnight.
5. To make the turkey
6. Following the manufacturer's specific start-up procedure, preheat the smoker to 250°F, and add apple or mesquite wood.
7. Remove the turkey from the refrigerator and place it directly on the smoker rack. Do not rinse it.
8. Smoke the turkey for 3½ to 4 hours (about 30 minutes per pound), basting it with the butter twice during smoking, until the skin is browned and the internal temperature registers 165°F.
9. Remove the turkey from the heat and let it rest for 10 minutes.
10. Sprinkle with the remaining scallions before serving.

Nutrition:

Calories: 165 call

Fat: 14g

Carbohydrates: 0.5g

Fiber: 0 g

Protein: 15.2g

99. Juicy Beer Can Turkey

Preparation Time: 20 Minutes

Cooking Time: 6 hours

Servings: 6-8

Ingredients:

For the rub

- 4 garlic cloves, minced.
- 2 teaspoons dry ground mustard
- 2 teaspoons smoked paprika.
- 2 teaspoons salt
- 2 teaspoons freshly ground black pepper.
- 1 teaspoon ground cumin
- 1 teaspoon ground turmeric
- 1 teaspoon onion powder
- ½ teaspoon sugar

For the turkey

- o (10-pound) fresh whole turkey, neck, giblets, and gizzard removed and discarded.
- o tablespoons olive oil
- 1 large, wide (24-ounce) can of beer, such as Foster's
     4 dried bay leaves
- 2 teaspoons ground sage
- 2 teaspoons dried thyme
- ¼ cup (½ stick) unsalted butter, melted.

Directions:

1. To make the rub
2. Following the manufacturer's specific start-up procedure, preheat the smoker to 250°F, and add cherry, peach, or apricot wood.
3. In a small bowl, stir together the garlic, mustard, paprika, salt, pepper, cumin, turmeric, onion powder, and sugar.
4. To make the turkey
5. Rub the turkey inside and out with the olive oil.

6. Apply the spice rub all over the turkey.
7. Pour out or drink 12 ounces of the beer.
8. Using a can opener, remove the entire top of the beer can.
9. Add the bay leaves, sage, and thyme to the beer.
10. Place the can of beer upright on the smoker grate. Carefully fit the turkey over it until the entire can is inside the cavity and the bird stands by itself. Prop the legs forward to aid in stability.
11. Smoke the turkey for 6 hours, basting with the butter every other hour.
12. Remove the turkey from the heat when the skin is browned and the internal temperature registers 165°F. Remove the beer can very carefully—it will be slippery, and the liquid inside extremely hot. Discard the liquid and recycle the can.
13. Let the turkey rest for 20 minutes before carving.

Nutrition:

Calories: 300 call

Fat: 12g

Carbohydrates: 1g

Fiber: 0g

Protein: 42g

100. Buttered Thanksgiving Turkey

Preparation Time: 25 minutes
Cooking Time: 5 or 6 hours
Servings: 12 to 14
Ingredients:

- 1 whole turkey (make sure the turkey is not pre-brined)
- 2 batches Garlic Butter Injectable
- 3 tablespoons olive oil
- 1 batch Chicken Rub
- 2 tablespoons butter

Directions:
1. Supply your smoker with Traeger's and follow the manufacturer's specific start-up procedure. Preheat the grill, with the lid closed to 180°F.
2. Inject the turkey throughout with the garlic butter injectable. Coat the turkey with olive oil and season it with the rub. Using your hands, work the rub into the meat and skin.
3. Place the turkey directly on the grill grate and smoke for 3 or 4 hours (for an 8- to 12-pound turkey, cook for 3 hours; for a turkey over 12 pounds, cook for 4 hours), basting it with butter every hour.
4. Increase the grill's temperature to 375°F and continue to cook until the turkey's internal temperature reaches 170°F.
5. Remove the turkey from the grill and let it rest for 10 minutes, before carving and serving.

Nutrition:

Calories: 97cal

Fat: 4 g

Protein: 13 g

Carbohydrates: 1 g

Fiber: 0 g

101. Jalapeno Injection Turkey

Preparation Time: 15 minutes
Cooking Time: 4 hours and 10 minutes
Servings: 6
Ingredients:

- 15 pounds whole turkey, giblet removed.
- ½ of medium red onion, peeled and minced.
- 8 jalapeño peppers
- 2 tablespoons minced garlic
- 4 tablespoons garlic powder
- 6 tablespoons Italian seasoning
  1 cup butter, softened, unsalted.
- ¼ cup olive oil
- 1 cup chicken broth

Directions:
1. Open hopper of the smoker, add dry pallets, make sure ashcan is in place, then open the ash damper, power on the smoker, and close the ash damper.
2. Set the temperature of the smoker to 200 degrees F, let preheat for 30 minutes or until the green light on the dial blinks that indicate smoker has reached to set temperature.
3. Meanwhile, place a large saucepan over medium-high heat, add oil and butter and when the butter melts, add onion, garlic, and peppers and cook for 3 to 5 minutes or until nicely golden brown.
4. Pour in broth, stir well, let the mixture boil for 5 minutes, then remove pan from the heat and strain the mixture to get just liquid.

5. Inject turkey generously with prepared liquid, then spray the outside of turkey with butter spray and season well with garlic and Italian seasoning.
6. Place turkey on the smoker grill, shut with lid, and smoke for 30 minutes, then increase the temperature to 325 degrees F and continue smoking the turkey for 3 hours or until the internal temperature of turkey reach to 165 degrees F.
7. When done, transfer turkey to a cutting board, let rest for 5 minutes, then carve into slices and serve.

Nutrition:

Calories: 131 call

Fat: 7 g

Protein: 13 g

Carbohydrates: 3 g

Fiber: 0.7 g

102. Turkey Meatballs

Preparation Time: 40 minutes

Cooking Time: 40 minutes

Servings: 8

Ingredients:

- 1 1/4 lb. ground turkey
- 1/2 cup breadcrumbs
- 1 egg, beaten.
- 1/4 cup milk
- 1 teaspoon onion powder
- 1/4 cup Worcestershire sauce
- Pinch garlic salt
- Salt and pepper to taste
- 1 cup cranberry jam
- 1/2 cup orange marmalade
- 1/2 cup chicken broth

Directions:

1. In a large bowl, mix the ground turkey, breadcrumbs, egg, milk, onion powder, Worcestershire sauce, garlic salt, salt, and pepper.
2. Form meatballs from the mixture.
3. Preheat the Pit boss grill to 350 degrees F for 15 minutes while the lid is closed.
4. Add the turkey meatballs to a baking pan.
5. Place the baking pan on the grill.
6. Cook for 20 minutes.
7. In a pan over medium heat, simmer the rest of the ingredients for 10 minutes.
8. Add the grilled meatballs to the pan.
9. Coat with the mixture.
10. Cook for 10 minutes.

Nutrition: Calories: 37 Fats: 1.8 g Cholesterol: 10 mg Carbohydrates: 3.1 g Fiber: 0.6 g Sugar: 1.3g Protein: 2.5 g

103. Pit boss simple Smoked Turkey

Preparation Time: 1 day and 1 hour

Cooking Time: 4 hours and 30 minutes

Servings: 6

Ingredients:

- 2 gallons of water, divided.
- 2 cups of sugar
- 2 cups salt
- Ice cubes
- 1 whole turkey
- ½ cup kosher salt
- ½ cup black pepper
- 3 sticks butter, sliced.

Directions:

1. Add one-quart water to a pot over medium heat.
2. Stir in the 2 cups each of sugar and salt.
3. Bring to a boil.
4. Remove from heat and let cool.
5. Add ice and the remaining water.
6. Stir to cool.
7. Add the turkey to the brine.
8. Cover and refrigerate for 24 hours.
9. Rinse the turkey and dry with paper towels.
10. Season with salt and pepper.
11. Preheat the Pit boss grill to 180 degrees F for 15 minutes while the lid is closed.
12. Smoke the turkey for 2 hours.
13. Increase temperature to 225 degrees. Smoke for another 1 hour.

14. Increase temperature to 325 degrees. Smoke for 30 minutes.
15. Place the turkey on top of a foil sheet.
16. Add butter on top of the turkey.
17. Cover the turkey with foil.
18. Reduce temperature to 165 degrees F.
19. Cook on the grill for 1 hour.

Nutrition: Calories: 48.2 Fats: 1.4 g Cholesterol: 21.5 mg Carbohydrates: 0 g Fiber: 0 g Sugar: 0 g Protein: 8.3 g

104. Maple Turkey Breast

Preparation Time: 4 hours and 30 minutes
Cooking Time: 2 hours
Servings: 4
Ingredients:

- 3 tablespoons olive oil
- 3 tablespoons dark brown sugar
- 3 tablespoons garlic, minced.
- 2 tablespoons Cajun seasoning
- 2 tablespoons Worcestershire sauce
- 6 lb. turkey breast fillets

Directions:
1. Combine olive oil, sugar, garlic, Cajun seasoning, and Worcestershire sauce in a bowl.
2. Soak the turkey breast fillets in the marinade.
3. Cover and marinate for 4 hours.
4. Grill the turkey at 180 degrees F for 2 hours.

Serving Suggestion: Let rest for 15 minutes before serving.
Preparation / Cooking Tips: You can also sprinkle dry rub on the turkey before grilling.
Nutrition:
Calories: 416 Cal
Fat: 13.3 g
Carbs: 0 g

Protein: 69.8 g
Fiber: 0 g

105. Turkey with Apricot Barbecue Glaze

Preparation Time: 30 minutes
Cooking Time: 30 minutes
Servings: 4
Ingredients:

- 4 turkey breast fillets
- 4 tablespoons chicken rub
- 1 cup apricot barbecue sauce

Directions:
1. Preheat the Pit boss grill to 365 degrees F for 15 minutes while the lid is closed.
2. Season the turkey fillets with the chicken run.
3. Grill the turkey fillets for 5 minutes per side.
4. Brush both sides with the barbecue sauce and grill for another 5 minutes per side.

Serving Suggestion: Serve with buttered cauliflower.
Preparation / Cooking Tips: You can sprinkle turkey with chili powder if you want your dish spicy.
Nutrition:
Calories: 316 Cal
Fat: 12.3 g
Carbs: 0 g

Protein: 29.8 g
Fiber: 0 g

106. Tandoori Chicken Wings

Preparation Time: 20 minutes
Cooking Time: 1 hour 20 minutes
Servings: 4-6
Ingredients:

- ¼ Cup Yogurt
- 1 Whole Scallions, minced
- 1 Tablespoon minced cilantro leaves
- 2 Teaspoon ginger, minced.
- 1 Teaspoon Masala
- 1 Teaspoon salt
- 1 Teaspoon ground black pepper
- 1 ½ pound chicken wings
- ¼ cup yogurt
- 2 tablespoon mayonnaise
- 2 tablespoon Cucumber
- 2 teaspoon lemon juice
- ½ teaspoon cumin
- ½ teaspoon salt
- 1/8 cayenne pepper

Directions:
1. Combine yogurt, scallion, ginger, garam masala, salt, cilantro, and pepper ingredients in the jar of a blender and process until smooth.
2. Put chicken and massage the bag to cat all the wings.
3. Refrigerate for 4 to 8 hours. Remove the excess marinade from the wings; discard the marinade.
4. Set the temperature to 350F and preheat, lid closed, for 10 to 15 minutes. Brush and oil the grill grate
5. Arrange the wings on the grill. Cook for 45 to 50 minutes, or until the skin is brown and crisp and meat is no longer pink at the bone. Turn once or twice during cooking to prevent the wings from sticking to the grill.
6. Meanwhile combine all sauce ingredients; set aside and refrigerate until ready to serve.
7. When wings are cooked through, transfer to a plate or platter. Serve with yogurt sauce.

Nutrition:

Calories 241kcal

Carbohydrates 11g

Protein 12g

Fat 16g

Saturated Fat 3g

107. Asian BBQ Chicken

Preparation Time: 12 to 24 hours
Cooking Time: 1 hour
Servings: 4-6
Ingredients:
- 1 whole chicken
- To taste Asian BBQ Rub
- 1 whole ginger ale

Direction:
1. Rinse chicken in cold water and pat dry with paper towels.
2. Cover the chicken all over with Asian BBQ rub; make sure to drop some in the inside too. Place in large bag or bowl and cover and refrigerate for 12 to 24 hours.
3. When ready to cook, set the Pit boss grill to 372F and preheat lid closed for 15 minutes.
4. Open can of ginger ale and take a few big gulps. Set the can of soda on a stable surface. Take the chicken out of the fridge and place the bird over top of the soda can. The base of the can and the two legs of the chicken should form a sort of tripod to hold the chicken upright.
5. Stand the chicken in the center of your hot grate and cook the chicken till the skin is golden brown and the internal temperature is about 165F on an instant-read thermometer, approximately 40 minutes to 1 hour.

Nutrition:

Calories 140kcal

Carbohydrates 18g

Protein 4g

Fat 4g

Sodium 806 mg

Potassium 682 mg

Fiber 5g

Sugar 8g

108. Homemade Turkey Gravy

Preparation Time: 20 minutes
Cooking Time: 3 hours 20 minutes
Servings: 8-12
Ingredients:
- 1 turkey, neck
- 2 large Onion, eight
- 4 celeries, stalks
- 4 large carrots, fresh
- 8 clove garlic, smashed.
- 8 thyme sprigs
- 4 cup chicken broth
- 1 teaspoon chicken broth
- 1 teaspoon salt
- 1 teaspoon cracked black pepper.
- 1 butter, sticks
- 1 cup all-purpose flour

Directions:
1. When ready to cook, set the temperature to 350F and preheat the Pit boss grill with the lid closed, for 15 minutes.
2. Place turkey neck, celery, carrot (roughly chopped), garlic, onion, and thyme on a roasting pan. Add four cups of chicken stock then season with salt and pepper.
3. Move the prepped turkey on the rack into the roasting pan and place in the Pit boss grill.
4. Cook for about 3-4 hours until the breast reaches 160F. The turkey will continue to cook, and it will reach a finished internal temperature of 165F.
5. Strain the drippings into a saucepan and simmer on low.

6. In a saucepan, mix butter (cut into 8 pieces) and flour with a whisk stirring until golden tan. This takes about 8 minutes, stirrings constantly.
7. Whisk the drippings into the roux then cook until it comes to a boil. Season with salt and pepper.

Nutrition:

Calories 160kcal

Carbohydrate 27g

Protein 55g

Fat 23g

Saturated Fat 6.1g

109. Bacon Wrapped Turkey Legs

Preparation Time: 10 minutes
Cooking Time: 3 hours
Servings: 4-6
Ingredients:

- Gallon water
- To taste Pit boss rub
- ½ cup pink curing salt
- ½ cup brown sugar
- 6 whole peppercorns

- 2 whole dried bay leaves
- ½ gallon ice water
- 8 whole turkey legs
- 16 sliced bacon

Directions:

1. In a large stockpot, mix one gallon of water, the rub, curing salt, brown sugar, peppercorns, and bay leaves.
2. Boil it to over high heat to dissolve the salt and sugar granules. Take off the heat then add in ½ gallon of ice and water.
3. The brine must be at least to room temperature, if not colder.
4. Place the turkey legs, completely submerged in the brine.
5. After 24 hours, drain the turkey legs then remove the brine.
6. Wash the brine off the legs with cold water, then dry thoroughly with paper towels.
7. When ready to cook, start the Pit boss grill according to grill instructions. Set the heat to 250F and preheat, lid closed for 10 to 15 minutes.
8. Place turkey legs directly on the grill grate.
9. After 2 ½ hours, wrap a piece of bacon around each leg then finish cooking them for 30 to 40 minutes of smoking.
10. The total smoking time for the legs will be 3 hours or until the internal temperature reaches 165F on an instant-read meat thermometer. Serve, Enjoy!

Nutrition:

Calories 390kcal

Total Fat 14g

Saturated Fat 0g

Cholesterol 64mg

Sodium 738mg

Carbohydrates 44g

110. Roasted Chicken

Preparation Time: 20 minutes
Cooking Time: 1 hour 20 minutes
Servings: 4-6
Ingredients:

- 8 tablespoon butter, room temperature
- 1 clove garlic, minced.
- 1 scallion, minced.
- 2 tablespoon fresh herbs such as thyme, rosemary, sage, or parsley

- As needed Chicken rub
- Lemon juice
- As needed vegetable oil

Directions:

1. In a small cooking bowl, mix the scallions, garlic, butter, minced fresh herbs, 1-1/2 teaspoon of the rub, and lemon juice. Mix with a spoon.
2. Remove any giblets from the cavity of the chicken. Wash the chicken inside and out with cold running water. Dry thoroughly with paper towels.
3. Sprinkle a generous amount of Chicken Rub inside the cavity of the chicken.
4. Gently loosen the skin around the chicken breast and slide in a few tablespoons of the herb butter under the skin and cover.
5. Cover the outside with the remaining herb butter.
6. Insert the chicken wings behind the back. Tie both legs together with a butcher's string.

Powder the outside of the chicken with more Chicken Rub then insert sprigs of fresh herbs inside the cavity of the chicken.

7. Set temperature to High and preheat, lid closed for 15 minutes.
8. Oil the grill with vegetable oil. Move the chicken on the grill grate, breast-side up then close the lid.
9. After chicken has cooked for 1 hour, lift the lid. If chicken is browning too quickly, cover the breast and legs with aluminum foil.
10. Close the lid then continue to roast the chicken until an instant-read meat thermometer inserted into the thickest part registers a temperature of 165F.
11. Take off chicken from grill and let rest for 5 minutes. Serve, Enjoy!

Nutrition:

Calories 222kcal

Carbohydrates 11g

Protein 29g

Fat 4g

Cholesterol 62mg

Sodium 616mg

Potassium 620mg

111. Grilled Asian Chicken Burgers

Preparation Time: 5 minutes

Cooking Time: 50 minutes

Servings: 4-6

Ingredients:

- Pound chicken, ground
- 1 cup panko breadcrumbs
- 1 cup parmesan cheese
- 1 small jalapeno, diced.
- 2 whole scallions, minced.
- 2 garlic cloves
- ¼ cup minced cilantro leaves
- 2 tablespoon mayonnaise
- 2 tablespoon chili sauce
- 1 tablespoon soy sauce
- 1 tablespoon ginger, minced.
- 2 teaspoon lemon juice
- 2 teaspoon lemon zest
- 1 teaspoon salt
- 1 teaspoon ground black pepper
- 8 hamburger buns
- 1 tomato, sliced.
- Arugula, fresh
- 1 red onion sliced.

Directions:

1. Align a rimmed baking sheet with aluminum foil then spray with nonstick cooking spray.
2. In a large bowl, combine the chicken, jalapeno, scallion, garlic, cilantro, panko, Parmesan, chili sauce, soy sauce ginger, mayonnaise, lemon juice and zest, and salt and pepper.
3. Work the mixture with your fingers until the ingredients are well combined. If the mixture looks too wet to form patties and add additional more panko.
4. Wash your hands under cold running water, form the meat into 8 patties, each about an inch larger than the buns and about ¾" thick. Use your thumbs or a tablespoon, make a wide, shallow depression in the top of each.
5. Put them on the prepared baking sheet. Spray the tops with nonstick cooking spray. If not cooking right away, cover with plastic wrap and refrigerate.
6. Set the Pit boss grill to 350F then preheat for 15 minutes, lid closed.
7. Order the burgers, depression-side down, on the grill grate. Remove and discard the foil on the baking sheet so you will have an uncontaminated surface to transfer the slider when cooked.
8. Grill the burgers for about 25 to 30 minutes, turning once, or until they release easily from the grill grate when a clean metal spatula is slipped under them. The internal temperature when read on an instant-read meat thermometer should be 160F.
9. Spread mayonnaise and arrange a tomato slice, if desired, and a few arugulas leaves on one-half of each bun. Top with a grilled burger and red onions, if using, then replace the top half of the bun. Serve immediately. Enjoy

Nutrition:

Calories 329kcal

Carbohydrates 10g

Protein 21g

Fat 23g

112. Grilled Sweet Cajun Wings

Preparation Time: 10 minutes
Cooking Time: 45 minutes
Servings: 4-6
Ingredients:

- 2-pound chicken wings
- As needed Pork and Poultry rub
- Cajun shake

Directions:

1. Coat wings in Sweet rub and Cajun shake.
2. When ready to cook, set the Pit boss grill to 350F and preheat, lid closed for 15 minutes.
3. Cook for 30 minutes until skin is brown and center is juicy, and an instant-read thermometer reads at least 165F. Serve, Enjoy!

113. The Grilled Chicken Challenge

Preparation Time: 15 minutes
Cooking Time: 1 hour and 10 minutes
Servings: 4-6
Ingredients:

- 1 (4-lbs.) whole chicken
- As needed chicken rub

Directions:

1. When ready to cook, set temperature to 375F then preheat, close the lid for 15 minutes.
2. Rinse and dry the whole chicken (remove and discard giblets, if any). Season the entire chicken, including the inside of the chicken using chicken rub.
3. Place the chicken on the grill and cook for 1 hour and 10 minutes.
4. Remove chicken from grill when internal temperature of breast reaches 160F. Check heat periodically throughout as cook times will vary based on the weight of the chicken.
5. Allow chicken to rest until the internal temperature of breast reaches 165F, 15-20 minutes. Enjoy!

Nutrition:

Calories 212kcal
Carbohydrates 42.6g
Protein 6.1g
Fat 2.4g

Saturated Fat 0.5g
Fiber 3.4g
Sugar 2.9g

114. Chicken Breast with Lemon

Preparation Time: 15min
Cooking Time: 15min
Servings: 6
Ingredients:

- 6 Chicken breasts, skinless and boneless
- ½ cup Oil
- 1 - 2 Fresh thyme sprigs
- 1 tsp. ground black pepper
- 2 tsp. Salt
- 2 tsp. of Honey
- 1 Garlic clove, chopped.
- 1 Lemon the juice and zest
- For service: Lemon wedges

Directions:

1. In a bowl combine the thyme, black pepper, salt, honey, garlic, and lemon zest and juice. Stir until dissolved and combined. Add the oil and whisk to combine.
2. Clean the breasts and pat dry. Place them in a plastic bag. Pour the pre-made marinade and massage to distribute evenly. Place in the fridge, 4 hours.
3. Preheat the grill to 400F with the lid closed.
4. Drain the chicken and grill until the internal temperature reaches 165F, about 15 minutes.
5. Serve with lemon wedges and a side dish of your choice.

Nutrition:

Calories: 230
Proteins: 38g

Carbohydrates: 1g Fat: 7g

115. Chicken Breasts with Dried Herbs

Preparation Time: 15 minutes
Cooking Time: 40 minutes
Servings: 4
Ingredients:

- 4 chicken breasts boneless
- 1/4 cup garlic-infused olive oil
- 2 clove garlic minced.
- 1/4 tsp of dried sage
- 1/4 tsp of dried lavender
- 1/4 tsp of dried thyme
- 1/4 tsp of dried mint
- 1/2 Tbsps. dried crushed red pepper
- Kosher salt to taste

Directions:

1. Place the chicken breasts in a shallow plastic container.
2. In a bowl, combine all remaining ingredients, and pour the mixture over the chicken breast and refrigerate for one hour.
3. Remove the chicken breast from the sauce (reserve sauce) and pat dry on kitchen paper.
4. Start your Pit boss grill on SMOKE (hickory Traeger) with the lid open until the fire is established). Set the temperature to 250F and preheat for 10 to 15 minutes.
5. Place chicken breasts on the smoker. Close Pit boss grill lid and cook for about 30 to 40 minutes or until chicken breasts reach 165F.
6. Serve hot with reserved marinade.

Nutrition:
Calories: 391
Carbohydrates: 0.7g
Fat: 3.21g
Fiber: 0.12g
Protein: 20.25g

116. Grilled Chicken with Pineapple

Preparation Time: 1 hour
Cooking Time: 1 hr. 15 mins
Servings: 6
Ingredients:

- 2 lbs. Chicken tenders
- 1 c. sweet chili sauce
- ¼ c. fresh pineapple juice
- ¼ c. honey

Directions:

1. Combine the honey, pineapple juice, and sweet chili sauce in a medium bowl. Whisk together thoroughly.
2. Put ¼ cup of the mixture to one side.
3. Coat the chicken in the sauce.
4. Place a lid over the bowl and leave it in the fridge for 30 minutes to marinate.
5. Heat the grill to high heat.
6. Separate the chicken from the marinade and grill for 5 minutes on each side.
7. Use the reserved sauce to brush over the chicken.
8. Continue to grill for a further 1 minute on each side.
9. Take the chicken off the grill and let it rest for 5 minutes before servings.

Nutrition:
Calories: 270
Fat: 2 g,
Carbohydrates: 25 g,
Protein: 33 g

117. Whole Orange Chicken

Preparation Time: 15 minutes + marinate time.
Cooking Time: 45 minutes
Servings: 4
Ingredients:

- 1 whole chicken, 3-4 pounds' backbone removed.
- 2 oranges
- ¼ cup oil
- 2 teaspoons Dijon mustard
- 1 orange, zest
- 2 tablespoons rosemary leaves, chopped.
- 2 teaspoons salt

Directions:

1. Clean and pat your chicken dry.
2. Take a bowl and mix in orange juice, oil, orange zest, salt, rosemary leaves, Dijon mustard and mix well.

3. Marinade chicken for 2 hours or overnight
4. Pre-heat your grill to 350 degrees F
5. Transfer your chicken to the smoker and smoke for 30 minutes' skin down. Flip and smoke until the internal temperature reaches 175 degrees F in the thigh and 165 degrees F in the breast.
6. Rest for 10 minutes and carve.
7. Enjoy!

Nutrition:

Calories: 290

Fats: 15g

Carbohydrates: 20g

Fiber: 1g

118. Turkey Patties

Preparation Time: 20 minutes
Cooking Time: 40 minutes
Servings: 6
Ingredients:

- 2 lbs. turkey minced meat
- 1/2 cup of parsley finely chopped.
- 2/3 cup of onion finely chopped.
- 1 red bell pepper finely chopped.

- 1 large egg at room temperature
- Salt and pepper to taste
- 1/2 tsp dry oregano
- 1/2 tsp dry thyme

Directions:

1. In a bowl, combine well all ingredients.
2. Make from the mixture patties.
3. Start Pit boss grill on (recommended apple or oak Traeger) lid open, until the fire is established (4-5 minutes). Increase the temperature to 350F and allow to pre-heat, lid closed, for 10 - 15 minutes.
4. Place patties on the grill racks and cook with lid covered for 30 to 40 minutes.
5. Your turkey patties are ready when you reach a temperature of 130F.
6. Serve hot.

Nutrition:

Calories: 251

Carbohydrates: 3.4g

Fat: 12.5

Fiber: 0.9g

Protein: 31.2g

119. Special Occasion's Dinner Cornish Hen

Preparation Time: 15 minutes
Cooking Time: 1 hour
Servings: 4
Ingredients:

- 4 Cornish game hens
- 4 fresh rosemary sprigs

- 4 tbsp. butter, melted.
- 4 tsp. chicken rub

Directions:

1. Set the temperature of Grill to 375 degrees F and preheat with closed lid for 15 mins.
2. With paper towels, pat dry the hens.
3. Tuck the wings behind the backs and with kitchen strings, tie the legs together.
4. Coat the outside of each hen with melted butter and sprinkle with rub evenly.
5. Stuff each hen with a rosemary sprig.
6. Place the hens onto the grill and cook for about 50-60 mins.
7. Remove the hens from grill and place onto a platter for about 10 mins.
8. Cut each hen into desired-sized pieces and serve.

Nutrition:

Calories: 430

Carbohydrates: 2.1g

Protein: 25.4g

Fat: 33g

Sugar: 0g

Sodium: 331mg

Fiber: 0.7g

120. Crispy & Juicy Chicken

Preparation Time: 15 minutes
Cooking Time: 5 hours
Servings: 6
Ingredients:

- ¾ C. dark brown sugar

- ½ C. ground espresso beans

- 1 tbsp. ground cumin
- 1 tbsp. ground cinnamon
- 1 tbsp. garlic powder
- 1 tbsp. cayenne pepper

- Salt and ground black pepper, to taste
- 1 (4-lb.) whole chicken, neck and giblets removed.

Directions:
1. Set the temperature of Grill to 200-225 degrees F and preheat with closed lid for 15 mins.
2. In a bowl, mix brown sugar, ground espresso, spices, salt, and black pepper.
3. Rub the chicken with spice mixture generously.
4. Put the chicken onto the grill and cook for about 3-5 hours.
5. Remove chicken from grill and place onto a cutting board for about 10 mins before carving.
6. Cut the chicken into desired-sized pieces and serve.

Nutrition:
Calories: 540
Carbohydrates: 20.7g
Protein: 88.3g
Fat: 9.6g

Sugar: 18.1g
Sodium: 226mg
Fiber: 1.2g

121. Ultimate Tasty Chicken

Preparation Time: 15 minutes
Cooking Time: 3 hours
Servings: 5
Ingredients:
For Brine:
- 1 C. brown sugar
- ½ C. kosher salt
- 16 C. water

For Chicken:
- 1 (3-lb.) whole chicken
- 1 tbsp. garlic, crushed.
- 1 tsp. onion powder

- Salt
- Ground black pepper, to taste
- 1 medium yellow onion, quartered.
- 3 whole garlic cloves, peeled.
- 1 lemon, quartered.
- 4-5 fresh thyme sprigs

Directions:
1. For brine: in a bucket, dissolve brown sugar and kosher salt in water.
2. Place the chicken in brine and refrigerate overnight.
3. Set the temperature of Grill to 225 degrees F and preheat with closed lid for 15 mins.
4. Remove the chicken from brine and with paper towels, pat it dry.
5. In a small bowl, mix crushed garlic, onion powder, salt, and black pepper.
6. Rub the chicken with garlic mixture evenly.
7. Stuff the inside of the chicken with onion, garlic cloves, lemon, and thyme.
8. With kitchen strings, tie the legs together.
9. Place the chicken onto grill and cook, covered for about 2½-3 hours.
10. Remove chicken from pallet grill and transfer onto a cutting board for about 10 mins before carving.
11. Cut the chicken in desired sized pieces and serve.

Nutrition:
Calories: 641
Carbohydrates: 31.7g
Protein: 79.2g
Fat: 20.2g

Sugar: 29.3g
Sodium: 11500mg
Fiber: 0.6g

122. South-East-Asian Chicken Drumsticks

Preparation Time: 15 minutes
Cooking Time: 2 hours
Servings: 6
Ingredients:
- 1 C. fresh orange juice
- ¼ C. honey
- 2 tbsp. sweet chili sauce
- 2 tbsp. hoisin sauce
- 2 tbsp. fresh ginger grated finely.

- 2 tbsp. garlic, minced.
- 1 tsp. Sriracha
- ½ tsp. sesame oil
- 6 chicken drumsticks

Directions:

1. Set the temperature of Grill to 225 degrees F and preheat with closed lid for 15 mins, using charcoal.
2. Mix all the ingredients except for chicken drumsticks and mix until well combined.
3. Set aside half of honey mixture in a small bowl.
4. In the bowl of remaining sauce, add drumsticks and mix well.
5. Arrange the chicken drumsticks onto the grill and cook for about 2 hours, basting with remaining sauce occasionally.
6. Serve hot.

Nutrition:

Calories: 385
Carbohydrates: 22.7g
Protein: 47.6g
Fat: 10.5g

Sugar: 18.6g
Sodium: 270mg
Fiber: 0.6g

123. Game Day Chicken Drumsticks

Preparation Time: 15 minutes
Cooking Time: 1 hour
Servings: 8
Ingredients:

For Brine:

- ½ C. brown sugar
- ½ C. kosher salt
- 5 C. water
- 2 (12-oz.) bottles beer
- 8 chicken drumsticks
- For Coating:

- ¼ C. olive oil
- ½ C. BBQ rub
- 1 tbsp. fresh parsley, minced.
- 1 tbsp. fresh chives, minced.
- ¾ C. BBQ sauce
- ¼ C. beer

Directions:

1. For brine: in a bucket, dissolve brown sugar and kosher salt in water and beer.
2. Place the chicken drumsticks in brine and refrigerate, covered for about 3 hours.
3. Set the temperature of Grill to 275 degrees F and preheat with closed lid for 15 mins.
4. Remove chicken drumsticks from brine and rinse under cold running water.
5. With paper towels, pat dry chicken drumsticks.
6. Coat drumsticks with olive oil and rub with BBQ rub evenly.
7. Sprinkle the drumsticks with parsley and chives.
8. Arrange the chicken drumsticks onto the grill and cook for about 45 mins.
9. Meanwhile, in a bowl, mix BBQ sauce and beer.
10. Remove from grill and coat the drumsticks with BBQ sauce evenly.
11. Cook for about 15 mins more.
12. Serve immediately.

Nutrition:

Calories: 448
Carbohydrates: 20.5g
Protein: 47.2g
Fat: 16.1g

Sugar: 14.9g
Sodium: 9700mg
Fiber: 0.2g

124. Glazed Chicken Thighs

Preparation Time: 15 minutes
Cooking Time: 2 hours and 5 minutes
Servings: 4
Ingredients:

- 2 garlic cloves, minced.
- ¼ C. honey
- 2 tbsp. soy sauce
- ¼ tsp. red pepper flakes, crushed.
- 4 (5-oz.) skinless, boneless chicken thighs

- 2 tbsp. olive oil
- 2 tsp. sweet rub
- ¼ tsp. red chili powder
- Freshly ground black pepper, to taste

Directions:

1. Set the temperature of Grill to 400 degrees F and preheat with closed lid for 15 mins.
2. In a bowl, add garlic, honey, soy sauce and red pepper flakes and with a wire whisk, beat until well combined.
3. Coat chicken thighs with oil and season with sweet rub, chili powder and black pepper generously.

4. Arrange the chicken drumsticks onto the grill and cook for about 15 mins per side.
5. In the last 4-5 mins of cooking, coat the thighs with garlic mixture.
6. Serve immediately.

Nutrition:

Calories: 309

Carbohydrates: 18.7g

Protein: 32.3g.

Fat: 12.1g

Sugar: 17.6g

Sodium: 504mg

Fiber: 0.2g

125. Cajun Chicken Breasts

Preparation Time: 10 minutes

Cooking Time: 6 hours

Servings: 6

Ingredients:

- 2 lb. skinless, boneless chicken breasts
- 2 tbsp. Cajun seasoning
- 1 C. BBQ sauce

Directions:

1. Set the temperature of Grill to 225 degrees F and preheat with closed lid for 15 mins.
2. Rub the chicken breasts with Cajun seasoning generously.
3. Put the chicken breasts onto the grill and cook for about 4-6 hours.
4. During last hour of cooking, coat the breasts with BBQ sauce twice.
5. Serve hot.

Nutrition:

Calories: 252

Carbohydrates: 15.1g

Protein: 33.8g; Fat: 5.5g

Sugar: 10.9g

Sodium: 570mg

Fiber: 0.3g

126. BBQ Sauce Smothered Chicken Breasts

Preparation Time: 15 minutes

Cooking Time: 30 minutes

Servings: 4

Ingredients:

- 1 tsp. garlic, crushed.
- ¼ C. olive oil
- 1 tbsp. Worcestershire sauce
- 1 tbsp. sweet mesquite seasoning
- 4 chicken breasts
- 2 tbsp. regular BBQ sauce
- 2 tbsp. spicy BBQ sauce
- 2 tbsp. honey bourbon BBQ sauce

Directions:

1. Set the temperature of Grill to 450 degrees F and preheat with closed lid for 15 mins.
2. In a large bowl, mix garlic, oil, Worcestershire sauce and mesquite seasoning.
3. Coat chicken breasts with seasoning mixture evenly.
4. Put the chicken breasts onto the grill and cook for about 20-30 mins.
5. Meanwhile, in a bowl, mix all 3 BBQ sauces.
6. In the last 4-5 mins of cooking, coat breast with BBQ sauce mixture.
7. Serve hot.

Nutrition:

Calories: 421

Carbohydrates: 10.1g

Protein: 41,2g

Fat: 23.3g

Sugar: 6.9g

Sodium: 763mg

Fiber: 0.2g

127. Budget Friendly Chicken Legs

Preparation Time: 15 minutes

Cooking Time: 1 hour and 30 minutes

Servings: 6

Ingredients:

For Brine:

- 1 C. kosher salt
- ¾ C. light brown sugar
- 16 C. water
- 6 chicken leg quarters

For Glaze:

- ½ C. mayonnaise
- 2 tbsp. BBQ rub
- 2 tbsp. fresh chives, minced.
- 1 tbsp. garlic, minced.

Directions

1. For brine: in a bucket, dissolve salt and brown sugar in water.
2. Place the chicken quarters in brine and refrigerate, covered for about 4 hours.
3. Set the temperature of Grill to 275 degrees F and preheat with closed lid for 15 mins.
4. Remove chicken quarters from brine and rinse under cold running water.
5. With paper towels, pat dry chicken quarters.
6. For glaze: in a bowl, add all ingredients and mix till ell combined.
7. Coat chicken quarters with glaze evenly.
8. Place the chicken leg quarters onto grill and cook for about 1-1½ hours.
9. Serve immediately.

Nutrition:

Calories: 399
Carbohydrates: 17.2g
Protein: 29.1g
Fat: 24.7g

Sugar: 14.2g
Sodium: 15000mg
Fiber: 0g

128. Thanksgiving Dinner Turkey

Preparation Time: 15 minutes
Cooking Time: 4 hours
Servings: 16
Ingredients:

- ½ lb. butter, softened.
- 2 tbsp. fresh thyme, chopped.
- 2 tbsp. fresh rosemary, chopped.
- 6 garlic cloves, crushed.
- 1 (20-lb.) whole turkey, neck and giblets removed.
- Salt and ground black pepper

Directions:

1. Set the temperature of Grill to 300 degrees F and preheat with closed lid for 15 mins, using charcoal.
2. In a bowl, place butter, fresh herbs, garlic, salt, and black pepper and mix well.
3. Separate the turkey skin from breast to create a pocket.
4. Stuff the breast pocket with ¼-inch thick layer of butter mixture.
5. Season turkey with salt and black pepper.
6. Arrange the turkey onto the grill and cook for 3-4 hours.
7. Remove the turkey from grill and place onto a cutting board for about 15-20 mins before carving.
8. Cut the turkey into desired-sized pieces and serve.

Nutrition:

Calories: 965
Carbohydrates: 0.6.
Protein: 106.5g
Fat: 52g

Sugar: 0g
Sodium: 1916mg
Fiber: 0.2g

129. Roasted Turkey with Herb

Preparation Time: 15 Minutes
Cooking Time: 3 Hours 30 Minutes
Servings: 12
Ingredients:

- 14 pounds turkey, cleaned.
- 2 tablespoons chopped mixed herbs.
- Pork and poultry rub as needed.
- ¼ teaspoon ground black pepper
- 3 tablespoons butter, unsalted, melted.
- 8 tablespoons butter, unsalted, softened.
- 2 cups chicken broth

Directions:

1. Clean the turkey by removing the giblets, wash it inside out, pat dry with paper towels, then place it on a roasting pan and tuck the turkey wings by tiring with butcher's string.
2. Switch on the grill, fill the grill hopper with hickory flavored Traeger's, power the grill on by using the control panel, select 'smoke' on the temperature dial, or set the temperature to 325 degrees F and let it preheat for a minimum of 15 minutes.
3. Meanwhile, prepared herb butter and for this, take a small bowl, place the softened butter in it, add black pepper and mixed herbs and beat until fluffy.
4. Place some of the prepared herb butter underneath the skin of turkey by using a handle of a wooden spoon and massage the skin to distribute butter evenly.

5. Then rub the exterior of the turkey with melted butter, season with pork and poultry rub, and pour the broth in the roasting pan.
6. When the grill has preheated, open the lid, place roasting pan containing turkey on the grill grate, shut the grill and smoke for 3 hours and 30 minutes until the internal temperature reaches 165 degrees F and the top has turned golden brown.
7. When done, transfer turkey to a cutting board, let it rest for 30 minutes, then carve it into slices and serve.

Nutrition: Calories: 154.6 Fat: 3.1 g Carbs: 8.4 g Protein: 28.8 g

130. Turkey Legs

Preparation Time: 10 Minutes
Cooking Time: 5 Hours
Servings: 4
Ingredients:

- 4 turkey legs
- For the Brine:
- ½ cup curing salt.
- 1 tablespoon whole black peppercorns
- 1 cup BBQ rub
- ½ cup brown sugar

- 2 bay leaves
- 2 teaspoons liquid smoke
- 16 cups of warm water
- 4 cups ice
- 8 cups of cold water

Directions:

1. Prepare the brine and for this, take a large stockpot, place it over high heat, pour warm water in it, add peppercorn, bay leaves, and liquid smoke, stir in salt, sugar, and BBQ rub and bring it to a boil.
2. Remove pot from heat, bring it to room temperature, then pour in cold water, add ice cubes, and let the brine chill in the refrigerator.
3. Then add turkey legs in it, submerge them completely, and let soak for 24 hours in the refrigerator.
4. After 24 hours, remove turkey legs from the brine, rinse well and pat dry with paper towels.
5. When ready to cook, switch on the grill, fill the grill hopper with hickory flavored Traeger's, power the grill on by using the control panel, select 'smoke' on the temperature dial, or set the temperature to 250 degrees F and let it preheat for a minimum of 15 minutes.
6. When the grill has preheated, open the lid, place turkey legs on the grill grate, shut the grill, and smoke for 5 hours until nicely browned and the internal temperature reaches 165 degrees F. Serve immediately.

Nutrition: Calories: 416 Fat: 13.3 g Carbs: 0 g Protein: 69.8 g

131. Turkey Breast

Preparation Time: 12 Hours
Cooking Time: 8 Hours
Servings: 6
Ingredients:
For the Brine:

- 2 pounds turkey breast, deboned.
- 2 tablespoons ground black pepper
- ¼ cup salt
- 1 cup brown sugar
- 4 cups cold water

For the BBQ Rub:

- 2 tablespoons dried onions
- 2 tablespoons garlic powder

- ¼ cup paprika
- 2 tablespoons ground black pepper
- 1 tablespoon salt
- 2 tablespoons brown sugar
- 2 tablespoons red chili powder
- 1 tablespoon cayenne pepper
- 2 tablespoons sugar
- 2 tablespoons ground cumin

Directions:

1. Prepare the brine and for this, take a large bowl, add salt, black pepper, and sugar in it, pour in water, and stir until sugar has dissolved.
2. Place turkey breast in it, submerge it completely and let it soak for a minimum of 12 hours in the refrigerator.
3. Meanwhile, prepare the BBQ rub and for this, take a small bowl, place all its ingredients in it and then stir until combined, set aside until required.
4. Then remove turkey breast from the brine and season well with the prepared BBQ rub.
5. When ready to cook, switch on the grill, fill the grill hopper with apple flavored Traeger's, power the grill on by using the control panel, select 'smoke' on the temperature dial, or set the temperature to 180 degrees F and let it preheat for a minimum of 15 minutes.

6. When the grill has preheated, open the lid, place turkey breast on the grill grate, shut the grill, change the smoking temperature to 225 degrees F, and smoke for 8 hours until the internal temperature reaches 160 degrees F.
7. When done, transfer turkey to a cutting board, let it rest for 10 minutes, then cut it into slices and serve.

Nutrition: Calories: 250 Fat: 5 g Carbs: 31 g Protein: 18 g

132. Apple wood-Smoked Whole Turkey

Preparation Time: 10 minutes
Cooking Time: 5 hours
Servings: 6
Ingredients:

- 1 (10- to 12-pound) turkey, giblets removed.
- Extra-virgin olive oil, for rubbing.
- ¼ cup poultry seasoning
- 8 tablespoons (1 stick) unsalted butter, melted.
- ½ cup apple juice
- 2 teaspoons dried sage
- 2 teaspoons dried thyme

Directions:

1. Supply your smoker with Pit boss and follow the manufacturer's specific start-up procedure. Preheat, with the lid closed to 250°F.
2. Rub the turkey with oil and season with the poultry seasoning inside and out, getting under the skin.
3. In a bowl, combine the melted butter, apple juice, sage, and thyme to use for basting.
4. Put the turkey in a roasting pan, place on the grill, close the lid, and grill for 5 to 6 hours, basting every hour, until the skin is brown and crispy, or until a meat thermometer inserted in the thickest part of the thigh reads 165°F.
5. Let the turkey meat rest for about 15 to 20 minutes before carving.

Nutrition: Calories: 180 Carbs: 3g Fat: 2g Protein: 39g

133. Savory-Sweet Turkey Legs

Preparation Time: 10 minutes
Cooking Time: 5 hours
Servings: 4
Ingredients:

- 1-gallon hot water
- 1 cup curing salt (such as Morton Tender Quick)
- ¼ cup packed light brown sugar.
- 1 teaspoon freshly ground black pepper.
- 1 teaspoon ground cloves
- 1 bay leaf
- 2 teaspoons liquid smoke
- 4 turkey legs
- Mandarin Glaze, for serving

Directions:

1. In a huge container with a lid, stir together the water, curing salt, brown sugar, pepper, cloves, bay leaf, and liquid smoke until the salt and sugar are dissolved; let come to room temperature.
2. Submerge the turkey legs in the seasoned brine, cover, and refrigerate overnight.
3. When ready to smoke, remove the turkey legs from the brine and rinse them; discard the brine.
4. Supply your smoker with Pit boss and follow the manufacturer's specific start-up procedure. Preheat, with the lid closed to 225°F.
5. Arrange the turkey legs on the grill, close the lid, and smoke for 4 to 5 hours, or until dark brown and a meat thermometer inserted in the thickest part of the meat reads 165°F.
6. Serve with Mandarin Glaze on the side or drizzled over the turkey legs.

Nutrition: Calories: 190 Carbs: 1g Fat: 9g Protein: 24g

134. Marinated Smoked Turkey Breast

Preparation Time: 15 minutes
Cooking Time: 4 hours
Servings: 6
Ingredients:

- 1 (5 pounds) boneless chicken breast
- 4 cups water
- 2 tablespoons kosher salt
- 1 teaspoon Italian seasoning
- 2 tablespoons honey
- 1 tablespoon cider vinegar
- Rub:
- ½ teaspoon onion powder

- 1 teaspoon paprika
- 1 teaspoon salt
- 1 teaspoon ground black pepper
- 1 tablespoon brown sugar
- ½ teaspoon garlic powder
- 1 teaspoon oregano

Directions:
1. In a huge container, combine the water, honey, cider vinegar, Italian seasoning, and salt.
2. Add the chicken breast and toss to combine. Cover the bowl and place it in the refrigerator and chill for 4 hours.
3. Rinse the chicken breast with water and pat dry with paper towels.
4. In another mixing bowl, combine the brown sugar, salt, paprika, onion powder, pepper, oregano, and garlic.
5. Generously season the chicken breasts with the rub mix.
6. Preheat the grill to 225°F with lid closed for 15 minutes. Use cherry Traeger's.
7. Arrange the turkey breast into a grill rack. Place the grill rack on the grill.
8. Smoke for about 3 to 4 hours or until the internal temperature of the turkey breast reaches 165°F.
9. Remove the chicken breast from heat and let them rest for a few minutes. Serve.

Nutrition: Calories 903 Fat: 34g Carbs: 9.9g Protein 131.5g

135. Maple Bourbon Turkey

Preparation Time: 15 minutes
Cooking Time: 3 hours
Servings: 8
Ingredients:
- 1 (12 pounds) turkey
- 8 cup chicken broth
- 1 stick butter (softened)
- 1 teaspoon thyme
- 2 garlic cloves (minced)
- 1 teaspoon dried basil
- 1 teaspoon pepper
- 1 teaspoon salt
- 1 tablespoon minced rosemary
- 1 teaspoon paprika
- 1 lemon (wedged)
- 1 onion
- 1 orange (wedged)
- 1 apple (wedged)
- Maple Bourbon Glaze:
- ¾ cup bourbon
- 1/2 cup maple syrup
- 1 stick butter (melted)
- 1 tablespoon lime

Directions:
1. Wash the turkey meat inside and out under cold running water.
2. Insert the onion, lemon, orange, and apple into the turkey cavity.
3. In a mixing bowl, combine the butter, paprika, thyme, garlic, basil, pepper, salt, basil, and rosemary.
4. Brush the turkey generously with the herb butter mixture.
5. Set a rack into a roasting pan and place the turkey on the rack. Put a 5 cups of chicken broth into the bottom of the roasting pan.
6. Preheat the grill to 350°F with lid closed for 15 minutes, using maple Traeger's.
7. Place the roasting pan in the grill and cook for 1 hour.
8. Meanwhile, combine all the maple bourbon glaze ingredients in a mixing bowl. Mix until well combined.
9. Baste the turkey with glaze mixture. Continue cooking, basting turkey every 30 minutes and adding more broth as needed for 2 hours, or until the internal temperature of the turkey reaches 165°F.
10. Take off the turkey from the grill and let it rest for a few minutes. Cut into slices and serve.

Nutrition: Calories 1536 Fat 58.6g Carbs: 24g Protein 20.1g

136. Thanksgiving Turkey

Preparation Time: 15 minutes
Cooking Time: 4 hours
Servings: 6
Ingredients:
- 2 cups butter (softened)
- 1 tablespoon cracked black pepper.
- 2 teaspoons kosher salt
- 2 tablespoons freshly chopped rosemary
- 2 tablespoons freshly chopped parsley
- 2 tablespoons freshly chopped sage
- 2 teaspoons dried thyme
- 6 garlic cloves (minced)
- 1 (18 pound) turkey

Directions:
1. In a mixing bowl, combine the butter, sage, rosemary, 1 teaspoon black pepper, 1 teaspoon salt, thyme, parsley, and garlic.

2. Use your fingers to loosen the skin from the turkey.
3. Generously, Rub butter mixture under the turkey skin and all over the turkey as well. 4. Season turkey generously with herb mix. 5. Preheat the grill to 300°F with lid closed for 15 minutes.
4. Place the turkey on the grill and roast for about 4 hours, or until the turkey thigh temperature reaches 160°F.
5. Take out the turkey meat from the grill and let it rest for a few minutes. Cut into sizes and serve.

Nutrition: Calories 278 Fat 30.8g Carbs: 1.6g Protein 0.6g

137. Spatchcock Smoked Turkey

Preparation Time: 15 minutes
Cooking Time: 4 hours 3 minutes
Servings: 6
Ingredients:

- 1 (18 pounds) turkey
- 2 tablespoons finely chopped fresh parsley.
- 1 tablespoon finely chopped fresh rosemary.
- 2 tablespoons finely chopped fresh thyme.
- ½ cup melted butter.
- 1 teaspoon garlic powder
- 1 teaspoon onion powder
- 1 teaspoon ground black pepper
- 2 teaspoons salt or to taste.
- 2 tablespoons finely chopped scallions

Directions:

1. Remove the turkey giblets and rinse turkey, in and out, under cold running water.
2. Place the turkey on a working surface, breast side down. Use a poultry shear to cut the turkey along both sides of the backbone to remove the turkey back bone.
3. Flip the turkey over, back side down. Now, press the turkey down to flatten it.
4. In a mixing bowl, combine the parsley, rosemary, scallions, thyme, butter, pepper, salt, and garlic and onion powder.
5. Rub butter mixture over all sides of the turkey.
6. Preheat your grill to HIGH (450°F) with lid closed for 15 minutes.
7. Place the turkey directly on the grill grate and cook for 30 minutes. Reduce the heat to 300°F and cook for an additional 4 hours, or until the internal temperature of the thickest part of the thigh reaches 165°F.
8. Take out the turkey meat from the grill and let it rest for a few minutes. Cut into sizes and serve.

Nutrition: Calories: 780 Fat: 19g Carbs: 29.7g Protein 116.4g

138. Hoisin Turkey Wings

Preparation Time: 15 minutes
Cooking Time: 1 hour
Servings: 8
Ingredients:

- 2 pounds turkey wings
- ½ cup hoisin sauce
- 1 tablespoon honey
- 2 teaspoons soy sauce
- 2 garlic cloves (minced)
- 1 teaspoon freshly grated ginger
- 2 teaspoons sesame oil
- 1 teaspoons pepper or to taste.
- 1 teaspoons salt or to taste.
- ¼ cup pineapple juice
- 1 tablespoon chopped green onions.
- 1 tablespoon sesame seeds
- 1 lemon (cut into wedges)

Directions:

1. In a huge container, combine the honey, garlic, ginger, soy, hoisin sauce, sesame oil, pepper, and salt. Put all the mixture into a zip lock bag and add the wings. Refrigerate for 2 hours.
2. Remove turkey from the marinade and reserve the marinade. Let the turkey rest for a few minutes, until it is at room temperature.
3. Preheat your grill to 300°F with the lid closed for 15 minutes.
4. Arrange the wings into a grilling basket and place the basket on the grill.
5. Grill for 1 hour or until the internal temperature of the wings reaches 165°F.
6. Meanwhile, pour the reserved marinade into a saucepan over medium-high heat. Stir in the pineapple juice.
7. Wait to boil then reduce heat and simmer for until the sauce thickens.
8. Brush the wings with sauce and cook for 6 minutes more. Remove the wings from heat.
9. Serve and garnish it with green onions, sesame seeds and lemon wedges.

Nutrition: Calories: 115 Fat: 4.8g Carbs: 11.9g Protein 6.8g

139. Pit boss Turkey Jerky

Preparation Time: 15 minutes
Cooking Time: 4 hours
Servings: 6
Ingredients:

- Marinade:
- 1 cup pineapple juice
- ½ cup brown sugar
- 2 tablespoons Sirach
- 2 teaspoons onion powder
- 2 tablespoons minced garlic
- 2 tablespoons rice wine vinegar
- 2 tablespoons hoisin
- 1 tablespoon red pepper flakes
- 1 tablespoon coarsely ground black pepper flakes.
- 2 cups coconut amino
- 2 jalapenos (thinly sliced)
- Meat:
- 3 pounds turkey boneless skinless breasts (sliced to ¼ inch thick)

Directions:

1. Pour the marinade mixture ingredients in a container and mix until the ingredients are well combined.
2. Put the turkey slices in a gallon sized zip lock bag and pour the marinade into the bag. Massage the marinade into the turkey. Seal the bag and refrigerate for 8 hours.
3. Remove the turkey slices from the marinade.
4. Activate the Pit boss grill for smoking and leave lip opened for 5 minutes until fire starts.
5. Close the lid and preheat your Pit boss grill to 180°F, using hickory Traeger.
6. Remove the turkey slices from the marinade and pat them dry with a paper towel.
7. Arrange the turkey slices on the grill in a single layer. Smoke the turkey for about 3 to 4 hours, turning often after the first 2 hours of smoking. The jerky should be dark and dry when it is done.
8. Remove the jerky from the grill and let it sit for about 1 hour to cool. Serve immediately or store in refrigerator.

Nutrition: Calories: 109 Carbs: 12g Fat: 1g Protein: 14g

140. Whole Turkey

Preparation Time: 20 Minutes
Cooking Time: 8 Hours
Servings: 6
Ingredients:

- 1 Whole Turkey of about 12 to 16 lb.
- 1 Cup of your Favorite Rub
- 1 Cup of Sugar
- 1 Tablespoon of minced garlic
- ½ Cup of Worcestershire sauce
- 2 Tablespoons of Canola Oil

Directions:

1. Thaw the Turkey and remove the giblets.
2. Pour in 3 gallons of water in a non-metal bucket of about 5 gallons.
3. Add the BBQ rub and mix very well.
4. Add the garlic, the sugar, and the Worcestershire sauce; then submerge the turkey into the bucket.
5. Refrigerate the turkey in the bucket for an overnight.
6. Place the Grill on a High Smoke and smoke the Turkey for about 3 hours.
7. Switch the grilling temp to about 350 degrees F; then push a metal meat thermometer into the thickest part of the turkey breast.
8. Cook for about 4 hours; then take off the Pit boss grill and let rest for about 15 minutes.
9. Slice the turkey, then serve and enjoy your dish!

Nutrition: Calories: 165 Fat: 14g Carbs: 0.5g Protein: 15.2g

141. Herbed Turkey Breast

Preparation Time: 8 Hours And 10 Minutes
Cooking Time: 3 Hours
Servings: 12
Ingredients:

- 7 pounds turkey breast, bone-in, skin-on, fat trimmed.
- 3/4 cup salt
- 1/3 cup brown sugar
- 4 quarts water, cold
- For Herbed Butter:
- 1 tablespoon chopped parsley.
- ½ teaspoon ground black pepper
- 8 tablespoons butter, unsalted, softened.
- 1 tablespoon chopped sage.

- ½ tablespoon minced garlic
- 1 tablespoon chopped rosemary.
- 1 teaspoon lemon zest
- 1 tablespoon chopped oregano.
- 1 tablespoon lemon juice

Directions:

1. Prepare the brine and for this, pour water in a large container, add salt, and sugar and stir well until salt and sugar has completely dissolved.
2. Add turkey breast in the brine, cover with the lid and let soak in the refrigerator for a minimum of 8 hours.
3. Then remove turkey breast from the brine, rinse well and pat dry with paper towels.
4. Open hopper of the smoker, add dry pallets, make sure ashcan is in place, then open the ash damper, power on the smoker, and close the ash damper.
5. Set the temperature of the smoker to 350 degrees F, let preheat for 30 minutes or until the green light on the dial blinks that indicate smoker has reached to set temperature.
6. Meanwhile, take a roasting pan, pour in 1 cup water, then place a wire rack in it and place turkey breast on it.
7. Prepare the herb butter and for this, place butter in a heatproof bowl, add remaining ingredients for the butter and stir until just mix.
8. Loosen the skin of the turkey from its breast by using your fingers, then insert 2 tablespoons of prepared herb butter on each side of the skin of the breastbone and spread it evenly, pushing out all the air pockets.
9. Place the remaining herb butter in the bowl into the microwave wave and heat for 1 minute or more at high heat setting or until melted.
10. Then brush melted herb butter on the outside of the turkey breast and place roasting pan containing turkey on the smoker grill.
11. Shut the smoker with lid and smoke for 2 hours and 30 minutes or until the turkey breast is nicely golden brown and the internal temperature of turkey reach to 165 degrees F, flipping the turkey and basting with melted herb butter after 1 hour and 30 minutes smoking.
12. When done, transfer the turkey breast to a cutting board, let it rest for 15 minutes, then carve it into pieces and serve.

Nutrition: Calories: 97 Fat: 4 g Protein: 13 g Carbs: 1 g

Chapter 6.   Smoking Recipes

142. Smoked Ribs

Preparation Time: 20 minutes
Cooking Time: 6 hours
Servings: 8
Ingredients:
- Four baby back ribs
- 1 cup pork rubs
- 1 cup barbecue sauce

Directions:
1. Preheat your grill to 180 tiers F for 15 minutes simultaneously as the lid is closed.
2. Sprinkle toddler again ribs with beef rub.
3. Smoke the ribs for 5 hours.
4. Brush the ribs with barbecue sauce.
5. Wrap the ribs with foil.
6. Put the ribs again on the grill.
7. Increase temperature to 350 levels F.
8. Cook for forty-five minutes to at least one hour.
9. Let rest before slicing and serving.

Nutrition:
Energy (calories): 493 kcal
Protein: 38.78 g
Fat: 30.94 g
Carbohydrates: 14.97 g

143. Smoked Pot Roast

Preparation Time: 30 minutes
Cooking Time: 6 hours
Servings: 4
Ingredients:
- Salt and pepper to taste
- 1 tsp. Onion powder 1 tsp. garlic powder
- 3 lb. chuck roast
- 2 cups potatoes sliced in half.
- 2 cups carrots, sliced.
- Two onions, peeled.
- 1 tsp. chili powder
- 1 cup red wine
- 1 tbsp. fresh rosemary, chopped.
- 1 tbsp. fresh thyme, chopped.
- Two dried chipotle peppers
- 2 cups beef stock

Directions:
1. Mix the salt, pepper, onion powder, and garlic powder in a bowl.
2. Rub chuck roast with this aggregate.
3. Preheat your pellet grill to 180 ranges F for 15 minutes while the lid is closed.
4. Smoke the pork for 1 hour.
5. Increase temperature to 275 tiers F.
6. Place the pork and the relaxation of the ingredients in a Dutch oven.
7. Seal the Dutch oven and area on the grill.
8. Braise for five hours.

Nutrition:
Energy (calories): 733 kcal
Protein: 95.53 g
Fat: 29.17 g
Carbohydrates: 20.59 g

144. Smoked Brisket

Preparation Time: 30 minutes
Cooking Time: 12 hours
Servings: 8
Ingredients:
- Salt and pepper to taste
- 2 tbsp. beef rub
- 1 tbsp. Worcestershire sauce
- 6 lb. brisket
- 1 cup beef broth

Directions:
1. Mix salt, pepper, beef rub, and Worcestershire sauce in a bowl.
2. Rub brisket with this combination.
3. Preheat your wood pellet grill to 180 levels F for 15 minutes while the lid is closed.

4. Smoke the brisket for 7 hours.
5. Transfer brisket on top of a foil.
6. Pour the broth over the brisket.
7. Wrap it with foil.
8. Smoke for five hours.
9. Let rest before slicing.

Nutrition:

Energy (calories): 464 kcal

Protein: 73.34 g

Fat: 17.43 g

Carbohydrates: 3.54 g

145. Pit boss Smoked Potatoes.

Preparation Time: 30 minutes
Cooking Time: 1 hour
Servings: 6
Ingredients:

- 2 tbsp. butter
- 1/2 cup milk
- 1 cup heavy cream
- Two cloves' garlic crushed and minced.
- 2 tbsp. flour
- Four potatoes sliced thinly.
- Salt and pepper to taste
- 1 cup cheddar cheese, grated.

Directions:

1. Preheat your wood pellet grill to 375 levels F for 15 minutes at the same time as the lid is closed.
2. Add butter to your forged iron pan.
3. In a bowl, blend the milk, cream, garlic, and flour.
4. Arrange some of the potatoes in a pan.
5. Season with salt and pepper.
6. Pour some of the sauce over the potatoes.
7. Repeat layers till elements were used.
8. Grill for 50 minutes.
9. Sprinkle cheese on top and prepare dinner for 10 minutes.

Nutrition:

Energy (calories): 176 kcal

Protein: 2.78 g

Fat: 12 g

Carbohydrates: 15.14 g

146. Pit boss Smoked devil Eggs.

Preparation Time: 30 minutes
Cooking Time: 45 minutes
Servings: 8
Ingredients:

- 12 hard-boiled eggs peeled and sliced in half.
- Two jalapeño peppers
- Two slices bacon, cooked crisp and chopped.
- 1/2 cup mayonnaise
- 2 tsp. white vinegar
- 2 tsp. mustard
- 1/2 teaspoon chili powder
- 1/2 teaspoon paprika
- Salt to taste
- Pinch paprika
- Chopped chives.

Directions:

1. With the roasted peppers, Serving Set the wood pellet grill to 180 ranges F.
2. Preheat for 15 minutes while the lid is closed.
3. Smoke the eggs and peppers for forty-five minutes.
4. Transfer to a plate.
5. Scoop out the egg yolks and location in a bowl.
6. Stir in the rest of the substances.
7. Mash the eggs and blend well.
8. Scoop the egg combination on top of the egg whites.

Nutrition:

Energy (calories): 182 kcal

Protein: 10.94 g

Fat: 14.1 g

Carbohydrates: 2.12 g

147. Cajun Smoked Turkey Recipe

Preparation Time: 10 minutes
Cooking Time: 2-3 hours
Servings: 8
Ingredients

For the injection
- 1 ounce 12- bottle beer, at room temperature
- 1/2 cup butter, melted.
- Six large garlic cloves
- 2 tbsp. Worcestershire sauce
- 2 tbsp. creole seasonings
- 1 tbsp. liquid crab boil
- 1 tbsp. Louisiana-style hot sauce
- 1 tbsp. kosher salt
- 1/2 teaspoon cayenne pepper
- 1 pound 12-14 natural turkeys

For the rub
- 1 tsp. paprika
- 1/2 teaspoon garlic powder
- 1/2 teaspoon onion powder
- 1/2 teaspoon dried thyme
- 1/4 teaspoon dried oregano
- 1/4 teaspoon cumin
- 1/4 teaspoon kosher salt
- 1/4 teaspoon freshly ground black pepper.
- 1/8 teaspoon cayenne pepper
- 1 tbsp. vegetable oil
- Two fist-sized chunks of applewood or other light smoking wood

Directions
1. To make the injection, place beer, butter, garlic, Worcestershire, Creole seasoning, liquid crab boil, hot sauce, salt, and cayenne pepper in the jar of a blender and puree until completely smooth. Utilizing a meat injection syringe, inject the mixture into the turkey's meat around with each injection spaced about 1-inch apart.
2. To help make the rub, combine paprika, garlic powder, onion powder, thyme, oregano, cumin, salt, black pepper, and cayenne in a little bowl—season turkey inside and out with rub. Fold wings beneath the body, tie the legs together, and brush the turkey lightly with vegetable oil.
3. Turn up smoker or grill to 325degrees F, adding smoking wood chunks when at temperature. When wood is ignited and smoked, place turkey in smoker or grill and smoke until an instantaneous read thermometer registers 165degrees F in the thickest part of the breast, about 2-3 hours.
4. Take away the turkey from the smoker and invite to rest, uncovered, for 20 to 30 minutes. Carve and serve.

Nutrition:

Energy (calories): 391 kcal
Protein: 11.57 g

Fat: 36.76 g
Carbohydrates: 2.54 g

148. Cryer's Cider-Smoked Ribs Recipe

Preparation Time: 10 minutes
Cooking Time: 2 hours
Servings: 12
Ingredients

- 3 tbsp. white sugar
- 3 tbsp. packed brown sugar.
- 2 tbsp. of sea salt
- 1 1/2 tablespoons ground New Mexico Chile powder
- 1 tbsp. garlic powder
- 1 tbsp. onion powder
- 1 tbsp. Hungarian paprika
- 1 tbsp. ground ancho Chile powder
- 1 tbsp. ground black pepper

- 1 1/2 tsp. dried rosemary
- 1 1/2 tsp. dried thyme, or more to taste
- 1 1/2 tsp. ground cumin, or more to taste
- 1 1/2 tsp. ground nutmeg, or more to taste
- 1 1/2 tsp. ground allspice
- 1/2 tsp. cayenne pepper, or more to taste
- Three slabs of baby back pork ribs
- 4 cups apple cider, or as needed.
- 2 cups barbeque sauces

Directions
1. Combine the white sugar, brown sugar, sea salt, Chile powder, garlic powder, onion powder, paprika, ancho Chile powder, black pepper, rosemary, thyme, cumin, nutmeg, allspice, and cayenne pepper in a bowl to help make the rib rub.
2. Coat ribs evenly with the rub. Close it with plastic wrap and let marinate in the refrigerator, 8 hours to overnight.
3. Turn to heat the smoker to 300 degrees F (150 degrees C) per manufacturer's instructions. Put the ribs on smoker meat-side up. Cook until browned, about 1 1/2 hour. Then remove from smoker.
4. Pour apple cider into an aluminum roasting pan—position ribs in the pan, sitting on end if needed. Cover with aluminum foil. Go back to the smoker. Just continue smoking ribs until tender, about 2 hours more.
5. Transfer ribs to a grill. Brush barbeque sauce at the top. Grill until darkish, about 10 minutes per side.

Nutrition:

Energy (calories): 296 kcal

Protein: 4.69 g

Fat: 1.55 g

Carbohydrates: 68.52 g

149. Fat Boy's Smoked Baby Backs Recipe

Preparation Time: 10 minutes

Cooking Time: 3 hours and 30 minutes

Servings: 3

Ingredients

- Three racks of baby back pork ribs, outer membrane removed.
- 1/4 cup water
- 1/2 cup vinegar
- 1/3 cup Worcestershire sauce
- 1 tsp. olive oil
- 1/2 cup finely chopped onions
- 1 cup ketchup
- 1/4 cup honey
- 3 tbsp. steak sauces (such as a.1)
- 1 tbsp. hot sauces (such as a crystal)
- One clove garlic, chopped.
- 1 tsp. ground cayenne pepper

Directions

1. Turn to heat the oven to 200 degrees F (95 degrees C).
2. Place marinated ribs in a shallow baking dish; add water—tent aluminum foil over a baking dish.
3. Bake ribs in the preheated oven until heated through, about 1 1/4 hour.
4. Preheat smoker to 225 degrees F (110 degrees C) according to manufacturer's instructions.
5. Combine vinegar and Worcestershire sauce in a little bowl and pour right into a spray bottle.
6. Transfer ribs to the smoker. Let cook, spraying generously with vinegar mixture every 30 minutes, until tender, about 3 hours.
7. Preheat an outdoor grill for medium-high heat and lightly oil the grate.
8. Heat essential olive oil in a skillet over medium heat. Put an onion; cook and stir until softened, about five minutes. Add ketchup, honey, steak sauce, hot sauce, garlic, and cayenne pepper. Simmer sauce until flavors combine, about 20 minutes.
9. Brush sauce over ribs. Grill until deeply browned, about 15 minutes.

Nutrition:

Energy (calories): 336 kcal

Protein: 15.36 g

Fat: 5.39 g

Carbohydrates: 58.84 g

150. Hickory Smoked Cornish Game Hen Recipe

Preparation Time: 10 minutes

Cooking Time: 1 hour

Servings: 4

Ingredients

- 1 tbsp. Neely's dry rub
- 1 tbsp. kosher salt, plus more for seasonings
- 1 tsp. freshly ground black pepper, plus more for seasonings.
- 4 (1 1/2 to 2 lbs.) Cornish game hens washed and dried well.
- 2 tbsp. butter
- One shallot finely chopped.
- 1 cup chicken broth
- 3/4 cup freshly squeezed orange juice
- 2 tbsp. apple cider vinegar
- hot sauce dash

Directions

1. Whisk together the dry mixture, salt, and pepper in a small mixing bowl. Then season the washed and dried game hens with the rub and place them on a baking sheet. Close with plastic wrap and refrigerate for 1 hour.
2. Meanwhile, in a little saucepan over medium heat, add butter to melt. When melted, add the shallots and sauté until tender season with salt and pepper, to taste. Then add the chicken broth and orange juice. Boil and reduce to 1/2 cup, about ten minutes. It will quickly coat the trunk of a spoon and become slightly syrupy. When it reduced, add the apple cider vinegar and hot sauce—taste for seasoning.
3. Prepare your grill/smoker for indirect heat with charcoal and hickory chips. Sustain your temperature at 275 degrees F.
4. Arrange the overall game hens on the grill and cover—smoke for 40 minutes. Open the cover and brush the hens with the glaze, making sure to find yourself in all the nooks and crannies. Then cover the grill and smoke for an additional 15 minutes. Take away the hens from the grill to a serving platter and let rest, covered with foil for a quarter-hour before serving.

Nutrition:

Energy (calories): 177 kcal

Protein: 13.43 g

Fat: 9.98 g

Carbohydrates: 8.04 g

151. Pastrami-Rubbed Smoked Tri-Tip Recipe

Preparation Time: 10 minutes
Cooking Time: 1 hour 30 minutes
Servings: 4
Ingredients

- 4 tbsp. Fresh coarsely ground black pepper.
- 2 tbsp. coarse rock salt
- 2 tbsp. coriander seeds
- 2 tsp. mustard seeds
- 1 tbsp. brown sugar
- 1 tbsp. paprika
- 2 tsp. granulated garlic powder
- 2 tsp. granulated onion powder
- 3 one - to 4-pound tri-tip roast
- store-bought BBQ sauce, for serving.

Directions

1. Mix the pepper, salt, coriander seeds and mustard seeds in a mortar and pestle and grind until coarsely ground. Mix the brown sugar, and the paprika, garlic powder and onion powder. Dry the roast with paper towels and cover evenly with the spiced sauce, making sure to find the sides too. Placed on a rimmed baking sheet, cover and let sit in the refrigerator for at least thirty minutes or overnight.
2. Turn heat a grill for indirect cooking to 225 to 250 degrees F. As the grill is heating, make a smoker box with hickory or mesquite wood chips. If the wood chips begin to smoke, put the box on the back of the grill over direct heat.
3. Put the tri-tip on the grill's indirect heat side, leaving the dampers of the grill open. When your grill does not have a damper, leave a gap in the lid to let the air in. However, not allow smoke out. By using a probe thermometer, bring the meat to 130 degrees F, about 1 hour and 15 minutes.
4. Allow meat rest 10 to 15 minutes, then slice against the grain and enjoy with BBQ sauce alongside.

Nutrition:

Energy (calories): 550 kcal
Protein: 73.21 g

Fat: 25.07 g
Carbohydrates: 4.65 g

152. Rosemary and Garlic Smoked Pork Roast Recipe

Preparation Time: 10 minutes
Cooking Time: 1 hour 30 minutes
Servings: 8
Ingredients

- 4 cups apples or hickory wood chips
- 1 2.5 lbs. boneless pork top loin roast (single loin)
- 2 tbsp. snipped fresh rosemary.
- 1 tbsp. olive oil
- Four cloves' garlic, minced.
- 1/2 teaspoon pepper
- 1/4 teaspoon salt
- Four sprigs of fresh rosemary
- 1/2 lemon or lime
- Reynolds wrap aluminum foil

Directions

1. Sink the wood chips in water to cover at least 1 hour before grilling. Drain wood chips after soaking.
2. Trim fat from meat. For rub, combine the snipped rosemary, olive oil, garlic, pepper, and salt. Sprinkles rub evenly over meat; rub in together with your fingers. Insert a meat thermometer into its center.
3. For a charcoal grill and arrange medium coals around a drip pan. Pour 1 inch of water into a drip pan.
4. Test for medium-low heat above the pan. (Hold your hand, palm side down, in where the meat will cook. Count "1000 one, 1000 two," etc. Having the ability to keep your hand there for a count of five is equal to medium-low.) Pour half sprinkle of the wood chips over the coals, sprinkle rosemary sprigs over chips. Place meat on grill rack over drip pan. Cover: grill for 1 to 1-1/4 hours or until meat thermometer registers 155 degrees F. Add remaining wood chips halfway through grilling.
5. For a gas grill, preheat the grill. Reduce heat to medium-low. Adjust for indirect cooking, following manufacturer's directions—grill as above, except place meat on a rack in a roasting pan.
6. Remove meat from the grill. Squeeze juice from lime or lemon over meat. Cover with Reynolds Wrap® Aluminum Foil; let are a symbol of ten minutes before carving.

Nutrition:

Energy (calories): 307 kcal
Protein: 44.67 g

Fat: 9.87 g
Carbohydrates: 8 g

153. Slow-Smoked Barbecue Chicken Recipe

Preparation Time: 40 minutes
Cooking Time: 6 hours
Servings: 5
Ingredients

- 3/4 cup packed dark brown sugar.
- 1/2 cup kosher salt
- 1/2 cup ground espresso beans
- 2 tbsp. freshly ground black pepper.
- 2 tbsp. garlic powder
- 1 tbsp. ground cinnamon
- 1 tbsp. ground cumin
- 1 tbsp. cayenne pepper
- One whole chicken (about 4 pounds), giblets removed.

hardwood charcoal, charcoal kettle grill, chimney starter, wood chunks or soaked wood chips, heavy-duty fireproof gloves, disposable aluminum tray, instant-read thermometer, large non-reactive 5-gallon container.

Directions

1. Put altogether all the ingredients except for the chicken in a resealable container, cover tightly, and shake well to combine. (Dry rub could be stored, covered, in a cool, dry place for two months.)
2. Bring 1-gallon water and 1 cup dry rub to a boil in a stockpot, stirring before sugar and salt are dissolved. Allow the brine to let it cool to room temperature, transfer it to a non-reactive container and refrigerate until it cools. Place the chicken in the cold salt solution and refrigerate for 4 to 8 hours.
3. Set a wire rack on a baking sheet. Take away the chicken from the brine, pat dry with paper towels, and put on the wire rack. Discard the brine. Refrigerate for 6 hours.
4. Place the chicken on a peeled baking tray and coat the chicken lightly around with 1/2 cup dry rub (you might not need the entire rub) and reserve.
5. Remove any ash and debris if the smoker has been used and clean the grates. Fill a chimney starter about halfway with hardwood charcoal. Loosely crumple a couple of newspapers and drizzle pieces or spray them with vegetable oil (this can help the paper burn longer and speeds up the charcoal-lighting process). Stuff the paper into the chimney's lower chamber, place the vent on the smoker's top grate, and light it. Allow charcoal burn until the coals are glowing red and coated in gray ash, about a quarter-hour. Put on a couple of heavy-duty fireproof gloves and carefully dump the charcoal into one side of the grill-over underneath the air vent if your grill has one-leaving the spouse free of coals. Place a disposable aluminum tray on the other side to use as a drip pan.
6. Place a few hardwood chunks or a foil packet of wood chips over the coals. Add the top grate and put your meat over the drip pan. Cover the grill, placing the air vents in the lid over the flesh meat. Open both vents about halfway.
7. Place the chicken in the smoker and then smoke, maintaining a smoker temperature between 200 ° and 225 ° F, replenishing the pieces of wood or shavings as needed, until an instant-read thermometer inserted in the center of one leg registers 165 ° F, three to five hours. Transfer the chicken to a cutting board and let rest for 10 minutes.
8. At this time, you can slice the chicken into quarters or tear the meat into shreds to make pulled chicken. Or, if you want extra-crispy skin, you can briefly roast the chicken in a 450degrees F oven, or create a grill with hot and cool sides, put the chicken over the cool side, cover the grill, and cook for 5 to 10 minutes.

Nutrition:

Energy (calories): 489 kcal
Protein: 74.99 g

Fat: 10.37 g
Carbohydrates: 20.84 g

154. Smoked Apple Pork Butt Recipe

Preparation Time: 10 minutes
Cooking Time: 4-6 hours
Servings: 7
Ingredients:

- 1 1/2 cups brown sugar
- 1/2 cup kosher salt
- 1/3 cup ground black pepper
- 1/4 cup ground paprika
- 1/4 cup garlic powder
- 1/4 cup Italian seasoning
- 2 tbsp. onion powder
- 2 tbsp. chili powder
- 2 tbsp. cayenne pepper
- 1 tbsp. ground cumin
- 1 tsp. dried sage
- 1/2 cup apple cider
- 1/4 cup apple juice concentrate
- 2 tbsp. honey
- 2 tbsp. Worcestershire sauce
- 3 drops liquid smoke flavoring.
- 7 pounds bone-in pork butt
- 1/2 cup yellow mustard
- 1 tbsp. honey

- 1 cup of whiskey barrel wood chips (such as jack Daniel's)
- 1/2 cup applewood chips
- 1/2 cup apple juice concentrate
- 1/2 cup water

Directions

1. Combine brown sugar, salt, pepper, paprika, garlic, Italian seasoning, onion powder, chili powder, cayenne pepper, cumin, and sage in a little container—measure one tablespoon of the dry rub mixture into a huge box that may fit the pork butt. Refrigerate the remaining dry rub.
2. Mix the apple cider, 1/4 cup apple juice concentrate, two tablespoons honey, Worcestershire sauce, and liquid smoke into the large container to create the marinade.
3. String the top of the pork butt in a checkerboard pattern. Inject a few of the marinade into the bottom, sides, and the surface of the pork butt—place pork in the jar with the remaining marinade. Put the marinate in the refrigerator, 8 hours to overnight.
4. Combine whiskey barrel wood chips, applewood chips, 1/2 cup apple juice concentrate, and water in a sizable resealable bag. Seal and let soak, about 20 minutes.
5. Turn heat an electric smoker to 225 degrees F (110 degrees C). Fill the smoker box with wood chips according to the manufacturer's instructions.
6. Remove pork from marinade; rub mustard and one tablespoon honey evenly at the top. Coat pork butts heavily with dry rub—place fat-side through to a rack.
7. Put the shelf in the smoker; Cook until the center inserted instant thermometer reads 160 ° F (71 ° C) to an average or 170 ° F (77 ° C), 4 to 6 hours. Add more soaked wood chips midway through the cooking period. Place pork butt fat-side through to a sizable platter. Let rest for 20 minutes then cover it with aluminum foil and turning over halfway through resting time.

Nutrition:

Energy (calories): 1535 kcal

Protein: 117.27 g

Fat: 82.29 g

Carbohydrates: 77.74 g

155. Smoked Beer-Can Turkey Recipe

Preparation Time: 30 minutes

Cooking Time: 2-3 hours

Servings: 8

Ingredients

For the brine
- 2 quarts apple juice
- 1 cup kosher salt
- 1/2 cup brown sugar
- 1/4 cup molasses
- 3 quarts ice cold water
- One whole natural turkey, 12 to 14 pounds

For the rub
- 1 tbsp. paprika
- 1 tsp. kosher salt
- 1 tsp. chili powder

- 1 tsp. garlic powder
- 1 tsp. freshly ground black pepper.
- 1/2 teaspoon onion powder
- 1/2 teaspoon dried thyme
- 1/2 teaspoon dried oregano
- 1/4 teaspoon ground cumin
- 1/4 teaspoon cayenne pepper

One medium chunk of applewood or other light smoking wood
- 1 (24 ounces) tall can of beer

Type of fire: indirect

Grill heat: medium

Directions

To make the brine:

1. Whisk together the apple juice, salt, brown sugar, and molasses in a large container until the salt and sugar have dissolved. Mix 3 liters of ice-cold water. Dip the turkey, breast side down, into the brine. Put the container in the refrigerator and salt for 12 hours. To help make the rub: In a little bowl, combine paprika, salt, chili powder, garlic powder, black pepper, onion powder, thyme, oregano, cumin, and cayenne pepper. Reserve.
2. Remove the turkey from the brine. Dry inside and outside with paper towels. I use fingers to gently separate the skin from the flesh under the breasts and around the thighs. Spread about 1 1/2 tablespoons of rubbing under your chest and thighs. Sprinkle remaining friction around the turkey inside and out.
3. Turn up smoker or grill to 325degrees F, adding smoking wood chunks when at temperature. When the wood is ignited and generating smoke, drink or empty 1/3 of beer and place the smokers can. Carefully lower turkey onto beer can, legs down. Adjust turkey legs, so it stands vertical stably. Cover and smoke until an instant-read thermometer register 160degrees F in the breast's thickest portion, about 2-3 hours.
4. Take away the turkey from the smoker and invite to rest, uncovered, for 20 to 30 minutes. Remove beer can carve and serve.

Nutrition:

Energy (calories): 325 kcal

Protein: 9.61 g

Fat: 21.98 g

Carbohydrates: 22.51 g

156. Sweet Smoked Pork Ribs Recipe

Preparation Time: 30 minutes
Cooking Time: 3-4 hours
Servings: 10
Ingredients

- 1/4 cup salt
- 1/4 cup white sugar
- 2 tbsp. packed brown sugar.
- 2 tbsp. ground black pepper
- 2 tbsp. ground white peppers
- 2 tbsp. onion powder
- 1 tbsp. garlic powder
- 1 tbsp. chili powder
- 1 tbsp. ground paprika
- 1 tbsp. ground cumin
- 10 pounds of baby back pork ribs
- 1 cup apple juice
- 1/4 cup packed brown sugar.
- 1/4 cup barbeque sauces

Directions

1. Stir salt, white sugar, two tablespoons brown sugar, black pepper, white pepper, onion powder, garlic powder, chili powder, paprika, and cumin together in a little bowl to help make the dry rub. Rub the spice blend into the back ribs on all sides. Wrap the ribs generously with plastic wrap and refrigerate for at least 30 minutes just before cooking.
2. Unwrap baby back ribs and place them onto the wire racks of the smoker within a layer.
3. Place the racks right into a smoker, fill the smoker pan with apple, grape, pear, or cherry chips, and bring the smoker to 270 degrees F (130 degrees C)—smoke for one hour.
4. Stir in the apple juice, 1/4 cup of brown sugar and barbecue sauce. Brush the ribs with the sauce every 30 to 45 minutes following the first hour. Cook the smoker's ribs before the meat is no longer pink and begins to "shrink" back from the bones, 3 to 4 hours. Brush the sauce onto the ribs one final time 30 minutes before the ribs will be ready to be taken from the smoker.
5. Once the ribs are done, wrap them tightly with aluminum foil, and invite them to rest 10 to a quarter-hour. It allows the juices to reabsorb into the meat and make the ribs moist.

Nutrition:

Energy (calories): 869 kcal

Protein: 95.47 g

Fat: 26.98 g

Carbohydrates: 56.95 g

157. Baked Green Bean Casserole

Preparation Time: 10 minutes
Cooking Time: 50 minutes
Servings: 12
Ingredients:

- 3 lbs. trimmed green beans - Kosher salt - 2 tbsps. olive oil.
- 2 tbsps. unsalted butter - 1/2 lb. shitake or king trumpet mushrooms, sliced.
- 1/4 cup minced shallot - 1/4 cup rice flour
- 2 cups chicken stock - 1/2 cup sherry cooking wine
- 1 cup heavy cream - 1 cup grated Parmigiano Reggiano.
- 1 cup slivered almonds, for topping - 4 cups canola or vegetable oil
- Eight whole, peeled shallots - 1/2 cup rice flour - 1 tsp. kosher salt

Intolerances:

- Egg-Free

Directions:

1. Make the temperature to High and preheat, lid closed for 15 minutes.
2. Fill a large stockpot 2/3 full of water and bring to a boil over high heat. Prepare a large ice bath. If the water is already boiling, add 1 tbsp. of salt.
3. Once the water has come to a boil, add half the green beans. Cook until al dente, about 2 minutes. Remove with a colander and place the beans in the ice bath to cool.
4. Take the green beans out of the water and place them on paper towels to dry. Repeat with the rest of the green beans.

To make the Sauce:

1. Melt the butter and olive oil in a small saucepan over medium heat.
2. Add the shallots and mushrooms and a generous pinch of salt and cook, stirring, until the mushrooms are soft, about 5 minutes.

3. Sprinkle such rice flour over the top and then stir to coat the mushrooms, and cook off the raw flour taste, about 2 minutes.
4. Add some sherry, stir, and reduce, then slowly stir in the stock, allowing thickening and ensuring there are no lumps, about 3 minutes.
5. Stir in the cream and Parmigiano-Reggiano. Taste, adding salt and pepper as needed.
6. Combine the green beans with the sauce. Then pour into a large oven-proof serving dish. Sprinkle with almonds.
7. Bake until the sauce is bubbling, and the almonds are browned about 30 minutes.
8. The moment that the green beans are on the grill, fry the shallots. Put the oil in a deep saucepan or Dutch oven and heat oil to 350degrees F.
9. Put the rice flour and salt in a shallow bowl and mix with a fork. Cut the shallots into 1/8-inch rings. Mix the shallots to cover them with the rice flour, shaking them off in a colander. Fry the shallots in batches until golden brown, about 30 seconds to one minute. Drain on paper towels.
10. Prepare casserole and ready, garnish with the fried shallots. Enjoy!

Nutrition:

Calories: 190 Fats: 10g

Protein: 5g

Cholesterol: 1mg Carbs: 20g

158. Corn and Cheese Chile Rellenos

Preparation Time: 30 minutes
Cooking Time: 1 hour and 10 minutes
Servings: 12
Ingredients:

- 2 lbs. Ripe Tomatoes, Chopped
- Four cloves' garlic, chopped.
- 1/2 cup sweet onion, chopped.
- One jalapeno stemmed, seeded, and chopped.
- Eight large Green New Mexican Or Poblano Chiles
- Three ears sweet corn, husked.
- 1/2 tsp. Dry Oregano, Mexican, Crumbled
- 1 tsp. ground cumin
- 1 tsp. Mild chili powder
- 1/8 tsp. Ground Cinnamon
- Salt and Freshly Ground Pepper
- 3 cups grated Monterey Jack.
- 1/2 cup Mexican Crema
- 1 cup queso fresco, crumbled.
- Fresh Cilantro Leaves

Intolerances:
- Gluten-Free - Egg-Free
- Lactose-Free

Directions:

1. Put the tomatoes, garlic, jalapeno, and onion in a shallow baking dish and place them on the grill rack.
2. Start grill on Smoke with the lid open until the fire is established (4 to 5 minutes).
3. Set the temperature to 450degrees F and preheat, lid closed, for 10 to 15 minutes.
4. Arrange the New Mexican chilis and the sweet corn on the grate and grill until the chilis are blistered and blackened in spots and the corn is lightly browned, 15 to 20 minutes for the chilis and 10 to 15 minutes for the corn, turning with tongs as needed.
5. Whip the tomato-onion mixture once or twice and then remove it from the grill grate when the tomatoes begin to break down. Let all the vegetables cool.
6. Reduce the heat to 350degrees F if you intend to bake the Rellenos right away.
7. Put the cooled mixed tomato in a blender and then liquefy. Pour into a saucepan.
8. Add cumin, thyme, chili powder, cinnamon, salt, and pepper to taste. Let boil on medium heat for 15 to 20 minutes, or until the sauce thickens slightly, stirring occasionally.
9. A small paring knife slit each chili lengthwise from the shoulder (just below the stem) to the tip. Pull out the seeds and set the chilis aside while you make the filling.
10. Slice the corn off the cobs and put it in a large mixing bowl. Mix with 2 cups of the cheese, reserving 1 cup.
11. Gently stir in the sour cream—season with salt and pepper. Generously stuff the chilis with the corn-cheese mixture and arrange shoulder to shoulder, cut sides up, in a baking dish or on a rimmed baking sheet.
12. Pour some of the reserved cheese or sprinkle on top of each Relleno.
13. Cook the Rellenos for 25-30 minutes or until the filling boils and the cheese has melted. Reheat the tomato sauce if necessary.
14. To serve, put a small pool of tomato sauce on each plate and arrange a Relleno in the center of it. Enjoy!

Nutrition: Calories: 500 Fat: 30g Cholesterol: 165mg Carbs: 60g Protein: 20g

159. Mashed Potatoes

Preparation Time: 5 minutes
Cooking Time: 40 minutes
Servings: 12
Ingredients:

- 5 lbs. Yukon gold potatoes, large dice
- 1 1/2 sticks butter, softened.
- 1 1/2 cup cream, room temperature
- Kosher salt, to taste

- White pepper, to taste

Intolerances:
- Gluten-Free
- Egg-Free

Directions:

1. When ready to cook, set temperature to 300degrees F and preheat, lid closed for 15 minutes.
2. Peel off and dice potatoes into 1/2" cubes.
3. Place the potatoes in a foil tin and cover. Roast in the pellet grill until tender (about 40 minutes).
4. In a medium saucepan, combine cream and butter. Cook over medium heat until butter is melted.
5. Mash potatoes using a potato masher. Gradually add in cream and butter mixture, and mix using the masher. Be careful not to overwork, or the potatoes will become gluey.
6. Season with salt and pepper to taste. Enjoy!

Nutrition:
Calories: 230
Fat: 2g
Carbs: 45g
Protein: 9g

160. Smoked Apple Cinnamon

Preparation Time: 15 minutes
Cooking Time: 4 hours
Servings: 10
Ingredients:

- Golden apples (5-lbs. 2.3-kgs)
- The Rub
- 1/4 cup Lemon juice
- 2 tsp. Lemon zest
- 1/4 cup Cinnamon

- 3 cups Sugar

Intolerances:
- Gluten-Free
- Egg-Free
- Lactose-Free

Directions:

1. Preheat the smoker until it reaches the desired temperature before smoking.
2. Use applewood chips for smoking.
3. Cut the apples into halves, and then discard the seeds.
4. Combine lemon juice, lemon zest, and sugar, and then mix well.
5. Rub the apples with the mixture, then marinate for about 2 hours or until the sugar mixture becomes liquid.
6. Select "smoke" on the wood pellet smoker and fill the hopper with applewood chips. Do not forget to soak the wood chips before using them.
7. Set the temperature to 225degrees F (107°C).
8. Arrange the apples on the smoker's rack, then smoke for 2 hours or until the apples are tender and golden brown.
9. Once it is done, remove it from the smoker and arrange it on a serving dish.
10. Serve and enjoy.

Nutrition:
Calories: 100
Fat: 5g
Protein: 7g

161. Sweet Smoked Beans

Preparation Time: 15 minutes
Cooking Time: 45 minutes
Servings: 10
Ingredients:

- 1 lb. Dried navy beans (1-lbs. 0.45-kgs)
- The Spice
- 1 cup Chopped onion.
- 3/4 cup Brown sugar
- 1/4 cup Red wine vinegar
- 1/4 cup Molasses
- 1 tbsp. Mustard

- 1 tbsp. Garlic powder
- 1/2 teaspoon salt
- 3 cups Water

Intolerances:
- Gluten-Free
- Egg-Free
- Lactose-Free

Directions:
1. Preheat the smoker until it reaches the desired temperature before smoking.
2. Use applewood chips for smoking.
3. Place the beans in a container, and then pour water to cover.
4. Soak the navy beans overnight, then wash and rinse the beans.
5. Place the beans in a bowl, add chopped onion, brown sugar, red wine vinegar, mustard, garlic powder, and salt. Toss to combine.
6. Transfer the beans to a disposable aluminum pan, and then spread evenly. Pour water over the beans.
7. Fill the hopper with soaked applewood chips, then select "smoke" on the wood pellet smoker. Let the lid open.
8. Set the temperature to 225degrees F (107°C).
9. Place the aluminum pan on the lowest rack of the wood pellet smoker, then smoke for 45 minutes or until the beans are tender.
10. Once it is done, transfer the smoked beans to a serving dish, then serve. Enjoy.

Nutrition:

Calories: 140

Fat: 0.3g

Carbs: 35g

Protein: 3g

162. Smoked Stuffed Avocado with Shredded Chicken

Preparation Time: 15 minutes

Cooking Time: 45 minutes

Servings: 10

Ingredients:
- 3 lbs. ripe avocados

Stuffing:
- 5 cups Pulled chicken.
- 2 cups Grated cheese.
- One ¼ cups Salsa

- 20 Quail eggs

Intolerances:
- Gluten-Free
- Egg-Free

Directions:
1. Preheat the smoker until it reaches the desired temperature before smoking.
2. Use applewood chips for smoking.
3. Cut the ripe avocados into halves, then discard the seeds.
4. Preheat a wood pellet smoker, then add peach wood pellet to the hopper. Let the lid open.
5. Program the temperature to 375degrees F (191°C), then close the lid for about 10 minutes.
6. While waiting for the smoke, combine the pulled chicken with salsa and grated cheese, then mix well.
7. Top the halved avocado with the chicken and cheese mixture but leave the center.
8. Arrange the stuffed avocados in the smoker, and then smoke for 25 minutes.
9. After 25 minutes, open the lid.
10. Crack a quail egg, and then drop in the center of the avocados. Repeat with the remaining avocados and quail eggs.
11. Smoke the avocado again for about 10 minutes or until the eggs are set.
12. Once it is done, take the smoked avocados out from the smoker and arrange on a serving dish.
13. Enjoy right away.

Nutrition:

Calories: 350

Fat: 20g

Carbs: 18g

Protein: 25g

163. Smoked Buttery Potatoes

Preparation Time: 15 minutes

Cooking Time: 50 minutes

Servings: 10

Ingredients:
- 4 lbs. Potatoes
- 1 cup Butter
- 1/4 cup Salt
- 2 ½ tablespoons Black pepper

Intolerances:
- Gluten-Free
- Egg-Free

Directions:
1. Preheat the smoker until it reaches the desired temperature before smoking.
2. Use cherry wood chips for smoking.
3. Melt butter over low heat, and then set aside.

4. Peel the potatoes, and then cut into slices.
5. Arrange the sliced potato in a disposable aluminum pan, then brush with melted butter.
6. Sprinkle salts, and black pepper on top, then repeat with the remaining potatoes and spices.
7. Preheat a wood pellet smoker, then add soaked cherry wood pellet to the hopper. Let the lid open.
8. Program the temperature to 375degrees F (191°C), then close the lid.
9. Place the pan on the smoker's rack, then smoke for 40 minutes.
10. Once it is done, take the pan out from the smoker, then serve. Enjoy.

Nutrition:

Calories: 250

Carbs: 40g

Fat: 10g

164. Oktoberfest Pretzel Mustard Chicken

Preparation Time: 15 minutes
Cooking Time: 25 minutes
Servings: 4
Ingredients:

- 1/4 Pound pretzel sticks
- 3 Tablespoon Dijon mustard
- 3 Tablespoon apple cider or brown ale
- 1 Tablespoon honey
- 3/2 teaspoon fresh thyme, plus more for garnish
- 4 boneless, skinless chicken breasts

Directions

1. Preheat oven to 400 degrees F (200 degrees C). Flatten pretzel sticks on a baking sheet. Bake until toasted and slightly browned about 15 minutes; set aside to cool.
2. Meanwhile, in a small saucepan, melt honey with mustard and beer. Cook over medium heat until just bubbly, about 3 minutes; remove from heat and stir in thyme. Brush both sides of chicken with mustard mixture; return to heat and cook until chicken is no longer pink in the center, turning once just 3-4 minutes total.
3. Place pretzel sticks on a plate. Slice chicken breasts crosswise, and place atop pretzels. Drizzle with remaining mustard mixture and garnish with thyme. Serve warm.

Nutrition

Energy (calories): 1253 kcal

Protein: 226.07 g

Fat: 26.83 g

Carbohydrates: 11.39 g

Calcium, Ca61 mg

Magnesium, Mg288 mg

Phosphorus, P2150 mg

Iron, Fe4.26 mg

165. Smoked Turkey with Fig BBQ Sauce

Preparation Time: 4 hours
Cooking Time: 2 hours
Servings: 4
Ingredients

- 1 Gallon water
- 1/2 Cup sugar
- 2 dried bay leaves
- 2 large thyme sprigs
- 6 peppercorns
- 1/2 Cup salt
- 6 Turkey Thighs
- 1/2 Cup Ras El Hangout
- 6 Tablespoon extra-virgin olive oil
- 1 Cup Pit boss Apricot BBQ Sauce
- 4 Figs, fresh

Directions:

1. In a large pot, bring the water and sugar to a boil. Add the peppercorns, thyme, bay leaves, salt, and stir to dissolve the salt. Mix in the turkey thighs and place a lid on top, weight it down if possible. Simmer over medium-low heat for one hour. Remove the lid and let cool. Remove the turkey thighs from the pot and refrigerate until cool enough to handle.
2. Increase the heat to a medium-high and reduce the syrup by half, about 40 minutes. Strain through a fine sieve into a small bowl. Discard the solids. Return the syrup to low heat and add the Pit boss Apricot BBQ Sauce and Ras El Hangout. Stir well and cook an additional 5 minutes, remove from heat.
3. Preheat Pit boss to 275F and place the turkey thighs back in the pot for 30 minutes to crisp up slightly. Remove and towel dry with paper towels. Slice the figs in half, quarter the thighs, and assemble each plate with a thigh, a fig, and 2 tablespoons of sauce. Serve immediately.

Nutrition

Energy (calories): 2102 kcal

Protein: 14.55 g

Fat: 205.81 g
Carbohydrates: 57.98 g
Calcium, Ca215 mg

Magnesium, Mg65 mg
Phosphorus, P303 mg
Iron, Fe6.64 mg

166. Smoking' Thai Curry Chicken

Preparation Time: 4 hours
Cooking Time: 20 minutes
Servings: 6
Ingredients

- 1/4 Cup soy sauce
- 3 Tablespoon brown sugar
- 2 Tablespoon lime juice
- 2 Tablespoon extra-virgin olive oil
- 2 teaspoon curry powder
- 1/2 Teaspoon Cardamom
- 2 Clove garlic, minced.

- 1 Teaspoon Lemon Grass
- 1 teaspoon freshly grated ginger
- 1 jalapeño seeded and diced.
- As Needed Pit boss Thai Red Curry Rub
- 3 Pound Chicken Breast
- cilantro
- Coconut

Directions:

1. Drain and rinse the glass noodles with cool water and place noodles in a large bowl. Set aside.
2. Prepare the Pit boss Thai Red Curry Rub by placing all the ingredients in a bowl and tossing to combine.
3. Cut the chicken into strips or desired size pieces and place in a large resealable plastic bag. Add a few tablespoons of the curry rub to the bag and close, gently shaking to evenly coat the chicken.
4. Pour the coconut cream into a large bowl and add 1/4 cup of the red curry paste. Once mixed, add to the bowl with the glass noodles and toss to coat.
5. Place the chicken and the remaining red curry paste in a Ziploc bag. Gently pound the bag with a meat tenderizer, rolling pin, or the back of a cast-iron pan to ensure the chicken pieces are evenly coated.
6. Add the chicken and glass noodles to the Pit boss smoker, close the lid, and smoke for 2-4 hours at 275 degrees.

Nutrition
Energy (calories): 326 kcal
Protein: 31.46 g
Fat: 17.52 g
Carbohydrates: 9.27 g
Calcium, Ca34 mg

Magnesium, Mg53 mg
Phosphorus, P278 mg
Iron, Fe1.48 mg
Potassium, K457 mg

167. Honey Lime Chicken Adobo Skewers

Preparation Time: 15 minutes
Cooking Time: 15 minutes
Servings: 6
Ingredients

- 4 Chicken Breast, Diced
- 1 Tablespoon vegetable oil
- 2 Teaspoon garlic, minced.
- 2 Teaspoon onion powder
- 3/4 Cup rice vinegar
- 1/4 Cup soy sauce

- 3 Tablespoon honey
- 2 Whole lime, juiced.
- As Needed salt
- As Needed black pepper
- 8 Pit boss Skewers

Directions:

1. In a large bowl, mix the diced chicken breast with 1 tablespoon oil, minced garlic & onion powder, mix until all the chicken is coated evenly.
2. Place in the fridge while you prepare the sauce.
3. In a medium-sized bowl, combine vinegar, honey, lime juice, soy sauce, and remaining 1 tablespoon oil & mix thoroughly until all ingredients are combined.
4. Add chicken to the honey-lime marinade and allow to marinate for 10 minutes or in the fridge for up to 24 hours.
5. Preheat Pit boss BBQ to 375 degrees and oil the grill.
6. On each skewer place approximately 1/4 cup of the honey lime chicken.
7. Place the chicken skewers on the grill and cook for 12 -15 minutes until bacon is light brown and chicken is cooked through.
8. Enjoy!

Nutrition

Energy (calories): 429 kcal
Protein: 41.3 g
Fat: 22.1 g
Carbohydrates: 13.75 g

Calcium, Ca33 mg
Magnesium, Mg58 mg
Phosphorus, P358 mg
Iron, Fe1.71 mg

168. Braised Brunswick Stew

Preparation Time: 30 minutes
Cooking Time: 2 hours
Servings: 4
Ingredients

- 8 Tablespoon butter
- 1 Large onion
- 1 green bell pepper, diced.
- 2 Celery, stalks
- 4 Clove garlic, minced.
- 1 Teaspoon smoked paprika.
- 1/2 Teaspoon cayenne pepper
- Tablespoon Worcestershire sauce
- 45 Ounce Diced Tomatoes, Canned
- Cup Pit bosque BBQ Sauce
- Pound pulled pork.

- Pound Pulled Chicken
- Pound beef brisket
- Cup chicken broth
- 10 Ounce Lima Beans, frozen
- 10 Ounce Corn, frozen
- 1 Cup Okra, frozen
- To Taste salt
- To Taste black pepper
- Tablespoon apple cider vinegar
- hot sauce

Directions

1. Heat butter in a large pot over medium-high heat
2. Add in onion, green bell pepper, celery, minced garlic, smoked paprika, and cayenne pepper and cook until tender.
3. Add in tomatoes. Bring to a boil and then add Worcestershire sauce.
4. Reduce heat to low and simmer for 20 minutes.
5. Add in BBQ sauce, pork, beef, chicken, and simmer for 30 minutes.
6. Add in beef broth to thin the stew. If needed, add more broth to the thin stew.
7. Add in corn, okra, stir, and cover. Simmer for 30 minutes.
8. Add in lima beans, stir, and cover. Simmer for 30 minutes.
9. Add in corn, stir, and cover. Simmer for another 15 minutes.
10. Taste and season with salt and peppers as needed.
11. Before serving, add in apple cider vinegar and hot sauce to taste.
12. Serve with toasted bread.

Nutrition

Energy (calories): 1381 kcal
Protein: 119.94 g
Fat: 61.91 g
Carbohydrates: 95.55 g

Calcium, Ca195 mg
Magnesium, Mg308 mg
Phosphorus, P1532 mg
Iron, Fe14.65 mg

169. Quick Rotisserie Chicken

Preparation Time: 15 minutes
Cooking Time: 1 hour 30 minutes
Servings: 6
Ingredients

- 1 whole chicken
- 1 pinch salt
- One-fourth cup butter, melted.

- One-fourth tablespoon ground black pepper
- 1 tablespoon salt
- 1 tablespoon paprika

Directions

1. First, season the inner side of the chicken with a pinch of salt and put the chicken on to rotisserie and arrange the grill on high. Cook it well for ten minutes.
2. During this, rapidly merge the paprika, one tablespoon salt, butter, and pepper and then turn the grill down to intermediate and baste the chicken with a mixture of butter.
3. Seal the lid and cook for one to one and a half hours and then basting infrequently until inner temperature reaches 180 degrees.
4. Eliminate from the rotisserie and allow standing for ten to fifteen minutes before slicing into pieces and serve.

Nutrition

Energy (calories): 617 kcal
Protein: 27.58 g
Fat: 42.51 g
Carbohydrates: 34.08 g

Calcium, Ca94 mg
Magnesium, Mg80 mg
Phosphorus, P319 mg
Iron, Fe2.66 mg
Potassium, K462 mg

170. Smoked Hot Paprika Pork Tenderloin

Preparation Time: 20-35 minutes
Cooking Time: 2 ½ to 3 hours
Servings: 6
Ingredients:

- 2-pound pork tenderloin
- 3/4 cup chicken stock
- 1/2 cup tomato-basil sauce
- 2 tbsp. smoked hot paprika (or to taste)
- 1 tbsp. oregano
- Salt and pepper to taste

Directions:

1. In a bowl, combine the chicken stock, tomato-basil sauce, paprika, oregano, salt, and pepper together.
2. Brush over tenderloin.
3. Smoke grill for 4-5 minutes. Pre head, lid closed for 10-14 minutes.
4. Place pork for 2 ½ to 3 hours.
5. Rest for 10 minutes.

Nutrition:
Calories: 360.71 Cal
Fat: 14.32 g
Carbohydrates: 3.21 g
Protein: 52.09 g
Fiber: 1.45 g

171. Smoked Pork Tenderloin with Mexican Pineapple Sauce

Preparation Time: 10-15 minutes
Cooking Time: 3 hours and 55 minutes
Servings: 6
Ingredients:

- Pineapple Sauce
- 1 can (11 oz.) unsweetened crushed pineapple
- 1 can (11 oz.) roasted tomato or tomatillo.
- 1/2 cup port wine
- 1/4 cup orange juice
- 1/4 cup packed brown sugar.
- 1/4 cup lime juice
- 2 tbsp. Worcestershire sauce
- 1 tsp garlic powder
- 1/4 tsp cayenne pepper
- PORK
- 2 pork tenderloin (1 pound each)
- 1 tsp ground cumin
- 1/2 tsp pepper
- 1/4 tsp cayenne pepper
- 2 tbsp. lime juice (freshly squeezed)

Directions:

1. Combine cumin, pepper, cayenne pepper and lime juice and rub over tenderloins.
2. Smoke grill for 4-5 minutes. Preheat, lid closed for 10-15 minutes.
3. Smoke tenderloin for 2 ½ to 3 hours.
4. Rest for 5 minutes
5. For Sauce:
6. Combine ingredients and boil for 25 minutes.
7. Remove from heat and cool.
8. Serve pork slices with pineapple sauce and lime wedges.

Nutrition:
Calories: 277.85 Cal
Fat: 3.49 g
Carbohydrates: 24.31 g
Protein: 32.42 g
Fiber: 0.67 g

172. Garlic Aioli and Smoked Salmon Sliders

Preparation Time: 15 minutes
Cooking Time: 1 hour and 30 minutes
Servings: 12
Ingredients:

- For Brine:
- Water as needed.
- ½ a cup of salt
- 1 tablespoon of dried tarragon
- 1 and a ½ pound of salmon fillets
- For Aioli:
- 1 cup of mayonnaise
- 3 tablespoon of fresh lemon juice
- 3 minced garlic cloves
- 1 and a ½ teaspoon of ground black pepper
- ½ a teaspoon of lemon zest
- Salt as needed.
- ½ a cup of apple wood chips
- 12 slide burger buns

Directions:

1. Take a large sized baking dish and add ½ a cup of salt alongside about half water.
2. Add tarragon, salmon in the brine mix and keep adding more water.
3. Cover up the dish and freeze for 2-12 hours. Take a small bowl and add lemon juice, mayonnaise, pepper, garlic, 1 pinch of salt and lemon zest.
4. Mix and chill for 30 minutes.
5. Remove your Salmon from the brine and place it on a wire rack and let it sit for about 30 minutes.
6. Smoke them over low heat for 1 and a ½ to 2 hours. Assemble sliders by dividing the salmon among 12 individual buns.
7. Top each of the pieces with a spoonful of aioli and place another bun on top.

Nutrition:

Calories: 320 Cal

Protein: 22 g

Fat: 22 g

Fiber: 0 g

Carbohydrates: 13 g

173. Texas Styled Smoked Flounder

Preparation Time: 20 minutes
Cooking Time: 20 minutes
Servings: 6
Ingredients:

- 1 whole flounder
- 1 halved lemon
- Ground black pepper as needed.
- 2 tablespoons of chopped up fresh dill.
- 1 tablespoon of olive oil
- 1 cup of soaked wood chips

Directions:

1. Preheat your smoker to a temperature of 350 degrees Fahrenheit.
2. Slice half of your lemon and place them into the slices. Rub the fish with a coating of olive oil. Squeeze another half of the lemon all over the fish. Season with some black pepper.
3. Rub 1 tablespoon of dill into the slits and insert the lemon slices firmly. Place the flounder on top of a large piece of aluminum foil and fold the sides all around the fish.
4. Place the fish in your smoker and throw a couple handful of soaked wood chips into the coals. And smoke for 10 minutes
5. Once done, seal up the foil and smoke it until it is fully done. Remove fish and garnish with some extra dill.

Nutrition:

Calories: 226 Cal

Protein: 28 g

Fat: 4 g

Fiber: 0 g

Carbohydrates: 28 g

174. Fire and Ice Smoked Salmon

Preparation Time: 6 hours
Cooking Time: 50 minutes
Servings: 7
Ingredients:

- ½ a cup of brown sugar
- 2 tablespoons of salt
- 2 tablespoon of crushed red pepper flakes
- Mint leaves
- ¼ cup of brandy
- 1 (4 pounds) salmon side with bones removed.
- 2 cups of alder wood chips soaked up in water.

Directions:

1. Take a medium bowl and mix in the brown sugar, crushed red pepper flakes, salt, mint leaves and brandy until a paste form. Coat the paste on all sides of the salmon and wrap the Salmon up in plastic wrap.
2. Let it refrigerate for at least 4 hours or overnight. Preheat your smoker to high heat and oil up the grate. Add soaked alder chips to your heat box and wait until smoke starts to appear.
3. Turn the heat to your lowest setting and place the salmon on the grate. Lock up the lid and let your Salmon smoke for about 45 minutes.

Nutrition:

Calories: 370 Cal

Protein: 23 g

Fat: 28 g

Fiber: 0 g

Carbohydrates: 1 g

175. Bradley Maple Cure Smoked Salmon

Preparation Time: 2 hours
Cooking Time: 1 hour and 30 minutes
Servings: 6
Ingredients:

- 1 large sized salmon fillet
- 1 quart of water
- ½ a cup of pickling and canning salt
- ½ a cup of maple syrup
- ¼ cup of dark rum
- ¼ cup of lemon juice
- 10 whole cloves
- 10 whole allspice berries
- 1 bay leaf

Directions:

1. Take a medium sized bowl and add the brine ingredients. Mix them well. Place the salmon fillet in a cover with brine.
2. Cover it up and let it refrigerate for about 2 hours. Remove the Salmon and pat dry then air dry for 1 hour.
3. Preheat your smoker to a temperature of 180 degrees Fahrenheit and add Bradley Maple-Flavored briquettes. Smoke the salmon for about 1 and a ½ hour.

Nutrition:

Calories: 223 Cal
Fat: 7 g
Carbohydrates: 15 g

Protein: 21 g
Fiber: 0 g

176. Smoked Teriyaki Tuna

Preparation Time: 5-7 hours
Cooking Time: 2 hours
Servings: 4
Ingredients:

- Tuna steaks, 1 oz.
- 2 c. marinade, teriyaki
- Alder wood chips soaked in water.

Directions:

1. Slice tuna into thick slices of 2 inch. Place your tuna slices and marinade then set in your fridge for about 3 hours.
2. After 3 hours, remove the tuna from the marinade and pat dry. Let the tuna air dry in your fridge for 2-4 hours. Preheat your smoker to 180 degrees Fahrenheit.
3. Place the Tuna on a Teflon-coated fiberglass and place them directly on your grill grates. Smoke the Tuna for about an hour until the internal temperature reaches 145 degrees Fahrenheit.
4. Remove the tuna from your grill and let them rest for 10 minutes. Serve!

Nutrition:

Calories: 249 Cal
Fat: 3 g
Carbohydrates: 33 g

Protein: 21 g
Fiber: 0 g

177. Cold Hot Smoked Salmon

Preparation Time: 16 hours
Cooking Time: 8 hours
Servings: 4
Ingredients:

- 5 pound of fresh sockeye (red) salmon fillets
- For trout Brine
- 4 cups of filtered water
- 1 cup of soy sauce
- ½ a cup of pickling kosher salt
- ½ a cup of brown sugar
- 2 tablespoon of garlic powder
- 2 tablespoon of onion powder
- 1 teaspoon of cayenne pepper

Directions:

1. Combine all the ingredients listed under trout brine in two different 1-gallon bags. Store it in your fridge. Cut up the Salmon fillets into 3-4-inch pieces. Place your salmon pieces into your 1-gallon container of trout brine and let it keep in your fridge for 8 hours.
2. Rotate the Salmon and pat them dry using a kitchen towel for 8 hours.
3. Configure your pellet smoker for indirect cooking. Remove your salmon pieces of from your fridge Preheat your smoker to a temperature of 180 degrees Fahrenheit.

4. Once a cold smoke at 70 degrees Fahrenheit starts smokes your fillets
5. Keep smoking it until the internal temperature reaches 145 degrees Fahrenheit.
6. Remove the Salmon from your smoker and let it rest for 10 minutes.

Nutrition:

Calories: 849 Cal

Fat: 45 g

Carbohydrates: 51 g

Protein: 46 g

Fiber: 0 g

178. Smoked Up Salmon and Dungeness Crab Chowder

Preparation Time: 30 minutes
Cooking Time: 45 minutes
Servings: 6
Ingredients:

- 4 gallons of water
- 3 fresh Dungeness crabs
- 1 cup of rock salt
- 3 cups of Cold-Hot Smoked Salmon
- 3 cups of ocean clam juice
- 5 diced celery stalks

- 1 yellow diced onion
- 2 peeled and diced large sized russet potatoes.
- 14 ounces of sweet corn
- 12 ounce of clam chowder dry soup mix
- 4 bacon slices crumbled and cooked.

Directions:

1. Bring 4 gallons of water and rock salt to a boil. Add the Dungeness crab and boil for 20 minutes.
2. Remove the crabs, let it cool and clean the crabs and pick out crab meat. Place it over high heat.
3. Add clam juice, 5 cups of water, diced potatoes, diced celery, and onion. Bring the mix to a boil as well. Add corn to the liquid and boil.
4. Whisk in the clam chowder and keep mixing everything. Simmer on low for about 15 minutes and add the crumbled bacon. Add bacon, garnish with ½ cup flaked smoked salmon and ½ cup Dungeness crabmeat. Serve!

Nutrition:

Calories: 174 Cal

Fat: 5 g

Carbohydrates: 12 g

Protein: 8 g

Fiber: 0 g

179. Alder Wood Smoked Bony Trout

Preparation Time: 4 hours
Cooking Time: 2 hours
Servings: 4
Ingredients:

- 4 fresh boned whole trout with their skin on
- For trout Brine
- 4 cups of filtered water
- 1 cup of soy sauce
- ½ a cup of pickling kosher salt

- ½ a cup of brown sugar
- 2 tablespoon of garlic powder
- 2 tablespoon of onion powder
- 1 teaspoon of cayenne pepper

Directions:

1. Combine all the ingredients listed under trout brine in two different 1-gallon bags.
2. Store it in your fridge.
3. Place your trout in the sealable bag with trout brine and place the bag in a shallow dish.
4. Let it refrigerate for about 2 hours, making sure to rotate it after 30 minutes.
5. Remove them from your brine and pat them dry using kitchen towels.
6. Air Dry your brine trout in your fridge uncovered for about 2 hours.
7. Preheat your smoker to a temperature of 180 degrees Fahrenheit using alder pellets.
8. The pit temperature of should be 180 degrees Fahrenheit and the cold smoke should be 70 degrees Fahrenheit.
9. Cold smoke your prepared trout for 90 minutes.
10. After 90 minutes transfer the cold smoked boned trout pellets to your smoker grill are and increase the smoker temperature to 225 degrees Fahrenheit.
11. Keep cooking until the internal temperature reaches 145 degrees Fahrenheit in the thickest parts.
12. Remove the trout from the grill and let them rest for 5 minutes.
13. Serve!

Nutrition:

Calories: 508 Cal

Fat: 23 g

Carbohydrates: 47 g

Protein: 15 g

Fiber: 0 g

Chapter 7.   Fish and seafood Recipes

180. Halibut

Preparation Time: 10 minutes
Cooking Time: 30 minutes
Servings: 4
Ingredients:

- 1-pound fresh halibut filet (cut into 4 equal sizes)
- 1 tbsp. fresh lemon juice
- 2 garlic cloves (minced)
- 2 tsp soy sauce
- ½ tsp ground black pepper
- ½ tsp onion powder
- 2 tbsp. honey
- ½ tsp oregano
- 1 tsp dried basil
- 2 tbsp. butter (melted)
- Maple syrup for serving.

Directions:

1. Combine the lemon juice, honey, soy sauce, onion powder, oregano, dried basil, pepper, and garlic.
2. Brush the halibut filets generously with the filet the mixture. Wrap the filets with aluminum foil and refrigerate for 4 hours.
3. Remove the filets from the refrigerator and let them sit for about 2 hours, or until they are at room temperature.
4. Activate your wood pellet grill on smoke, leaving the lid opened for 5 minutes or until fire starts.
5. The lid must not be opened for it to be preheated and reach 275°F 15 minutes, using fruit wood pellets.
6. Place the halibut filets directly on the grill grate and smoke for 30 minutes.
7. Remove the filets from the grill and let them rest for 10 minutes.
8. Serve and top with maple syrup to taste.

Nutrition:
Calories: 180 Cal
Fat: 6.3 g
Carbohydrates: 10 g
Protein: 20.6 g
Fiber: 0.3 g

181. Barbeque Shrimp

Preparation Time: 20 minutes
Cooking Time: 8 minutes
Servings: 6
Ingredients:

- 2-pound raw shrimp (peeled and deveined)
- ¼ cup extra virgin olive oil
- ½ tsp paprika
- ½ tsp red pepper flakes
- 2 garlic cloves (minced)
- 1 tsp cumin
- 1 lemon (juiced)
- 1 tsp kosher salt
- 1 tbsp. chili paste
- Bamboo or wooden skewers (soaked for 30 minutes, at least)

Directions:

1. Combine the pepper flakes, cumin, lemon, salt, chili, paprika, garlic and olive oil. Add the shrimp and toss to combine.
2. Transfer the shrimp and marinade into a zip-lock bag and refrigerate for 4 hours.
3. Let shrimp rest in room temperature after pulling it out from marinade.
4. Start your grill on smoke, leaving the lid opened for 5 minutes, or until fire starts. Use hickory wood pellet.
5. Keep lid unopened and preheat the grill to "high" for 15 minutes.
6. Thread shrimps onto skewers and arrange the skewers on the grill grate.
7. Smoke shrimps for 8 minutes, 4 minutes per side.
8. Serve and enjoy.

Nutrition:
Calories: 267 Cal
Fat: 11.6 g
Carbohydrates: 4.9 g
Protein: 34.9 g
Fiber: 0.4 g

182. Oyster in Shells

Preparation Time: 25 minutes
Cooking Time: 8 minutes
Servings: 4
Ingredients:

- 12 medium oysters
- 1 tsp oregano
- 1 lemon (juiced)
- 1 tsp freshly ground black pepper.
- 6 tbsp. unsalted butter (melted)
- 1 tsp salt or more to taste
- 2 garlic cloves (minced)
- 2 ½ tbsp. grated parmesan cheese
- 2 tbsp. freshly chopped parsley

Directions:

1. Remove dirt.
2. Open the shell completely. Discard the top shell.
3. Gently run the knife under the oyster to loosen the oyster foot from the bottom shell.
4. Repeat step 2 and 3 for the remaining oysters.
5. Combine melted butter, lemon, pepper, salt, garlic, and oregano in a mixing bowl.
6. Pour ½ to 1 tsp of the butter mixture on each oyster.

7. Start your wood pellet grill on smoke, leaving the lid opened for 5 minutes, or until fire starts.
8. Keep lid unopened to preheat in the set "HIGH" with lid closed for 15 minutes.
9. Gently arrange the oysters onto the grill grate.
10. Grill oyster for 6 to 8 minutes or until the oyster juice is bubbling and the oyster is plump.
11. Remove oysters from heat. Serve and top with grated parmesan and chopped parsley.

Nutrition:
Calories: 200 Cal
Fat: 19.2 g
Carbohydrates: 3.9 g
Protein: 4.6 g
Fiber: 0.8 g

183. Cajun Smoked Catfish

Preparation Time: 15 minutes
Cooking Time: 2 hours
Servings: 4
Ingredients:
- 4 catfish fillets (5 ounces each)
- ½ cup Cajun seasoning
- 1 tsp ground black pepper
- 1 tbsp. smoked paprika.
- 1/4 tsp cayenne pepper
- 1 tsp hot sauce
- 1 tsp granulated garlic
- 1 tsp onion powder
- 1 tsp thyme
- 1 tsp salt or more to taste
- 2 tbsp. chopped fresh parsley.

Directions:
1. Pour water into the bottom of a square or rectangular dish. Add 4 tbsp. salt. Arrange the catfish fillets into the dish. Cover the dish and refrigerate for 3 to 4 hours.
2. Combine the paprika, cayenne, hot sauce, onion, salt, thyme, garlic, pepper, and Cajun seasoning in a mixing bowl.
3. Remove the fish from the dish and let it sit for a few minutes, or until it is at room temperature. Pat the fish fillets dry with a paper towel.
4. Rub the seasoning mixture over each fillet generously.
5. Start your grill on smoke, leaving the lid opened for 5 minutes, or until fire starts.
6. Keep lid unopened and preheat to 200°F, using mesquite hardwood pellets.
7. Arrange the fish fillets onto the grill grate and close the grill. Cook for about 2 hours, or until the fish is flaky.
8. Remove the fillets from the grill and let the fillets rest for a few minutes to cool.
9. Serve and garnish with chopped fresh parsley.

Nutrition:
Calories: 204 Cal
Fat: 11.1 g
Carbohydrates: 2.7 g
Protein: 22.9 g
Fiber: 0.6 g

184. Smoked Scallops

Preparation Time: 10 minutes
Cooking Time: 15 minutes
Servings: 6
Ingredients:
- 2 pounds sea scallops
- 4 tbsp. salted butter
- 2 tbsp. lemon juice
- ½ tsp ground black pepper
- 1 garlic clove (minced)
- 1 kosher tsp salt
- 1 tsp freshly chopped tarragon

Directions:
1. Let the scallops dry using paper towels and drizzle all sides with salt and pepper to season.
2. Place you are a cast iron pan in your grill and preheat the grill to 400°F with lid closed for 15 minutes.
3. Combine the butter and garlic in hot cast iron pan. Add the scallops and stir. Close grill lid and cook for 8 minutes.
4. Flip the scallops and cook for an additional 7 minutes.
5. Remove the scallop from heat and let it rest for a few minutes.
6. Stir in the chopped tarragon. Serve and top with lemon juice.

Nutrition:
Calories: 204 Cal
Fat: 8.9 g
Carbohydrates: 4 g
Protein: 25.6 g
Fiber: 0.1 g

185. Pit boss Salmon with Togarashi

Preparation Time: 5 Minutes
Cooking Time: 20 Minutes
Servings: 3
Ingredients:
- One salmon fillet
- 1/4 cup olive oil
- 1/2 tbsp kosher salt
- 1 tbsp Togarashi seasoning

Directions:
1. Preheat your Pit boss to 400oF.
2. Place the salmon on a sheet lined with non-stick foil with the skin side down.
3. Rub the oil into the meat, then sprinkle salt and Togarashi.
4. Place the salmon on the grill and cook for 20 minutes or until the internal temperature reaches 145oF with the lid closed.

5. Remove from the Pit boss and serve when hot.

Nutrition:
Calories 119
Total fat 10g
Saturated fat 2g
Sodium 720mg

186. Trager Rockfish

Preparation Time: 10 Minutes
Cooking Time: 20 Minutes
Servings: 6
Ingredients:

- Six rockfish fillets
- One lemon, sliced.
- 3/4 tbsp salt
- 2 tbsp fresh dill, chopped.
- 1/2 tbsp garlic powder
- 1/2 tbsp onion powder
- 6 tbsp butter

Directions:
1. Preheat your Pit boss to 400OF.
2. Season the fish with salt, dill, garlic, and onion powder on both sides, then place it in a baking dish.
3. Place a pat of butter and a lemon slice on each fillet. Place the baking dish in the Pit boss and close the lid.
4. Cook for 20 minutes or until the fish is no longer translucent and is flaky.
5. Remove from Pit boss and let rest before serving.

Nutrition:
Calories 270
Total fat 17g
Saturated fat 9g
Total carbs 2g
Net carbs 2g
Protein 28g
Sodium 381mg

187. Pit boss Grilled Lingcod

Preparation Time: 10 Minutes
Cooking Time: 15 Minutes
Servings: 6
Ingredients:

- 2 lb. lingcod fillets
- 1/2 tbsp salt
- 1/2 tbsp white pepper
- 1/4 tbsp cayenne pepper
- Lemon wedges

Directions:
1. Preheat your Pit boss to 375OF.
2. Place the lingcod on a parchment paper or a grill mat.
3. Season the fish with salt, pepper, and top with lemon wedges.
4. Cook the fish for 15 minutes or until the internal temperature reaches 145OF.

Nutrition:
Calories 245
Total fat 2g
Total carbs 2g

Protein 52g
Sugars 1g
Fiber 1g
Sodium 442mg

188. Crab Stuffed Lingcod

Preparation Time: 20 Minutes
Cooking Time: 30 Minutes
Servings: 6
Ingredients:
Lemon cream sauce

- Four garlic cloves
- One shallot
- One leek
- 2 tbsp olive oil
- 1 tbsp salt
- 1/4 tbsp black pepper
- 3 tbsp butter
- 1/4 cup white wine
- 1 cup whipping cream
- 2 tbsp lemon juice
- 1 tbsp lemon zest

Crab mix

- 1 lb. crab meat
- 1/3 cup mayo
- 1/3 cup sour cream
- 1/3 cup lemon cream sauce
- 1/4 green onion, chopped.
- 1/4 tbsp black pepper
- 1/2 tbsp old bay seasoning

Fish

- 2 lb. lingcod
- 1 tbsp olive oil
- 1 tbsp salt
- 1 tbsp paprika
- 1 tbsp green onion, chopped.
- 1 tbsp Italian parsley

Directions:
Lemon cream sauce
1. Chop garlic, shallot, and leeks, then add to a saucepan with oil, salt, pepper, and butter.
2. Sauté over medium heat until the shallot is translucent.
3. Deglaze with white wine, then add whipping cream. Bring the sauce to boil, reduce heat, and simmer for 3 minutes.
4. Remove from heat and add lemon juice and lemon zest. Transfer the sauce to a blender and blend until smooth.
5. Set aside 1/3 cup for the crab mix.
Crab mix
1. Add all the fixings to a mixing bowl and mix thoroughly until well combined.
2. Set aside.
Fish
1. Fire up your Pit boss to high heat, then slice the fish into 6-ounce portions.

85

2. Lay the fish on its side on a cutting board and slice it 3/4 way through the middle leaving a 1/2 inch on each end to have a nice pouch.
3. Rub the oil into the fish, then place them on a baking sheet. Sprinkle with salt.
4. Stuff crab mix into each fish, then sprinkle paprika and place it on the grill.
5. Cook for 15 minutes or more if the fillets are more than 2 inches thick.
6. Remove the fish and transfer to serving platters. Pour the remaining lemon cream sauce on each fish and garnish with onions and parsley.

Nutrition:
Calories 476
Total fat 33g
Saturated fat 14g
Total carbs 6g
Net carbs 5g
Protein 38g
Sugars 3g
Fiber 1g
Sodium 1032mg

189. Pit boss Smoked Shrimp.

Preparation Time: 10 Minutes
Cooking Time: 10 Minutes
Servings: 6
Ingredients:
- 1 lb. tail-on shrimp, uncooked
- 1/2 tbsp onion powder
- 1/2 tbsp garlic powder
- 1/2 tbsp salt
- 4 tbsp teriyaki sauce
- 2 tbsp green onion, minced.
- 4 tbsp sriracha mayo

Directions:
1. Peel the shrimp shells leaving the tail on, then wash well and rise.
2. Drain well and pat dry with a paper towel.
3. Preheat your Pit boss to 450OF.
4. Season the shrimp with onion powder, garlic powder, and salt. Place the shrimp in the Pit boss and cook for 6 minutes on each side.
5. Remove the shrimp from the Pit boss and toss with teriyaki sauce, then garnish with onions and mayo.

Nutrition:
Calories 87
Total carbs 2g
Net carbs 2g
Protein 16g
Sodium 1241mg

190. Grilled Shrimp Kabobs

Preparation Time: 5 Minutes
Cooking Time: 10 Minutes
Servings: 4
Ingredients:
- 1 lb. colossal shrimp peeled and deveined.
- 2 tbsp. oil

- 1/2 tbsp. garlic salt
- 1/2 tbsp. salt
- 1/8 tbsp. pepper
- Six skewers

Directions:
1. Preheat your Pit boss to 3750F.
2. Pat the shrimp dry with a paper towel.
3. In a mixing bowl, mix oil, garlic salt, salt, and pepper.
4. Toss the shrimp in the mixture until well coated.
5. Skewer the shrimps and cook in the Pit boss with the lid closed for 4 minutes.
6. Open the lid, flip the skewers, cook for another 4 minutes, or wait until the shrimp is pink and the flesh is opaque.
7. Serve.

Nutrition:
Calories 325
Protein 20g
Sodium 120mg

191. Sweet Bacon-Wrapped Shrimp

Preparation Time: 20 Minutes
Cooking Time: 10 Minutes
Servings: 12
Ingredients:
- 1 lb. raw shrimp
- 1/2 tbsp salt
- 1/4 tbsp garlic powder
- 1 lb. bacon cut into halves.

Directions:
1. Preheat your Pit boss to 3500F.
2. Remove the shells and tails from the shrimp, then pat them dry with the paper towels.
3. Sprinkle salt and garlic on the shrimp, then wrap with bacon and secure with a toothpick.
4. Place the shrimps on a baking rack greased with cooking spray.
5. Cook for 10 minutes, flip and cook for another 10 minutes, or until the bacon is crisp enough.
6. Remove from the Pit boss and serve.

Nutrition:
Calories 204
Total fat 14g
Saturated fat 5g
Total carbs 1g
Net carbs 1g
Protein 18g
Sodium 939mg

192. Pit boss Spot Prawn Skewers

Preparation Time: 10 Minutes
Cooking Time: 10 Minutes
Servings: 6
Ingredients:
- 2 lb. spot prawns
- 2 tbsp oil
- Salt and pepper to taste

Directions:

1. Preheat your Pit boss to 400OF.
2. Skewer your prawns with soaked skewers, then generously sprinkle with oil, salt, and pepper.
3. Place the skewers on the grill, then cook with the lid closed for 5 minutes on each side.
4. Remove the skewers and serve when hot.

Nutrition:

Calories 221
Total fat 7g
Saturated fat 1g
Total carbs 2g
Net carbs 2g
Protein 34g
Sodium 1481mg

193. Pit boss Bacon-wrapped Scallops

Preparation Time: 15 Minutes
Cooking Time: 20 Minutes
Servings: 8
Ingredients:

- 1 lb. sea scallops
- 1/2 lb. bacon
- Sea salt

Directions:

1. Preheat your Pit boss to 375OF.
2. Pat dries the scallops with a towel, then wrap them with a piece of bacon and secure with a toothpick.
3. Lay the scallops on the grill with the bacon side down. Close the lid and cook for 5 minutes on each side.
4. Keep the scallops on the bacon side so that you will not get grill marks on the scallops.
5. Serve and enjoy.

Nutrition:

Calories 261
Total fat 14g
Saturated fat 5g
Total carbs 5g
Net carbs 5g
Protein 28g
Sodium 1238mg

194. Pit boss Lobster Tail

Preparation Time: 10 Minutes
Cooking Time: 15 Minutes
Servings: 2
Ingredients:

- 10 oz lobster tail
- 1/4 tbsp old bay seasoning
- 1/4 tbsp Himalayan salt
- 2 tbsp butter, melted.
- 1 tbsp fresh parsley, chopped.

Directions:

1. Preheat your Pit boss to 450OF.
2. Slice the tail down the middle, then season it with bay seasoning and salt.

3. Place the tails directly on the grill with the meat side down. Grill for 15 minutes or until the internal temperature reaches 140OF.
4. Remove from the Pit boss and drizzle with butter.
5. Serve when hot garnished with parsley.

Nutrition:

Calories 305
Total fat 14g
Saturated fat 8g
Total carbs 5g
Net carbs 5g
Protein 38g
Sodium 684mg

195. Roasted Honey Salmon

Preparation Time: 5 Minutes
Cooking Time: 1 Hour
Servings: 4
Ingredients:

- Two cloves' garlic, grated.
- Two tablespoon ginger, minced.
- One teaspoon honey
- One teaspoon sesame oil
- Two tablespoon lemon juice
- One teaspoon chili paste
- Four salmon fillets
- Two tablespoon soy sauce

Directions:

1. Set your wood pellet grill to smoke while the lid is open.
2. Do this for 5 minutes.
3. Preheat your wood pellet grill to 400 degrees F.
4. Combine all the ingredients except salmon in a sealable plastic bag.
5. Shake to mix the ingredients.
6. Add the salmon.
7. Marinate inside the refrigerator for 30 minutes.
8. Add the salmon to a roasting pan and place it on top of the grill.
9. Close the lid and cook for 3 minutes.
10. Flip the salmon and cook for another 3 minutes.

Nutrition:

Calories 119
Total fat 10g
Saturated fat 2g
Sodium 720mg

196. Blackened Salmon

Preparation Time: 10 Minutes
Cooking Time: 20 Minutes
Servings: 4
Ingredients:

- 2 lb. salmon, fillet, scaled and deboned.
- Two tablespoons olive oil
- Four tablespoons sweet dry rub

- One tablespoon cayenne pepper
- Two cloves' garlic, minced.

Directions:
1. Turn on your wood pellet grill.
2. Set it to 350 degrees F.
3. Brush the salmon with the olive oil.
4. Sprinkle it with the dry rub, cayenne pepper, and garlic.
5. Grill for 5 minutes per side.

Nutrition:
Calories 119
Total fat 10g
Saturated fat 2g
Sodium 720mg

197. Grilled Cajun Shrimp

Preparation Time: 5 Minutes
Cooking Time: 25 Minutes
Servings: 8
Ingredients:
Dip
- 1/2 cup mayonnaise
- One teaspoon lemon juice
- 1 cup sour cream
- One clove garlic, grated.
- One tablespoon Cajun seasoning
- One tablespoon hickory bacon rub
- One tablespoon hot sauce
- Chopped scallions.

Shrimp
- 1/2 lb. shrimp peeled and deveined.
- Two tablespoons olive oil
- 1/2 tablespoon hickory bacon seasoning
- One tablespoon Cajun seasoning

Directions:
1. Turn on your wood pellet grill.
2. Set it to 350 degrees F.
3. Mix the dip ingredients in a bowl.
4. Transfer to a small pan.
5. Cover with foil.
6. Place on top of the grill.
7. Cook for 10 minutes.
8. Coat the shrimp with the olive oil and sprinkle with the seasonings.
9. Grill for 5 minutes per side.
10. Pour the dip on top or serve with the shrimp.

Nutrition:
Calories 87
Total carbs 2g
Net carbs 2g
Protein 16g
Sodium 1241mg

198. Salmon Cakes

Preparation Time: 5 Minutes
Cooking Time: 25 Minutes
Servings: 4
Ingredients:
- 1 cup cooked salmon, flaked.

- 1/2 red bell pepper, chopped.
- Two eggs, beaten.
- 1/4 cup mayonnaise
- 1/2 tablespoon dry sweet rub
- 1 1/2 cups breadcrumbs
- One tablespoon mustard
- Olive oil

Directions:
1. Combine all the fixings except the olive oil in a bowl.
2. Form patties from this mixture.
3. Let sit for 15 minutes.
4. Turn on your wood pellet grill.
5. Set it to 350 degrees F.
6. Add a baking pan to the grill.
7. Drizzle a little olive oil on top of the pan.
8. Add the salmon cakes to the pan.
9. Grill each side for 3 to 4 minutes.

Nutrition:
Calories 119
Total fat 10g
Saturated fat 2g
Sodium 720mg

199. Pineapple Maple Glaze Fish

Preparation Time: 10 minutes
Cooking Time: 15 Minutes
Servings: 6
Ingredients:
- 3 pounds of fresh salmon
- 1/4 cup maple syrup
- 1/2 cup pineapple juice
- Brine Ingredients
- 3 cups of water
- Sea salt, to taste
- 2 cups of pineapple juice
- ½ cup of brown sugar
- 5 tablespoons of Worcestershire sauce
- 1 tablespoon of garlic salt

Directions:
1. Combine all the brine ingredients in a large cooking pan.
2. Place the fish into the brine and let it sit for 2 hours for marinating.
3. After 2 hours, take out the fish and pat dry with a paper towel and set aside.
4. Preheat the smoker grill to 250 degrees Fahrenheit, until the smoke started to appear.
5. Put salmon on the grill and cook for 15 minutes.
6. Meanwhile, mix pineapple and maple syrup in a bowl and baste fish every 5 minutes.
7. Once the salmon is done, serve and enjoy.

Nutrition:
Calories 123
Total Fat 4.9g6 %
Saturated Fat 1.5g8 %
Cholesterol 60mg20 %

Sodium 29mg1 %
Total Carbohydrate 0g0 %
Dietary Fiber 0g0 %
Sugar 0g

200. Smoked Catfish Recipe

Preparation Time: 10 minutes
Cooking Time: 5 Minutes
Servings: 3
Ingredients:
Ingredients for The Rub
- 2 tablespoons paprika
- 1/4 teaspoon salt
- 1 tablespoon garlic powder
- 1 tablespoon onion powder
- 1/2 tablespoon dried thyme
- 1/2 tablespoon cayenne

Other ingredients
- 2 pounds fresh catfish fillets
- 4 tablespoons butter, soften.

Directions:
1. Take a mixing bowl, and combine all the rub ingredients in it, including the paprika, salt, garlic powder, onion powder, and thyme and cayenne paper.
2. Rub the fillet with the butter, and then sprinkle a generous amount of rub on top.
3. Coat fish well with the rub.
4. Preheat the smoker grill at 200 degrees Fahrenheit for 15 minutes.
5. Cook fish on the grill for 10 minutes, 5minutes per side.
6. Once done, serve and enjoy.

Nutrition:
Calories 146 - Total Fat 4.2g - Saturated Fat 2.5g - Cholesterol 61mg
Sodium 28mg

201. Classic Smoked Trout

Preparation Time: 10 minutes
Cooking Time: 1 Hour
Servings: 3
Ingredients:
Ingredients for The Brine
- 4 cups of water
- 1-2 cups dark-brown sugar
- 1 cup of sea salt

Ingredients for The Trout's
- 3 pounds of trout, backbone and pin bones removed.
- 4 tablespoons of olive oil

Directions:
1. Preheat the electrical smoker grill, by setting the temperature to 250 degrees F, for 15 minutes by closing the lid.
2. Take a cooking pot, and combine all the brine ingredients, including water, sugar, and salt.
3. Submerged the fish in the brine mixture for a few hours.

4. Afterward, take out the fish, and pat dry with the paper towel.
5. Drizzle olive oil over the fish, and then place it over the grill grate for cooking.
6. Smoke the fish, until the internal temperature reaches 140 degrees Fahrenheit for 1 hour.
7. Then serve.

Nutrition:
Calories 254 - Total Fat 4.8g - Saturated Fat 1.5g - Cholesterol 81mg - Sodium 18mg

202. Cajun Smoked Shrimp

Preparation Time: 10 minutes
Cooking Time: 10 Minutes
Servings: 2 Servings:
Ingredients:
- 2 tablespoons of virgin olive oil
- 1/2 lemon, juiced.
- 3 cloves garlic, finely minced
- 2 tablespoons of Cajun spice
- Salt, to taste
- 1.5 pounds of shrimp, raw, peeled, deveined.

Directions:
1. Take a zip lock bag and combine olive oil, lemon juice, garlic cloves, Cajun spice, salt, and shrimp.
2. Toss the ingredients well for fine coating.
3. Preheat the smoker grill for 10 minutes until the smoke starts to establish.
4. Put the fish on the grill grate and close lid.
5. Turn the temperature to high and allow the fish to cook the shrimp for 10 minutes, 5 minutes per side.
6. Once done, serve.

Nutrition:
Calories 446
Total Fat 4.8g
Saturated Fat 6.5g
Cholesterol 53mg
Sodium 48mg

203. Candied Smoked Salmon with Orange Ginger Rub

Preparation Time: 10 minutes
Cooking Time: 2 Hours 10 Minutes
Servings: 10
Ingredients:
The Marinade
- Brown sugar – ¼ cup
- Salt – ½ teaspoon

The Rub
- Minced garlic – 2 tablespoons
- Grated fresh ginger – 1 teaspoon.
- Grated orange zest – ½ teaspoon
- Chili powder – ½ teaspoon
- Cayenne pepper – ½ teaspoon

The Glaze
- Red wine – 2 tablespoons
- Dark rum – 2 tablespoons

- Brown sugar – 1 ½ cups
- Honey – 1 cup

Directions:
1. Mix salt with brown sugar then apply over the salmon fillet. Let it rest for approximately an hour or until the sugar is melted.
2. In the meantime, combine minced garlic with grated fresh ginger, orange zest, chili powder, and cayenne pepper. Mix well.
3. Rub the salmon fillet with the spice mixture then set aside.
4. Plug the wood pellet smoker then fill the hopper with the wood pellet. Turn the switch on.
5. Set the wood pellet smoker for indirect heat then adjust the temperature to 225°F (107°C).
6. Place the seasoned salmon in wood pellet smoker and smoke for 2 hours.
7. Mix red wine with dark rum, brown sugar, and honey then stir until dissolved.
8. During the smoking process, baste the honey mixture over the salmon fillet for several times.
9. Once the smoked salmon flakes, remove it from the wood pellet smoker and transfer it to a serving dish.
10. Serve and enjoy.

Nutrition:
Calories: 433
Fats: 39g
Carbs: 4g
Fiber: 0g

204. Juicy Lime Smoked Tuna Belly

Preparation Time: 10 minutes
Cooking Time: 2 Hours 10 Minutes
Servings: 10
Ingredients:
- Tuna belly (3-lb., 1.4-kg.)

The Marinade
- Fresh limes – 2
- White sugar – 2 tablespoons
- Brown sugar – 3 tablespoons
- Pepper – ½ teaspoon
- Soy sauce – 1 tablespoon
- Sriracha sauce – 2 tablespoons

Directions:
1. Cut the limes into halves then squeeze the juice over the tuna belly. Marinate the tuna belly with the juice for 10 minutes. Meanwhile, combine white sugar with brown sugar, pepper, soy sauce, and Sriracha sauce then mix well. Wash and rinse the tuna belly then pat it dry. Then, plug the wood pellet smoker then fill the hopper with the wood pellet. Turn the switch on.
2. Set the wood pellet smoker for indirect heat then adjust the temperature to 225°F (107°C).
3. Wait until the wood pellet smoker reaches the desired temperature then place the seasoned tuna belly in it. Smoke the tuna belly for 2 hours or until it flakes and once it is done, remove it from the wood pellet smoker.
4. Serve and enjoy.

Nutrition:
Calories: 392
Fats: 27g
Carbs: 2g
Fiber: 0g

205. Lemon Butter Smoked Mackerel with Juniper Berries Brine

Preparation Time: 10 minutes
Cooking Time: 2 Hours 10 Minutes
Servings: 10
Ingredients:
- Mackerel fillet (4-lbs., 1.8-kg.)

The Brine
- Cold water – 4 cups
- Mustard seeds – 1 tablespoon
- Dried juniper berries – 1 tablespoon
- Bay leaves – 3
- Salt – 1 tablespoon

The Glaze
- Butter – 2 tablespoons
- Lemon juice – 2 tablespoons

Directions:
1. Pour cold water into a container, then season with salt, bay leaves, dried juniper berries, and mustard seeds, then stir well.
2. Add the mackerel fillet to the brine mixture, then soak for approximately 20 minutes, then wash and rinse it. Pat the mackerel dry.
3. Then, plug the wood pellet smoker then fill the hopper with the wood pellet. Turn the switch on.
4. Set the wood pellet smoker for indirect heat then adjust the temperature to 225°F (107°C).
5. Place the seasoned mackerel on a sheet of aluminum foil then baste butter over it.
6. Drizzle lemon juice then wraps the mackerel fillet with the aluminum foil.
7. Smoke the wrapped mackerel for 2 hours or until it flakes and once it is done, remove from the wood pellet smoker. Unwrap the smoked mackerel and serve. Enjoy!

Nutrition:
Calories: 467
Fats: 55g
Carbs: 4g
Fiber: 0g

206. Smoked Crab Paprika Garlic with Lemon Butter Flavor

Preparation Time: 5 minutes
Cooking Time: 30 Minutes
Servings: 10
Ingredients:
- Fresh Crabs (7-lb., 3.2-kg.)

The Sauce
- Salt – 1 tablespoon
- Cayenne pepper – 1 ½ teaspoon
- Salted butter – 2 cups
- Lemon juice – ½ cup
- Worcestershire sauce – 1 tablespoon
- Garlic powder – 2 teaspoons

- Smoked paprika – 2 teaspoons.

Directions:
1. Preheat a saucepan over low heat then melt the butter. Let it cool.
2. Season the melted butter with salt, cayenne pepper, Worcestershire sauce, garlic powder, and smoked paprika, then pour lemon juice into the melted butter. Stir until incorporated and set aside.
3. Then, plug the wood pellet smoker then fill the hopper with the wood pellet. Turn the switch on.
4. Set the wood pellet smoker for indirect heat then adjust the temperature to 350°F (177°C).
5. Arrange the crabs in a disposable aluminum pan then drizzle the sauce over the crabs.
6. Smoke the crabs for 30 minutes then remove from the wood pellet smoker.
7. Transfer the smoked crabs to a serving dish then serve.
8. Enjoy!

Nutrition:
Calories: 455
Fats: 53g
Carbs: 3g
Fiber: 0g

207. Cayenne Garlic Smoked Shrimp

Preparation Time: 5 minutes
Cooking Time: 15 Minutes
Servings: 10
Ingredients:
- Fresh Shrimps (3-lb., 1.4-kg.)

The Spices
- Olive oil – 2 tablespoons
- Lemon juice – 2 tablespoons
- Salt – ¾ teaspoon
- Smoked paprika – 2 teaspoons.
- Pepper – ½ teaspoon
- Garlic powder – 2 tablespoons
- Onion powder – 2 tablespoons
- Dried thyme – 1 teaspoon
- Cayenne pepper – 2 teaspoons

Directions:
1. Combine salt, smoked paprika, pepper, garlic powder, onion powder, dried thyme, and cayenne pepper then mix well. Set aside. Then, peel the shrimps and discard the head. Place in a disposable aluminum pan. Drizzle olive oil and lemon juice over the shrimps and shake to coat. Let the shrimps rest for approximately 5 minutes. Then, plug the wood pellet smoker then fill the hopper with the wood pellet. Turn the switch on.
2. Set the wood pellet smoker for indirect heat then adjust the temperature to 350°F (177°C).
3. Sprinkle the spice mixture over the shrimps then stir until the shrimps are completely seasoned.

4. Place the disposable aluminum pan with shrimps in the wood pellet smoker and smoke the shrimps for 15 minutes. The shrimps will be opaque and pink. Remove the smoked shrimps from the wood pellet smoker and transfer to a serving dish.
5. Serve and enjoy.

Nutrition: Calories: 233 - Fats: 25g - Carbs: 7g - Fiber: 0g

208. Cinnamon Ginger Juicy Smoked Crab

Preparation Time: 10 minutes
Cooking Time: 30 Minutes
Servings: 10
Ingredients:
- Fresh Crabs (7-lb., 3.2-kg.)

The Spices
- Salt – 1 tablespoon
- Ground celery seeds – 3 tablespoons
- Ground mustard – 2 teaspoons
- Cayenne pepper – ½ teaspoon
- Black pepper – ½ teaspoon
- Smoked paprika – 1 ½ teaspoon.
- Ground clove – A pinch
- Ground allspice – ¾ teaspoon
- Ground ginger – 1 teaspoon
- Ground cardamom – ½ teaspoon
- Ground cinnamon – ½ teaspoon
- Bay leaves - 2

Directions:
1. Combine the entire spices—salt, ground celery seeds, mustard, cayenne pepper, black pepper, smoked paprika, clove, allspice, ginger, cardamom, and cinnamon in a bowl then mix well. Sprinkle the spice mixture over the crabs then wrap the crabs with aluminum foil. Then, plug the wood pellet smoker then fill the hopper with the wood pellet. Turn the switch on. Set the wood pellet smoker for indirect heat then adjust the temperature to 350°F (177°C). Place the wrapped crabs in the wood pellet smoker and smoke for 30 minutes. Once it is done, remove the wrapped smoked carbs from the wood pellet smoker and let it rest for approximately 10 minutes.
2. Unwrap the smoked crabs and transfer it to a serving dish.
3. Serve and enjoy!

Nutrition: Calories: 355 - Fats: 22g - Carbs: 8g - Fiber: 0g

209. Roasted Yellowtail

Preparation Time: 10 minutes
Cooking Time: 30 minutes
Servings: 4
Ingredients:
- 4 Yellowtail Filets (6 oz.)
- 1 lb. new Potatoes
- 2 tbsp. Olive oil

- 1 lb. Mushrooms, oyster
- 1 tsp. ground Black pepper
- 4 tbsp. of olive oil

Salsa Verde:
- 1 tbsp. Cilantro, chopped.
- 2 tbsp. Mint, chopped.
- ½ cup Parsley, chopped.
- 2 cloves of garlic, minced.
- 1 tbsp. Oregano, chopped.
- 1 Lemon, the juice
- 1 cup of Olive oil
- 1/8 tsp. Pepper Flake
- Salt

Directions:
1. Preheat the grill to high with closed lid.
2. Place an iron pan directly on the grill. Let it heat for 10 minutes.
3. Rub the fish with oil. Season with black pepper and salt.
4. In a 2 different bowls place the mushrooms and potatoes, drizzle with oil and season with black pepper and salt. Toss.
5. Place the potatoes in the pan. Cook 10 minutes. Add the mushrooms.
6. Place the fillets on the grate with the skin down. Cook for 6 minutes and flip. Cook for 4 minutes more.
7. While the potatoes, mushrooms, and fish are cooking make the Salsa Verde. In a bowl combine all the ingredients and stir to combine.
8. Place the mushrooms and potatoes on a plate, top with a fillet and drizzle with the Salsa Verde.
9. Serve and Enjoy!

Nutrition: Calories: 398 Protein: 52g Carbs: 20g Fat: 18gg

210. Baked Steelhead

Preparation Time: 15 minutes
Cooking Time: 20 minutes
Servings: 4 - 6
Ingredients:
- 1 Lemon
- 2 Garlic cloves, minced.
- ½ Shallot, minced.
- 3 tbsp. Butter, unsalted
- Saskatchewan seasoning, blackened.
- Italian Dressing
- 1 Steelhead, (a fillet)

Directions:
1. Preheat the grill to 350F with closed lid.
2. In an iron pan place the butter. Place the pan in the grill while preheating so that the butter melts. Coat the fillet with Italian dressing. Rub with Saskatchewan rub. Make sure the layer is thin.

3. Mince the garlic and shallot. Remove the pan from the grill and add the garlic and shallots.
4. Spread the mixture on the fillet. Slice the lemon into slices. Place the slice on the butter mix.
5. Place the fish on the grate. Cook 20 - 30 minutes.
6. Remove from the grill and serve. Enjoy!

Nutrition: Calories: 230 Protein: 28g Carbs 2g: Fat: 14g

211. Wine Brined Salmon

Preparation Time: 15 minutes
Cooking Time: 5 hours
Servings: 4
Ingredients:
- 2 cups low-sodium soy sauce
- 1 cup dry white wine
- 1 cup water
- ½ teaspoon Tabasco sauce
- 1/3 cup sugar
- ¼ cup salt
- ½ teaspoon garlic powder
- ½ teaspoon onion powder
- Ground black pepper, as required.
- 4 (6-ounce) salmon fillets

Directions:
1. In a large bowl, add all ingredients except salmon and stir until sugar is dissolved.
2. Add salmon fillets and coat with brine well.
3. Refrigerate, covered overnight.
4. Remove salmon from bowl and rinse under cold running water.
5. With paper towels, pat dry the salmon fillets.
6. Arrange a wire rack in a sheet pan.
7. Place the salmon fillets onto wire rack, skin side down and set aside to cool for about 1 hour.
8. Preheat the Z Grills Pit Boss Grill & Smoker on smoke setting to 165 degrees F, using charcoal.
9. Arrange the salmon fillets onto the grill, skin side down and cook for about 3-5 hours or until desired doneness.
10. Remove the salmon fillets from grill and serve hot.

Nutrition:
Calories 379
Total Fat 10.5 g
Saturated Fat 1.5 g
Cholesterol 75 mg
Sodium 14000 mg
Total Carbs 26.8 g
Fiber 0.1 g
Sugar 25.3 g
Protein 41.1 g

212. Citrus Salmon

Preparation Time: 15 minutes
Cooking Time: 30 minutes
Servings: 6
Ingredients:
- 2 (1-pound) salmon fillets
- Salt and ground black pepper, as required.

- 1 tablespoon seafood seasoning
- 2 lemons, sliced.
- 2 limes, sliced.

Directions:
1. Preheat the Z Grills Pit Boss Grill & Smoker on grill setting to 225 degrees F.
2. Season the salmon fillets with salt, black pepper and seafood seasoning evenly.
3. Place the salmon fillets onto the grill and top each with lemon and lime slices evenly.
4. Cook for about 30 minutes.
5. Remove the salmon fillets from grill and serve hot.

Nutrition:
Calories 327
Total Fat 19.8 g
Saturated Fat 3.6 g
Cholesterol 81 mg
Sodium 237 mg
Total Carbs 1 g
Fiber 0.3 g
Sugar 0.2 g
Protein 36.1 g

213. Simple Mahi-Mahi

Preparation Time: 10 minutes
Cooking Time: 10 minutes
Servings: 4
Ingredients:
- 4 (6-ounce) mahi-mahi fillets
- 2 tablespoons olive oil
- Salt and ground black pepper, as required.

Directions:
1. Preheat the Z Grills Pit Boss Grill & Smoker on grill setting to 350 degrees F.
2. Coat fish fillets with olive oil and season with salt and black pepper evenly.
3. Place the fish fillets onto the grill and cook for about 5 minutes per side.
4. Remove the fish fillets from grill and serve hot.

Nutrition:
Calories 195
Total Fat 7 g
Saturated Fat 1 g
Cholesterol 60 mg
Sodium 182 mg
Total Carbs 0 g
Fiber 0 g
Sugar 0 g
Protein 31.6g

214. Rosemary Trout

Preparation Time: 10 minutes
Cooking Time: 5 hours
Servings: 8
Ingredients:
- 1 (7-pound) whole lake trout, butterflied.
- ½ cup kosher salt

- ½ cup fresh rosemary, chopped.
- 2 teaspoons lemon zest grated finely.

Directions:
1. Rub the trout with salt generously and then, sprinkle with rosemary and lemon zest.
2. Arrange the trout in a large baking dish and refrigerate for about 7-8 hours.
3. Remove the trout from baking dish and rinse under cold running water to remove the salt.
4. With paper towels, pat dry the trout completely.
5. Arrange a wire rack in a sheet pan.
6. Place the trout onto the wire rack, skin side down and refrigerate for about 24 hours.
7. Preheat the Z Grills Pit Boss Grill & Smoker on grill setting to 180 degrees F, using charcoal.
8. Place the trout onto the grill and cook for about 2-4 hours or until desired doneness.
9. Remove the trout from grill and place onto a cutting board for about 5 minutes before serving.

Nutrition:
Calories 633
Total Fat 31.8 g
Saturated Fat 7.9 g
Cholesterol 153 mg
Sodium 5000 mg
Total Carbs 2.4 g
Fiber 1.6 g
Sugar 0 g
Protein 85.2 g

215. Sesame Seeds Flounder

Preparation Time: 15 minutes
Cooking Time: 2½ hours
Servings: 4
Ingredients:
- ½ cup sesame seeds, toasted.
- ½ teaspoon kosher salt flakes
- 1 tablespoon canola oil
- 1 teaspoon sesame oil
- 4 (6-ounce) flounder fillets

Directions:
1. Preheat the Z Grills Pit Boss Grill & Smoker on grill setting to 225 degrees F.
2. With a mortar and pestle, crush sesame seeds with kosher salt slightly.
3. In a small bowl, mix both oils.
4. Coat fish fillets with oil mixture generously and then, rub with sesame seeds mixture.
5. Place fish fillets onto the lower rack of grill and cook for about 2-2½ hours.
6. Remove the fish fillets from grill and serve hot.

Nutrition:
Calories 343
Total Fat 16.2 g
Saturated Fat 2.3 g

Cholesterol 116 mg
Sodium 476 mg
Total Carbs 4.2 g
Fiber 2.1 g
Sugar 0.1 g
Protein 44.3 g

216. Parsley Prawn Skewers

Preparation Time: 15 minutes
Cooking Time: 8 minutes
Servings: 5
Ingredients:
- ¼ cup fresh parsley leaves, minced.
- 1 tablespoon garlic, crushed.
- 2½ tablespoons olive oil
- 2 tablespoons Thai chili sauce
- 1 tablespoon fresh lime juice
- 1½ pounds prawns peeled and deveined.

Directions:
1. In a large bowl, add all ingredients except for prawns and mix well.
2. In a resealable plastic bag, add marinade and prawns.
3. Seal the bag and shake to coat well.
4. Refrigerate for about 20-30 minutes.
5. Preheat the Z Grills Pit Boss Grill & Smoker on grill setting to 450 degrees F.
6. Remove the prawns from marinade and thread onto metal skewers.
7. Arrange the skewers onto the grill and cook for about 4 minutes per side.
8. Remove the skewers from grill and serve hot.

Nutrition:
Calories 234
Total Fat 9.3 g
Saturated Fat 1.7 g
Cholesterol 287 mg
Sodium 562 mg
Total Carbs 4.9 g
Fiber 0.1 g
Sugar 1.7 g
Protein 31.2 g

217. Buttered Shrimp

Preparation Time: 15 minutes
Cooking Time: 30 minutes
Servings: 6
Ingredients:
- 8 ounces salted butter, melted.
- ¼ cup Worcestershire sauce
- ¼ cup fresh parsley, chopped.
- 1 lemon, quartered.
- 2 pounds jumbo shrimp peeled and deveined.
- 3 tablespoons BBQ rub

Directions:
1. In a metal baking pan, add all ingredients except for shrimp and BBQ rub and mix well.
2. Season the shrimp with BBQ rub evenly.

3. Add shrimp in the pan with butter mixture and coat well.
4. Set aside for about 20-30 minutes.
5. Preheat the Z Grills Pit Boss Grill & Smoker on grill setting to 250 degrees F.
6. Place the pan onto the grill and cook for about 25-30 minutes.
7. Remove the pan from grill and serve hot.

Nutrition:
Calories 462
Total Fat 33.3 g
Saturated Fat 20.2 g
Cholesterol 400 mg
Sodium 485 mg
Total Carbs 4.7 g
Fiber 0.2 g
Sugar 2.1 g
Protein 34.9 g

218. Prosciutto Wrapped Scallops

Preparation Time: 15 minutes
Cooking Time: 40 minutes
Servings: 4
Ingredients:
- 8 large scallops shelled and cleaned.
- 8 extra-thin prosciutto slices

Directions:
1. Preheat the Z Grills Pit Boss Grill & Smoker on grill setting to 225-250 degrees F.
2. Arrange the prosciutto slices onto a smooth surface.
3. Place 1 scallop on the edge of 1 prosciutto slice and roll it up tucking in the sides of the prosciutto to cover completely.
4. Repeat with remaining scallops and prosciutto slices.
5. Arrange the wrapped scallops onto a small wire rack.
6. Place the wire rack onto the grill and cook for about 40 minutes.
7. Remove the scallops from grill and serve hot.

Nutrition:
Calories 160
Total Fat 6.7 g
Saturated Fat 2.3 g
Cholesterol 64 mg
Sodium 1000 mg
Total Carbs 1.4 g
Fiber 0 g
Sugar 0 g
Protein 23.5 g

219. Buttered Clams

Preparation Time: 15 minutes
Cooking Time: 8 minutes
Servings: 6
Ingredients:
- 24 littleneck clams
- ½ cup cold butter, chopped.
- 2 tablespoons fresh parsley, minced.

- 3 garlic cloves, minced.
- 1 teaspoon fresh lemon juice

Directions:
1. Preheat the Z Grills Pit Boss Grill & Smoker on grill setting to 450 degrees F.
2. Scrub the clams under cold running water.
3. In a large casserole dish, mix remaining ingredients.
4. Place the casserole dish onto the grill.
5. Now, arrange the clams directly onto the grill and cook for about 5-8 minutes or until they are opened. (Discard any that fail to open).
6. With tongs, carefully transfer the opened clams into the casserole dish and remove from the grill.
7. Serve immediately.

Nutrition:
Calories 306
Total Fat 17.6 g
Saturated Fat 9.9 g
Cholesterol 118 mg
Sodium 237 mg
Total Carbs 6.4 g
Fiber 0.1 g
Sugar 0.1 g
Protein 29.3 g

220. Lemony Lobster Tails

Preparation Time: 15 minutes
Cooking Time: 25 hours
Servings: 4
Ingredients:
- ½ cup butter, melted.
- 2 garlic cloves, minced.
- 2 teaspoons fresh lemon juice
- Salt and ground black pepper, as required.
- 4 (8-ounce) lobster tails

Directions:
1. Preheat the Z Grills Pit Boss Grill & Smoker on grill setting to 450 degrees F.
2. In a metal pan, add all ingredients except for lobster tails and mix well.
3. Place the pan onto the grill and cook for about 10 minutes.
4. Meanwhile, cut down the top of the shell and expose lobster meat.
5. Remove pan of butter mixture rom grill.
6. Coat the lobster meat with butter mixture.
7. Place the lobster tails onto the grill and cook for about 15 minutes, coating with butter mixture once halfway through.
8. Remove from the grill and serve hot.

Nutrition:
Calories 409
Total Fat 24.9 g
Saturated Fat 15.1 g
Cholesterol 392 mg
Sodium 1305 mg
Total Carbs 0.6 g
Fiber 0 g

Sugar 0.1 g
Protein 43.5 g

221. Chile Lime Clams with Tomatoes and Grilled Bread

Preparation Time: 10 minutes
Cooking Time: 25 minutes
Servings: 4
Ingredients:
- 6 tbsp unsalted pieces of butter
- 2 large shallots, chopped.
- 4 thinly sliced garlic cloves
- 1 tbsp of tomato paste
- 1 cup of beer
- 1 cup cherry tomatoes
- 1 1/2 ounce can-chickpeas, rinsed.
- 2 tbsp sambal oiled.
- 24 scrubbed littleneck clams
- 1 tbsp fresh lime juice
- 4 thick slices of country-style bread
- 2 tbsp olive oil
- Kosher salt
- ½ cup cilantro leaves
- lime wedges

Intolerances:
- Gluten-Free
- Egg-Free

Directions:
1. Set up the grill for medium, indirect heat. Put a large skillet on the grill over direct heat and melt 4 tbsp of butter in it.
2. Add the shallots and garlic and keep cooking, often stirring, until they soften, about 4 minutes.
3. Add the tomato paste and keep cooking, continually stirring, until paste darkens to a rich brick red color. Add the beer and tomatoes.
4. Cook until the beer is reduced nearly by half, about 4 minutes. Add in the chickpeas and sambal oiled, then the clams.
5. Cover and keep cooking until clams have opened, maybe from 5 to 10 minutes depending on the size of clams and the heat. Discard any clams that do not open. Pour in the lime juice and the remaining 2 tbsp of butter.
6. While grilling the clams, you can sprinkle the bread with oil and season with salt. Grill until it becomes golden brown and crisp.
7. Put the toasts onto plates and spoon with clam mixture, then top with cilantro. Serve with lime wedges.

Nutrition:
Calories: 400
Fat: 21g
Carbs: 33g
Protein: 17g

222. Grilled Fish with Salsa Verde

Preparation Time: 15 minutes
Cooking Time: 30 minutes
Servings: 4
Ingredients:

- 2 garlic cloves
- 3 tbsp fresh orange juice
- 1 tsp dried oregano
- 2 cups of chopped white onion.
- ¾ cup chopped cilantro.
- ¼ cup extra virgin olive oil and more for the grill
- 5 tbsp fresh lime juice
- 1 lb. of tilapia, striped bass, or sturgeon fillets
- Kosher salt and grounded pepper
- 1 cup of mayonnaise
- 1 tbsp of milk
- 4 corn tortillas
- 2 avocados peeled and sliced.
- ½ small head of cabbage, cored and thinly sliced.
- Salsa Verde
- Lime wedges

Intolerances:

- Gluten-Free
- Egg-Free

Directions:

1. Mix the garlic, orange juice, oregano, one cup onion, ¼ cup cilantro, ¼ cup oil, and 3 tbsp of lime juice in a medium bowl.
2. Season the fish with salt and grounded pepper. Spoon the 1/2 onion mixture on a glass baking dish then put the fish on it.
3. Spoon the remaining onion mixture over the fish and chill for half hour. Turn the fish, cover, and chill for another half hour.
4. Mix the mayo, milk, and the remaining two tbsp of lime juice in a little bowl.
5. Set up the grill for medium-high heat and brush the grate with oil.
6. Grill the fish, with some marinade on, till opaque in the center, about 3–5 minutes for each side.
7. Grill the tortillas till slightly burned, about ten seconds per side. Coarsely chop the fish and put it onto a platter.
8. Serve with lime mayonnaise, tortillas, avocados, cabbage, Salsa Verde, lime wedges and the remaining cup of sliced onion and ½ cup cilantro.

Nutrition:
Calories: 270
Fat: 22g
Cholesterol: 11mg
Carbs: 2g
Protein: 20g

223. Grilled Salmon Steaks with Cilantro Yogurt Sauce

Preparation Time: 10 minutes
Cooking Time: 20 minutes
Servings: 4
Ingredients:

- Vegetable oil (for the grill)
- 2 serrano chilis
- 2 garlic cloves
- 1 cup cilantro leaves
- ½ cup plain whole-milk Greek yogurt
- 1 tbsp of extra virgin olive oil
- 1 tsp honey
- Kosher salt
- 2 12oz bone-in salmon steaks

Intolerances:

- Gluten-Free
- Egg-Free

Directions:

1. Set up the grill for medium-high heat, then oil the grate.
2. Expel and dispose of seeds from one chili. Mix the two chilis, garlic, cilantro, the yogurt, oil, the nectar, and ¼ cup water in a blender until it becomes smooth, then season well with salt.
3. Move half of the sauce to a little bowl and put it aside. Season the salmon steaks with salt.
4. Grill it, turning more than once, until it is beginning to turn dark, about 4 minutes.
5. Keep on grilling, turning frequently, and seasoning with residual sauce for at least 4 minutes longer.

Nutrition:
Calories: 290
Fat: 14g
Cholesterol: 80g
Carbs: 1g
Protein: 38g

224. Grilled Scallops with Lemony Salsa Verde

Preparation Time: 15 minutes
Cooking Time: 15 minutes
Servings: 2
Ingredients:

- 2 tbsp of vegetable oil and more for the grill
- 12 large sea scallops, side muscle removed.
- Kosher salt and grounded black pepper
- Lemony Salsa Verde

Intolerances:

- Gluten-Free - Egg-Free - Lactose-Free

Directions:

1. Set up the grill for medium-high heat, then oil the grate. Toss the scallops with 2 tbsp of oil on a rimmed baking sheet and season with salt and pepper.

2. Utilizing a fish spatula or your hands, place the scallops on the grill.
3. Grill them, occasionally turning, until gently singed and cooked through, around 2 minutes for each side.
4. Serve the scallops with Lemony Salsa Verde.

Nutrition:
Calories: 30 Fat: 1g Cholesterol: 17mg · Carbs: 1g Protein: 6g

225. Grilled Shrimp with Shrimp Butter

Preparation Time: 15 minutes
Cooking Time: 15 minutes
Servings: 4
Ingredients:
- 6 tbsp unsalted butter
- 1/2 cup finely chopped red onion.
- 1 1/2 tsp crushed red pepper
- 1 tsp Malaysian shrimp paste
- 1 1/2 tsp lime juice
- salt
- grounded black pepper
- 24 shelled and deveined large shrimp
- 6 wooden skewers (better if soaked in water for 30 minutes)
- Torn mint leaves and assorted sprouts.

Intolerances:
- Gluten-Free
- Egg-Free

Directions:
1. In a little skillet, liquefy 3 tbsp of butter. Add the onion then cook over moderate heat for about 3 minutes.
2. Add in the squashed red pepper and shrimp paste and cook until fragrant, about 2 minutes.
3. Add in the lime juice and the remaining 3 tbsp of butter and season with salt. Keep the shrimp sauce warm.
4. Set up the grill. Season the shrimp with salt and pepper and string onto the skewers, not too tightly.
5. Grill over high heat, turning once until gently singed and cooked through, around 4 minutes.
6. Move onto a platter and spoon with shrimp sauce. Spread on the mint leaves and sprouts and serve.

Nutrition:
Calories: 224
Fat: 10g
Cholesterol: 260mg
Carbs: 1g
Protein: 30g

226. Grilled Sea Scallops with Corn Salad

Preparation Time: 25 minutes
Cooking Time: 30 minutes
Servings: 6
Ingredients:
- 6 shucked ears of corn
- 1-pint grape tomatoes, halved.
- 3 sliced scallions, white and light green parts only
- 1/3 cup basil leaves, finely shredded
- Salt and grounded pepper
- 1 small shallot, minced.
- 2 tbsp balsamic vinegar
- 2 tbsp hot water
- 1 tsp Dijon mustard 1/4 cup
- 3 tbsp sunflower oil
- 1 1/2 pounds sea scallops

Intolerances:
- Gluten-Free
- Egg-Free
- Lactose-Free

Directions:
1. In a pot of boiling salted water, cook the corn for about 5 minutes. Drain and cool.
2. Place the corn into a big bowl and cut off the kernels. Add the tomatoes, the scallions and basil then season with salt and grounded pepper.
3. In a blender, mix the minced shallot with the vinegar, heated water, and mustard. With the blender on, gradually add 6 tbsp of the sunflower oil.
4. Season the vinaigrette with salt and pepper; at that point, add it to the corn salad.
5. In a huge bowl, toss the remaining 1 tbsp of oil with the scallops, then season with salt and grounded pepper.
6. Heat a grill pan. Put on half of the scallops and grill over high heat, turning once, until singed, around 4 minutes.
7. Repeat with the other half of the scallops. Place the corn salad on plates, then top with the scallops and serve.

Nutrition:
Calories: 230
Fat: 5g
Cholesterol: 60mg
Carbs: 13g
Protein: 33g

227. Grilled Oysters with Tequila Butter

Preparation Time: 20 minutes
Cooking Time: 25 minutes
Servings: 6
Ingredients:
- 1/2 tsp fennel seeds
- 1/4 tsp crushed red pepper
- 7 tbsp of unsalted butter

- 1/4 cup of sage leaves, plus 36 small leaves for the garnish
- 1 tsp of dried oregano
- 2 tbsp lemon juice
- 2 tbsp of tequila
- Kosher salt
- rock salt, for the serving
- 3 dozen scrubbed medium oysters.

Intolerances:
- Gluten-Free
- Egg-Free
- Lactose-Free

Directions:
1. Using a skillet, toast the fennel seeds and squashed red pepper over moderate heat until fragrant for 1 minute.
2. Move onto a mortar and let it cool. With a pestle, pound the spices to a coarse powder, then move into a bowl.
3. Using the same skillet, cook 3 1/2 tbsp of the butter over moderate heat until it becomes dark-colored, about two minutes.
4. Add 1/4 cup of sage and keep cooking, occasionally turning, for about 2 minutes. Move the sage onto a plate.
5. Transfer the butter into the bowl with the spices. Repeat with the remaining butter and sage leaves. Put some aside for decoration.
6. Put the fried sage leaves onto the mortar and squash them with the pestle. Add the squashed sage to the butter along with the oregano, lemon juice, and tequila and season with salt. Keep warm.
7. Set up the grill. Line a platter with rock salt. Grill the oysters over high heat until they open, about 1 to 2 minutes.
8. Dispose of the top shell and spot the oysters on the rock salt, being careful not to spill their juice.
9. Spoon the warm tequila sauce over the oysters, decorate with a fresh sage leaf, and serve.

Nutrition:
Calories: 68
Fat: 3g
Carbs: 4g
Protein: 10g

228. Citrus Soy Squid

Preparation Time: 15 minutes
Cooking Time: 45 minutes
Servings: 4
Ingredients:
- 1 cup mirin
- 1 cup of soy sauce
- 1/3 cup yuzu juice or fresh lemon juice
- 2 cups of water
- 2 pounds squid tentacles left whole; bodies cut crosswise 1 inch thick.

Intolerances:
- Gluten-Free
- Egg-Free
- Lactose-Free

Directions:
1. In a bowl, mix the mirin, soy sauce, the yuzu juice, and water.
2. Put a bit of the marinade in a container and refrigerate it for later use.
3. Add the squid to the bowl with the rest of the marinade and let it sit for about 30 minutes or refrigerate for 4 hours.
4. Set up the grill. Drain the squid.
5. Grill over medium-high heat, turning once until white all through for 3 minutes.
6. Serve hot.

Nutrition:
Calories: 110
Fat: 6g
Carbs: 6g
Protein: 8g

229. Spiced Salmon Kebabs

Preparation Time: 20 minutes
Cooking Time: 25 minutes
Servings: 4
Ingredients:
- 2 tbsp of chopped fresh oregano.
- 2 tsp of sesame seeds
- 1 tsp ground cumin
- 1 tsp Kosher salt
- 1/4 tsp crushed red pepper flakes
- 1 1/2 pounds of skinless salmon fillets cut into 1" pieces.
- 2 lemons thinly sliced into rounds.
- 2 tbsp of olive oil
- 16 bamboo skewers soaked in water for one hour.

Intolerances:
- Gluten-Free
- Egg-Free
- Lactose-Free

Directions:
1. Set up the grill for medium heat. Mix the oregano, sesame seeds, cumin, salt, and red pepper flakes in a little bowl. Put the spice blend aside.
2. String the salmon and the lemon slices onto 8 sets of parallel skewers to make 8 kebabs.
3. Spoon with oil and season with the spice blend.
4. Grill and turn at times until the fish is cooked.

Nutrition:
Calories: 230
Fat: 10g

Carbs: 1g
Protein: 30g

230. Grilled Onion Butter Cod

Preparation Time: 10 minutes
Cooking Time: 15 minutes
Servings: 4
Ingredients:

- 1/4 cup butter
- 1 finely chopped small onion.
- 1/4 cup white wine
- 4 (6ounce) cod fillets
- 1 tbsp of extra virgin olive oil
- 1/2 tsp salt (or to taste)
- 1/2 tsp black pepper
- Lemon wedges

Intolerances:

- Gluten-Free
- Egg-Free

Directions:

1. Set up the grill for medium-high heat.
2. In a little skillet liquefy the butter. Add the onion and cook for 1or 2 minutes.
3. Add the white wine and let stew for an extra 3 minutes. Take away and let it cool for 5 minutes.
4. Spoon the fillets with extra virgin olive oil and sprinkle with salt and pepper. Put the fish on a well-oiled rack and cook for 8 minutes.
5. Season it with sauce and cautiously flip it over. Cook for 6 to 7 minutes more, turning more times or until the fish arrives at an inside temperature of 145ºF.
6. Take away from the grill, top with lemon wedges, and serve.

Nutrition:
Calories: 140
Fat: 5g
Cholesterol: 46mg
Carbs: 4g
Protein: 20g

231. Grilled Calamari with Mustard Oregano and Parsley Sauce

Preparation Time: 10 minutes
Cooking Time: 35 minutes
Servings: 6
Ingredients:

- 8 Calamari, cleaned.
- 2 cups of milk
- Sauce
- 4 tsp of sweet mustard
- Juice from 2 lemons
- 1/2 cup of olive oil
- 2 tbsp fresh oregano finely chopped.
- Pepper, ground
- 1/2 bunch of parsley finely chopped.

Intolerances:

- Gluten-Free
- Egg-Free
- Lactose-Free

Directions:

1. Clean calamari well and cut into slices.
2. Place calamari in a large metal bow, cover and marinate with milk overnight.
3. Remove calamari from the milk and drain well on paper towel. Grease the fish lightly with olive oil.
4. In a bowl, combine mustard and the juice from the two lemons.
5. Beat lightly and pour the olive oil very slowly; stir until all the ingredients are combined well.
6. Add the oregano and pepper and stir well.
7. Start the Pit boss grill and set the temperature to moderate; preheat, lid closed, for 10 to 15 minutes.
8. Place the calamari on the grill and cook for 2-3 minutes per side or until it has a bit of char and remove from the grill.
9. Transfer calamari to serving platter and pour them over with mustard sauce and chopped parsley.

Nutrition:
Calories: 212
Fat: 19g
Cholesterol: 651mg
Carbs: 7g
Protein: 3g

232. Grilled Cuttlefish with Spinach and Pine Nuts Salad

Preparation Time: 15 minutes
Cooking Time: 30 minutes
Servings: 6
Ingredients:

- 1/2 cup of olive oil
- 1 tbsp of lemon juice
- 1 tsp oregano
- Pinch of salt
- 8 large cuttlefish, cleaned.
- Spinach, pine nuts, olive oil and vinegar for serving.

Intolerances:

- Gluten-Free
- Egg-Free
- Lactose-Free

Directions:

1. Prepare marinade with olive oil, lemon juice, oregano, and a pinch of salt pepper (be careful, cuttlefish do not need too much salt).
2. Place the cuttlefish in the marinade, tossing to cover evenly. Cover and marinate for about 1 hour.
3. Remove the cuttlefish from marinade and pat dry them on paper towel.
4. Start the Pit boss grill, and set the temperature to high and preheat, lid closed, for 10 to 15 minutes.

5. Grill the cuttlefish just 3 - 4 minutes on each side.
6. Serve hot with spinach, pine nuts, olive oil, and vinegar.

Nutrition:
Calories: 299
Fat: 19g
Cholesterol: 186mg
Carbs: 3g
Protein: 28g

233. Grilled Dijon Lemon Catfish Fillets

Preparation Time: 15 minutes
Cooking Time: 25 minutes
Servings: 6
Ingredients:
- 1/2 cup olive oil
- Juice of 4 lemons
- 2 tbsp Dijon mustard
- 1/2 tsp salt
- 1 tsp paprika
- Fresh rosemary chopped.
- 4 (6- to 8-oz.) catfish fillets, 1/2-inch thick

Intolerances:
- Gluten-Free
- Egg-Free
- Lactose-Free

Directions:
1. Set the temperature to Medium and preheat, lid closed, for 10 to 15 minutes.
2. Whisk the olive oil, lemon juice, mustard, salt, paprika and chopped rosemary in a bowl.
3. Brush one side of each fish fillet with half of the olive oil-lemon mixture; season with salt and pepper to taste.
4. Grill fillets, covered, 4 to 5 minutes. Turn fillets and brush with remaining olive oil-lemon mixture.
5. Grill 4 to 5 minutes more (do not cover).
6. Remove fish fillets to a serving platter, sprinkle with rosemary and serve.

Nutrition:
Calories: 295
Fat: 24g
Cholesterol: 58mg
Carbs: 3g
Protein: 16g

234. Grilled Halibut Fillets in Chili Rosemary Marinade

Preparation Time: 15 minutes
Cooking Time: 55 minutes
Servings: 6
Ingredients:
- 1 cup of virgin olive oil
- 2 large red chili peppers, chopped.
- 2 cloves garlic cut into quarters.
- 1 bay leaf
- 1 twig of rosemary
- 2 lemons
- 4 tbsp of white vinegar
- 4 halibut fillets

Intolerances:
- Gluten-Free
- Egg-Free
- Lactose-Free

Directions:
1. In a large container, mix olive oil, chopped red chili, garlic, bay leaf, rosemary, lemon juice and white vinegar.
2. Submerge halibut fillets and toss to combine well.
3. Cover and marinate in the refrigerator for several hours or overnight.
4. Remove anchovies from marinade and pat dry on paper towels for 30 minutes.
5. Start the Pit boss grill, set the temperature to medium and preheat, lid closed for 10 to 15 minutes.
6. Grill the anchovies, skin side down for about 10 minutes, or until the flesh of the fish becomes white (thinner cuts and fillets can cook in as little time as 6 minutes).
7. Turn once during cooking to avoid having the halibut fall apart.
8. Transfer to a large serving platter, pour a little lemon juice over the fish, sprinkle with rosemary and serve.

Nutrition:
Calories: 259
Fat: 4g
Cholesterol: 133mg
Carbs: 5g
Protein: 51g

235. Grilled Lobster with Lemon Butter and Parsley

Preparation Time: 15 minutes
Cooking Time: 40 minutes
Servings: 4
Ingredients:
- 1 lobster (or more)
- 1/2 cup fresh butter
- 2 lemons juice (freshly squeezed)
- 2 tbsp parsley
- Salt and freshly ground pepper to taste

Intolerances:
- Gluten-Free
- Egg-Free

Directions:
1. Use a pot large enough large to hold the lobsters and fill water and salt. Bring to boil and put in lobster. Boil for 4 - 5 minutes.
2. Remove lobster to the working surface.

3. Pull the body to the base of the head and divide the head.
4. Firmly hold the body, with the abdomen upward, and with a sharp knife cut it along in the middle.
5. Start your Pit boss grill with the lid open until the fire is established (4 to 5 minutes). Set the temperature to 350°F and preheat, lid closed for 10 to 15 minutes.
6. Melt the butter and beat it with a lemon juice, parsley, salt, and pepper. Spread butter mixture over lobster and put directly on a grill grate.
7. Grill lobsters cut side down about 7 - 8 minutes until the shells are bright in color (also, depends on its size).
8. Turn the lobster over and brush with butter mixture. Grill for another 4 - 5 minutes.
9. Serve hot sprinkled with lemon butter and parsley finely chopped.

Nutrition:
Calories: 385
Fat: 24g
Cholesterol: 346mg
Carbs: 2g
Protein: 37g

236. Grilled Trout in White Wine and Parsley Marinade

Preparation Time: 20 minutes
Cooking Time: 45 minutes
Servings: 4
Ingredients:
- 1/4 cup olive oil
- 1 lemon juice
- 1/2 cup of white wine
- 2 cloves garlic minced.
- 2 tbsp fresh parsley finely chopped.
- 1 tsp fresh basil finely chopped.
- Salt and freshly ground black pepper to taste.
- 4 trout fish, cleaned.
- Lemon slices for garnish

Intolerances:
- Gluten-Free
- Egg-Free
- Lactose-Free

Directions:
1. In a large container, stir olive oil, lemon juice, wine, garlic, parsley, basil, and salt and freshly ground black pepper to taste.
2. Submerge fish in sauce and toss to combine well.
3. Cover and marinate in refrigerate overnight.
4. When ready to cook, start the Pit boss grill on Smoke with the lid open for 4 to 5 minutes.

Set the temperature to 400°F and preheat, lid closed, for 10 to 15 minutes.
5. Remove the fish from marinade and pat dry on paper towel, reserve marinade.
6. Grill trout for 5 minutes from both sides (be careful not to overcook the fish).
7. Pour fish with marinade and serve hot with lemon slices.

Nutrition:
Calories: 267
Fat: 18g
Carbs: 3g
Protein: 16g

237. Stuffed Squid on Pit boss Grill

Preparation Time: 15 minutes
Cooking Time: 30 minutes
Servings: 8
Ingredients:
- 2 lbs. of squid
- 4 cloves garlic
- 10 sprigs parsley
- 4 slices old bread
- 1/3 cup of milk
- Salt and ground white pepper
- 4 slices of prosciutto
- 4 slices of cheese
- 3 tbsp of olive oil
- 1 lemon

Intolerances:
- Egg-Free

Directions:
1. Wash and clean your squid and pat dry on paper towel. Finely chop parsley and garlic.
2. Cut bread into cubes and soak in milk.
3. Add parsley, garlic, white pepper, and salt. Stir well together.
4. Cut the cheese into larger pieces (the pieces should be large enough that they can be pushed through the opening of the squid).
5. Mix the cheese with prosciutto slices and stir well together with remaining ingredients.
6. Use your fingers to open the bag pack of squid and pushed the mixture inside. At the end add some more bread.
7. Close the openings with toothpicks.
8. Start your Pit boss grill on smoke with the lid open for 5 minutes.
9. Set the temperature to the highest setting and preheat, lid closed, for 10 – 15 minutes.
10. Grill squid for 3 – 4 minutes being careful not to burn the squid. Serve hot.

Nutrition:
Calories: 290
Fat: 13g

Cholesterol: 288mg
Carbs: 13g
Protein: 25g

238. Fish Stew

Preparation Time: 20 minutes
Cooking Time: 25 minutes
Servings: 8
Ingredients:

- 1 jar (28oz.) Crushed Tomatoes
- 2 oz. of Tomato paste
- ¼ cup of White wine
- ¼ cup of Chicken Stock
- 2 tbsp. Butter
- 2 Garlic cloves, minced.
- ¼ Onion, diced.
- ½ lb. Shrimp divined and cleaned.
- ½ lb. of Clams
- ½ lb. of Halibut
- Parsley
- Bread

Directions:

1. Preheat the grill to 300F with closed lid.
2. Place a Dutch oven over medium heat and melt the butter.
3. Sauté the onion for 4 - 7 minutes. Add the garlic. Cook 1 more minute.
4. Add the tomato paste. Cook until the color becomes rust red. Pour the stock and wine. Cook 10 minutes. Add the tomatoes, simmer.
5. Chop the halibut and together with the other seafood add in the Dutch oven. Place it on the grill and cover with a lid.
6. Let it cook for 20 minutes.
7. Season with black pepper and salt and set aside.
8. Top with chopped parsley and serve with bread.
9. Enjoy!

Nutrition:
Calories: 188
Protein: 25g
Carbohydrates: 7g
Fat: 12g

239. Smoked Shrimp

Preparation Time: 4 hours and 15 minutes
Cooking Time: 10 minutes
Servings: 4
Ingredients:

- 4 tablespoons olive oil
- 1 tablespoon Cajun seasoning
- 2 cloves garlic, minced.
- 1 tablespoon lemon juice
- Salt to taste
- 2 lb. shrimp peeled and deveined.

Direction:

1. Combine all the ingredients in a sealable plastic bag.

2. Toss to coat evenly.
3. Marinate in the refrigerator for 4 hours.
4. Set the Pit boss grill to high.
5. Preheat it for 15 minutes while the lid is closed.
6. Thread shrimp onto skewers.
7. Grill for 4 minutes per side.

Serving Suggestion: Garnish with lemon wedges.
Preparation / Cooking Tips: Soak skewers first in water if you are using wooden skewers.
Nutrition:
Calories: 298
Protein: 42g
Carbohydrates: 10g
Fat: 10g
Fiber 0g

240. Cod with Lemon Herb Butter

Preparation Time: 30 minutes
Cooking Time: 15 minutes
Servings: 4
Ingredients:

- 4 tablespoons butter
- 1 clove garlic, minced.
- 1 tablespoon tarragon, chopped.
- 1 tablespoon lemon juice
- 1 teaspoon lemon zest
- Salt and pepper to taste
- 1 lb. cod fillet

Direction:

1. Preheat the Pit boss grill too high for 15 minutes while the lid is closed.
2. In a bowl, mix the butter, garlic, tarragon, lemon juice and lemon zest, salt, and pepper.
3. Place the fish in a baking pan.
4. Spread the butter mixture on top.
5. Bake the fish for 15 minutes.

Serving Suggestion: Spoon sauce over the fish before serving.
Preparation / Cooking Tips: You can also use other white fish fillet for this recipe.
Nutrition:
Calories: 218
Protein: 22g
Carbohydrates: 20g
Fat: 12g
Fiber 0g

241. Salmon with Avocado Salsa

Preparation Time: 30 minutes
Cooking Time: 20 minutes
Servings: 6
Ingredients:

- 3 lb. salmon fillet
- Garlic salt and pepper to taste
- 4 cups avocado sliced into cubes.
- 1 onion, chopped.
- 1 jalapeño pepper, minced.

- 1 tablespoon lime juice
- 1 tablespoon olive oil
- ¼ cup cilantro, chopped.
- Salt to taste

Direction:
1. Sprinkle both sides of salmon with garlic salt and pepper.
2. Set the Pit boss grill to smoke.
3. Grill the salmon for 7 to 8 minutes per side.
4. While waiting, prepare the salsa by combining the remaining ingredients in a bowl.
5. Serve salmon with the avocado salsa.

Serving Suggestion: Garnish with lemon wedges.
Preparation / Cooking Tips: You can also use tomato salsa for this recipe if you do not have avocados.

Nutrition:
Calories: 278
Protein: 20g
Carbohydrates: 17g
Fat: 11g
Fiber 0g

242. Buttered Crab Legs

Preparation Time: 30 minutes
Cooking Time: 10 minutes
Servings: 4
Ingredients:
- 12 tablespoons butter
- 1 tablespoon parsley, chopped.
- 1 tablespoon tarragon, chopped.
- 1 tablespoon chives, chopped.
- 1 tablespoon lemon juice
- 4 lb. king crab legs split in the center.

Direction:
1. Set the Pit boss grill to 375 degrees F.
2. Preheat it for 15 minutes while lid is closed.
3. In a pan over medium heat, simmer the butter, herbs, and lemon juice for 2 minutes.
4. Place the crab legs on the grill.
5. Pour half of the sauce on top.
6. Grill for 10 minutes.
7. Serve with the reserved butter sauce.

Serving Suggestion: Garnish with lemon wedges.
Preparation / Cooking Tips: You can also use shrimp for this recipe.

Nutrition:
Calories: 218
Protein: 28g
Carbohydrates: 18g
Fat: 10g
Fiber 0g

243. Grilled Blackened Salmon

Preparation Time: 15 minutes
Cooking Time: 30 minutes
Servings: 4
Ingredients:
- 4 salmon fillets
- Blackened dry rub.

- Italian seasoning powder

Direction:
1. Season salmon fillets with dry rub and seasoning powder.
2. Grill in the Pit boss grill at 325 degrees F for 10 to 15 minutes per side.

Serving Suggestion: Garnish with lemon wedges.
Preparation / Cooking Tips: You can also drizzle salmon with lemon juice.

Nutrition:
Calories: 258
Protein: 23g
Carbohydrates: 20g
Fat: 12g
Fiber 0g

244. Spicy Shrimp

Preparation Time: 45 minutes
Cooking Time: 10 minutes
Servings: 4
Ingredients:
- 3 tablespoons olive oil
- 6 cloves garlic
- 2 tablespoons chicken dry rub
- 6 oz. chili
- 1 1/2 tablespoons white vinegar
- 1 1/2 teaspoons sugar
- 6 lb. shrimp peeled and deveined.

Direction:
1. Add olive oil, garlic, dry rub, chili, vinegar, and sugar in a food processor.
2. Blend until smooth.
3. Transfer mixture to a bowl.
4. Stir in shrimp.
5. Cover and refrigerate for 30 minutes.
6. Preheat the Pit boss grill to hit for 15 minutes while the lid is closed.
7. Thread shrimp onto skewers.
8. Grill for 3 minutes per side.

Serving Suggestion: Garnish with chopped herbs.
Preparation / Cooking Tips: You can also add vegetables to the skewers.

Nutrition:
Calories: 250
Protein: 24g
Carbohydrates: 18g
Fat: 13g
Fiber 0g

245. Grilled Herbed Tuna

Preparation Time: 4 hours and 15 minutes
Cooking Time: 10 minutes
Servings: 6
Ingredients:
- 6 tuna steaks
- 1 tablespoon lemon zest
- 1 tablespoon fresh thyme, chopped.
- 1 tablespoon fresh parsley, chopped.
- Garlic salt to taste

Direction:

1. Sprinkle the tuna steaks with lemon zest, herbs, and garlic salt.
2. Cover with foil.
3. Refrigerate for 4 hours.
4. Grill for 3 minutes per side.

Serving Suggestion: Top with lemon slices before serving.

Preparation / Cooking Tips: Take the fish out of the refrigerator 30 minutes before cooking.

Nutrition:

Calories: 234
Protein: 25g
Carbohydrates: 17g
Fat: 11g
Fiber 0g

246. Roasted Snapper

Preparation Time: 30 minutes
Cooking Time: 15 minutes
Servings: 4
Ingredients:

- 4 snapper fillets
- Salt and pepper to taste
- 2 teaspoons dried tarragon
- Olive oil
- 2 lemons, sliced.

Direction:

1. Set the Pit boss grill to high.
2. Preheat it for 15 minutes while the lid is closed.
3. Add 1 fish fillet on top of a foil sheet.
4. Sprinkle with salt, pepper, and tarragon.
5. Drizzle with oil.
6. Place lemon slices on top.
7. Fold and seal the packets.
8. Put the foil packets on the grill.
9. Bake for 15 minutes.
10. Open carefully and serve.

Serving Suggestion: Drizzle with melted butter before serving.

Preparation / Cooking Tips: You can also add asparagus spears or broccoli in the packet to cook with the fish.

Nutrition:

Calories: 222
Protein: 18g
Carbohydrates: 12g
Fat: 10g
Fiber 0g

247. Fish Fillets with Pesto

Preparation Time: 15 minutes
Cooking Time: 15 minutes
Servings: 6
Ingredients:

- 2 cups fresh basil
  - cup parsley, chopped.
- 1/2 cup walnuts

- 1/2 cup olive oil
- 1 cup Parmesan cheese, grated.
- Salt and pepper to taste
- 4 white fish fillets

Direction:

1. Preheat the Pit boss grill too high for 15 minutes while the lid is closed.
2. Add all the ingredients except fish to a food processor.
3. Pulse until smooth. Set aside.
4. Season fish with salt and pepper.
5. Grill for 6 to 7 minutes per side.
6. Serve with the pesto sauce.

Serving Suggestion: Garnish with fresh basil leaves.

Preparation / Cooking Tips: You can also spread a little bit of the pesto on the fish before grilling.

Nutrition:

Calories: 279
Protein: 32g
Carbohydrates: 20g
Fat: 14g
Fiber 0g

248. Halibut with Garlic Pesto

Preparation Time: 20 minutes
Cooking Time: 10 minutes
Servings: 4
Ingredients:

- 4 halibut fillets
- 1 cup olive oil
- Salt and pepper to taste
- 1/4 cup garlic, chopped.
- 1/4 cup pine nuts

Direction:

1. Set the Pit boss grill to smoke.
2. Establish fire for 5 minutes.
3. Set temperature to high.
4. Place a cast iron on a grill.
5. Season fish with salt and pepper.
6. Add fish to the pan.
7. Drizzle with a little oil.
8. Sear for 4 minutes per side.
9. Prepare the garlic pesto by pulsing the remaining ingredients in the food processor until smooth.
10. Serve fish with garlic pesto.

Serving Suggestion: Sprinkle with fresh herbs before serving.

Preparation / Cooking Tips: You can also use other white fish fillets for this recipe.

Nutrition:

Calories: 298
Protein: 32g
Carbohydrates: 20g
Fat: 16g
Fiber 0g

249. Whole Vermillion Snapper

Preparation Time: 15 minutes
Cooking Time: 25 minutes
Servings: 6
Ingredients:

- 2 Rosemary springs
- 4 Garlic cloves, chopped (peeled)
- 1 Lemon thinly sliced.
- Black pepper
- Sea Salt
- 1 Vermillion Snapper gutted and scaled.

Directions:

1. Preheat the grill to high with closed lid.
2. Stuff the fish with garlic. Sprinkle with rosemary, black pepper, sea salt and stuff with lemon slices.
3. Grill for 25 minutes.

Nutrition:
Calories: 240
Protein: 43g
Carbohydrates: 0g
Fat: 3g
Fiber: 0g

250. Smoked Sea Bass

Preparation Time: 10 minutes
Cooking Time: 40 minutes
Servings: 4
Ingredients:

- Marinade
- 1 teaspoon Blackened Saskatchewan
- 1 tablespoon Thyme, fresh
- 1 tablespoon Oregano, fresh
- 8 cloves of Garlic, crushed.
- 1 lemon, the juice
- ¼ cup oil
- Sea Bass
- 4 Sea bass fillets, skin off
- Chicken Rub Seasoning
- Seafood seasoning (like Old Bay)
- 8 tablespoon Gold Butter
- For garnish
- Thyme
- Lemon

Directions:

1. Make the marinade: In a Ziploc bag combine the ingredients and mix. Add the fillets and marinate for 30 min in the fridge. Turn once.
2. Preheat the grill to 325F with closed lid.
3. In a dish for baking add the butter. Remove the fish from marinade and pour it in the baking dish. Season the fish with chicken and seafood rub. Place it in the baking dish and on the grill. Cook 30 minutes. Baste 1 - 2 times.
4. Remove from the grill when the internal temperature is 160F.
5. Garnish with lemon slices and thyme.

Nutrition
Calories: 220

Protein: 32g
Carbohydrates: 1g
Fiber: 0g
Fat: 8g

251. Tuna Burgers

Preparation Time: 30 minutes
Cooking Time: 15 minutes
Servings: 4 - 6
Ingredients:

- 2 lbs. Tuna steak, ground
- 2 Eggs
- 1 Bell pepper, diced.
- 1 teaspoon Worcestershire or soy sauce
- 1 Onion, Diced.
- 1 tablespoon Salmon rub seasoning
- 1 tablespoon Saskatchewan Seasoning

Directions:

1. In a large bowl combine the salmon seasoning, Saskatchewan seasoning, bell pepper, onion, soy/Worcestershire sauce, eggs, and tuna. Mix well. Oil the hands, make patties.
2. Preheat the grill to high.
3. Grill the tuna patties for 10 - 15 min. Flip after 7 minutes.

Nutrition:
Calories: 236
Protein: 18g
Carbohydrates: 1g
Fat: 5g
Fiber: 0.7g

252. Grilled Clams with Garlic Butter

Preparation Time: 10 minutes
Cooking Time: 8 minutes
Servings: 6 - 8
Ingredients:

  1 Lemon cut wedges.
- 1 - 2 teaspoon Anise - flavored Liqueur
  2 tablespoon Parsley, minced.
  o 2- 3 Garlic cloves, minced.
- 8 tablespoon butter, chunks
- 24 of Littleneck Clams

Directions:

1. Clean the clams with cold water. Discard those who are with broken shells or do not close.
2. Preheat the grill to 450F with closed lid.
3. In a casserole dish squeeze juice from 2 wedges, and add parsley, garlic, butter, and liqueur. Arrange the littleneck clams on the grate. Grill 8 minutes, until open. Discard those that will not open.
4. Transfer the clams in the baking dish.
5. Serve in a shallow dish with lemon wedges. Enjoy!

Nutrition:
Calories: 273

Protein: 4g
Carbohydrates: 0.5g
Fiber: 0g
Fat: 10g

253. Simple but Delicious Fish Recipe

Preparation Time: 45 minutes
Cooking Time: 10 minutes
Servings: *4 - 6*
Ingredients:

- 4 lbs. fish cut it into pieces (portion size)
- 1 tablespoon minced Garlic
- 1/3 cup of Olive oil
- 1 cup of Soy Sauce
- Basil, chopped.
- 2 Lemons, the juice

Directions:

1. Preheat the grill to 350F with closed lid.
2. Combine the ingredients in a bowl. Stir to combine. Marinade the fish for 45 min.
3. Grill the fish until it reaches 145F internal temperature.
4. Serve with your favorite side dish and enjoy!

Nutrition:
Calories: 153
Protein: 25g
Carbohydrates: 1g
Fiber: 0.3g
Fat: 4g

254. Crab Legs on The Grill

Preparation Time: 15 minutes
Cooking Time: 30 minutes
Servings: *4 - 6*
Ingredients:

- 1 cup melted Butter.
- 3 lb. Halved Crab Legs
- 2 tablespoon Lemon juice, fresh
- 1 tablespoon Old Bay
- 2 Garlic cloves, minced.
- For garnish, chopped parsley.
- For **Servings:** Lemon wedges

Directions:

1. Place the crab legs in a roasting pan.
2. In a bowl combine the lemon juice, butter, and garlic. Mix. Pour over the legs. Coat well. Sprinkle with old bay.
3. Preheat the grill to 350F with closed lid.
4. Place the roasting pan on the grill and cook 20 - 30 minutes busting two times with the sauce in the pan.
5. Place the legs on a plate. Divide the crab sauce among 4 bowls for dipping.

Nutrition:
Calories: 170
Proteins: 20g
Carbohydrates: 0
Fiber: 0g
Fat: 8g

255. Seared Tuna Steaks

Preparation Time: 5 minutes
Cooking Time: 5 minutes
Servings: *2 - 4*
Ingredients:

- 3 -inch Tuna
- Black pepper
- Sea Salt
- Olive oil
- Sriracha
- Soy Sauce

Directions:

1. Baste the tuna steaks with oil and sprinkle with black pepper and salt.
2. Preheat the grill to high with closed lid.
3. Grill the tuna for 2 ½ minutes per side.
4. Remove from the grill. Let it rest for 5 minutes.
5. Cut into thin pieces and serve with Sriracha and Soy Sauce. Enjoy.

Nutrition:
Calories: 120
Proteins: 34g
Carbohydrates: 0g
Fiber: 0g
Fat: 1.5g

256. Roasted Shrimp Mix

Preparation Time: 30 minutes
Cooking Time: 1h 30 minutes
Servings: *8 - 12*
Ingredients:

- 3 lb. Shrimp (large), with tails, divided.
- 2 lb. Kielbasa Smoked Sausage
- 6 corns cut into 3 pieces.
- 2 lb. Potatoes, red
- Old Bay

Directions:

1. Preheat the grill to 275F with closed lid.
2. First, cook the sausage on the grill. Cook for 1 hour.
3. Increase the temperature to high. Season the corn and potatoes with Old Bay. Now roast until they become tender.
4. Season the shrimp with the Old Bay and cook on the grill for 20 minutes.
5. In a bowl combine the cooked ingredients. Toss.
6. Adjust seasoning with Old Bay and serve. Enjoy!

Nutrition:
Calories: 530
Proteins: 20g
Carbohydrates: 32g
Fat: 35g
Fiber: 1g

257. Seasoned Shrimp Skewers

Preparation Time: 10 minutes
Cooking Time: 35 minutes.
Servings: 4
Ingredients:

- 1 ½ pound fresh large shrimp, peeled, deveined, and rinsed.
- 2 tablespoons minced basil
- 2 teaspoons minced garlic
- 1/2 teaspoon sea salt
- 1/2 teaspoon ground black pepper
- 1/3 cup olive oil
- 2 tablespoons lemon juice

Directions:

1. Place basil, garlic, salt, black pepper, and oil in a large bowl, whisk until well combined, then add shrimps and toss until well coated.
2. Then plug in the smoker, fill its tray with hickory woodchips and water pan with water and white wine halfway through, and place dripping pan above the water pan.
3. Then open the top vent, shut with lid, and use temperature settings to preheat smoker at 225 degrees F.
4. In the meantime, thread shrimps on wooden skewers, six shrimps on each skewer.
5. Place shrimp skewers on smoker rack, then shut with lid and set the timer to smoke for 35 minutes or shrimps are opaque.
6. When done, drizzle lemon juice over shrimps and serve.

Nutrition:
Calories: 168 Cal
Carbohydrates: 2 g
Fat: 11 g
Protein: 14 g
Fiber: 0 g

Chapter 8.   Vegetarian recipes

258. Kale Chips

Preparation Time: 30 Minutes
Cooking Time: 20 Minutes
Servings: 4
Ingredients:

- 4 cups kale leaves
- Olive oil
- Salt to taste

Directions:

1. Drizzle kale with oil and sprinkle it with salt.
2. Set the Pit basswood pellet grill to 250 degrees F.
3. Preheat it for 15 minutes while the lid is closed.
4. Add the kale leaves to a baking pan.
5. Place the pan on the grill.
6. Cook the kale for 20 minutes or until crispy.

Nutrition:
Calories 118
Total fat 7.6g
Total carbs 10.8g
Protein 5.4g,
Sugars 3.7g
Fiber 2.5g,
Sodium 3500mg
Potassium 536mg

259. Sweet Potato Fries

Preparation Time: 30 Minutes
Cooking Time: 40 Minutes
Servings: 4
Ingredients:

- Three sweet potatoes sliced into strips.
- Four tablespoons olive oil
- Two tablespoons fresh rosemary, chopped.
- Salt and pepper to taste

Directions:

1. Set the Pit basswood pellet grill to 450 degrees F.
2. Preheat it for 10 minutes.
3. Spread the sweet potato strips in the baking pan.
4. Toss in olive oil and sprinkle with rosemary, salt, and pepper.
5. Cook for 15 minutes.
6. Flip and cook for another 15 minutes.
7. Flip and cook for ten more minutes.

Nutrition:
Calories 118
Total fat 7.6g
Total carbs 10.8g
Protein 5.4g
Sugars 3.7g
Fiber 2.5g,
Sodium 3500mg
Potassium 536mg

260. Potato Fries with Chipotle Peppers

Preparation Time: 30 Minutes
Cooking Time: 30 Minutes
Servings: 4
Ingredients:

- Four potatoes sliced into strips.
- Three tablespoons olive oil
- Salt and pepper to taste
- 1 cup mayonnaise
- Two chipotle peppers in adobo sauce
- Two tablespoons lime juice

Directions:

1. Set the Pit basswood pellet grill to high.
2. Preheat it for 15 minutes while the lid is closed.
3. Coat the potato strips with oil.
4. Sprinkle with salt and pepper.
5. Put a baking pan on the grate.
6. Transfer potato strips to the pan.
7. Cook potatoes until crispy.
8. Mix the remaining ingredients.
9. Pulse in a food processor until pureed.
10. Serve potato fries with chipotle dip.

Nutrition:
Calories 118
Total fat 7.6g
Total carbs 10.8g
Protein 5.4g
Sugars 3.7g
Fiber 2.5g,
Sodium 3500mg
Potassium 536mg

261. Pit boss Grilled Zucchini

Preparation Time: 30 Minutes
Cooking Time: 10 Minutes
Servings: 4
Ingredients:

- Four zucchinis sliced into strips.
- One tablespoon sherry vinegar
- Two tablespoons olive oil
- Salt and pepper to taste
- Two fresh thyme, chopped.

Directions:

1. Place the zucchini strips in a bowl.
2. Mix the remaining fixings and pour them into the zucchini.
3. Coat evenly.
4. Set the Pit basswood pellet grill to 350 degrees F.
5. Preheat for 15 minutes while the lid is closed.
6. Place the zucchini on the grill.
7. Cook for 3 minutes per side.

Nutrition:
Calories 118
Total fat 7.6g

Total carbs 10.8g
Protein 5.4g
Sugars 3.7g
Fiber 2.5g,
Sodium 3500mg
Potassium 536mg

262. Smoked Potato Salad

Preparation Time: 1 Hour and 15 Minutes
Cooking Time: 40 Minutes
Servings: 4
Ingredients:

- 2 lb. potatoes
- Two tablespoons olive oil
- 2 cups mayonnaise
- One tablespoon white wine vinegar
- One tablespoon dry mustard
- 1/2 onion, chopped.
- Two celery stalks, chopped.
- Salt and pepper to taste

Directions:

1. Coat the potatoes with oil.
2. Smoke the potatoes in the Pit basswood pellet grill at 180 degrees F for 20 minutes.
3. Increase temperature to 450 degrees F and cook for 20 more minutes.
4. Transfer to a bowl and let cool.
5. Peel potatoes.
6. Slice into cubes.
7. Refrigerate for 30 minutes.
8. Stir in the rest of the ingredients.

Nutrition:
Calories 118
Total fat 7.6g
Total carbs 10.8g
Protein 5.4g
Sugars 3.7g
Fiber 2.5g,
Sodium 3500mg
Potassium 536mg

263. Baked Parmesan Mushrooms

Preparation Time: 15 Minutes
Cooking Time: 15 Minutes
Servings: 8
Ingredients:

- Eight mushroom caps
- 1/2 cup Parmesan cheese, grated.
- 1/2 teaspoon garlic salt
- 1/4 cup mayonnaise
- Pinch paprika
- Hot sauce

Directions:

1. Place mushroom caps in a baking pan.
2. Mix the remaining ingredients in a bowl.
3. Scoop the mixture onto the mushroom.
4. Place the baking pan on the grill.

5. Cook in the Pit basswood pellet grill at 350 degrees F for 15 minutes while the lid is closed.

Nutrition:
Calories 118
Total fat 7.6g
Total carbs 10.8g
Protein 5.4g
Sugars 3.7g
Fiber 2.5g,
Sodium 3500mg
Potassium 536mg

264. Roasted Spicy Tomatoes

Preparation Time: 30 Minutes
Cooking Time: 1 Hour and 30 Minutes
Servings: 4
Ingredients:

- 2 lb. large tomatoes sliced in half.
- Olive oil
- Two tablespoons' garlic, chopped.
- Three tablespoons parsley, chopped.
- Salt and pepper to taste
- Hot pepper sauce

Directions:

1. Set the temperature to 400 degrees F.
2. Preheat it for 15 minutes while the lid is closed.
3. Add tomatoes to a baking pan.
4. Drizzle with oil and sprinkle with garlic, parsley, salt, and pepper.
5. Roast for 1 hour and 30 minutes.
6. Drizzle with hot pepper sauce and serve.

Nutrition:
Calories 118
Total fat 7.6g
Total carbs 10.8g
Protein 5.4g
Sugars 3.7g
Fiber 2.5g,
Sodium 3500mg
Potassium 536mg

265. Grilled Corn with Honey and Butter

Preparation Time: 30 Minutes
Cooking Time: 10 Minutes
Servings: 4
Ingredients:

- Six pieces of corn
- Two tablespoons olive oil
- 1/2 cup butter
- 1/2 cup honey
- One tablespoon smoked salt
- Pepper to taste

Directions:

1. Preheat the wood pellet grill too high for 15 minutes while the lid is closed.
2. Brush the corn with oil and butter.

3. Grill the corn for 10 minutes, turning from time to time.
4. Mix honey and butter.
5. Brush corn with this mixture and sprinkle with smoked salt and pepper.

Nutrition:
Calories 118
Total fat 7.6g
Total carbs 10.8g
Protein 5.4g
Sugars 3.7g
Fiber 2.5g,
Sodium 3500mg
Potassium 536mg

266. Grilled Sweet Potato Planks

Preparation Time: 30 Minutes
Cooking Time: 30 Minutes
Servings: 8
Ingredients:

- Five sweet potatoes sliced into planks.
- One tablespoon olive oil
- One teaspoon onion powder
- Salt and pepper to taste

Directions:
1. Set the Pit basswood pellet grill to high.
2. Preheat it for 15 minutes while the lid is closed.
3. Coat the sweet potatoes with oil.
4. Sprinkle with onion powder, salt, and pepper.
5. Grill the sweet potatoes for 15 minutes.

Nutrition:
Calories 118
Total fat 7.6g
Total carbs 10.8g
Protein 5.4g
Sugars 3.7g
Fiber 2.5g,
Sodium 3500mg
Potassium 536mg

267. Roasted Veggies and Hummus

Preparation Time: 30 Minutes
Cooking Time: 20 Minutes
Servings: 4
Ingredients:

- One white onion sliced into wedges.
- 2 cups butternut squash
- 2 cups cauliflower sliced into florets.
- 1 cup mushroom buttons
- Olive oil
- Salt and pepper to taste
- Hummus

Directions:
1. Set the Pit basswood pellet grill to high.
2. Preheat it for 10 minutes while the lid is closed.
3. Add the veggies to a baking pan.
4. Roast for 20 minutes.

5. Serve roasted veggies with hummus.

Nutrition:
Calories 118
Total fat 7.6g
Total carbs 10.8g
Protein 5.4g
Sugars 3.7g
Fiber 2.5g,
Sodium 3500mg
Potassium 536mg

268. Pit boss Smoked Mushrooms.

Preparation Time: 15 Minutes
Cooking Time: 45 Minutes
Servings: 2
Ingredients:

- 4 cups whole baby portobello, cleaned.
- 1 tbsp canola oil
- 1 tbsp onion powder
- 1 tbsp garlic, granulated.
- 1 tbsp salt
- 1 tbsp pepper

Directions:
1. Place all the ingredients in a bowl, mix, and combine.
2. Set your Pit boss to 180oF.
3. Place the mushrooms on the grill directly and smoke for about 30 minutes.
4. Increase heat to high and cook the mushroom for another 15 minutes.
5. Serve warm and enjoy!

Nutrition:
Calories 118
Total fat 7.6g
Total carbs 10.8g
Protein 5.4g
Sugars 3.7g
Fiber 2.5g,
Sodium 3500mg
Potassium 536mg

269. Grilled Zucchini Squash Spears

Preparation Time: 5 Minutes
Cooking Time: 10 Minutes
Servings: 4
Ingredients:

- Four zucchinis, medium
- 2 tbsp olive oil
- 1 tbsp sherry vinegar
- Two thyme leaves pulled.
- Salt to taste
- Pepper to taste

Directions:
1. Clean zucchini cut ends off, half each lengthwise, and cut each half into thirds.
2. Combine all the other ingredients in a zip lock bag, medium, then add spears.
3. Toss well and mix to coat the zucchini.
4. Preheat Pit boss to 350oF with the lid closed for 15 minutes.
5. Remove spears from the zip lock bag and place them directly on your grill grate with the cut side down.

6. Cook for about 3-4 minutes until zucchini is tender and grill marks show.
7. Remove them from the grill and enjoy.

Nutrition:
Calories 93
Total fat 7.4g
Total carbs 7.1g
Protein 2.4g
Sugars 3.4g
Fiber 2.5g,
Sodium 3500mg
Potassium 536mg

270. Grilled Asparagus & Honey-Glazed Carrots

Preparation Time: 15 Minutes
Cooking Time: 35 Minutes
Servings: 4
Ingredients:
- One bunch asparagus, woody ends removed.
- 2 tbsp olive oil
- 1 lb. peeled carrots
- 2 tbsp honey
- Sea salt to taste
- Lemon zest to taste

Directions:
1. Rinse the vegetables under cold water.
2. Splash the asparagus with oil and generously with a splash of salt.
3. Drizzle carrots generously with honey and splash lightly with salt.
4. Preheat your Pit boss to 350oF with the lid closed for about 15 minutes.
5. Place the carrots first on the grill and cook for about 10-15 minutes.
6. Now place asparagus on the grill and cook both for about 15-20 minutes and until done to your liking.
7. Top with lemon zest and enjoy.

Nutrition:
Calories 184
Total fat 7.3g
Total carbs 28.6g
Protein 6g
Sugars 18.5g
Fiber 7.6g,
Sodium 142mg
Potassium 826mg

271. Pit boss Grilled Vegetables

Preparation Time: 5 Minutes
Cooking Time: 15 Minutes
Servings: 12
Ingredients:
- One veggie tray
- 1/4 cup vegetable oil
- 1-2 tbsp Pit boss veggie seasoning

Directions:
1. Preheat your Pit boss to 375oF.
2. Meanwhile, toss the veggies in oil placed on a sheet pan, large, then splash with the seasoning.

3. Place on the Pit boss and grill for about 10-15 minutes.
4. Remove, serve, and enjoy.

Nutrition:
Calories 44
Total fat 5g
Total carbs 10.8g
Protein 0g
Sugars 0g
Fiber 0g,
Sodium 36mg
Potassium 116mg

272. Smoked Acorn Squash

Preparation Time: 10 Minutes
Cooking Time: 2 Hours
Servings: 6
Ingredients:
- Three acorn squash seeded and halved.
- 3 tbsp olive oil
- 1/4 cup butter, unsalted
- 1 tbsp cinnamon, ground
- 1 tbsp chili powder
- 1 tbsp nutmeg, ground
- 1/4 cup brown sugar

Directions:
1. Brush the cut sides of your squash with olive oil, then cover with foil poking holes for smoke and steam to get through.
2. Preheat your Pit boss to 225oF.
3. Place the squash halves on the grill with the cut side down and smoke for about 1½- 2 hours. Remove from the Traeger.
4. Let it sit while you prepare spiced butter. Melt butter in a saucepan, then adds spices and sugar, stirring to combine.
5. Remove the foil from the squash halves.
6. Place 1 tbsp of the butter mixture onto each half.
7. Serve and enjoy!

Nutrition:
Calories 149
Total fat 10g
Total carbs 14g
Protein 2g
Sugars 2g
Fiber 2g,
Sodium 19mg
Potassium 101mg

273. Roasted Green Beans with Bacon

Preparation Time: 15 minutes
Cooking Time: 20 minutes
Servings: 6
Ingredients:
- 1-pound green beans
- 4 strips bacon cut into small pieces.
- 4 tablespoons extra virgin olive oil
- 2 cloves garlic, minced.
- 1 teaspoon salt

Directions:

1. Fire the Pit boss Grill to 4000F. Use desired wood pellets when cooking. Keep lid unopened and let it preheat for at most 15 minutes.
2. Toss all ingredients on a sheet tray and spread out evenly.
3. Place the tray on the grill grate and roast for 20 minutes.

Nutrition:
Calories: 65 Cal
Fat: 5.3 g
Carbohydrates: 3 g
Protein: 1.3 g
Fiber: 0 g

274. Smoked Watermelon

Preparation Time: 15 minutes
Cooking Time: 45-90 minutes
Servings: 5
Ingredients:

- 1 small seedless watermelon
- Balsamic vinegar
- Wooden skewers

Directions:

1. Slice ends of small seedless watermelons.
2. Slice the watermelon in 1-inch cubes. Put the cubes in a container and drizzle vinegar on the cubes of watermelon.
3. Preheat the smoker to 225°F. Add wood chips and water to the smoker before starting preheating.
4. Place the cubes on the skewers.
5. Place the skewers on the smoker rack for 50 minutes.
6. Cook
7. Remove the skewers.
8. Serve!

Nutrition:
Calories: 20 Cal
Fat: 0 g
Carbohydrates: 4 g
Protein: 1 g
Fiber: 0.2 g

275. Grilled Corn with Honey Butter

Preparation Time: 15 minutes
Cooking Time: 10 minutes
Servings: 6
Ingredients:

- 6 pieces corn, husked.
- 2 tablespoons olive oil
- Salt and pepper to taste
- ½ cup butter, room temperature
- ½ cup honey

Directions:

1. Fire the Pit boss Grill to 3500F. Use desired wood pellets when cooking. Keep lid unopened to preheat until 15 minutes.

2. Coat corn with oil and add salt and pepper.
3. Place the corn on the grill grate and cook for 10 minutes. Make sure to flip the corn halfway through the cooking time for even cooking.
4. Meanwhile, mix the butter and honey on a small bowl. Set aside.
5. Remove corn from grill and coat with honey butter sauce.

Nutrition:
Calories: 387 Cal
Fat: 21.6 g
Carbohydrates: 51.2 g
Protein: 5 g
Fiber: 0 g

276. Smoked Mushrooms

Preparation Time: 20 minutes
Cooking Time: 2 hours
Servings: 6
Ingredients:

- 6-12 large Portobello mushrooms
- Sea salt
- black pepper
- Extra virgin olive oil
- Herbs de Provence.

Directions:

1. Preheat the smoker to 200°F while adding water and wood chips to the smoker bowl and tray, respectively.
2. Wash and dry mushrooms
3. Rub the mushrooms with olive oil, salt, and pepper seasoning with herbs in a bowl.
4. Place the mushrooms with the cap side down on the smoker rack. Smoke the mushrooms for 2 hours while adding water and wood chips to the smoker after every 60 minutes.
5. Remove the mushrooms and serve.

Nutrition:
Calories: 106 Cal
Fat: 6 g
Carbohydrates: 5 g
Protein: 8 g
Fiber: 0.9 g

277. Smoked Cherry Tomatoes

Preparation Time: 20 minutes
Cooking Time: 1 ½ hours
Servings: 8-10
Ingredients:

- 2 pints of tomatoes

Directions:

1. Preheat the electric smoker to 225°F while adding wood chips and water to the smoker.
2. Clean the tomatoes with clean water and dry them off properly.
3. Place the tomatoes on the pan and place the pan in the smoker.
4. Smoke for 90 minutes while adding water and wood chips to the smoker.

Nutrition:
Calories: 16 Cal
Fat: 0 g
Carbohydrates: 3 g
Protein: 1 g
Fiber: 1 g

278. Smoked and Smashed New Potatoes

Preparation Time: 5 minutes
Cooking Time: 8 hours
Servings: 4
Ingredients:

- 1-1/2 pounds small new red potatoes or fingerlings
- Extra virgin olive oil
- Sea salt and black pepper
- 2 tbsp softened butter

Directions:

1. Let the potatoes dry. Once dried, put in a pan and coat with salt, pepper, and extra virgin olive oil.
2. Place the potatoes on the topmost rack of the smoker.
3. Smoke for 60 minutes.
4. Once done, take them out and smash each one.
5. Mix with butter and season.

Nutrition:
Calories: 258 Cal
Fat: 2.0 g
Carbohydrates: 15.5 g
Protein: 4.1 g
Fiber: 1.5 g

279. Smoked Brussels Sprouts

Preparation Time: 15 minutes
Cooking Time: 45 minutes
Servings: 6
Ingredients:

- 1-1/2 pounds Brussels sprouts
- 2 cloves of garlic minced.
- 2 tbsp extra virgin olive oil
- Sea salt and cracked black pepper.

Directions:

1. Rinse sprouts
2. Remove the outer leaves and brown bottoms off the sprouts.
3. Place sprouts in a large bowl then coat with olive oil.
4. Add a coat of garlic, salt, and pepper and transfer them to the pan.
5. Add to the top rack of the smoker with water and woodchips.
6. Smoke for 45 minutes or until reaches 250°F temperature.
7. Serve

Nutrition:
Calories: 84 Cal
Fat: 4.9 g

Carbohydrates: 7.2 g
Protein: 2.6 g
Fiber: 2.9 g

280. Apple Veggie Burger

Preparation Time: 10 minutes
Cooking Time: 35 minutes
Servings: 6
Ingredients:

- 3 tbsp ground flax or ground chia
- 1/3 cup of warm water
- 1/2 cups rolled oats.
- 1 cup chickpeas, drained and rinsed.
- 1 tsp cumin
- 1/2 cup onion
- 1 tsp dried basil
- 2 granny smith apples
- 1/3 cup parsley or cilantro, chopped.
- 2 tbsp soy sauce
- 2 tsp liquid smoke
- 2 cloves garlic, minced.
- 1 tsp chili powder
- 1/4 tsp black pepper

Directions:

1. Preheat the smoker to 225°F while adding wood chips and water to it.
2. In a separate bowl, add chickpeas and mash. Mix the remaining ingredients along with the dipped flax seeds.
3. Form patties from this mixture.
4. Put the patties on the rack of the smoker and smoke them for 20 minutes on each side.
5. When brown, take them out, and serve.

Nutrition:
Calories: 241 Cal
Fat: 5 g
Carbohydrates: 40 g
Protein: 9 g
Fiber: 10.3 g

281. Smoked Tofu

Preparation Time: 10 minutes
Cooking Time: 41 hour and 30 minutes
Servings: 4
Ingredients:

- 400g plain tofu
- Sesame oil

Directions:

1. Preheat the smoker to 225°F while adding wood chips and water to it.
2. Till that time, take the tofu out of the packet and let it rest.
3. Slice the tofu in one-inch-thick pieces and apply sesame oil.
4. Place the tofu inside the smoker for 45 minutes while adding water and wood chips after one hour.
5. Once cooked, take them out and serve!

Nutrition:
Calories: 201 Cal
Fat: 13 g
Carbohydrates: 1 g
Protein: 20 g
Fiber: 0 g

282. Easy Smoked Vegetables

Preparation Time: 15 minutes
Cooking Time: 1 ½ hour
Servings: 6
Ingredients:

- 1 cup of pecan wood chips
- 1 ear fresh corn, silk strands removed, and husks, cut corn into 1-inch pieces.
- 1 medium yellow squash, 1/2-inch slices
- 1 small red onion, thin wedges
- 1 small green bell pepper, 1-inch strips
- 1 small red bell pepper, 1-inch strips
- 1 small yellow bell pepper, 1-inch strips
- 1 cup mushrooms, halved.
- 2 tbsp vegetable oil
- Vegetable seasonings

Directions:

1. Take a large bowl and toss all the vegetables together in it.
2. Sprinkle it with seasoning and coat all the vegetables well with it.
3. Place the wood chips and a bowl of water in the smoker.
4. Preheat the smoker at 100°F or ten minutes.
5. Put the vegetables in a pan and add to the middle rack of the electric smoker.
6. Smoke for thirty minutes until the vegetable becomes tender.
7. When done, serve, and enjoy.

Nutrition:
Calories: 97 Cal
Fat: 5 g
Carbohydrates: 11 g
Protein: 2 g
Fiber: 3 g

283. Zucchini with Red Potatoes

Preparation Time: 15 minutes
Cooking Time: 4 hours
Servings: 4
Ingredients:

- 2 zucchinis sliced in 3/4-inch-thick disks.
- 1 red pepper cut into strips.
- 2 yellow squash sliced in 3/4-inch-thick disks.
- 1 medium red onion cut into wedges.
- 6 small red potatoes cut into chunks.
- Balsamic Vinaigrette:
- ⅓ cup extra virgin olive oil
- ¼ teaspoon salt
- ¼ cup balsamic vinegar
- 2 tsp Dijon mustard
- ⅛ teaspoon pepper

Directions:

1. For Vinaigrette: Take a medium-sized bowl and blend together olive oil, Dijon mustard, salt, pepper, and balsamic vinegar.
2. Place all the veggies into a large bowl and pour the vinaigrette mixture over it and evenly toss.
3. Put the vegetable in a pan and then smoke for 4 hours at a temperature of 225°F.
4. Serve and enjoy the food.

Nutrition:
Calories: 381 Cal
Fat: 17.6 g
Carbohydrates: 49 g
Protein: 6.7 g
Fiber: 6.5 g

284. Shiitake Smoked Mushrooms

Preparation Time: 15 minutes
Cooking Time: 45 minutes
Servings: 4-6
Ingredients:

- 4 Cup Shiitake Mushrooms
- 1 tbsp canola oil
- 1 tsp onion powder
- 1 tsp granulated garlic
- 1 tsp salt
- 1 tsp pepper

Directions:

1. Combine all the ingredients together.
2. Apply the mix over the mushrooms generously.
3. Preheat the smoker at 180°F. Add wood chips and half a bowl of water in the side tray.
4. Place it in the smoker and smoke for 45 minutes.
5. Serve warm and enjoy.

Nutrition:
Calories: 301 Cal
Fat: 9 g
Carbohydrates: 47.8 g
Protein: 7.1 g
Fiber: 4.8 g

285. Coconut Bacon

Preparation Time: 10 minutes
Cooking Time: 30 minutes
Servings: 2
Ingredients:

- 3 1/2 cups flaked coconut.
- 1 tbsp pure maple syrup
- 1 tbsp water
- 2 tbsp liquid smoke
- 1 tbsp soy sauce
- 1 tsp smoked paprika (optional)

Directions:

1. Preheat the smoker at 325°F.
2. Take a large mixing bowl and combine liquid smoke, maple syrup, soy sauce, and water.

3. Pour flaked coconut over the mixture. Add it to a cooking sheet.
4. Place in the middle rack of the smoker.
5. Smoke it for 30 minutes and every 7-8 minutes, keep flipping the sides.
6. Serve and enjoy.

Nutrition:
Calories: 1244 Cal
Fat: 100 g
Carbohydrates: 70 g
Protein: 16 g
Fiber: 2 g

286. Garlic and Herb Smoke Potato

Preparation Time: 5 minutes
Cooking Time: 2 hours
Servings: 6
Ingredients:
- 1.5 pounds bag of Gemstone Potatoes
- 1/4 cup Parmesan, fresh grated
- For the Marinade
- 2 tbsp olive oil
- 6 garlic cloves freshly chopped.
- 1/2 tsp dried oregano
- 1/2 tsp dried basil
- 1/2 tsp dried dill
- 1/2 tsp salt
- 1/2 tsp dried Italian seasoning
- 1/4 tsp ground pepper

Directions:
1. Preheat the smoker to 225°F.
2. Wash the potatoes thoroughly and add them to a sealable plastic bag.
3. Add garlic cloves, basil, salt, Italian seasoning, dill, oregano, and olive oil to the zip lock bag. Shake.
4. Place in the fridge for 2 hours to marinate.
5. Next, take an Aluminum foil and put 2 tbsp of water along with the coated potatoes. Fold the foil so that the potatoes are sealed in.
6. Place in the preheated smoker.
7. Smoke for 2 hours
8. Remove the foil and pour the potatoes into a bowl.
9. Serve with grated Parmesan cheese.

Nutrition:
Calories: 146 Cal
Fat: 6 g
Carbohydrates: 19 g
Protein: 4 g
Fiber: 2.1 g

287. Smoked Baked Beans

Preparation Time: 15 minutes
Cooking Time: 3 hours
Servings: 12
Ingredients:
- 1 medium yellow onion diced.
- 3 jalapenos

- 56 oz pork and beans
- 3/4 cup barbeque sauce
- 1/2 cup dark brown sugar
- 1/4 cup apple cider vinegar
- 2 tbsp Dijon mustard
- 2 tbsp molasses

Directions:
1. Preheat the smoker to 250°F.
2. Pour the beans along with all the liquid in a pan. Add brown sugar, barbeque sauce, Dijon mustard, apple cider vinegar, and molasses.
3. Stir
4. Place the pan on one of the racks.
5. Smoke for 3 hours until thickened
6. Remove after 3 hours.
7. Serve

Nutrition:
Calories: 214 Cal
Fat: 2 g
Carbohydrates: 42 g
Protein: 7 g
Fiber: 7 g

288. Corn & Cheese Chile Rellenos

Preparation Time: 30 minutes
Cooking Time: 65 minutes
Servings: 8-12
Ingredients:
- Pellet: hardwood, maple
- 2 lbs. Ripe tomatoes, chopped.
- Four cloves' garlic, chopped.
- 1/2 cup sweet onion, chopped.
- One jalapeno stemmed, seeded, and chopped.
- Eight large green new Mexican or poblano chiles
- Three ears sweet corn, husked.
- 1/2 tsp. Dry oregano, Mexican, crumbled.
- 1 tsp. ground cumin
- 1 tsp. Mild Chile powder
- 1/8 tsp. Ground cinnamon
- Salt and freshly ground pepper
- 3 cups grated Monterey jack.
- 1/2 cup Mexican crema
- 1 cup queso fresco, crumbled.
- Fresh cilantro leaves

Directions:
1. Place the tomatoes, garlic, onions, and jalapeno in a shallow baking dish and place it on the grill grate before starting. This vegetable will expose more wood smoke.
2. When prepared to cook, start the grill on Smoke with the lid open until the fire is established (4 to 5 minutes). S
3. Mix the cooled tomato mixture in a blender and liquefy. Put in a pot.
4. Stir in the cumin, oregano, some chile powder, cinnamon, and some salt and pepper to taste.

5. Carefully peel the New Mexican chiles' blistered outer skin: Leave the stem ends intact and try not to tear the flesh.
6. Cut the corn off the cobs and put it in a large mixing bowl.
7. Bake or cook the Rellenos for 25 to 30 minutes or until the filling is bubbling and the cheese has melted.
8. Sprinkle with queso fresco and garnish it with fresh cilantro leaves, if desired. Enjoy!

Nutrition:
Calories: 206
Carbs: 5g
Fat: 14g
Protein: 9g

289. Roasted Tomatoes with Hot Pepper Sauce

Preparation Time: 20 minutes
Cooking Time: 90 minutes
Servings: 4-6
Ingredients:
- Pellet: hardwood, alder
- 2 lbs. roman fresh tomatoes
- 3 tbsps. parsley, chopped.
- 2 tbsps. garlic, chopped.
- Black pepper, to taste
- 1/2 cup olive oil
- Hot pepper, to taste
- 1 lb. spaghetti or other pasta

Directions:
1. Prepare and ready to cook, set the temperature to 400degrees F and preheat, lid closed for 15 minutes.
2. Rinse with water the tomatoes and cut them in half, length width and then place them in a baking dish cut side up.
3. Sprinkle with chopped parsley, garlic, then add salt and black pepper, and then pour 1/4 cup of olive oil over them.
4. Place on pre-heated and bake for 1 1/2 hours and then tomatoes will shrink, and the skins will be partly blackened.
5. Take the tomatoes from the baking dish and place them in a food processor, leaving the cooking oil and puree them.
6. Put the pasta into boiling salted water and cook until tender. Then drain and mix immediately with the pureed tomatoes.
7. Add the remaining 1/4 cup of raw olive oil and crumbled hot red pepper to taste. Toss and serve. Enjoy!

Nutrition:
Calories: 111
Carbs: 5g
Fat: 11g
Protein: 1g

290. Grilled Fingerling Potato Salad

Preparation Time: 15 minutes
Cooking Time: 15 minutes
Servings: 6-8
Ingredients:
- Pellet: hardwood, pecan
- 1-1/2 lbs. Fingerling potatoes cut in half lengthwise
- Ten scallions
- 2/3 cup Evo (extra virgin olive oil), divided use
- 2 tbsps. rice vinegar
- 2 tsp. lemon juice
- One small jalapeno, sliced.
- 2 tsp. kosher salt

Directions:
1. Prepare and ready to cook, turn temperature to High and preheat, lid closed for 15 minutes.
2. Brush the spring onions with the oil and place them on the grill. Cook for about 2-3 minutes until they are slightly charred. Remove and let cool. Once the spring onions have cooled, slice them, and set aside.
3. Brush the Fingerlings with oil (reserving 1/3 cup for later use), then salt and pepper. Place cut side down on the grill cooked through, about 4-5 minutes.
4. In a bowl, mix the remaining 1/3 cup of olive oil, rice vinegar, salt, and lemon juice, then mix the green onions, potatoes, and slices jalapeno.
5. Season with salt and pepper and serve. Enjoy!

Nutrition:
Calories: 270
Carbs: 18g
Fat: 18g
Protein: 3g

291. Smoked Jalapeño Poppers

Preparation Time: 15 minutes
Cooking Time: 60 minutes
Servings: 4-6
Ingredients:
- Pellet: hardwood, mesquite
- 12 medium jalapeños
- Six slices bacon cut in half.
- 8 oz. cream cheese, softened.
- 1 cup cheese, grated.
- 2 tbsps. pork & poultry rub

Directions:
1. Prepare and ready to cook, turn temperature up to 180 degrees F and preheat, lid closed for 15 minutes.
2. Cut jalapeños in half lengthwise. Remove the seeds and ribs.
3. Combine softened cream cheese with Pork & Poultry rub and grated cheese.
4. Divide the mixture over each jalapeño half. Wrap in bacon and secure with a toothpick.

5. Put the jalapeños on a rimmed baking sheet. Place on the grill and smoke for 30 minutes.
6. Increase the temperature of the grill to 375 encores and cook for another 30 minutes or until the bacon is cooked to the desired doneness. Serve hot, enjoy!

Nutrition:
Calories: 280
Carbs: 24g
Fat: 19g
Protein: 4g

292. Grilled Veggie Sandwich

Preparation Time: 30 minutes
Cooking Time: 30 minutes
Servings: 4-6
Ingredients:
- Pellet: hardwood, pecan
- Smoked hummus
- 1-1/2 cups chickpeas
- 1/3 cup tahini
- 1 tbsp. minced garlic
- 2 tbsps. olive oil
- 1 tsp. kosher salt
- 4 tbsps. lemon juice
- Grilled veggie sandwich
- One small eggplant sliced into strips.
- One small zucchini cut into strips.
- One small yellow squash sliced into strips.
- Two large Portobello mushrooms
- Olive oil
- Salt and pepper to taste
- Two heirloom tomatoes, sliced.
- One bunch of basil leaves pulled.
- Four ciabatta buns
- 1/2 cup ricotta
- Juice of 1 lemon
- One garlic clove minced.
- Salt and pepper to taste

Directions:
1. Ready to cook, turn temperature to 180 degrees F and preheat, lid closed for 15 minutes.
2. In a prepared bowl of a food processor, combine the smoked chickpeas, tahini, garlic, olive oil, salt and lemon juice and blend until smooth but not completely smooth. Transfer to a bowl and reserve.
3. Increase grill temp to high (400-500 degrees F).
4. While the vegetables are cooking, mix the ricotta, the lemon juice, garlic, salt, and some pepper.
5. Cut the ciabatta buns in half and then open them up—spread the hummus on one side and ricotta on the other. Stack the grilled veggies and top with tomatoes and basil. Enjoy!

Nutrition:
Calories: 376
Carbs: 57g

Fat: 16g
Protein: 10g

293. Smoked Healthy Cabbage

Preparation Time: 10 minutes
Cooking Time: 2 hours
Servings: 5
Ingredients:
- Pellet: maple pellets
- One head cabbage, cored.
- 4 tbsp. butter
- 2 tbsp. rendered bacon fat.
- One chicken bouillon cube
- 1 tsp. fresh ground black pepper
- One garlic clove, minced.

Directions:
1. Pre-heat your smoker to 240 degrees Fahrenheit using your preferred wood.
2. Fill the hole of your cored cabbage with butter, bouillon cube, bacon fat, pepper, and garlic.
3. Wrap the cabbage in foil about two-thirds of the way up.
4. Make sure to leave the top open.
5. Transfer to your smoker rack and smoke for 2 hours
6. Unwrap and enjoy!

Nutrition:
Calories: 231
Fats: 10g
Carbs: 26g
Fiber: 1g

294. Garlic and Rosemary Potato Wedges

Preparation Time: 15 minutes
Cooking Time: 1 hour 30 minutes
Servings: 4
Ingredients:
- Pellet: maple pellets
- 4-6 large russet potatoes cut into wedges.
- ¼ cup olive oil
- Two garlic cloves, minced.
- 2 tbsp. rosemary leaves, chopped.
- 2 tsp. salt
- 1 tsp. fresh ground black pepper
- 1 tsp. sugar
- 1 tsp. onion powder

Directions:
1. Pre-heat your smoker to 250 degrees Fahrenheit using maple wood.
2. Take a large bowl and add potatoes and olive oil.
3. Toss well.
4. Take another small bowl and stir garlic, salt, rosemary, pepper, sugar, onion powder.
5. Sprinkle the mix on all sides of the potato wedge.
6. Transfer the seasoned wedge to your smoker rack and smoke for one and a ½ hours.
7. Serve and enjoy!

Nutrition:
Calories: 291
Fats: 10g
Carbs: 46g
Fiber: 2g

295. Smoked Tomato and Mozzarella Dip

Preparation Time: 5 minutes
Cooking Time: 1 hour
Servings: 4
Ingredients:
- Pellet: mesquite
- 8 ounces smoked mozzarella cheese, shredded.
- 8 ounces Colby cheese, shredded.
- ½ cup parmesan cheese, grated.
- 1 cup sour cream
- 1 cup sun-dried tomatoes
- 1 and ½ tsp. salt
- 1 tsp. fresh ground pepper
- 1 tsp. dried basil
- 1 tsp. dried oregano
- 1 tsp. red pepper flakes
- One garlic clove, minced.
- ½ teaspoon onion powder
- French toast, serving.

Directions:
- Pre-heat your smoker to 275 degrees Fahrenheit using your preferred wood.
- Take a large bowl and stir in the cheeses, tomatoes, pepper, salt, basil, oregano, red pepper flakes, garlic, and onion powder and mix well.
- Transfer the mix to a small metal pan and transfer to a smoker.
- Smoke for 1 hour
- Serve with toasted French bread Enjoy!

Nutrition:
Calories: 174
Fats: 11g
Carbs: 15g
Fiber: 2g

296. Feisty Roasted Cauliflower

Preparation Time: 15 minutes
Cooking Time: 10 minutes
Servings: 4
Ingredients:
- Pellet: maple
- One cauliflower head cut into florets.
- 1 tbsp. oil
- 1 cup parmesan, grated.
- Two garlic cloves, crushed.
- ½ teaspoon pepper
- ½ teaspoon salt
- ¼ teaspoon paprika

Directions:
1. Pre-heat your Smoker to 180 degrees F
2. Transfer florets to smoker and smoke for 1 hour

3. Take a bowl and add all ingredients except cheese.
4. Once smoking is done, remove florets.
5. Increase temperature to 450 degrees F, brush florets with the brush, and transfer to grill.
6. Smoke for 10 minutes more
7. Sprinkle cheese on top and let them sit (Lid closed) until cheese melts.
8. Serve and enjoy!

Nutrition:
Calories: 45
Fats: 2g
Carbs: 7g
Fiber: 1g

297. Savory Applesauce on the Grill

Preparation Time: 0 minutes
Cooking Time: 45 minutes
Servings: 2
Ingredients:
- 1½ pounds whole apples
- Salt

Directions:
1. Start the coals or turn a gas grill for medium direct cooking. Just make sure the grates are clean.
2. Put the apples on the grill directly over the fire. Close the lid and cook until the fruit feels soft when gently squeezed with tongs, 10 to 20 minutes total, depending on their size. Move to a cutting board and then let sit until cool enough to touch.
3. Cut the flesh from around the core of each apple; discard the cores. Put the chunks in a blender or food processor and process until smooth or put them in a bowl and purée with an immersion blender until as chunky or smooth as you like. Add some salt and then taste adjusts the seasoning. Serve or refrigerate in a container for up to 3 days.

Nutrition:
Calories: 15
Fats: 0 g
Cholesterol: 0 mg
Carbohydrates: 3 g
Fiber: 0 g
Sugars: 3 g
Proteins: 0 g

298. Avocado with Lemon

Preparation Time: 5 minutes
Cooking Time: 20 minutes
Servings: 4
Ingredients:
- Two ripe avocados
- Good-quality olive oil for brushing
- One lemon halved.
- Salt and pepper

Directions:
1. Start the coals or turn a gas grill for medium direct cooking. Just make sure the grates are clean.
2. Cut the avocados in half lengthwise. Carefully strike a chef's knife into the pit, then wiggle it a bit to lift and remove it. Insert a spoon underneath the flesh against the skin and run it all the way around to separate the entire half of the avocado. Repeat with the other avocado. Brush with oil, and then squeeze one of the lemon halves over them thoroughly on both sides so they do not discolor. Cut the other lemon half into four wedges.
3. Put the avocados on the grill directly over the fire, cut side down. Cover with lid and cook, turning once, until browned in places, 5 to 10 minutes total. Serve the halved avocados as is, or slice and fan them for a prettier presentation. Sprinkle with salt and pepper and garnish with the lemon wedges.

Nutrition:
Calories: 50.3
Fats: 4.6 g
Cholesterol: 0 mg
Carbohydrates: 2.8 g
Fiber: 1.7 g
Sugars: 0.2 g
Proteins: 0.6 g

299. Simplest Grilled Asparagus

Preparation Time: 0 minutes
Cooking Time: 25 minutes
Servings: 4
Ingredients:
- 1½–2 pounds asparagus
- 1–2 tablespoons good-quality olive oil or melted butter
- Salt

Directions:
1. Start the coals or turn the heat of a gas grill for direct hot cooking. Make sure the grates are clean.
2. Cut the tough bottoms from the asparagus. If they are thick, trim the ends with a vegetable peeler. Mix with the oil and then sprinkle with salt.
3. Put the asparagus on the grill directly over the fire, perpendicular to the grates, so they do not fall through. Cover with the lid and cook, turning once, until the thick part of the stalks can barely be pierced with a skewer or thin knife, 5 to 10 minutes total. Transfer to a platter and serve.

Nutrition:
Calories: 225
Fats: 20.6 g
Cholesterol: 0 mg
Carbohydrates: 9.1 g
Fiber: 4.2 g
Sugars: 0 g
Proteins: 4.6 g

300. Beets and Greens with Lemon Dill Vinaigrette

Preparation Time: 0 minutes
Cooking Time: 1 hour
Servings: 4
Ingredients:
- 1½ pounds small beets, with fresh-looking greens still attached if possible.
- ½ cup plus 2 tbsp. good-quality olive oil
- Salt and pepper
- 3 tbsp. fresh lemon juice
- 2 tbsp. minced fresh dill.

Directions:
1. Start the coals or turn a gas grill for medium to medium-low direct cooking. Make sure the grates are clean.
2. Cut the greens off the beets. Throw away any wilted or discolored leaves; rinse the remainder thoroughly to remove any grit and drain. Trim the root ends of the beets and scrub well under running water. Pat the leaves and beets dry. Toss the beets with two tablespoons of oil and a sprinkle of salt until evenly coated.
3. Put the beets on the grill directly over the fire. (No need to wash the bowl.) Close the lid and cook, turning them every 5 to 10 minutes, until a knife inserted in the center goes through with no resistance, 30 to 40 minutes total. Transfer to a plate and then let sit until cool enough to handle.
4. Toss the beet greens in the reserved bowl to coat in oil. Put them on the grill directly over the fire. Close the lid and cook, tossing once or twice, until they are bright green and browned in spots, 2 to 5 minutes total. Look; if they are on too long, they will crisp up to the point where they will shatter. Transfer to a plate.
5. Put the remaining ½ cup oil and the lemon juice in a serving bowl and whisk until thickened. Stir in the dill and some salt and pepper. Peel off the skin from the beets and cut into halves or quarters. Cut the stems from the leaves in 1-inch lengths; cut the leaves across into ribbons. Put the beets, leaves, and stems in the bowl and toss with the vinaigrette until coated. Serve warm or at room temperature. Or makeup to several hours ahead, covers, and refrigerates to serve chilled.

Nutrition:
Calories: 73
Fats: 3.8 g
Cholesterol: 0 mg
Carbohydrates: 9.6 g
Fiber: 3.6 g
Sugars: 2 g
Proteins: 2.2 g

301. Baby Bok Choy with Lime Miso Vinaigrette

Preparation Time: 10 minutes
Cooking Time: 25 minutes
Servings: 4
Ingredients:
- ¼ cup good-quality vegetable oil
- Grated zest of 1 lime
- 2 tbsp. fresh lime juice
- 2 tbsp. white or light miso
- 1 tbsp. rice vinegar
- Salt and pepper
- 1½ pounds baby book choy

Directions:
1. Start the coals or turn a gas grill for medium direct cooking. Make sure the grates are clean.
2. Whisk together the oil, lime zest and juice, miso, and vinegar in a small bowl until combined and thickened. Taste and adjust the seasoning with salt and pepper.
3. Trim the bottoms from the book choy and cut them into halves or quarters as needed. Pour half of the vinaigrette into a baking dish. Add the book choy and twist in the vinaigrette until completely coated.
4. Put the book choy on the grill directly over the fire. Close the lid and cook, turning once, until the leaves brown, and you can insert a knife through the core with no resistance, 5 to 10 minutes per side, depending on their size. Transfer to a platter; drizzle with the reserved vinaigrette and serve warm or at room temperature.

Nutrition:
Calories: 209.7
Fats: 9.4 g
Cholesterol: 7.4 mg
Carbohydrates: 25.9 g
Fiber: 4.5 g
Sugars: 3 g
Proteins: 10.1 g

302. Grilled Carrots

Preparation Time: 5 minutes
Cooking Time: 20 minutes
Servings: 6
Ingredients:
- 1 lb. carrots, large
- 1/2 tbsp. salt
- 6 oz. butter
- 1/2 tbsps. black pepper
- Fresh thyme

Directions:
1. Thoroughly wash the carrots and do not peel. Pat them dry and coat with olive oil.
2. Add salt to your carrots.
3. Meanwhile, preheat a pellet grill to 350oF.
4. Now place your carrots directly on the grill or on a raised rack.
5. Close and cook for about 20 minutes.
6. While carrots cook, cook butter in a saucepan, small, over medium heat until browned. Stir frequently to avoid burning. Remove from heat.
7. Remove carrots from the grill onto a plate, and then drizzle with browned butter.
8. Add pepper and splash with thyme.
9. Serve and enjoy.

Nutrition:
Calories: 250
Total Fat: 25 g
Saturated Fat: 15 g
Total Carbs: 6 g
Net Carbs: 4g
Protein: 1 g
Sugars: 3 g
Fiber: 2 g
Sodium: 402 mg

303. Grilled Brussels Sprouts

Preparation Time: 15 minutes
Cooking Time: 20 minutes
Servings: 8
Ingredients:
- 1/2 lb. bacon, grease reserved.
- 1 lb. Brussels Sprouts
- 1/2 tbsp. pepper
- 1/2 tbsp. salt

Directions:
1. Cook bacon until crispy on a stovetop, reserve its grease, and then chop into small pieces.
2. Meanwhile, wash the Brussels sprouts, trim off the dry end, and remove dried leaves, if any. Half of them and set aside.
3. Place 1/4 cup reserved grease in a pan, cast-iron, over medium-high heat.
4. Season the Brussels sprouts with pepper and salt.
5. Brown the sprouts on the pan with the cut side down for about 3-4 minutes.
6. In the meantime, preheat your pellet grill to 350-3750F.
7. Place bacon pieces and browned sprouts into your grill-safe pan.
8. Cook for about 20 minutes.
9. Serve immediately.

Nutrition:
Calories: 153
Total Fat: 10 g
Total Carbs: 5 g
Protein: 11 g
Sugars: 1 g

304. Wood pellet Spicy Brisket

Preparation Time: 20 minutes
Cooking Time: 9 hours
Servings: 10
Ingredients:
- 2 tbsps. garlic powder
- 2 tbsps. onion powder
- 2 tbsps. paprika
- 2 tbsps. chili powder
- 1/3 cup salt
- 1/3 cup black pepper
- 12 lb. whole packer brisket, trimmed.
- 1-1/2 cup beef broth

Directions:
1. Set your wood pellet temperature to 225degrees F. Let preheat for 15 minutes with the lid closed.
2. Meanwhile, mix garlic, onion, paprika, chili, salt, and pepper in a mixing bowl.
3. The brisket generously on all sides.
4. Place the meat on the grill with the fat side down and let it cool until the internal temperature reaches 160degrees F.
5. Remove the meat from the grill and double wrap it with foil. Return it to the grill and cook until the internal temperature reaches 204degrees F.
6. Remove from grill, unwrap the brisket and let rest for 15 minutes.
7. Slice and serve.

Nutrition:
Calories: 270
Saturated Fat: 8 g
Net Carbs: 3 g
Protein: 20 g

305. Smoky Caramelized Onions on the Pellet Grill

Preparation Time: 5 minutes
Cooking Time: 1 hour
Servings: 4
Ingredients:
- Five large, sliced onions
- 1/2 cup fat of your choice
- Pinch of Sea salt

Directions:
1. Place all the ingredients into a pan. For a deep rich brown, caramelized onion, cook them off for about 1hour on a stovetop.
2. Keep the grill temperatures not higher than 250 - 275oF.
3. Now transfer the pan into the grill.
4. Cook for about 1-1½ hours until brown. Check and stir with a spoon, wooden, after every 15 minutes. Make sure not to run out of pellets.
5. Now remove from the grill and season with more salt if necessary.

6. Serve immediately or place in a refrigerator for up to 1 week.

Nutrition:
Calories: 286
Saturated Fat: 10.3 g
Total Carbs: 12.8 g
Protein: 1.5 g

306. Hickory Smoked Green Beans

Preparation Time: 15 minutes
Cooking Time: 3 hours
Servings: 10
Ingredients:
- 6 cups fresh green beans halved, and ends cut off.
- 2 cups chicken broth
- 1 tbsp. pepper, ground
- 1/4 tbsp. salt
- 2 tbsps. apple cider vinegar
- 1/4 cup diced onion.
- 6-8 bite-size bacon slices
- Optional: sliced almonds

Directions:
1. Add green beans to a colander, then rinse thoroughly. Set aside.
2. Place chicken broth, pepper, salt, and apple cider in a large pan. Add green beans.
3. Blanch over medium heat for about 3-4 minutes, and then remove from heat.
4. Transfer the mixture into an aluminum pan, disposable. Make sure all of them go into the pan, so do not drain them.
5. Place bacon slices over the beans and place the pan into the wood pellet smoker,
6. Smoke for about 3 hours uncovered.
7. Remove from the smoker and top with almond slices.
8. Serve immediately.

Nutrition:
Calories: 57
Total Fat: 3 g
Net Carbs: 4 g
Protein: 4 g

307. Easy Grilled Corn

Preparation Time: 5 minutes
Cooking Time: 40 minutes
Servings: 6
Ingredients:
- Six fresh corn ears, still in the husk
- Pepper, salt, and butter

Directions:
1. Preheat your wood pellet grill to 375-400oF.
2. Cut off the large silk ball from the corn top and any hanging or loose husk pieces.
3. Place the corn on your grill grate directly, and do not peel off the husk.
4. Grill for about 30-40 minutes. Flip a few times to grill evenly all rounds.
5. Transfer the corn to a platter, serve.
6. Now top with pepper, salt, and butter.

7. Enjoy!

Nutrition:
Calories: 77
Total Fat: 1 g
Saturated Fat: 1 g
Total Carbs: 17 g
Net Carbs: 15 g
Protein: 3 g

308. Seasoned Potatoes on Smoker

Preparation Time: 10 minutes
Cooking Time: 45 minutes
Servings: 6
Ingredients:
- 1-1/2 lb. creamer potatoes
- 2 tbsps. olive oil
- 1 tbsp. garlic powder
- 1/4 tbsp. oregano
- 1/2 tbsp. thyme, dried
- 1/2 tbsp. parsley, dried

Directions:
1. Preheat your pellet grill to 350oF.
2. Spray an 8x8 inch foil pan using non-stick spray.
3. Mix all ingredients in the pan and place it into the grill.
4. Cook for about 45 minutes until potatoes are done. Stir after every 15 minutes.
5. Serve and enjoy!

Nutrition:
Calories: 130
Total Fat: 4 g
Saturated Fat: 2 g
Total Carbs: 20 g
Net Carbs: 18 g
Protein: 2 g

309. Smoked Deviled Eggs

Preparation Time: 15 minutes
Cooking Time: 30 minutes
Servings: 5
Ingredients
- 7 hard-boiled eggs, peeled.
- 3 tbsp mayonnaise
- 3 tbsp chives, diced.
- 1 tbsp brown mustard
- 1 tbsp apple cider vinegar
- Dash of hot sauce
- Salt and pepper
- 2 tbsp cooked bacon, crumbled.
- Paprika to taste

Directions:
1. Preheat the Pit boss to 180°F for 15 minutes with the lid closed.
2. Place the eggs on the grill grate and smoke the eggs for 30 minutes. Remove the eggs from the grill and let cool.
3. Half the eggs and scoop the egg yolks into a zip lock bag.
4. Add all other ingredients in the zip lock bag except bacon and paprika. Mix until smooth.

5. Pipe the mixture into the egg whites then top with bacon and paprika.
6. Let rest then serve and enjoy.

Nutrition:
Calories 140, Total fat 12g, Saturated fat 3g, Total Carbs 1g, Net Carbs 1g, Protein 6g, Sugar 0g, Fiber 0g, Sodium: 210mg, Potassium 100mg

310. Pit boss Grilled Stuffed Zucchini

Preparation Time: 5 minutes
Cooking Time: 11 minutes
Servings: 8
Ingredients
- 4 zucchinis
- 5 tbsp olive oil
- 2 tbsp red onion, chopped.
- 1/4 tbsp garlic, minced.
- 1/2 cup breadcrumbs
- 1/2 cup mozzarella cheese, shredded.
- 1 tbsp fresh mint
- 1/2 tbsp salt
- 3 tbsp parmesan cheese

Directions:
1. Cut the zucchini lengthwise and scoop out the pulp then brush the shells with oil.
2. In a non-stick skillet sauté pulp, onion, and remaining oil. Add garlic and cook for a minute.
3. Add breadcrumbs and cook until golden brown. Remove from heat and stir in mozzarella cheese, fresh mint, and salt.
4. Spoon the mixture into the shells and sprinkle parmesan cheese.
5. *Place in a grill and grill for 10 minutes or until the zucchini are tender.*

Nutrition:
Calories 186, Total fat 10g, Saturated fat 5g, Total Carbs 17g, Net Carbs 14g, Protein 9g, Sugar 4g, Fiber 3g, Sodium: 553mg

311. Pit boss Bacon Wrapped Jalapeno Poppers

Preparation Time: 10 minutes
Cooking Time: 20 minutes
Servings: 6
Ingredients
- 6 jalapenos, fresh
- 4 oz cream cheese
- 1/2 cup cheddar cheese, shredded.
- 1 tbsp vegetable rub
- 12 slices cut bacon.

Directions:
1. Preheat the Pit boss smoker and grill to375°F.
2. Slice the jalapenos lengthwise and scrape the seed and membrane. Rinse them with water and set aside.

3. In a mixing bowl, mix cream cheese, cheddar cheese, vegetable rub until well mixed.
4. Fill the jalapeno halves with the mixture then wrap with the bacon pieces.
5. Smoke for 20 minutes or until the bacon crispy.
6. Serve and enjoy.

Nutrition:
Calories 1830, Total fat 11g, Saturated fat 6g, Total Carbs 5g, Net Carbs 4g, Protein 6g, Sugar 4g, Fiber 1g

312. Green Beans with Bacon

Preparation Time: 10 minutes
Cooking Time: 20 minutes
Servings: 6
Ingredients:
- 4 strips of bacon, chopped.
- 1 1/2-pound green beans, ends trimmed.
- 1 teaspoon minced garlic
- 1 teaspoon salt
- 4 tablespoons olive oil

Directions:
1. Switch on the Pit boss grill fill the grill hopper with flavored Traeger's, power the grill on by using the control panel, select 'smoke' on the temperature dial, or set the temperature to 450 degrees F and let it preheat for a minimum of 15 minutes.
2. Meanwhile, take a sheet tray, place all the ingredients in it and toss until mixed.
3. When the grill has preheated, open the lid, place prepared sheet tray on the grill grate, shut the grill and smoke for 20 minutes until lightly browned and cooked.
4. When done, transfer green beans to a dish and then serve.

Nutrition:
Calories: 93 Cal
Fat: 4.6 g
Carbs: 8.2 g
Protein: 5.9 g
Fiber: 2.9 g

313. Grilled Potato Salad

Preparation Time: 15 minutes
Cooking Time: 10 minutes
Servings: 8
Ingredients:
- 1 ½ pound fingerling potatoes, halved lengthwise.
- 1 small jalapeno, sliced.
- 10 scallions
- 2 teaspoons salt
- 2 tablespoons rice vinegar
- 2 teaspoons lemon juice
- 2/3 cup olive oil, divided.

Directions:
1. Switch on the Pit boss grill fill the grill hopper with pecan flavored Traeger's,

power the grill on by using the control panel, select 'smoke' on the temperature dial, or set the temperature to 450 degrees F and let it preheat for a minimum of 5 minutes.
2. Meanwhile, prepare scallions, and for this, brush them with some oil.
3. When the grill has preheated, open the lid, place scallions on the grill grate, shut the grill and smoke for 3 minutes until lightly charred.
4. Then transfer scallions to a cutting board, let them cool for 5 minutes, then cut into slices and set aside until required.
5. Brush potatoes with some oil, season with some salt and black pepper, place potatoes on the grill grate, shut the grill and smoke for 5 minutes until thoroughly cooked.
6. Then take a large bowl, pour in remaining oil, add salt, lemon juice, and vinegar, and stir until combined.
7. Add grilled scallion and potatoes, toss until well mixed, taste to adjust seasoning and then serve.

Nutrition:
Calories: 223.7 Cal
Fat: 12 g
Carbs: 27 g
Protein: 1.9 g
Fiber: 3.3 g

314. Vegetable Sandwich

Preparation Time: 30 minutes
Cooking Time: 45 minutes
Servings: 4
Ingredients:
For the Smoked Hummus:
- 1 1/2 cups cooked chickpeas.
- 1 tablespoon minced garlic
- 1 teaspoon salt
- 4 tablespoons lemon juice
- 2 tablespoon olive oil
- 1/3 cup tahini

For the Vegetables:
- 2 large portobello mushrooms
- 1 small eggplant, destemmed, sliced into strips.
- 1 teaspoon salt
- 1 small zucchini, trimmed, sliced into strips.
- ½ teaspoon ground black pepper
- 1 small yellow squash, peeled, sliced into strips.
- ¼ cup olive oil

For the Cheese:
- 1 lemon, juiced.
- ½ teaspoon minced garlic

- ¼ teaspoon ground black pepper
- ¼ teaspoon salt
- 1/2 cup ricotta cheese

To Assemble:

- 1 bunch basil, leaves chopped.
- 2 heirloom tomatoes, sliced.
- 4 ciabatta buns, halved.

Directions:

1. Switch on the Pit boss grill fill the grill hopper with pecan flavored Traeger's, power the grill on by using the control panel, select 'smoke' on the temperature dial, or set the temperature to 180 degrees F and let it preheat for a minimum of 15 minutes.
2. Meanwhile, prepare the hummus, and for this, take a sheet tray and spread chickpeas on it.
3. When the grill has preheated, open the lid, place sheet tray on the grill grate, shut the grill and smoke for 20 minutes.
4. When done, transfer chickpeas to a food processor, add remaining ingredients for the hummus in it, and pulse for 2 minutes until smooth, set aside until required.
5. Change the smoking temperature to 500 degrees F, shut with lid, and let it preheat for 10 minutes.
6. Meanwhile, prepare vegetables and for this, take a large bowl, place all the vegetables in it, add salt and black pepper, drizzle with oil and lemon juice and toss until coated.
7. Place vegetables on the grill grate, shut with lid and then smoke for eggplant, zucchini, and squash for 15 minutes and mushrooms for 25 minutes.
8. Meanwhile, prepare the cheese and for this, take a small bowl, place all its ingredients in it and stir until well combined.
9. Assemble the sandwich for this, cut buns in half lengthwise, spread prepared hummus on one side, spread cheese on the other side, then stuff with grilled vegetables and top with tomatoes and basil.
10. Serve straight away.

Nutrition:
Calories: 560 Cal
Fat: 40 g
Carbs: 45 g
Protein: 8.3 g
Fiber: 6.8 g

315. Grilled Zucchini

Preparation Time: 5 minutes
Cooking Time: 10 minutes
Servings: 6
Ingredients:

- 4 medium zucchinis
- 2 tablespoons olive oil
- 1 tablespoon sherry vinegar
- 2 sprigs of thyme, leaves chopped.
- ½ teaspoon salt
- 1/3 teaspoon ground black pepper

Directions:

1. Switch on the Pit boss grill fill the grill hopper with oak flavored Traeger's, power the grill on by using the control panel, select 'smoke' on the temperature dial, or set the temperature to 350 degrees F and let it preheat for a minimum of 5 minutes.
2. Meanwhile, cut the ends of each zucchini, cut each in half and then into thirds and place in a plastic bag.
3. Add remaining ingredients, seal the bag, and shake well to coat zucchini pieces.
4. When the grill has preheated, open the lid, place zucchini on the grill grate, shut the grill and smoke for 4 minutes per side.
5. When done, transfer zucchini to a dish, garnish with more thyme and then serve.

Nutrition:
Calories: 74 Cal
Fat: 5.4 g
Carbs: 6.1 g
Protein: 2.6 g
Fiber: 2.3 g

316. Grilled Sugar Snap Peas

Preparation Time: 15 minutes
Cooking Time: 10 minutes
Servings: 4
Ingredients:

- 2-pound sugar snap peas, ends trimmed.
- ½ teaspoon garlic powder
- 1 teaspoon salt
- 2/3 teaspoon ground black pepper
- 2 tablespoons olive oil

Directions:

1. Switch on the Pit boss grill fill the grill hopper with apple flavored Traeger's, power the grill on by using the control panel, select 'smoke' on the temperature dial, or set the temperature to 450 degrees F and let it preheat for a minimum of 15 minutes.
2. Meanwhile, take a medium bowl, place peas in it, add garlic powder and oil, season with salt and black pepper, toss until mixed and then spread on the sheet pan.
3. When the grill has preheated, open the lid, place the prepared sheet pan on the grill grate,

shut the grill and smoke for 10 minutes until slightly charred.

4. Serve straight away.

Nutrition:
Calories: 91 Cal
Fat: 5 g
Carbs: 9 g
Protein: 4 g
Fiber: 3 g

317. Cauliflower with Parmesan and Butter

Preparation Time: 15 minutes
Cooking Time: 45 minutes
Servings: 4
Ingredients:
- 1 medium head of cauliflower
- 1 teaspoon minced garlic
- 1 teaspoon salt
- ½ teaspoon ground black pepper
- 1/4 cup olive oil
- 1/2 cup melted butter, unsalted.
- 1/2 tablespoon chopped parsley.
- 1/4 cup shredded parmesan cheese

Directions:
1. Switch on the Pit boss grill fill the grill hopper with flavored Traeger's, power the grill on by using the control panel, select 'smoke' on the temperature dial, or set the temperature to 450 degrees F and let it preheat for a minimum of 15 minutes.
2. Meanwhile, brush the cauliflower head with oil, season with salt and black pepper and then place in a skillet pan.
3. When the grill has preheated, open the lid, place prepared skillet pan on the grill grate, shut the grill and smoke for 45 minutes until golden brown and the center has turned tender.
4. Meanwhile, take a small bowl, place melted butter in it, and then stir in garlic, parsley, and cheese until combined.
5. Baste cheese mixture frequently in the last 20 minutes of cooking and, when done, remove the pan from heat and garnish cauliflower with parsley.
6. Cut it into slices and then serve.

Nutrition:
Calories: 128 Cal
Fat: 7.6 g
Carbs: 10.8 g
Protein: 7.4 g
Fiber: 5 g

318. Smoked Cauliflower

Preparation Time: 15 Minutes
Cooking Time: 10 Minutes
Servings: 3-4
Ingredients:
- 1 Head of cauliflower

- 1 Cup of parmesan cheese
- 1 Tablespoon of olive oil
- 2 Crushed garlic cloves
- ¼ Teaspoon of Paprika
- ½ Teaspoon of salt
- ½ Teaspoon of pepper

Directions:
1. Start your Pit boss smoker grill with the lid open for about 4 to 5 minutes.
2. Set the temperature on about 180°F and preheat with the lid closed for about 10 to 15 minutes.
3. Cut the cauliflower into florets of medium-sized; then place the cauliflower right on top of the grate and mix all the ingredients except for the cheese.
4. After about 1 hour, remove the cauliflower; then turn the smoker grill on high for about 10 to 15 minutes.
5. Brush the cauliflower with the mixture of the ingredients and place it on a sheet tray.
6. Place the cauliflower back on the grate for about 10 minutes.
7. Sprinkle with the parmesan cheese
8. Serve and enjoy your smoked cauliflower!

Nutrition:
- Calories: 60
- Fat: 3.6g
- Carbohydrates: 3.1g
- Dietary Fiber: 1g
- Protein: 4g

319. Grilled Asparagus

Preparation Time: 5 minutes
Cooking Time: 20 minutes
Servings: 4
Ingredients:
- 3 cups of vegetables sliced.
- 2 tbsp. of olive oil
- 2 tbsp. of garlic & herb seasoning

Directions:
1. Preheat your Pit boss grill to a temperature of about 350°F.
2. While your Pit bosses heating, slice the vegetables. Cut the spears from the Broccoli and the Zucchini; then wash the outsides and slice into spears; cut the peppers into wide strips. You can also grill carrots, corn, asparagus, and potatoes -grill at a temperature of about 350°F for about 20 minutes. Serve and enjoy!

Nutrition
- Calories: 47,
- Fat: 3g,
- Carbohydrates: 1g,
- Dietary Fiber: 1g,
- Protein: 2.2g

320. Grill Eggplants

Preparation Time: 5 minutes
Cooking Time: 12 minutes
Servings: 6
Ingredients:

- 1 to 2 large eggplants
- 3 tablespoons of extra virgin olive oil
- 2 tablespoons of balsamic vinegar
- 2 finely minced garlic cloves
- 1 pinch of each thyme, dill; oregano, and basil

Directions:

1. Gather your ingredients.
2. Heat your Pit boss grill to a medium-high.
3. When the Pit boss grill becomes hot; slice the eggplant into slices of about 1/2-inch of thickness.
4. In a bowl, whisk the olive oil with the balsamic vinegar, the garlic, the herbs, the salt, and the pepper.
5. Brush both sides of the sliced eggplant with oil and with the vinegar mixture.
6. Place the eggplant over the preheated grill.
7. Grill the eggplant for about 12 minutes.
8. Serve and enjoy!

Nutrition
Calories: 56,
Fat: 0.8g,
Carbohydrates: 11g,
Dietary Fiber: 4.1g,
Protein: 4g

321. Roasted Fall Vegetables

Preparation Time: 10 minutes
Cooking Time: 35 minutes
Servings: 8
Ingredients:

- Potatoes – ½ pound
- Brussels sprouts halved – ½ pound.
- Butternut squash, dice – ½ pound
- Cremini mushrooms halved – 1 pint.
- Salt – 1 tablespoon
- Ground black pepper – ¾ tablespoon
- Olive oil – 2 tablespoons

Directions:

1. In the meantime, take a large bowl, place potatoes in it, add salt and black pepper, drizzle with oil and then toss until coated.
2. Take a sheet tray and then spread seasoned potatoes on it.
3. When the grill has preheated, place sheet pan containing potatoes on the grilling rack and then grill for 15 minutes.
4. Then add mushrooms and sprouts into the pan, toss to coat and then continue grilling for 20 minutes until all the vegetables have turned nicely browned and thoroughly cooked.
5. Serve immediately.

Nutrition:
Calories: 80
Carbs: 7g
Fat: 6g
Protein: 1g

322. Cinnamon Almonds

Preparation Time: 15 minutes
Cooking Time: 1 hour and 30 minutes
Servings: 4
Ingredients:

- Almonds – 1 pound
- Granulated sugar – ½ cup
- Brown sugar – ½ cup
- Cinnamon – 1 tablespoon
- Salt – 1/8 teaspoon
- Egg white – 1

Directions:

1. In the meantime, take a small bowl, place egg white in it, and then whisk until frothy.
2. Add remaining ingredients for the seasoning in it, whisk until blended, then add almonds and toss until well coated.
3. Take a sheet pan and then spread almonds mixture in it.
4. When the grill has preheated, place sheet pan containing almonds mixture on the grilling rack and grill for 90 minutes until almonds have roasted, stirring every 10 minutes.
5. Check the fire after one hour of smoking and add more wood pallets if required.
6. When done, remove sheet pan from grill, let it cool slightly and then serve.

Nutrition:

- Calories 136.9
- Carbs: 15g
- Fat: 8g
- Protein: 3g

323. Roasted Pumpkin Seeds

Preparation Time: 10 minutes
Cooking Time: 40 minutes
Servings: 8
Ingredients:

- Pumpkin seeds – 1 pound
- Salt – 1 tablespoon
- Olive oil – 1 tablespoon

Directions:

1. In the meantime, take a baking sheet, grease it with oil, spread pumpkin seeds on it and then stir until coated.
2. When the grill has preheated, place baking sheet containing pumpkin sees on the grilling rack and let grill for 20 minutes.
3. Season pumpkin seeds with salt, switch temperature of the grill to 325 degrees F, and continue grilling for 20 minutes until roasted.
4. When done, let pumpkin seeds cool slightly and then serve.

Nutrition:
Calories: 130
Carbs: 13g
Fat: 5g
Protein 8g

324. Crispy Garlic Potatoes

Preparation Time: 15 minutes
Cooking Time: 40 minutes
Servings: 4
Ingredients:

- Baby potatoes scrubbed – 1 pound.
- Large white onion, peeled, sliced – 1.
- Garlic, peeled, sliced – 3.
- Chopped parsley – 1 teaspoon.
- Butter, unsalted, sliced – 3 tablespoons.

Directions:

1. In the meantime, cut potatoes in slices and then arrange them on a large piece of foil or baking sheet, separating potatoes by onion slices and butter.
2. Sprinkle garlic slices over vegetables, and then season with salt, black pepper, and parsley.
3. When the grill has preheated, place a baking sheet containing potato mixture on the grilling rack and grill for 40 minutes until potato slices have turned tender.
4. Serve immediately.

Nutrition:
Calories: 150
Carbs: 15g
Fat: 10g
Protein: 1g

325. Stuffed Avocados

Preparation Time: 5 minutes
Cooking Time: 10 to 15 minutes
Servings: 3 to 4
Ingredients:

- 4 Avocados, Halved, Pit Removed
- 8 Eggs
- 2 Cups Shredded Cheddar Cheese
- 4 Slices Bacon, Cooked and Chopped
- 1/4 Cup Cherry Tomatoes, Halved
- Green Onions, Sliced Thin
- Salt and Pepper, To Taste

Directions:

1. When ready to cook, set the temperature to High and preheat, lid closed for 15 minutes.
2. After removing the pit from the avocado, scoop out a little of the flesh to make enough room to fit 1 egg per half.
3. Fill the bottom of a cast iron pan with kosher salt and nestle the avocado halves into the salt, cut side up. The salt helps to keep them in place while cooking, like ice with oysters.
4. Crack egg into each half, top with a hand full of shredded cheddar cheese, some cherry tomatoes and bacon. Season with salt and pepper to taste.
5. Place the cast iron pan directly on the grill grate and bake the avocados for 12-15 minutes until the cheese is melted and the egg is just set.
6. Remove from the grill and let rest 5-10 minutes. Enjoy!

Nutrition:

- Carbs: 50g
- Fat: 103g
- Protein: 58g

326. Pit boss Bacon-Wrap Asparagus

Preparation Time: 10 minutes
Cooking Time: 25 to 30 minutes
Servings: 3
Ingredients:

- 1-pound fresh thick asparagus (15 to 20 spears)
- extra-virgin olive oil
- 5 slices thinly sliced bacon
- 1 teaspoon Pete's Western Rub (page 169) or salt and pepper

Directions:

1. Snap off the woody ends of asparagus and trim so they are all about the same length.
2. Divide the asparagus into bundles of 3 spears and spritz with olive oil. Wrap each bundle with 1 piece of bacon and then dust with the seasoning or salt and pepper to taste.
3. Configure your Pit boss smoker-grill for indirect cooking, placing Teflon coated fiberglass mats on top of the grates (to prevent the asparagus from sticking to the grill grates). Preheat to 400°F using any type of Traeger's. The grill can be preheated while prepping the asparagus.
4. Grill the bacon-wrapped asparagus for 25 to 30 minutes, until the asparagus is tender, and the bacon is cooked and crispy.

Nutrition:

- Calories: 94
- Carbs: 5g
- Fat: 7g
- Protein: 4g

327. Brisket Baked Beans

Preparation Time: 15 minutes
Cooking Time: 1 to 2 hours
Servings: 5
Ingredients:

- 2 tablespoons extra-virgin olive oil 1 large yellow onion, diced.
- 1 medium green bell pepper, diced.
- 1 medium red bell pepper, diced.
- 2 to 6 jalapeño peppers, diced.

- 3 cups chopped Texas-Style Brisket Flat (page 91) 1 (28-ounce) can baked beans, like Bush's Country.
- Style Baked Beans 1 (28-ounce) can pork and beans
- 1 (14-ounce) can red kidney beans, rinsed and drained 1 cup barbecue sauce, like Sweet Baby Ray's
- Barbecue Sauce ½ cup packed brown sugar.
- 3 garlic cloves, chopped.
- 2 teaspoons ground mustard
- ½ teaspoon kosher salt
- ½ teaspoon black pepper

Directions:

1. In a skillet over medium heat, warm the olive oil and then add the diced onion, peppers, and jalapeños. Cook until the onions are translucent, about 8 to 10 minutes, stirring occasionally.
2. In a 4-quart casserole dish, mix the chopped brisket, baked beans, pork and beans, kidney beans, cooked onion and peppers, barbecue sauce, brown sugar, garlic, ground mustard, salt, and black pepper.
3. Configure your Pit boss smoker-grill for indirect cooking and preheat to 325°F using your Traeger's of choice. Cook the brisket baked beans uncovered for 1½ to 2 hours, until the beans are thick and bubbly. Allow to rest for 15 minutes before serving.

Nutrition:

- Carbs: 35g
- Fat: 2g
- Protein: 9g

Chapter 9.   Red Meat Recipes

328. Chipotle Honey Smoked Beef Roast

Preparation Time: 10 minutes
Cooking Time: 4 hours 20 minutes
Servings: 10
Ingredients:
- Beef roast (5-lbs., 2.3-kg.)
- The Rub Vegetable oil – 2 tablespoons
- Black pepper – 1 ½ tbsp.
- Salt – 1 ½ tbsp.
- Brown sugar – ¾ tablespoon
- Onion powder – ¾ tablespoon
- Mustard – 1 teaspoon
- Garlic powder – 1 ½ tsp.
- Chipotle powder – 1 ½ tsp.
- The Glaze Honey – ½ cup
- Water – 2 tablespoons
- Minced garlic – 1 ½ tbsp.

The Heat
- Hickory wood pellets

Directions:
1. Place the rub ingredients—vegetable oil, black pepper, salt, brown sugar, onion powder, mustard, garlic powder, and chipotle powder in a bowl, and then mix until combined.
2. Rub the beef roast with the spice mixture, and then set aside. Plug the wood pellet smoker and place the wood pellet inside the hopper.
3. Turn the switch on. Set the "Smoke" setting and prepare the wood pellet smoker for indirect heat.
4. Wait until the smoke is ready and adjust the temperature to 275degrees F (135°C). Once the wood pellet smoker has reached the desired temperature, place the seasoned beef roast directly on the grate inside the wood pellet smoker and smoke for 2 hours.
5. In the meantime, combine honey, water, and minced garlic in a bowl, then stir until incorporated. After 2 hours, take the beef roast out of the wood pellet smoker and place it on a sheet of aluminum foil.
6. Leave the wood pellet smoker on and adjust the temperature to 300degrees F (149°C). Baste the beef roast with the glaze mixture, and then wrap it with the aluminum foil. Return the wrapped beef roast to the wood pellet smoker, then smoke for another 2 hours.
7. Once the smoked beef roast's internal temperature has reached 165degrees F (74°C), remove it from the wood pellet smoker.
8. Let the smoked beef roast rest for about 10 minutes, then unwrap it. Transfer the smoked beef roast to a serving dish, then serve. Enjoy!

Nutrition:
Energy (calories): 324 kcal
Protein: 27.7 g
Fat: 13.23 g
Carbohydrates: 26.4 g

329. Lemon Chili Smoked Beef Brisket

Preparation Time: 10 minutes
Cooking Time: 4 hours 10 minutes
Servings: 10
Ingredients:
- Beef brisket (4.5-lbs., 2-kg.)
- The Rub Lemon juice – 3 tablespoons
- Chili powder – ¼ cup
- Salt – 1 ½ tbsp.
- Garlic powder – 2 tablespoons
- Cayenne – 2 teaspoons
- Pepper – 2 teaspoons

The Heat
- Alder wood pellets

Directions:
1. Combine chili powder with salt, garlic powder, cayenne, and pepper, and then mix well. Rub the beef brisket with lemon juice, and then sprinkle the dry spice mixture over the beef brisket.
2. Plug the wood pellet smoker and fill the hopper with wood pellets. Turn the switch on. Set the "Smoke" setting and prepare the wood pellet smoker for indirect heat.
3. Adjust the wood pellet smoker's temperature to 275degrees F (135°C) and wait until it reaches the desired temperature. Place the seasoned beef brisket directly on the grate in the wood pellet smoker and smoke for approximately 3 hours or until the internal temperature has reached 125degrees F (52°C).
4. After 2 hours, take the beef brisket out of the wood pellet smoker and transfer it to a sheet of aluminum foil. Wrap the beef brisket with the aluminum foil, and then return it to the wood pellet smoker.
5. Smoke the wrapped beef brisket for another 2 hours or until the internal temperature has reached 165degrees F (74°C). Once it is done, remove the wrapped smoked beef brisket from the wood pellet smoker and let it rest for about 10 minutes.
6. Unwrap the smoked beef brisket, and then cut into slices.
7. Serve and enjoy.

Nutrition:
Energy (calories): 425 kcal
Protein: 30.96 g
Fat: 30.98 g
Carbohydrates: 4.66 g

330. Strip Steak Smoked and Seared

Preparation Time: 10 minutes
Cooking Time: 3 hours 10 minutes
Servings: 2
Ingredients:
- Strip streaks – 2 (At least 1" thick)
- Olive oil – 2 teaspoons
- Kosher salt to taste
- Freshly ground pepper to taste

Directions:
1. Use a teaspoon of olive oil to brush strip steaks on both sides of the season with freshly ground black pepper and salt.
2. Repeat the same process with the other strip steak, then set aside. Place the steaks over the lower rack of the wood pellet grill, and then set the temperature to about 2250F.
3. Smoke the steaks for about an hour or until the internal temperature reaches 1000F. Remove from the grill when ready, and then let them stay warm as you preheat the wood pellet grill to 7000F.
4. Once the grill is heated, switch it to open flame cooking mode, remove the lower racks, and replace it with a direct flame insert. Place back the grates on the grill at the lower position.
5. Sear the steaks as you use tongs to turn them until it develops a nice crust on the outside. Once cooked, transfer the steak strips to a cutting board and rest for about 5 minutes.
6. Add a pinch of kosher salt to the meat, then serve and enjoy.

Nutrition:
Energy (calories): 499 kcal
Protein: 28.95 g
Fat: 41.2 g
Carbohydrates: 1.05 g

331. Smoked Corned Beef Brisket

Preparation Time: 10 minutes
Cooking Time: 4 hours 10 minutes
Servings: 6
Ingredients:
- Corned beef brisket – 4 lb.
- Dijon or horseradish mustard
- Jeff's original rub
- Jeff's original barbecue sauce
- Foil pan or stainless steel

Direction:
1. Put the beef brisket in cold water in the refrigerator and change the water after 30 minutes to remove the extra salt. You can soak it for about 3 hours. You can then coat the entire beef brisket using horseradish mustard.
2. Liberally apply Jeff's original rub to all the sides. You can pat the rub instead of massaging it into the meat. Set smoker to 2250F with wood pellet smoke, then place

corned beef brisket over the smoker grate and let it smoke for about 3 hours or until the temperature of the thickest part reaches 1400F.
3. Make a sauce by mixing Jeff's original barbecue sauce with Dijon, and then create a mustard pad at the pan's bottom and place the meat over the pad with the flat side up.
4. Brush it with more of the mustard sauce, and then cover with foil. Please place it in a smoker and continue cooking for about one hour or until the thickest part's temperature reaches 1850F.
5. Allow the meat rest for about 30 minutes, then slice it and serve.

Nutrition:
Energy (calories): 599 kcal
Protein: 44.42 g
Fat: 45.09 g
Carbohydrates: 0.47 g

332. Sugar and Garlic Braised Brisket

Preparation Time: 10 minutes
Cooking Time: 7 hours
Servings: 12
Ingredients:
- Garlic—2 cloves, thinly sliced.
- Beef brisket—1 7lb. brisket
- Pepper and salt—according to taste
- They dried oregano—1 tsp.
- Brisket rub—as per your choice
- Beef stock—1 ½ cups
- Dried thyme—1 tsp.
- Kosher salt—according to taste
- Ketchup—1 cup
- Paprika—1 tsp.
- Butter—2 tbsps.
- Brown sugar—¼ cup
- Cayenne pepper—1 pinch
- Yellow onion—½, sliced thinly.

Directions:
1. Prepare your Wood Pellet Smoker-Grill by preheating it to a high temperature as per factory instructions. Close the top lid and leave for 12–15 minutes.
2. Use the available rub along with kosher salt to properly season the beef.
3. Transfer the seasoned meat straight to the heated grilling grate with the fat side facing downward and cook for about 35–48 minutes.
4. During this time, melt some butter in a saucepan and cook onion pieces for about 4–8 minutes. Add garlic and keep cooking for another 1–2 minutes.
5. Add thyme, oregano, cayenne, paprika, pepper, and salt to the pan and cook for an additional 30 seconds.
6. Use the available stock to deglaze and add brown sugar and ketchup. Simmer for a while.

7. Please take out the cooked brisket and put it in a large enough baking dish. Cover it with the prepared sauce and tightly seal the plate with aluminum foil.
8. Bring the temperature of your smoker-grill to 225degrees F and transfer the covered baking dish to the grilling grate. Braise for about 4–6 hours.
9. Remove and create a vent in the aluminum foil. Let it cool, and then serve.

Nutrition:
Carbohydrate—26 g Protein—53 g Fat—10 g Sodium—2,295 mg Cholesterol—93 mg

333. Beef Tenderloin Roasted with Herbs and Honey

Preparation Time: 10 minutes
Cooking Time: 81 minutes
Servings: 12
Cooking Time: about 81 minutes
Ingredients:
- Kosher salt—2 tsp.
- Beef tenderloin—1 5lb.
- tenderloin trimmed and tied.
- Ground pepper—1 tsp.,
- Fresh Olive oil—3 tbsps.

For the herb mix:
- Kosher salt—according to taste
- Honey—2 tsp.
- Extra virgin olive oil—½ cup
- Parsley—1 cup, fresh, finely chopped.
- Lemon juice—2 tbsps.
- Ground pepper—fresh
- Shallot—¼ cup, chopped finely.

Directions:
1. Take out a large enough baking dish and put the tenderloin in it. Grease properly with olive oil.
2. Generously coat all sides of the meat with salt and pepper.
3. Prepare your Wood Pellet Smoker-Grill by preheating it to a high temperature as per factory instructions. Close the top lid and leave for 12–18 minutes.
4. Put the meat straight onto your grilling grate and let it sear properly.
5. Reduce the temperature to 300degrees F and let the meat roast for about 60–76 minutes. The internal temperature should reach about 135degrees F.
6. Take out the cooked meat and let it rest for about 15–20 minutes.
7. Using a medium-sized bowl, prepare a mixture with lemon juice, honey, salt, shallot, herbs, and oil. Stir properly and adjust salt and pepper to taste.
8. Slice the cooked meat and pour the herb and honey mixture over the slices.
9. Your dish is ready to be served.

Nutrition:
Calories: 704 Carbohydrate—14 g Protein—50 g Fat—51 g Sodium—631 mg Cholesterol—159 mg

334. Red Wine Braised Lamb

Preparation Time: 10 minutes
Cooking Time: 4 hours
Servings: 6
Ingredients:
- Rib rub—any of your choice
- Lamb shanks 4
- Red wine—1 cup
- Beef broth—1 cup
- Olive oil—as per your choice
- Thyme—4 sprigs, fresh
- Rosemary—4 sprigs, fresh

Directions:
1. Use the rib rub to coat the shanks of lamb properly.
2. Prepare your Wood Pellet Smoker-Grill by preheating it to a high temperature as per factory instructions. Close the top lid and leave for 12–18 minutes.
3. Transfer the shanks straight to the grilling grate and cook them for about 19–20 minutes.
4. Put the cooked shanks in a large Dutch oven and fill it with beef broth, herbs, and wine. Put the lid on the Dutch oven and transfer it to your smoker-grill. This time, reduce the cooking temperature to about 325degrees F.
5. Let the shanks cook for about 3–4 hours. Its internal temperature should reach about 180degrees F.
6. Take out and serve the shanks with the juices.

Nutrition:
Calories: 160 Carbohydrate—13 g Protein—19 g Fat—4 g Sodium—440 mg Cholesterol—48 mg

335. Mustard Anchovy Rib Eye Steaks

Preparation Time: 10 minutes
Cooking Time: 2 hours12 minutes
Servings: 6
Ingredients:
- Ribeye—4 steaks, about 1-inch thick
- Garlic powder—1 tsp.
- Dry mustard—1 tbsp.
- Black pepper—2 tsp.
- Onion powder—2 tsp.
- Brown sugar—1 tbsp.
- Warm water—2 tbsps.
- Anchovy—10 fillets, minced.

Directions:
1. Take a large enough bowl to mix everything except the steaks.
2. Use the prepared paste to coat the steaks on all sides. Put the steaks in your refrigerator to marinate for at least 2 hours.
3. Prepare your Wood Pellet Smoker-Grill by preheating it to a high temperature as per factory instructions. Close the top lid and leave for about 12–18 minutes.
4. Put the steaks on the grilling grate and cook for about 5 minutes on each side.

5. Once the internal temperature reaches 135degrees F, remove the steaks from the smoker-grill and let them cool down for 10 minutes.
6. Your dish is ready to be served.

Nutrition:
Calories: 634 Carbohydrate—34 g Protein—67 g Fat—13 g Sodium—786 mg Cholesterol—160 mg

336. Tomato Vinegar Beef Tenderloin

Preparation Time: 10 minutes
Cooking Time: 55 minutes
Servings: 8
Ingredients:
- Tomatoes—6, cored, seeds removed, and peeled.
- Beef tenderloin 1, trimmed.
- Balsamic vinegar—2 tbsps.
- Extra virgin olive oil—2/3 cup Rib rub—any of your choice
- Fresh thyme—1 tsp., minced.

Directions:
1. Prepare your Wood Pellet Smoker-Grill by preheating it to a temperature of about 450degrees F. Close the top lid and leave for 12–18 minutes.
2. Coat the meat properly with olive oil, rib rub, pepper, and salt. Transfer the prepared meat to a shallow roasting pan.
3. Roast for about 18–20 minutes. Reduce the temperature to 350degrees F and keep roasting for another 18–20 minutes.
4. Remove and allow cooling for 6–10 minutes.
5. Cut thin slices and use thyme to garnish.
6. Make a mixture of balsamic vinegar, tomatoes, thyme leaves, and olive oil in your blender or food processor.
7. Pour it all over the sliced meat.
8. Enjoy.

Nutrition:
Calories: 412 Carbohydrate—0 g Protein—32 g Fat—30 g Sodium—256 mg Cholesterol—118 mg

337. Spicy Grilled Beef Steak

Preparation Time: 10 minutes
Cooking Time: 1 hour 22 minutes
Servings: 6
Ingredients:
- Chili powder—2 tbsps.
- Beef rib eye—4 steaks
- Brown sugar—1 tsp.
- Worcestershire sauce—2 tbsps.
- Garlic clove 2, minced.
- Ground cumin—1 tsp.
- Olive oil—2 tbsps.
- Salt—1 tsp.

Directions:
1. Mix salt and mashed garlic in a small mixing bowl. Add Worcestershire sauce, chili powder, brown sugar, olive oil, and cumin.

2. Use this mixture to coat the steaks.
3. Put the coated steaks and the rest of the rub, in a large zip-seal bag. Let it marinate in the refrigerator for about 5–24 hours.
4. Prepare your Wood Pellet Smoker-Grill by preheating it to about 225degrees F. close the top lid and leave for 12–18 minutes.
5. Smoke the steaks for about 50–60 minutes. Then, remove.
6. Increase the temperature to about 350degrees F and cook the steaks again to get an internal temperature of about 135degrees F.
7. Remove and allow the meat to cool.
8. Your dish is ready to be served.

Nutrition:
Calories: 634 Carbohydrate—34 g Protein—67 g Fat—13 g Sodium—786 mg Cholesterol—160 mg

338. Wood Pellet Smoked Meatloaf

Preparation Time: 10 minutes
Cooking Time: 1 hour
Servings: 8
Ingredients
- 1 and ½ lbs. of ground beef
- ½ lb. of sausage
- ½ Cup of breadcrumbs
- ¾ Cup of plain yogurt
- ¼ Cup of milk
- Two large eggs
- 2 Teaspoons of chopped garlic
- ½ Cup of Parmesan cheese
- 1 Tablespoon of dried parsley
- 1 Tsp. of dried oregano
- 1 and ½ tsp. of kosher salt
- Your favorite BBQ rub 1
- Pinch of black pepper

Directions
1. Start your pellet smoker grill and turn it to a temperature of about 350degrees F to heat it.
2. In a medium-size bowl, mix all your wet ingredients; then place the seasonings in it and mix the sausage and the ground beef altogether in a bowl Form a loaf of your mixture; then roll it into your favorite rub. Place the beef loaf on the pellet grill rack; then put the meat probe right into the center.
3. Smoke the Meatloaf on High smoke for about 30 minutes at a temperature of 350degrees F until the internal temperature displays 160° F; it may take an hour.
4. Slice your meatloaf; then serve and enjoy its delicious taste.

Nutrition:
Calories: 343, Fat: 25.6g, Carbohydrates: 10g, Protein: 17.2g, Dietary Fiber 0.5 g

339. Wood Pellet Corned Beef with Cabbage

Preparation Time: 10 minutes
Cooking Time: 30 minutes
Servings: 4
Ingredients
- A cut of corned beef
- 2 cups of water
- 5 to 6 red potatoes
- 1 head of cabbage
- 3 Tsp. of garlic salt
- 1 Tsp. of ground black pepper
- 3 to 4 tablespoons of whole grain mustard
- 3 Tablespoons of melted butter

Directions
1. Start by rinsing the two sides of the corned beef under cold water for about 2 minutes to excess any excess salt.
2. Coat both the sides of the corned beef with two tablespoons of mustard
3. Add the water and the corned beef to an aluminum pan and smoke it at a temperature of about 220° F.
4. Remove the stem and remove the core of the cabbage; then quarter it
5. Melt the butter; then stir in about one tablespoon of mustard and about one teaspoon of garlic salt.
6. Place the cabbage quarters into the aluminum pan in each of the corners and core it sides up so that it looks like bowls.
7. Chop the potatoes into half and season it with about two teaspoons of garlic salt and about ½ teaspoon of pepper.
8. Place the potatoes along the edges of the aluminum pan between the quarters of the cabbage.
9. Cover with the aluminum foil; then turn up your wood pellet grill to about 280degrees F and cook for about two additional hours until the internal temperature of the meat reaches about 200 to 205° F.
10. Remove the aluminum foil and cook for about 15 minutes. Slice the meat, then serve and enjoy it!

Nutrition:
Calories: 213.5, Fat: 15g, Carbohydrates: 8g, Protein: 7.9g, Dietary Fiber: 1.2g

340. Smoked Porterhouse Steak

Preparation Time: 10 minutes
Cooking Time: 50 minutes
Servings: 2-4
Ingredients:
The Meat
- Two porterhouse steaks (1 inch thick) (20 oz. or 1.25 lb.).

The Mixture
- Melted butter – 4 tbsp.
- Worcestershire Sauce – 2 tsp.
- Dijon Mustard – 1 tbsp.
- Coffee rub – 1 tsp.

The Fire
- Wood pellet smoker, hickory wood pellets.

Directions:
1. Start your wood pellet smoker on grill instructions when you are ready to cook.
2. Set the temperature to smoke setting. Preheat for 5 minutes while keeping the lid closed.
3. Mix the butter, Worcestershire sauce, and mustard until it is smooth. Brush the mixture on both sides of the steaks. Season the porterhouse steaks with coffee rub.
4. Arrange the steaks on the grill grate and smoke them for about 30 minutes. Remove the steaks using tongs.
5. Increase the heat to 450° F. Brush the steaks again with the butter sauce mixture prepared earlier.
6. When the grill comes up to the temperature, place the steaks back on the grill grate and cook until it is done according to your choice. Whichever doneness you prefer i.e., rare, medium rare or well done.
7. In case of medium rare, cook until the internal temperature is about 135° F. Before serving, let the steaks rest for 5 minutes.

Nutrition:
Energy (calories): 831 kcal
Protein: 58.26 g
Fat: 64.63 g
Carbohydrates: 1.59 g

341. Smoked Rib Eye with Bourbon Butter

Preparation Time: 10 minutes
Cooking Time: 1 hour 20 minutes
Servings: 4-6
Ingredients:
The Meat
- 4 Ribeye steaks (1 inch thick).

The Mixture
- Fresh ground pepper – 1/2 tsp.
- Garlic (minced) – 1-2 cloves.
- Green Onion (finely minced) – 1 tbsp.
- Parsley (finely minced) – 1 tbsp.
- Salt– 1/2 tsp.
- Bourbon – 2 tbsp.
- Butter – 1/2 cup.
- prime rub.

The Fire
- Wood pellet smoker, mesquite wood pellets.

Directions:
1. In a mixing bowl, add butter, parsley, chives, bourbon, garlic, salt, and pepper. Stir all the ingredients with a wooden spoon. Put the smoker on.

2. Until the fire is established, keep the lid open. The fire should be established in about 4-5 minutes.

3. Season the rib eye steaks with a prime rub. And then arrange the steaks on the grill and smoke them for about an hour.

4. Then temporarily remove the steaks from the smoker and set your smoker's temperature up to 450F. Place the steaks back on the grill. Give one side about 6-8 minutes and then turn it over.

5. Keep the other side for the same amount of time. Otherwise, if you like your steak medium rare then keep cooking and turning over until the internal temperature is 135 F.

6. Take the steak out of the smoker after they are cooked to your liking and immediately pat them with the bourbon butter sauce you made earlier.

7. Allow the meat rest for at least 3 minutes before serving it.

Nutrition:
Energy (calories): 613 kcal
Protein: 49.61 g
Fat: 43.85 g
Carbohydrates: 5.41 g

342. Greek Style Smoked Lamb Leg

Preparation Time: 10 minutes
Cooking Time: 2 hours
Servings: 8-12
Ingredients:
The Meat
- Lamb leg with bone in (6-7 lbs.) T

The Mixture
- Oregano – 1 tsp.
- Garlic – 8 cloves.
- Fresh rosemary (with no stem) – 2 tbsp.
- 2 Lemons.
- Extra virgin olive oil – 6 tbsp.
- Coarse kosher salt and pepper (as required).

The Fire
- Wood pellet smoker, oak wood pellets.

Directions:
1. Take the lamb leg and put small slits on it. Use a paring knife for this process. To make the herb and garlic paste, you must finely chop and mince garlic, rosemary, and oregano. You can also use a food processor to make the paste.

2. Now, you must stuff this paste in the slits you made on the meat. Take a roasting pan and put the lamb leg on it.

3. Rub the lemon juice on lamb leg. Then do the same with olive oil. Cover the whole leg with a plastic wrap and leave it to refrigerate overnight.

4. Take the lamb out of the refrigerator and leave it for as long as it adopts room temperature.

Then remove the wrap from lamb. Season the lamb with salt and pepper.

5. Start your wood pellet grill on smoke. Until the fire is established for 4-5 minutes, leave the lid open. Adjust the temperature to be 400F and preheat for 10-15 minutes.

6. Keep the lid closed this time. Leave the lab in for 30 minutes. Then reduce the heat to 350F. Continue to cook it, until it reaches the internal temperature that you want.

7. For medium rare, it must be about 140F. Take the lamb out of the smoker and serve.

Nutrition:
Energy (calories): 515 kcal
Protein: 78.18 g
Fat: 21.69 g
Carbohydrates: 2.53 g

343. Smoked Lamb Stew

Preparation Time: 10 minutes
Cooking Time: 2 hours
Servings: 4-6
Ingredients:
The Meat
- Lamb (1/2-inch chunks) – (3 lbs.)

The Mixture
- Beef Stock – 2 cups.
- 4 chopped Garlic cloves.
- Tomato paste – ¼ cup.
- Beer – 12 oz.
- 2 Bay leaves.
- Olive oil – 3 tbsp.
- 3 diced Large Carrots.
- Dried Thyme - 2 tsp.
- 1 diced turnip Peas - 2 cup
- 1 diced parsnip.
- Coarse kosher salt and pepper (as required).

The Fire
- Wood pellet smoker, oak wood pellets.

Directions:
1. Start your wood pellet grill on smoke. For 5 minutes keep the lid open until the fire is established.

2. Then take the temperature to 450 F. while keeping the lid closed preheats for 15 minutes more.

3. Use salt and pepper for seasoning the lamb. Heat oil in a wood pellet smoker and brown all sides separately for 6-8 minutes.

4. Now add all the lamb pieces in the Dutch oven. Add garlic and sauté for exactly 2 minutes. Then after that, put in tomato paste and cook for one more minute.

5. Then, collectively add beer, beef stock, thyme, bay leaves, salt, and pepper. Cook this now on a high heat.

6. The remaining vegetables are also browned while meat has been cooking. In the cooking

pot, put in all the vegetables and let it cook for one hour.

7. Finally, the dish is ready to serve.

Nutrition:
Energy (calories): 809 kcal
Protein: 62.3 g
Fat: 53.94 g
Carbohydrates: 16.02 g

344. Ground Lamb Kebabs

Preparation Time: 10 minutes
Cooking Time: 1 hour
Servings: 2-4
Ingredients:
The Meat
- Ground Lamb – 1-1/2 lb.

The Mixture
- Minced onions – 1/3 cup.
- Minced garlic – ½ cloves.
- Cilantro – 3 tbsp.
- Minced fresh mint – 1 tbsp.
- Ground cumin 1 tsp.
- Paprika – 1 tsp.
- Salt – 1 tsp.
- Ground coriander – ½ tsp.
- Cinnamon – ¼ tsp.
- Pita bread - to serve.

The Fire
- Wood pellet smoker, cherry wood pellets.

Directions:
1. Take a large mixing bowl. Put in all the ingredients except for the pita bread. Now start making meatballs out of the mixture. The meatballs should be about 2 inches in diameter.
2. Take a bamboo skewer for each of the meatballs. Now, wet your hands to easily mold the skewered meal. Mold them each into a cigar shape.
3. Place it in the refrigerator for at least 30 minutes at least or preferably overnight. Set your wood pellet smoker on the smoke option and with the lid open the fire establishes. It takes about 4-5 minutes.
4. Then after that set the temperature to 350F and preheat it for about 10-15 minutes. During preheating keep the lid closed. Place the kebabs on the grill.
5. After 30 minutes turn them over.
6. Also, if the internal temperature reads 160F then it is time to turn them over. Warm the bread before serving it with kebobs.

Nutrition:
Energy (calories): 173 kcal
Protein: 17.62 g
Fat: 10.76 g
Carbohydrates: 1.72 g

345. Lamb Lollipops with Mango Chutney

Preparation Time: 10 minutes
Cooking Time: 1 hour
Servings: 4-6
Ingredients:
The Meat
- 6 Lamb chops (frenched) – (3/4 inch thick).

The Mixture
- Olive oil – 2 tbsp.
- Kosher salt – ½ tsp.

For Mango chutney
- 1 chopped mango.
- 3 Garlic cloves (chopped).
- ½ chopped habanero pepper.
- Salt – 1 tsp.
- Fresh lime juice – 1 tbsp.
- Chopped fresh cilantro – 3 sprigs.
- Pepper – ½ tsp.

The Fire
- Wood pellet smoker, apple wood pellets.

Directions:
1. Put all the ingredients and mix the chutney and put them in a food processor. Pulse them till you get your desired consistency. Set this aside.
2. With the lid open, establish fire in your wood pellet smoker for about 4-5 minutes. Then preheat it at a high temperature.
3. Let the lid closed for about 15 minutes of preheating. Put the lamb chops on a baking sheet and drizzle olive oil on it. Then season with salt and pepper. Allow them to sit for 10 minutes at room temperature. On the grill grate place your lamb chops. Now close the lid and grill for 5 minutes.
4. Then flip the chops over and allow them to smoke for another 3 minutes. If you want precise internal temperature, it should be 130 F to indicate that it is cooked through.
5. Remove the meat from the grill after that. Allow it to rest at least 10 minutes before serving them with the delicious chutney and sprinkled chopped mint.

Nutrition:
Energy (calories): 690 kcal
Protein: 90.91 g
Fat: 35.74 g
Carbohydrates: 1.46 g

346. Smoked Lamb Leg

Preparation Time: 10 minutes
Cooking Time: 4 hours
Servings: 4-6
Ingredients:
The Meat
- 1 Lamb leg.

The Mixture
- Honey – ¼ cup.
- Sierra Dijon Mustard – 2 tbsp.
- Chopped rosemary – 2 tbsp.
- Lemon zest – 1 tsp.
- Garlic (minced) – 3 cloves.
- Ground black pepper – 1 tsp.

The Fire
- Wood pellet smoker.

Directions:
1. It is better to have frozen piece of lamb leg. So, you can shave off as much fat as you like.
2. Mix garlic, lemon zest, chopped rosemary, mustard, pepper, and honey in a bowl. Put a saran wrap and place the leg of lamb on top of it. Pour the mixture on top of it.
3. Alternatively, you can use zip lock bag for this process Wrap the lamb leg up and put it in the refrigerator.
4. Let it sit in the fridge overnight. Take the wrap off the meat or take it out of zip lock bag if you have used it.
5. Take 3-4 garlic cloves and insert it in the meat. Sprinkle over the meat some seasonings, which include salt, pepper, and cayenne. Slow smoking is the method of cooking used for the lamb meat in this recipe.
6. Set the temperature at 200 and watch your meat thermometer probe. When it reaches 130 degrees take it out and let it rest for 20 minutes.
7. Make ¼ inch standards cut for serving meat and pour the juices on top of it to serve.

Nutrition:
Energy (calories): 413 kcal
Protein: 51.28 g
Fat: 13.55 g
Carbohydrates: 19.99 g

Chapter 10. Baking Recipes

347. Quick Yeast Dinner Rolls

Preparation Time: 5 minutes
Cooking Time: 30 minutes
Servings: 8
Ingredients:

- 2 tablespoons yeast, quick rise
- 1 cup water, lukewarm
- 3 cups flour
- ¼ cup sugar
- 1 teaspoon salt
- ¼ cup unsalted butter, softened.
- 1 egg
- Cooking spray, as needed.
- 1 egg, for egg wash

Directions:

1. Combine the yeast and warm water in a small bowl to activate the yeast. Let sit for about 5 to 10 minutes, or until foamy.
2. Combine the flour, sugar, and salt in the bowl of a stand mixer fitted with the dough hook. Pour the water and yeast into the dry ingredients with the machine running on low speed.
3. Add the butter and egg and mix for 10 minutes, gradually increasing the speed from low to high.
4. Form the dough into a ball and place in a buttered bowl. Cover with a cloth and let the dough rise for approximately 40 minutes.
5. Transfer the risen dough to a lightly floured work surface and divide into 8 pieces, forming a ball with each.
6. Lightly spritz a cast iron pan with cooking spray and arrange the balls in the pan. Cover with a cloth and let rise for 20 minutes.
7. When ready to cook, set Pit boss temperature to 375 F (191 C) and preheat, lid closed for 15 minutes.
8. Brush the rolls with the egg wash. Place the pan on the grill and bake for 30 minutes, or until lightly browned.
9. Remove from the grill. Serve hot.

Nutrition:
Energy (calories): 413 kcal
Protein: 51.28 g
Fat: 13.55 g
Carbohydrates: 19.99 g

348. Baked Cornbread with Honey Butter

Preparation Time: 10 minutes
Cooking Time: 35 to 45 minutes
Servings: 6
Ingredients:

- 4 ears whole corn
- 1 cup all-purpose flour
- 1 cup cornmeal
- 2/3 cup white sugar
- 1½ teaspoons baking powder
- ½ teaspoon baking soda
- ½ teaspoon salt
- 1 cup buttermilk
- ½ cup butter, softened.
- 2 eggs
- ½ cup butter, softened.
- ¼ cup honey

Directions:

1. When ready to cook, set Pit boss temperature to High and preheat, lid closed for 15 minutes.
2. Peel back the outer layer of the corn husk, keeping it attached to the cob. Remove the silk from the corn and place the husk back into place. Soak the corn in cold water for 10 minutes.
3. Place the corn directly on the grill grate and cook for 15 to 20 minutes, or until the kernels are tender, stirring occasionally. Remove from the grill and set aside.
4. In a large bowl, stir together the flour, cornmeal, sugar, baking powder, baking soda and salt.
5. In a separate bowl, whisk together the buttermilk, butter, and eggs. Pour the wet mixture into the cornmeal mixture and fold together until there are no dry spots. Pour the batter into a greased baking dish.
6. Cut the kernels from the corn and sprinkle over the top of the batter, pressing the kernels down with a spoon to submerge.
7. Turn Pit boss temperature down to 350 F (177 C). Place the baking dish on the grill. Bake for about 20 to 25 minutes, or until the top is golden brown and a toothpick inserted into the middle of the cornbread comes out clean.
8. Remove the cornbread from the grill and let cool for 10 minutes before serving.
9. To make the honey butter, mix the butter and honey until combined. Serve the cornbread with the honey butter.

Nutrition:
Energy (calories): 690 kcal
Protein: 90.91 g
Fat: 35.74 g
Carbohydrates: 1.46 g

349. S'mores Dip with Candied Pecans

Preparation Time: 10 minutes
Cooking Time: 37 to 45 minutes
Servings: 4
Ingredients:
Candied Smoked Pecans:

- ½ cup sugar
- ½ cup brown sugar
- 1 tablespoon ground cinnamon

- 1 teaspoon salt
- ¼ teaspoon cayenne pepper
- 1 egg white
- 1 teaspoon water
- 1-pound (454 g) pecans

S'mores Dip:
- 1 tablespoon butter
- 2 cups milk chocolate chips
- 10 large marshmallows cut in half.
- Graham crackers, for serving.

Directions:
1. When ready to cook, set Pit boss temperature to 300 F (149 C) and preheat, lid closed for 15 minutes.
2. In a small bowl, stir together the sugars, cinnamon, salt, and cayenne pepper. In a medium bowl, whisk together the egg white and water until frothy.
3. Pour the pecans into a large bowl. Pour in the egg white mixture and sugar mixture and toss to coat well.
4. Spread the coated pecans on a sheet tray lined with parchment paper. Place the tray directly on the grill grate. Smoke for 30 to 35 minutes, stirring often.
5. Remove from the grill and let cool. Break apart and roughly chop. Set aside.
6. When ready to cook, set Pit boss temperature to 400 F (204 C) and preheat, lid closed for 15 minutes.
7. Place a cast iron skillet directly on the grill grate while the grill heats up.
8. When the cast iron skillet is hot, melt the butter in the skillet and swirl around the skillet to coat.
9. Add the chocolate chips to the skillet, then top with the marshmallows. Cook for 7 to 10 minutes, or until the chocolate is melted and marshmallows are lightly browned. Remove from the grill.
10. Spread a handful of the candied pecans over the top and serve with the dip with the graham crackers.

Nutrition:
Energy (calories): 173 kcal
Protein: 17.62 g
Fat: 10.76 g
Carbohydrates: 1.72 g

350. Brown Sugared Bacon Cinnamon Rolls

Preparation Time: 5 minutes
Cooking Time: 25 to 35 minutes
Servings: 6
Ingredients:
- 12 slices bacon, sliced.
- 1/3 cup brown sugar
- 8 cinnamon rolls, store-brought

- 2 ounces (57 g) cream cheese, softened.

Directions:
1. When ready to cook, set Pit boss temperature to 350 F (177 C) and preheat, lid closed for 15 minutes.
2. Dredge 8 slices of the bacon in the brown sugar, making sure to cover both sides of the bacon.
3. Place the coated bacon slices along with the other bacon slices on a cooling rack placed on top of a large baking sheet.
4. Place the sheet on the grill and cook for 15 to 20 minutes, or until the fat is rendered, but the bacon is still pliable.
5. Open and unroll the cinnamon rolls. While bacon is still warm, place 1 slice of the brown sugared bacon on top of 1 of the unrolled rolls and roll back up. Repeat with the remaining rolls.
6. Turn Pit boss temperature down to 325 F (163 C). Place the cinnamon rolls in a greased baking dish and cook for 10 to 15 minutes, or until golden. Rotate the pan a half turn halfway through cooking time.
7. Meanwhile, crumble the cooked 4 bacon slices and add into the cream cheese.
8. Spread the cream cheese frosting over the warm cinnamon rolls. Serve warm.

Nutrition:
Energy (calories): 173 kcal
Protein: 17.62 g
Fat: 10.76 g
Carbohydrates: 1.72 g

351. Pit boss Soft Gingerbread Cookie

Preparation Time: 10 minutes
Cooking Time: 10 minutes
Servings: 8
Ingredients:
- 1¾ cups all-purpose flour
- 1½ teaspoons ground ginger
- ½ teaspoon ground cinnamon
- ½ teaspoon baking soda
- ¼ teaspoon ground cloves
- ¼ teaspoon kosher salt
- 1/3 cup brown sugar
- ¾ cup butter
- ½ cup plus 4 tablespoons granulated sugar, divided.
- ¼ cup molasses
- 1 egg

Directions:
1. When ready to cook, set Pit boss temperature to 325 F (163 C) and preheat, lid closed for 15 minutes.
2. In a medium bowl, stir together the flour, ginger, cinnamon, baking soda, cloves, and salt. Set aside.

3. In the bowl of a stand mixer, cream together the brown sugar, butter and ½ cup of the granulated sugar until light and fluffy. Stir in the molasses and egg and mix on medium speed until combined, scraping down the sides of the bowl.
4. Add the flour mixture to the bowl and mix on low speed until combined. Scrape the sides again and mix for 30 seconds longer.
5. Roll the dough into balls, 1 tablespoon at a time, and then roll the balls in the remaining 4 tablespoons of the sugar.
6. Place the dough balls on a baking sheet lined with parchment paper, leaving a couple inches between each cookie.
7. Place the sheet directly on the grill grate and cook for about 10 minutes, or until lightly browned but still soft in the center.
8. Remove from the grill and let cool on a wire rack. Serve.

Nutrition:
Energy (calories): 173 kcal
Protein: 17.62 g
Fat: 10.76 g
Carbohydrates: 1.72 g

352. Sweet Pull-Apart Rolls

Preparation Time: 5 minutes
Cooking Time: 10 to 12 minutes
Servings: 8
Ingredients:
- 1/3 cup vegetable oil
- ¼ cup warm water
- ¼ cup sugar
- 2 tablespoons active dry yeast
- 1 egg
- 3 1/2 cups all-purpose flour, divided.
- ½ teaspoon salt
- Cooking spray, as needed.

Directions:
1. When ready to cook, set Pit boss temperature to 400 F (204 C) and preheat, lid closed for 15 minutes.
2. Spritz a cast iron pan with cooking spray and set aside.
3. In the bowl of a stand mixer, combine the oil, warm water, sugar, and yeast. Let sit for 5 to 10 minutes, or until frothy and bubbly.
4. With a dough hook, mix in the egg, 2 cups of the flour and salt until combined. Add the remaining flour, ½ cup at a time.
5. Spritz your hands with cooking spray and shape the dough into 12 balls.
6. Arrange the balls in the prepared cast iron pan and let rest for 10 minutes. Place the pan in the grill and bake for about 10 to 12 minutes, or until the tops are lightly golden.
7. Serve immediately.

Nutrition:
Energy (calories): 690 kcal
Protein: 90.91 g
Fat: 35.74 g
Carbohydrates: 1.46 g

353. Baked Pulled Pork Stuffed Potatoes

Preparation Time: 10 minutes
Cooking Time: 50 minutes
Servings: 6
Ingredients:
- 4 russet potatoes
- Canola oil, as needed.
- Salt, to taste
- 2 tablespoons butter, melted.
- 3 cups pulled pork.
- 1 cup Cheddar cheese
- 1 cup Mozzarella cheese
- 4 tablespoons Pit boss Sweet & Heat BBQ Sauce

Topping:
- Sour cream
- Chopped bacon.
- Chopped green onion.

Directions:
1. When ready to cook, set Pit boss temperature to 450 F (232 C) and preheat, lid closed for 15 minutes.
2. Rub the potatoes with canola oil and sprinkle evenly with salt. Place the potatoes directly on the grill grate and cook for 45 minutes, or until fork tender.
3. Cut the potatoes in half and scoop the flesh out, leaving ¼ inch of the potato on the skin. Brush the inside of the skins with the melted butter and place on a baking tray. Place the tray on the grill and cook for 5 minutes, or until golden brown.
4. In a bowl, stir together the pulled pork, cheeses, and Pit boss Sweet & Heat BBQ Sauce.
5. Fill the potato skins with the mixture and return to the grill. Cook for 30 seconds, lid closed, or until the cheese is melted.
6. Serve topped with the sour cream, bacon, and green onion.

Nutrition:
Calories: 166 Cal
Fat: 8 g
Carbohydrates: 20 g
Protein: 3 g
Fiber: 0 g

354. Peanut Butter Cookies

Preparation Time: 5 minutes
Cooking Time: 25 minutes
Servings: 24
Ingredients:

- 1 egg
- 1 cup sugar
- 1 cup peanut butter

Directions:

1. Set your wood pellet grill to smoke.
2. Preheat too high.
3. Mix all the ingredients in one bowl.
4. Form cookies from the mixture.
5. Place in a baking pan.
6. Bake in the grill for 20 minutes.
7. Let cool for 5 minutes before serving.

Nutrition:
Calories: 166 Cal
Fat: 8 g
Carbohydrates: 20 g
Protein: 3 g
Fiber: 0 g

355. Pretzels

Preparation Time: 30 minutes
Cooking Time: 1 hour and 30 minutes
Servings: 6
Ingredients:

- 1 packet active instant dry yeast
- 1 tablespoon sugar
- 1 1/2 cups warm water
- 2 oz. melted butter
- 4 ½ cups all-purpose flour
- Cooking spray
- 1/2 cups baking soda.
- 10 cups boiling water.
- Egg yolks, beaten.
- Sea salt

Directions:

1. In a bowl, add the yeast, sugar, and warm water.
2. Combine using a mixer.
3. Let sit for 10 minutes.
4. Once it bubbles, stir in the butter and flour.
5. Mix for 3 minutes.
6. Transfer to a bowl.
7. Spray with oil.
8. Add a clean towel on top of the bowl.
9. Let it rise for 1 hour.
10. Roll the dough into long strips.
11. Form a knot to create a pretzel shape.
12. Start your wood pellet grill.
13. Set it to 350 degrees F.
14. Add the baking soda to the boiling water.
15. Drop the pretzels into the boiling water.
16. Transfer to a baking sheet.
17. Brush the top with the egg yolk and sprinkle with the salt.

18. Bake in the wood pellet grill for 20 minutes.

Nutrition:
Calories: 110 Cal
Fat: 1 g
Carbohydrates: 23 g
Protein: 3 g
Fiber: 1 g

356. Baked Pumpkin Seeds

Preparation Time: 15 minutes
Cooking Time: 45 minutes
Servings: 10
Ingredients:

- 10 cups pumpkin seeds
- 4 teaspoons melted butter.
- Java steak dry rub

Directions:

1. Set your wood pellet grill to smoke.
2. Preheat it to 300 degrees F.
3. Toss the seeds in steak rub and butter.
4. Place seeds
5. Cook for 45 minutes, stirring occasionally.

Nutrition:
Calories: 170 Cal
Fat: 15 g
Carbohydrates: 4 g
Protein: 9 g
Fiber: 2g

357. Cinnamon Pumpkin Seeds

Preparation Time: 5 minutes
Cooking Time: 20-25 minutes
Servings: 8
Ingredients:

- 8 cups pumpkin seeds
- 2 tablespoons melted butter.
- 2 tablespoons sugar
- 1 teaspoon ground cinnamon

Directions:

1. Set your wood pellet grill to smoke.
2. Preheat it to 350 degrees F.
3. Toss the pumpkin seeds in the butter, sugar, and cinnamon.
4. Spread in a baking pan.
5. Roast for 20 to 25 minutes.

Nutrition:
Calories: 285 Cal
Fat: 12 g
Carbohydrates: 34 g
Protein: 12 g
Fiber: 12 g

358. Cilantro and Lime Corn

Preparation Time: 15 minutes
Cooking Time: 15 minutes
Servings: 4
Ingredients:

- 4 corn cobs
- 1 tablespoon lime juice

- 2 tablespoons melted butter.
- Smoked paprika.
- 1 cup cilantro, chopped.

Directions:
1. Preheat your wood pellet grill to 400 degrees F.
2. Grill for 15 minutes, rotating every 5 minutes.
3. Brush the corn cobs with a mixture of lime juice and butter.
4. Season with the paprika.

Nutrition:
Calories: 100 Cal
Fat: 2 g
Carbohydrates: 19 g
Protein: 3 g
Fiber: 2 g

359. Roasted Trail Mix

Preparation Time: 10 minutes
Cooking Time: 15 minutes
Servings: 6
Ingredients:
- 1 cup pretzels
- 1 cup crackers
- 1 cup mixed nuts and seeds
- 3 tablespoons butter
- 1 teaspoon smoked paprika.

Directions:
1. Start your wood pellet grill.
2. Preheat it to 225 degrees F.
3. Toss all the ingredients in a roasting pan.
4. Smoke for 15 minutes.
5. Let cool and serve.

Nutrition:
Calories: 150 Cal
Fat: 11 g
Carbohydrates: 11 g
Protein: 5 g
Fiber: 2 g

360. Grilled Watermelon

Preparation Time: 5 minutes
Cooking Time: 6 minutes
Servings: 8
Ingredients:
- 1 watermelon, sliced.
- Feta cheese
- Mint leaves, chopped.

Directions:
1. Preheat your wood pellet grill to 450 degrees F.
2. Grill the watermelon for 3 minutes per side.
3. Slice into cubes.
4. Transfer to a bowl.
5. Top with the cheese and mint leaves.

Nutrition:
Calories: 14 Cal
Fat: 0 g
Carbohydrates: 3 g

Protein: 0 g
Fiber: 0 g

361. Grilled Peaches

Preparation Time: 5 minutes
Cooking Time: 10 minutes
Servings: 6
Ingredients:
- 1/2 tablespoon ground cinnamon
- 3 tablespoons brown sugar
- 3 peaches sliced in half and pitted.
- 1 tablespoon melted butter

Directions:
1. Turn on your wood pellet grill.
2. Set it to smoke.
3. Establish fire in the burn pot for 5 minutes.
4. Set it to 400 degrees F.
5. In a bowl, mix the cinnamon and brown sugar.
6. Coat the peaches with the butter.
7. Grill for 6 minutes.
8. Flip and sprinkle with the sugar mixture.
9. Grill for 2 minutes.

Nutrition:
Calories: 98 Cal
Fat: 6 g
Carbohydrates: 12 g
Protein: 1 g
Fiber: 1 g

362. Grilled Strawberries

Preparation Time: 5 minutes
Cooking Time: 5 minutes
Servings: 4
Ingredients:
- 1 tablespoon lemon juice
- 4 tablespoons honey
- 16 strawberries

Directions:
1. Turn on your wood pellet grill.
2. Set it to 450 degrees F.
3. Thread the strawberries into skewers.
4. Brush with the honey and lemon juice.
5. Grill for 5 minutes.

Nutrition:
Calories: 53 Cal
Fat: 0 g
Carbohydrates: 12 g
Protein: 1 g
Fiber: 3 g

363. Smoked Crepes

Preparation Time: 10 minutes
Cooking Time: 2 hours
Servings: 6
Ingredients:
- 2-pound apples sliced into wedges.
- Apple butter seasoning
- 1/2 cup apple juice

- 2 teaspoon lemon juice
- 5 tablespoon butter
- 3/4 teaspoon cinnamon, ground
- 2 tablespoon brown sugar
- 3/4 teaspoon cornstarch
- 6 crepes

Directions:
1. Preheat your wood pellet grill to 225 degrees F.
2. Season the apples with the apple butter seasoning.
3. Add to the grill.
4. Smoke for 1 hour.
5. Let cool and slice thinly.
6. Add to a baking pan.
7. Stir in the rest of the ingredients except the crepes. Roast for 15 minutes.
8. Add the apple mixture on top of the crepes. Roll and serve.

Nutrition:
Calories: 130 Cal
Fat: 5 g
Carbohydrates: 14 g
Protein: 7 g
Fiber: 1 g

364. Apple Crumble

Preparation Time: 30 minutes
Cooking Time: 1 hour and 30 minutes
Servings: 8
Ingredients:
- 2 cups and 2 tablespoons flour, divided.
- 1/2 cup shortening
- Pinch salt
- 1/4 cup cold water
- 8 cups apples sliced into cubes.
- 3 teaspoons lemon juice
- 1/2 teaspoon ground nutmeg
- 1 teaspoon apple butter seasoning
- 1/8 teaspoon ground cloves
- 1 teaspoon cinnamon
- 1/4 cup butter

Directions:
1. Set your wood pellet grill to smoke.
2. Preheat it to 350 degrees F.
3. Mix 1 1/2 cups flour, shortening and salt in a bowl until crumbly.
4. Slowly add cold water. Mix gently.
5. Wrap the dough in plastic and refrigerate for 20 to 30 minutes.
6. Place the apples in a bowl.
7. Toss in lemon juice. Take the dough out.
8. Press into a pan.
9. In a bowl, combine the 2 tablespoons flour, nutmeg, apple butter seasoning, ground cloves and cinnamon.
10. Add this to the bowl with apples.

11. Add the butter and mix with a mixer until crumbly.
12. Spread this on top of the dough.
13. Bake for 1 hour.

Nutrition:
Calories: 283 Cal
Fat: 6 g
Carbohydrates: 55 g
Protein: 1 g
Fiber: 0 g

365. Fruits on Bread

Preparation Time: 30 minutes
Cooking Time: 1 hour and 30 minutes
Servings: 8
Ingredients:
- 1/2 cup milk
- 1 teaspoon sugar
- 1/4 cup warm water
- 2 1/2 teaspoon active yeast, instant
- 2 1/2 cups all-purpose flour
- 2 tablespoon melted butter
- 1 egg
- 1/2 teaspoon vanilla
- 1/2 teaspoon salt
- Vegetable oil
- 1 tablespoon ground cinnamon
- Chocolate spread
- Fruits, sliced.

Directions:
1. Add the milk, sugar, water, and yeast in a bowl. Let sit for 10 minutes.
2. In another bowl, add the flour.
3. Create a well in the center.
4. Add the sugar mixture, butter, egg, vanilla, and salt.
5. Mix and knead.
6. Place in a bowl.
7. Cover with clean towel.
8. Let rise for 1 hour.
9. Start your wood pellet grill.
10. Set it to 450 degrees F.
11. Grease a cast iron skillet with the oil.
12. Create balls from the mixture.
13. Press and sprinkle with the cinnamon.
14. Fry for 1 minute per side.
15. Spread with chocolate and top with sliced fruits.

Nutrition:
Calories: 110 Cal
Fat: 2 g
Carbohydrates: 21 g
Protein: 5 g
Fiber: 2 g

366. Grilled Steak with American Cheese Sandwich

Preparation Time: 10 minutes
Cooking Time: 55 minutes
Servings: 4
Ingredients
1 pound of beef steak.
1/2 teaspoon of salt to taste.
1/2 teaspoon of pepper to taste.
1 tablespoon of Worcestershire sauce.
2 tablespoons of butter.
1 chopped onion.
1/2 chopped green bell pepper.
Salt and pepper to taste.
8 slices of American Cheese.
8 slices of white bread.
4 tablespoons of butter.

Directions:
Turn your Pit boss Smoker and Grill to smoke and fire up for about four to five minutes. Set the temperature of the grill to 450 degrees F and let it preheat for about ten to fifteen minutes with its lid closed.

Next, place a non-stick skillet on the griddle and preheat for about fifteen minutes until it becomes hot. Once hot, add in the butter and let melt. Once the butter melts, add in the onions and green bell pepper then cook for about five minutes until they become brown in color, set aside.

Next, still using the same pan on the griddle, add in the steak, Worcestershire sauce, salt, and pepper to taste then cook for about five to six minutes until it is cooked through. Add in the cooked bell pepper mixture; stir to combine then heat for another three minutes, set aside.

Use a sharp knife to slice the bread in half, butter each side then grill for about three to four minutes with its sides down. To assemble, add slices of cheese on each bread slice, top with the steak mixture then your favorite toppings, close the sandwich with another bread slice then serve.

Nutrition:
Calories 589 call
Carbohydrates 28g
Protein 24g
Fat 41g
Fiber 2g

367. Ground Turkey Burgers

Preparation Time: 15 minutes
Cooking Time: 50 minutes
Servings: 6
Ingredients
beaten egg.
2/3 cup of breadcrumbs.
1/2 cup of chopped celery
1/4 cup of chopped onion
1 tablespoon of minced parsley
1 teaspoon of Worcestershire sauce
1 teaspoon of dried oregano
1/2 teaspoon of salt to taste
1/4 teaspoon of pepper
1-1/4 pounds of lean ground turkey
6 hamburger buns
Optional topping
1 sliced tomato
1 sliced onion
Lettuce leaves

Directions:
Using a small mixing bowl, add in all the ingredients on the list aside from the turkey and buns then mix properly to combine.

Add in the ground turkey then mix everything to combine. Feel free to use clean hands for this. Make about six patties of the mixture then set aside.

Preheat your Pit boss Smoker and Grill to 375 degrees F, place the turkey patties on the grill and grill for about forty-five minutes until its internal temperature reads 165 degrees F. to assemble, use a knife to split the bun into two, top with the prepared burger and your favorite topping then close with another half of the buns, serve.

Nutrition:
Calories 293 call
Fat 11g
Carbohydrate 27g
Fiber 4g
Protein 22g

368. BBQ Shredded Beef Burger

Preparation Time: 10 minutes
Cooking Time: 5 hours 10 minutes
Servings: 4
Ingredients
3 pounds of boneless chuck roast.
Salt to taste
Pepper to taste
2 tablespoons of minced garlic
1 cup of chopped onion
28 oz. of barbeque sauce
6 buns

Directions:
Set the temperature of the Pit boss Smoker and Grill to 250 degrees F then preheat for about fifteen minutes with its lid closed.

Use a knife to trim off the excess fat present on the roast then place the meat on the preheated grill.

Grill the roast for about three and a half hours until it attains an internal temperature of 160 degrees F.

Next, place the chuck roast in an aluminum foil, add in the garlic, onion, barbeque sauce, salt, and pepper then stir to coat.

Place the roast bake on the grill and cook for another one and a half hour until an inserted thermometer reads 204 degrees F.

Once cooked, let the meat cool for a few minutes then shred with a fork. Fill the buns with the shredded beef then serve.

Nutrition:
Calories 593 call
Fat 31g
Carbohydrates 34g
Fiber 1g
Protein 44g

369. Grilled Pork Burgers

Preparation Time: 15 minutes
Cooking Time: 1 hour
Servings: 4 – 6
Ingredients
    1 beaten egg
    3/4 cup of soft breadcrumbs
    3/4 cup of grated parmesan cheese
    1 tablespoon of dried parsley
    1 teaspoons of dried basil
    1/2 teaspoon of salt to taste
    1/2 teaspoon of garlic powder
    1/4 teaspoon of pepper to taste
    2 pounds of ground pork
    6 hamburger buns
Toppings
    Lettuce leaves
    Sliced tomato
    Sliced sweet onion.
Directions:
Using a large mixing bowl, add in the egg, breadcrumbs, cheese, parsley, basil, garlic powder, salt, and pepper to taste then mix properly to combine.

Add in the ground pork then mix properly to combine using clean hands. Form about six patties out the mixture then set aside.

Next, set a Pit boss smoker and grill to smoke (250 degrees F) then let it fire up for about five minutes. Place the patties on the grill and smoke for about thirty minutes.

Flip the patties over, increase the temperature of the grill to 300 degrees F then grill the patties for a few minutes until an inserted thermometer reads 160 degrees F.

Serve the pork burgers on the buns, lettuce, tomato, and onion.
Nutrition:
Calories 522 call
Fat 28g
Carbohydrate 28g
Fiber 2g
Protein 38g

370. Delicious BLT Sandwich

Preparation Time: 15 minutes
Cooking Time: 35 minutes
Servings: 4-6
Ingredients
    8 slices of bacon
    1/2 romaine heart
        1sliced tomato
    4 slices of sandwich bread
        3 tablespoons of mayonnaise
    Salted butter
    Sea salt to taste
    Pepper to taste
Directions:
Preheat a Pit boss Smoker and Grill to 350 degrees F for about fifteen minutes with its lid closed.

Place the bacon slices on the preheated grill and cook for about fifteen to twenty minutes until they become crispy.

Next, butter both sides of the bread, place a grill pan on the griddle of the Traeger, and toast the bread for a few minutes until they become brown on both sides, set aside.

Using a small mixing bowl, add in the sliced tomatoes, season with salt and pepper to taste then mix to coat.

Next, spread mayo on both sides of the toasted bread, top with the lettuce, tomato, and bacon then enjoy.
Nutrition:
Calories 284 call
Protein 19g
Fat 19g
Carbohydrates 11g
Fiber 2g

371. Delicious Grilled Chicken Sandwich

Preparation Time: 15 minutes
Cooking Time: 50 minutes
Servings: 4
Ingredients
    1/4 cup of mayonnaise
        1 tablespoon of Dijon mustard
    1 tablespoon of honey
    4 boneless and skinless chicken breasts
    1/2 teaspoon of steak seasoning
    4 slices of American Swiss cheese
    4 hamburger buns
        2 bacon strips
    Lettuce leaves and tomato slices
Directions:
Using a small mixing bowl, add in the mayonnaise, mustard, and honey then mix properly to combine.

Use a meat mallet to pound the chicken into even thickness then slice into four parts. Season the chicken with the steak seasoning then set aside.

Preheat a Pit boss Smoker and Grill to 350 degrees F for about ten to fifteen minutes with its lid closed.

Place the seasoned chicken on the grill and grill for about twenty-five to thirty minutes until it reads an internal temperature of 165 degrees F. Grill the bacon until crispy then crumble.

Add the cheese on the chicken and cook for about one minute until it melts completely. At the same time, grill the buns for about one to two minutes until it is toasted as desired.

Place the chicken on the buns, top with the grilled bacon, mayonnaise mixture, lettuce, and tomato then serve.

Nutrition:
Calories 410 call
Fat 17g
Carbohydrate 29g
Fiber 3g
Protein 34g

372. Bacon, Egg, And Cheese Sandwich

Preparation Time: 15 minutes
Cooking Time: 20 minutes
Servings: 4
Ingredients
2 large eggs
2 tablespoons of milk or water
A pinch of salt to taste
A pinch of pepper to taste
3 teaspoons of butter
4 slices of white bread
2 slices of Jack cheese
4 slices of bacon

Directions:
Using a small mixing bowl, add in the eggs, milk, salt, and pepper to taste then mix properly to combine.

Preheat a Pit boss Smoker and Grill to 400 degrees F for about ten to fifteen minutes with its lid closed.

Place the bacon slices on the preheated grill and grill for about eight to ten minutes, flipping once until it becomes crispy. Set the bacon aside on a paper-lined towel.

Decrease the temperature of the grill to 350 degrees F, place a grill pan on the grill, and let it heat for about ten minutes.

Spread two tablespoons of butter on the cut side of the bread, place the bread on the skillet pan and toast for about two minutes until brown in color.

Place the cheese on the toasted bread, close the lid of the grill then cook for about one minute until the cheese melts completely, set aside. Still using the same grill pan, add in the rest of the butter then let melt. Pour in the egg mixture and cook for a few minutes until it is cooked as desired.

Assemble the sandwich as desired then serve.

Nutrition:
Calories 401 call
Fat 23g
Carbohydrates 26g
Fiber 3g
Protein 23g

Chapter 11. Cheese and Bread

373. Traeger-Grill Flatbread Pizza

Preparation Time: 10 minutes
Cooking Time: 20 minutes
Servings: 3
Ingredients
Dough
- 2 cups flour
    1 tbsp salt
- 1 tbsp sugar
    2 tbsp yeast
- 6 oz warm water

Toppings
- Green/red bell pepper
- 1/2 garlic
- zucchini
- 1/2 onion
- Olive oil
- 5 bacon strips
- 1 cup halved yellow cherry tomatoes.
- Sliced jalapenos
- Sliced green olives.
- Sliced kalamata olives
- Goat cheese
- *For drizzling:* Balsamic vinegar

Directions:
1. Combine all dough ingredients in a stand mixer bowl. Mix until the dough is smooth and elastic. Divide into 3 equal balls.
2. Roll each dough ball with a rolling pin into a thin round enough to fit a 12-inch skillet.
3. Grease the skillet using olive oil.
4. Meanwhile, turn your Pit boss grill on smoke for about 4-5 minutes with the lid open. Turn to high and preheat for about 10-15 minutes with the lid closed.
5. Once ready, arrange peppers, garlic, zucchini, and onion on the grill grate then drizzle with oil and salt. Check at 10 minutes.
6. Now remove zucchini from the grill and add bacon. Continue to cook for another 10 minutes until bacon is done.
7. Transfer the toppings on a chopping board to cool. Chop tomatoes, jalapenos, and olive.
8. Brush your crust with oil and smash garlic with a fork over the crust. Smear carefully not to tear the crust.
9. Add toppings to the crust in the skillet.
10. Place the skillet on the grill and cook for about 20 minutes until brown edges.
11. Repeat for the other crusts.
12. Now drizzle each with vinegar and slice.
13. Serve and enjoy.

Nutrition:
Calories 342, Total fat 1.2g, Saturated fat 0.2g, Total carbs 70.7g, Net carbs 66.8g, Protein 11.7g, Sugars 4.2g, Fiber 3.9g, Sodium 2333mg, Potassium 250mg

374. Pit boss Smoked Nut Mix

Preparation Time: 15 minutes
Cooking Time: 20 minutes
Servings: 8
Ingredients
- 3 cups mixed nuts (pecans, peanuts, almonds etc.)
- 1/2 tbsp brown sugar
    1 tbsp thyme, dried
- 1/4 tbsp mustard powder
- 1 tbsp olive oil, extra-virgin

Directions:
1. Preheat your Pit boss grill to 250oF with the lid closed for about 15 minutes.
2. Combine all ingredients in a bowl, large, then transfer into a cookie sheet lined with parchment paper.
3. Place the cookie sheet on a grill and grill for about 20 minutes.
4. Remove the nuts from the grill and let cool.
5. *Serve and enjoy.*

Nutrition:
Calories 249, Total fat 21.5g, Saturated fat 3.5g, Total carbs 12.3g, Net carbs 10.1g, Protein 5.7g, Sugars 5.6g, Fiber 2.1g, Sodium 111mg, Potassium 205mg

375. Pit boss Grill Chicken Flatbread

Preparation Time: 5 minutes
Cooking Time: 30 minutes
Servings: 6
Ingredients
- 6 mini breads
- 1-1/2 cups divided buffalo sauce.
- 4 cups cooked and cubed chicken breasts.
- For drizzling: mozzarella cheese

Directions:
1. Preheat your Pit boss grill to 375 - 400oF.
2. Place the breads on a surface, flat, then evenly spread 1/2 cup buffalo sauce on all breads.
3. Toss together chicken breasts and 1 cup buffalo sauce then top over all the breads evenly.
4. Top each with mozzarella cheese.
5. Place the breads directly on the grill but over indirect heat. Close the lid.
6. Cook for about 5-7 minutes until slightly toasty edges, cheese is melted and fully hated chicken.
7. Remove and drizzle with ranch or blue cheese.
8. *Enjoy!*

Nutrition:
Calories 346, Total fat 7.6g, Saturated fat 2g, Total Carbs 33.9g, Net Carbs 32.3g, Protein 32.5g, Sugars 0.8g, Fiber 1.6g, Sodium 642mg, Potassium 299mg

376. Grilled Homemade Croutons

Preparation Time: 10 minutes
Cooking Time: 30 minutes
Servings: 6
Ingredients
- 2 tbsp Mediterranean Blend Seasoning
- 1/4 cup olive oil
- 6 cups cubed bread.

Directions:
1. Preheat your Pit boss grill to 250oF.
2. Combine seasoning and oil in a bowl then drizzle the mixture over the bread cubes. Toss to evenly coat.
3. Layer the bread cubes on a cookie sheet, large, and place on the grill.
4. Bake for about 30 minutes. Stir at intervals of 5 minutes for browning evenly.
5. Once dried out and golden brown, remove from the grill.
6. *Serve and enjoy!*

Nutrition:
Calories 188, Total fat 10g, Saturated fat 2g, Total carbs 20g, Net carbs 19g, Protein 4g, Sugars 2g, Fiber 1g, Sodium 1716mg, Potassium 875mg

377. Smoked Cheddar Cheese

Preparation Time: 5 minutes
Cooking Time: 5 hours
Servings: 2
Ingredients
2, 8-oz, cheddar cheese blocks
Directions:
1. Preheat and set your Pit boss grill to 900F.
2. Place the cheese blocks directly on the grill grate and smoke for about 4 hours.
3. Remove and transfer into a plastic bag, resealable. Refrigerate for about 2 weeks to allow flavor from smoke to permeate your cheese.
4. *Now enjoy!*

Nutrition:
Calories 115, Total fat 9.5g, Saturated fat 5.4g, Total carbs 0.9g, Net carbs 0.9g, Protein 6.5g, Sugars 0.1g, Fiber 0g, Sodium 185mg, Potassium 79mg

378. Smoked Mac and Cheese

Preparation Time: 2 minutes
Cooking Time: 1 hour
Servings: 2
Ingredients
- 1/2 cup butter, salted.
- 1/3 cup flour
- 1/2 tbsp salt
- 6 cups whole milk
- Dash of Worcestershire
- 1/2 tbsp dry mustard
      1 lb. small, cooked shells, al dente in well-salted water

- 2 cups white cheddar, smoked.
- 2 cups cheddar jack cheese
- 1 cup crushed ritz

Directions:
1. Set your grill on "smoke" and run for about 5-10 minutes with the lid open until fire establishes. Now turn your grill to 325 of then close the lid.
2. Melt butter in a saucepan, medium, over low--medium heat then whisk in flour.
3. Cook while whisking for about 5-6 minutes over low heat until light tan color.
4. Whisk in salt, milk, Worcestershire, and mustard over low-medium heat stirring frequently until a thickened sauce.
5. Stir noodles, small shells, white sauce, and 1 cup cheddar cheese in a large baking dish, 10x3" high-sided, coated with butter.
6. Top with 1 cup cheddar cheese and ritz.
7. Place on the grill and bake for about 25-30 minutes until a bubbly mixture and cheese melts.
8. *Serve immediately. Enjoy!*

Nutrition:
Calories 628, Total fat 42g, Saturated fat 24g, Total carbs 38g, Net carbs 37g, Protein 25g, Sugars 11g, Fiber 1g, Sodium 807mg, Potassium 699mg

379. Berry Cobbler on a Pit boss grill

Preparation Time: 15 minutes
Cooking Time: 35 minutes
Servings: 8
Ingredients
For fruit filling
- 3 cups frozen mixed berries
- lemon juice
- 1 cup brown sugar
- 1 tbsp vanilla extract
- 1 tbsp lemon zest finely grated.
- A pinch of salt

For cobbler topping
- 1-1/2 cups all-purpose flour
- 1-1/2 tbsp baking powder
- 3 tbsp sugar, granulated.
- 1/2 tbsp salt
- 8 tbsp cold butter
- 1/2 cup sour cream
- 2 tbsp raw sugar

Directions:
1. Set your Pit boss grill on "smoke" for about 4-5 minutes with the lid open until fire establishes and your grill starts smoking.
2. Preheat your grill to 350 of for about 10-15 minutes with the grill lid closed.
3. Meanwhile, combine frozen mixed berries, Lemon juice, brown sugar, vanilla, lemon zest and pinch of salt. Transfer into a skillet and let the fruit sit and thaw.

4. Mix flour, baking powder, sugar, and salt in a bowl, medium. Cut cold butter into peas sizes using a pastry blender then add to the mixture. Stir to mix everything together.
5. Stir in sour cream until dough starts coming together.
6. Pinch small pieces of dough and place over the fruit until fully covered. Splash the top with raw sugar.
7. Now place the skillet directly on the grill grate, close the lid and cook for about 35 minutes until juices bubble, and a golden-brown dough topping.
8. Remove the skillet from the Pit boss grill and cool for several minutes.
9. *Scoop and serve warm.*

Nutrition:
Calories 371, Total fat 13g, Saturated fat 8g, Total carbs 60g, Net carbs 58g, Protein 3g, Sugars 39g, Fiber 2g, Sodium 269mg, Potassium 123mg

380. Pit boss Grill Apple Crisp

Preparation Time: 20 minutes
Cooking Time: 1 hour
Servings: 15
Ingredients
- *Apples*
- 10 large apples
- 1/2 cup flour
    1 cup sugar, dark brown
- 1/2 tbsp cinnamon
- 1/2 cup butter slices
- *Crisp*
    3 cups oatmeal, old-fashioned
- 1-1/2 cups softened butter, salted.
- 1-1/2 tbsp cinnamon
    1 cup brown sugar

Directions:
1. Preheat your grill to 350 of.
2. Wash, peel, core, and dice the apples into cubes, medium size.
3. Mix flour, dark brown sugar, and cinnamon then toss with your apple cubes.
4. Spray a baking pan, 10x13", with cooking spray then place apples inside. Top with butter slices.
5. Mix all crisp ingredients in a medium bowl until well combined. Place the mixture over the apples.
6. Place on the grill and cook for about 1-hour checking after every 15-20 minutes to ensure cooking is even. Do not place it on the hottest grill part.
7. Remove and let sit for about 20-25 minutes.
8. *It is very warm.*

Nutrition:
Calories 528, Total fat 26g, Saturated fat 16g, Total carbs 75g, Net carbs 70g, Protein 4g, Sugars 51g, Fiber 5g, Sodium 209mg, Potassium 122mg

381. Low Carb Almond Flour Bread

Preparation Time: 10 minutes
Cooking Time: 1 hour 15 minutes
Servings: 24 slices
Ingredients:
- 1tsp sea salt or to taste.
- 1tbsp apple cider vinegar
- ½ cup of warm water
- ¼ cup of coconut oil
- 4large eggs (beaten)
- 1tbsp gluten-free baking powder
- 2cup blanched almond flour.
- ¼ cup Psyllium husk powder
- 1tsp ginger (optional)

Directions:
1. Preheat the grill to 350°F with the lid closed for 15 minutes.
2. Line a 9 by 5-inch loaf pan with parchment paper. Set aside.
3. Combine the ginger, Psyllium husk powder, almond flour, salt, baking powder in a large mixing bowl.
4. In another mixing bowl, mix the coconut oil, apple cider vinegar, eggs, and warm water. Mix thoroughly.
5. Gradually pour the flour mixture into the egg mixture, stirring as you pour. Stir until it forms a smooth batter.
6. Fill the lined loaf pan with the batter and cover the batter with aluminum foil.
7. Place the loaf pan directly on the grill and bake for about 1 hour or until a toothpick or knife inserted in the middle of the bread comes out clean.

Nutrition: Calories: 93 Total Fat: 7.5 g Saturated Fat: 2.6 g Cholesterol: 31 mg Sodium: 139 mg Total Carbohydrate: 3.6 g Dietary Fiber: 2.2 g Total Sugars: 0.1 g Protein: 3.1 g

382. Rosemary Cheese Bread

Preparation Time: 10 minutes
Cooking Time: 12 minutes
Servings: 30 Breadstick
Ingredients:
- 1½ cup sunflower seeds
- ½ tsp sea salt
- 1egg
- 1tsp fresh rosemary (finely chopped)
- 2tsp xanthan gum
- 2tbsp cream cheese
- 2cups grated mozzarella

Directions:
1. Preheat the grill to 400°F with the lid closed for 15 minutes.
2. Toss the sunflower seeds into a powerful blender and blend until it smooth and flour-like.

3. Transfer the sunflower seed flour into a mixing bowl and add the rosemary and xanthan gum. Mix and set aside.
4. Melt the cheese in a microwave. To do this, combine the cream cheese and mozzarella cheese in a microwave-safe dish.
5. Place the microwave-safe dish in the grill and heat the cheese on high for 1 minute.
6. Bring out the dish and stir. Place the dish in the grill and heat for 30 seconds. Bring out the dish and stir until smooth.
7. Pour the melted cheese into a large mixing bowl.
8. Add the sunflower flour mixture to the melted cheese and stir the ingredients are well combined.
9. Add the salt and egg and mix thoroughly to form a smooth dough.
10. Measure out equal pieces of the dough and roll into sticks.
11. Grease a baking sheet with oil and arrange the breadsticks into the baking sheet in a single layer.
12. Use the back of a knife or metal spoon to make lines on the breadsticks.
13. Place the baking sheet on the grill and make for about 12 minutes or until the breadsticks turn golden brown.
14. Remove the baking sheet from the grill and let the breadsticks cool for a few minutes.
15. Serve.

Nutrition: Calories: 23 Total Fat: 1.9 g Saturated Fat: 0.5 g Cholesterol: 7 mg Sodium: 47 mg Total Carbohydrate: 0.6 g Dietary Fiber: 0.2 g Total Sugars: 0.1 g Protein: 1.2 g

383. Cinnamon Almond Shortbread

Preparation Time: 20 minutes
Cooking Time: 20 minutes
Servings: 5
Ingredients:
- 2tsp cinnamon
- ½ cup unsalted butter (softened)
- 1large egg (beaten)
- ½ tsp salt or to taste.
- 2cups almond flour
- ¼ cup sugar
- 1tsp ginger (optional)

Directions:
1. Preheat the grill to 300°F with the lid closed for 5 minutes.
2. Grease a cookie sheet with oil.
3. In a large bowl, combine the cinnamon, almond flour, sugar, ginger, and salt. Mix thoroughly to combine.
4. In another mixing bowl, whisk the egg and softened butter together.

5. Pour the egg mixture into the flour mixture and mix until the mixture forms a smooth batter.
6. Use a tablespoon to measure out equal amounts of the mixture and roll into balls.
7. Arrange the balls into the cookie sheet in a single layer.
8. Now, use the flat bottom of a clean glass cup to press each ball into a flat round cookie. Grease the bottom of the cup before using it to press the balls.
9. Place the cookie sheet on the grill and bake until browned. This will take about 20 to 25 minutes.
10. Remove the cookie sheet from the grill and let the shortbreads cool for a few minutes.
11. Serve and enjoy.

Nutrition: Calories: 152 Total Fat: 12.7 g Saturated Fat: 4.2 g Cholesterol: 27 mg Sodium: 124 mg Total Carbohydrate: 6.5 g Dietary Fiber: 1.7 g Total Sugars: 3.2 g Protein: 3.5 g

384. Simple Roasted Butternut Squash

Preparation Time: 5 minutes
Cooking Time: 25 minutes
Servings: 8
Ingredients:
- 1(2 pounds) butternut squash
- 2garlic cloves (minced)
- 2tablespoon extra olive virgin oil
- 1tsp paprika
- 1tsp oregano
- 1tsp thyme
- Salt and pepper to taste

Directions:
1. Start your grill on smoke mode and leave the grill open for 5 minutes, until fire Preheat the grill to 400°F.
2. Peel the butternut squash.
3. Cut the butternut squash into two (cut lengthwise).
4. Use a spoon to scoop out the seeds.
5. Cut the butternut squash into 1-inch chunks and wash the chunks with water.
6. In a big bowl, combine the butternut squash chunks and other ingredients.
7. Stir until the chunks are coated with the ingredients.
8. Spread the coated chunks on the sheet pan.
9. Place the sheet pan on the grill and bake for 25 minutes.
10. Remove the baked butternut squash from heat and let it sit to cool.
11. Serve.

Nutrition: Calories: 8 Total Fat: 3.7 g Saturated Fat: 0.5 g Cholesterol: 0 mg Sodium: 331 mg Total Carbohydrate 13.8 g Dietary Fiber 2.6 g Total Sugars: 2.5 g Protein: 1.2 g

385. Mango Bread

Preparation Time: 15 minutes
Cooking Time: 1 hour
Servings: 4
Ingredients:

- 2½ cup cubed ripe mangoes.
- 2cups all-purpose flour
- 1tsp baking powder.
- 1tsp baking soda.
- 2eggs (beaten)
- 1tsp cinnamon
- 1tsp vanilla extract
- ½ tsp nutmeg
- ¾ cup olive oil
- ¾ cup of sugar
- 1tbsp lemon juice
- ½ tsp salt
- ½ cup chopped dates.

Directions:

1. Start your grill on smoke mode and leave the lip opened for 5 minutes, or until the fire starts.
2. Close the lid and preheat the grill to 350°F for 15 minutes, using alder hair-triggers.
3. Grease an 8 by 4-inch loaf pan.
4. In a mixing bowl, combine the flour, baking powder, baking soda, cinnamon, salt, and sugar.
5. In another mixing bowl, whisk together the egg, lemon juice, oil, and vanilla.
6. Pour the egg mixture into the flour mixture and mix until you well combined.
7. Fold in the mangoes and dates.
8. Pour the mixture into the loaf pan and place the pan in the grill.
9. Place the loaf pan directly on the grill bake for about 50 to 60 minutes or until a toothpick inserted in the middle of the bread comes out clean.
10. After the baking cycle, remove the loaf pan from the grill and transfer the bread to a wire rack to cool completely.
11. Slice and serve.

Nutrition: Calories: 856 Total Fat: 41.2 g Saturated Fat: 6.4 g Cholesterol: 82 mg Sodium: 641 mg Total Carbohydrate 118.9 g Dietary Fiber 5.5 g Total Sugars: 66.3 g Protein: 10.7 g

386. Baked S'mores Donut

Preparation Time: 10 minutes
Cooking Time: 35 minutes
Servings: 8-12
Ingredients:
For the donuts:

- 1 cup all-purpose flour
- Cooking spray
- ¼ teaspoon baking soda
- 1/3 cup of sugar
- ¾ cup buttermilk
- 2 tbsp. butter (unsalted)
- One egg
- ½ tsp. vanilla extract
- Four chocolate bars (whatever kind you want)
- 24 marshmallows (sliced in half)
- For the Glaze
- ¼ cup whole milk
- 1 tsp. vanilla extract
- 2 cups confectioners' sugar

Directions:
Grill Prep:

1. Spray the donut pans with some cooking spray.
2. Mix sugar, flour, and baking soda.
3. Grab a different bowl; whisk your egg, melted butter, buttermilk, and vanilla.
4. Mix the dry and wet ingredients using a spatula, blending them perfectly.
5. Pipe your batter onto your greased donut pans.

On the Grill:

1. Set up your wood pellet smoker grill for indirect cooking.
2. Preheat your wood pellet smoker grill for 10 to 15 minutes at 350 degrees Fahrenheit.
3. Bake your batter for 25 minutes, till your donuts are nice and puffy, and the toothpick you insert to check it comes out nice and clean. Then let it cool in the pan.
4. Mix your vanilla and milk in a saucepan and heat it over low heat till it is a bit warm.
5. Sift your confectioner's sugar into your milk and vanilla mix till it is wonderfully combined.
6. Take your glaze off the fire, and let it set on a bowl of warm water.
7. Take your delicious donuts and dip them right into your glaze, then set your cooling rack over some foil, and then put your donuts on the shelf, letting them rest for 5 minutes.
8. Halve your donuts, and then place your halved marshmallows in between, as well as some chocolate.
9. Grill these sandwiches for 4 to 5 minutes. You want the chocolate and marshmallows to melt.
10. Take them off the grill, serve, and enjoy!

Nutrition:
Calories: 217 Cal
Fat: 5 g
Carbohydrates: 32 g
Protein: 11 g
Fiber: 2 g

387. Baked Cherry Cheesecake Galette

Preparation Time: 10 minutes
Cooking Time: 20 minutes
Servings: 6-8
Ingredients:
- For the cherry filling:
- 1-pound cherries (thawed, drained)
- ¼ cup of sugar
- 1 tsp. cornstarch
- 1 tsp. coriander
- A pinch of salt
- 1 tbsp. orange zest
- ½ tablespoon lemon zest
- For the cream cheese filling:
- 8 ounces of cream cheese (softened)
- 1 tsp. vanilla
- ¼ cup of sugar
- One egg
- For the galette:
- One refrigerated pie crust
- 1 egg, 1 tbsp. water, cream, or milk
- Granulated sugar
- Vanilla ice cream to serve.

Directions:
1. Grab a medium bowl; mix your cherries, orange zest, lemon zest, and coriander, half of the sugar, cornstarch, and a pinch of salt.
2. Grab another bowl, and in it, mix your egg, vanilla, and cream cheese. Whip it up.
3. Get your pie dough onto a sheet tray, and then stretch it out with a rolling pin. Get it to about 1 inch in diameter.
4. Spread out your cream cheese filling in the middle of the pie dough. Be careful to leave a border of an inch around the edge. Then pile your cherry mix on the cream cheese.
5. Now, you are going to fold in the pie dough's edges into little parts over the filling.
6. Next, brush the edges of the pie dough with egg wash, and then sprinkle on some granulated sugar.

On the Grill:
1. Set up your wood pellet smoker grill for indirect cooking.
2. Preheat your wood pellet smoker grill at a temperature of 350 degrees Fahrenheit, keeping it closed for 15 minutes.
3. Set your sheet to try right on the grill grate, and then bake that yummy goodness for 15 to 20 minutes. You want the crust to become nice and golden brown and for the cheesecake filling to be completely set.
4. Dish the galette while warm with some ice cream. And then enjoy.

Nutrition:
Calories: 400 Cal
Fat: 51 g
Carbohydrates: 18 g
Protein: 5 g
Fiber: 3 g

388. Smoked Salted Caramel Apple Pie

Preparation Time: 30 minutes
Cooking Time: 30 minutes
Servings: 4-6
Ingredients:
For the apple pie:
- One pastry (for double-crust pie)
- 6 Apples
- For the smoked, salted caramel:
- 1 cup brown sugar
- ¾ cup light corn syrup
- 6 tbsp. butter (unsalted, cut in pieces)
- 1 cup warm smoked cream
- 1 tsp. sea salt

Directions:
Grill Prep:
1. Fill a container with water and ice.
2. Grab a shallow, smaller pan, and then put in your cream. Take that smaller pan and place it in the large pan with ice and water.
3. Set this on your wood pellet smoker grill for 15 to 20 minutes.
4. For the caramel, mix your corn syrup and sugar in a saucepan, and then cook it all using medium heat. Be sure to stir every so often until the back of your spoon is coated and begins to turn copper.
5. Next, add the butter, salt, and smoked cream, and then stir.
6. Get your pie crust, apples, and salted caramel. Put a pie crust on a pie plate, and then fill it with slices of apples.
7. Pour on the caramel next.
8. Put on the top crust over all of that, and then crimp both crusts together to keep them locked in.
9. Create a few slits in the top crust so that the steam can be released as you bake.
10. Brush with some cream or egg, and then sprinkle with some sea salt and raw sugar.

On the Grill:
1. Set up your wood pellet smoker grill for indirect cooking.
2. Preheat your wood pellet smoker grill for 10 to 15 minutes at 375 degrees Fahrenheit, keeping the lid closed as soon as the fire gets started (should take 4 to 5 minutes, tops).
3. Set the pie on your grill, and then bake for 20 minutes.
4. At the 20-minute mark, lower the heat to 325 degrees Fahrenheit, and then let it cook for 35 minutes more. You want the crust to be a nice golden brown, and the filling should be bubbly when it is ready.
5. Take the pie off the grill and allow it to cool and rest.
6. Serve with some vanilla ice cream and enjoy!

Nutrition:
Calories: 149 Cal
Fat: 2 g
Carbohydrates: 30 g
Protein: 3 g
Fiber: 2 g

Chapter 12. Appetizers and Sides

389. Atomic Buffalo Turds

Preparation Time: 30 to 45 Minutes
Cooking Time: 1.5 Hours to 2 Hours
Servings: 6
Ingredients:

- 10 Medium Jalapeno Pepper
- 8 ounces regular cream cheese at room temperature
- ¾Cup Monterey Jack and Cheddar Cheese Blend Shred (optional)
- One teaspoon smoked paprika.
- One teaspoon garlic powder
- ½ teaspoon cayenne pepper
- Teaspoon red pepper flakes (optional)
- 20 smoky sausages
- Ten sliced bacon cut in half.

Directions:

1. Wear food service gloves when using. Jalapeno peppers are washed vertically and sliced. Carefully remove seeds and veins using a spoon or paring knife and discard. Place Jalapeno on a grilled vegetable tray and set aside.
2. A small bowl mix cream cheese, shredded cheese, paprika, garlic powder, cayenne pepper is used, and red pepper flakes if used until thoroughly mixed.
3. Mix cream cheese with half of the jalapeno pepper.
4. Place the Little Smokiness sausage on half of the filled jalapeno pepper.
5. Wrap half of the thin bacon around half of each jalapeno peppers.
6. Fix the bacon to the sausage with a toothpick so that the pepper does not pierce. Place the ABT on the grill tray or pan.
7. Set the wood pellet smoker and grill for indirect cooking and preheat to 250 degrees Fahrenheit using hickory pellets or blends.
8. Suck jalapeno peppers at 250 ° F for about 1.5 to 2 hours until the bacon is cooked and crisp.
9. Remove the ABT from the grill and let it rest for 5 minutes before hors d'oeuvres.

Nutrition: Calories: 131 Carbs: 1g Fat: 12g Protein: 5g

390. Grilled Corn

Preparation Time: 15 minutes
Cooking Time: 25 minutes
Servings: 6
Ingredients:

- Six fresh ears of corn
- Salt
- Black pepper
- Olive oil
- Vegetable seasoning
- Butter for serving.

Directions:

1. Preheat the grill to high with a closed lid.
2. Peel the husks. Remove the corn's silk. Rub with black pepper, salt, vegetable seasoning, and oil.
3. Close the husks and grill for 25 minutes. Turn them occasionally.
4. Serve topped with butter and enjoy.

Nutrition: Calories: 70 Protein: 3g Carbs: 18g Fat: 2g

391. Thyme - Rosemary Mash Potatoes

Preparation Time: 20 minutes
Cooking Time: 1 hour
Servings: 6
Ingredients:

- 4 ½ lbs. Potatoes, russet
- Salt
- 1 pint of Heavy cream
- 3 Thyme sprigs + 2 tablespoons for garnish
- 2 Rosemary sprigs
- 6 - 7 Sage leaves
- 6 - 7 Black peppercorns
- Black pepper to taste
- Two stick Butter softened.
- 2 Garlic cloves, chopped.

Directions:

1. Preheat the grill to 350F with a closed lid.
2. Peel the russet potatoes.
3. Cut into small pieces and place them in a baking dish. Fill it with water (1 ½ cups). Place on the grill and cook with a closed lid for about 1 hour.
4. In the meantime, in a saucepan, combine the garlic, peppercorns, herbs, and cream. Place on the grate and cook covered for about 15 minutes. Once done, strain to remove the garlic and herbs. Keep warm.
5. Take out the water of the potatoes and place them in a stockpot. Rice them with a fork and pour 2/3 of the mixture. Add one stick of softened butter and salt.
6. Serve right away.

Nutrition: Calories: 180 Protein: 4g Carbs: 28g Fat: 10g

392. Grilled Broccoli

Preparation Time: 15 minutes
Cooking Time: 10 minutes
Servings: 4 to 6
Ingredients:

- Four bunches of Broccoli
- Four tablespoons Olive oil
- Black pepper and salt to taste
- ½ Lemon, the juice
- ½ Lemon cut into wedges.

Directions:

1. Preheat the grill to High with a closed lid.

2. In a bowl, add the broccoli and drizzle with oil. Coat well—season with salt.
3. Grill for 5 minutes and then flip. Cook for 3 minutes more.
4. I have once done transfer on a plate. Squeeze lemon on top and serve with lemon wedges. Enjoy!

Nutrition: Calories: 35g Protein: 2.5g Carbs: 5g Fat: 1g

393. Smoked Coleslaw

Preparation Time: 15 minutes
Cooking Time: 25 minutes
Servings: 8
Ingredients:
- One shredded Purple Cabbage
- One shredded Green Cabbage
- 2 Scallions, sliced.
- 1 cup Carrots, shredded.

Dressing
- One tablespoon of Celery Seed
- 1/8 cup of White vinegar
- 1 ½ cups Mayo
- Black pepper and salt to taste

Directions:
1. Preheat the grill to 180F with a closed lid.
2. On a tray, spread the carrots and cabbage. Place the tray on the grate and smoke for about 25 minutes.
3. Transfer to the fridge to cool.
4. In the meantime, make the dressing. In a bowl, combine the ingredients. Mix well.
5. Transfer the veggies to a bowl. Drizzle with the sauce and toss
6. Serve sprinkled with scallions.

Nutrition: Calories: 35g Protein: 1g Carbs: 5g Fat: 5g

394. The Best Potato Roast

Preparation Time: 15 minutes
Cooking Time: 35 minutes
Servings: 6
Ingredients:
- 4 Potatoes, large (scrubbed)
- 1 ½ cups gravy (beef or chicken)
- Rib seasoning to taste
- 1 ½ cups Cheddar cheese
- Black pepper and salt to taste
- Two tablespoons sliced Scallions

Directions:
1. Preheat the grill to high with a closed lid.
2. Slice each potato into wedges or fries. Transfer into a bowl and drizzle with oil—season with Rib seasoning.
3. Spread the wedges/fries on a baking sheet (rimmed)—roast for about 20 minutes. Turn the wedges/fries and cook for 15 minutes more.
4. In the meantime, in a saucepan, warm the chicken/beef gravy. Cut the cheese into small cubes.

5. It was once done cooking, place the potatoes on a plate or into a bowl. Distribute the cut cheese and pour hot gravy on top.
6. Serve garnished with scallion—season with pepper. Enjoy!

Nutrition: Calories: 220 Protein: 3g Carbs: 38g Fat: 15g

395. Smoked Corn on the Cob

Preparation Time: 5 Minutes
Cooking Time: 60 Minutes
Servings: 4
Ingredients
- 4 corn ears, husk removed.
- 4 tbsp olive oil
- Pepper and salt to taste

Directions:
1. Preheat your smoker to 225°F.
2. Meanwhile, brush your corn with olive oil. Season with pepper and salt.
3. Place the corn on a smoker and smoke for about 1 hour 15 minutes.
4. Remove from the smoker and serve.
5. Enjoy!

Nutrition:
Calories 180, Total fat 7g, Saturated fat 4g, Total Carbs 31g, Net Carbs 27g, protein 5g, Sugars 5g, Fiber 4g, Sodium 23mg, Potassium 416mg

396. Pit boss Smoked Vegetables.

Preparation Time: 5 Minutes
Cooking Time: 20 Minutes
Servings: 4
Ingredients
- 1 head of broccoli
- 4 carrots
- 16 oz snow peas
- 1 tbsp olive oil
- 1 cup mushrooms, chopped.
- 1-1/2 tbsp pepper
- 1 tbsp garlic powder

Directions:
1. Cut broccoli and carrots into bite-size pieces. Add snow peas and combine.
2. Toss the veggies with oil and seasoning.
3. Now cover a pan, sheet, with parchment paper. Place veggies on top.
4. Meanwhile, set your wood pellet smoker to 180°F.
5. Place the pan into the smoker. Smoke for about 5 minutes.
6. Adjust smoker temperature to 400°F and continue cooking for another 10-15 minutes until slightly brown broccoli tips.
7. Remove, Serve, and enjoy.

Nutrition:
Calories 111, Total fat 4g, Saturated fat 1g, Total Carbs 15g, Net Carbs 9g, Protein 5g, Sugars 7g, Fiber 6g, Sodium 0mg, Potassium 109mg

397. Pit boss Smashed Potato Casserole 1

Preparation Time: 30-45 minutes
Cooking Time: 45-60 minutes
Servings: 8
Recommended pellet: Optional
Ingredients:

- 8-10 bacon slices
- ¼ cup (½ stick) salt butter or bacon grease
- 1 sliced red onion
- 1 sliced small pepper
- 1 sliced small red pepper
- 1 sliced small pepper
- 3 cups mashed potatoes.
- ¾ cup sour cream
- 1.5 teaspoon Texas BBQ Love
- 3 cups of sharp cheddar cheese
- 4 cups hashed brown potato.

Directions:

1. Cook the bacon in a large skillet over medium heat until both sides are crispy for about 5 minutes. Set the bacon aside.
2. Transfer the rendered bacon grease to a glass container.
3. In the same large frying pan, heat the butter or bacon grease over medium heat and fry the red onions and peppers until they become al dente. Set aside.
4. Spray a 9 x 11-inch casserole dish with a non-stick cooking spray and spread the mashed potatoes to the bottom of the dish.
5. Layer sour cream on mashed potatoes and season with Texas BBQ Love.
6. Layer the stir-fried vegetables on the potatoes and pour butter or bacon grease into a pan.
7. Sprinkle 1.5 cups of sharp cheddar cheese followed by frozen hash brown potatoes.
8. Spoon the remaining butter or bacon grease from the stir-fried vegetables over the hash browns and place the crushed bacon.
9. Place the remaining 1.5 cups of sharp cheddar cheese and cover the casserole dish with a lid or aluminum foil.
10. Using the selected pellets, set up a wood pellet smoking grill for indirect cooking and preheat to 350 ° F.
11. Bake the crushed potato casserole for 45-60 minutes until the cheese foams.
12. Rest for 10 minutes before eating.

Nutrition: Calories 77, Total fat 1g, Saturated fat 1g, Total carbs 17g, Net carbs 15g, Protein 3g, Sugars 6g, Fiber 2g, Sodium 14mg, Potassium 243mg

398. Mushrooms Stuffed with Crab Meat

Preparation Time: 20 minutes
Cooking Time: 30-45 minutes
Servings: 4-6
Recommended pellet: Optional
Ingredients:

- 6 medium-sized portobello mushrooms
- Extra virgin olive oil
- 1/3 Grated parmesan cheese cup
- Club Beat Staffing:
- 8 oz fresh crab meat or canned or imitation crab meat
- 2 tablespoons extra virgin olive oil
- 1/3 Chopped celery.
- Chopped red peppers.
- ½ cup chopped green onion.
- ½ cup Italian breadcrumbs
- ½Cup mayonnaise
- 8 oz cream cheese at room temperature
- 1/2 teaspoon of garlic
- 1 tablespoon dried parsley
- Grated parmesan cheese cup
- 1 1 teaspoon of Old Bay seasoning
- ¼ teaspoon of kosher salt
- ¼ teaspoon black pepper

Directions:

1. Clean the mushroom cap with a damp paper towel. Cut off the stem and save it.
2. Remove the brown gills from the bottom of the mushroom cap with a spoon and discard.
3. Prepare crab meat stuffing. If you are using canned crab meat, drain, rinse, and remove shellfish.
4. Heat the olive oil in a frying pan over medium high heat. Add celery, peppers and green onions and fry for 5 minutes. Set aside for cooling.
5. Gently pour the chilled sauteed vegetables and the remaining ingredients into a large bowl.
6. Cover and refrigerate crab meat stuffing until ready to use.
7. Put the crab mixture in each mushroom cap and make a mound in the center.
8. Sprinkle extra virgin olive oil and sprinkle parmesan cheese on each stuffed mushroom cap. Put the mushrooms in a 10 x 15-inch baking dish.
9. Use the pellets to set the wood pellet smoker grill to indirect heating and preheat to 375 ° F.
10. Bake for 30-45 minutes until the filling becomes hot (165 degrees Fahrenheit as measured by an instant-read digital thermometer) and the mushrooms begin to release juice.

Nutrition: Calories 77, Total fat 1g, Saturated fat 1g, Total carbs 17g, Net carbs 15g, Protein 3g, Sugars 6g, Fiber 2g, Sodium 14mg, Potassium 243mg

399. Bacon Wrapped with Asparagus

Preparation Time: 15 minutes
Cooking Time: 25-30 minutes
Servings: 4-6
Recommended pellet: Optional
- 1-pound fresh thick asparagus (15-20 spears)
- Extra virgin olive oil
- 5 sliced bacon
- 1 teaspoon of Western Love or salted pepper

Directions:
1. Cut off the wooden ends of the asparagus and make them all the same length.
2. Divide the asparagus into a bundle of three spears and split with olive oil. Wrap each bundle with a piece of bacon, then dust with seasonings or salt pepper for seasoning.
3. Set the wood pellet smoker grill for indirect cooking and place a Teflon coated fiberglass mat on the grate (to prevent asparagus from sticking to the grate grate). Preheat to 400 degrees Fahrenheit using all types of pellets. The grill can be preheated during asparagus Preparation Guide.
4. Bake the asparagus wrapped in bacon for 25-30 minutes until the asparagus is soft and the bacon is cooked and crispy.

Nutrition: Calories 77, Total fat 1g, Saturated fat 1g, Total carbs 17g, Net carbs 15g, Protein 3g, Sugars 6g, Fiber 2g, Sodium 14mg, Potassium 243mg

400. Bacon Cheddar Slider

Preparation Time: 30 minutes
Cooking Time: 15 minutes
Servings: 6-10 (1-2 sliders each as an appetizer)
Recommended pellet: Optional
Ingredients:
- 1-pound ground beef (80% lean)
- 1/2 teaspoon of garlic salt
- 1/2 teaspoon salt
- 1/2 teaspoon of garlic
- 1/2 teaspoon onion
- 1/2 teaspoon black pepper
- 6 bacon slices cut in half.
- ½Cup mayonnaise
- 2 teaspoons of creamy wasabi (optional)
- 6 (1 oz) sliced sharp cheddar cheese, cut in half (optional)
- Sliced red onion.
- ½Cup sliced kosher dill pickles.
- 12 mini breads sliced horizontally.
- Ketchup

Directions:
1. Place ground beef, garlic salt, seasoned salt, garlic powder, onion powder and black hope pepper in a medium bowl.

2. Divide the meat mixture into 12 equal parts, shape into small thin round patties (about 2 ounces each) and save.
3. Cook the bacon on medium heat over medium heat for 5-8 minutes until crunchy. Set aside.
4. To make the sauce, mix the mayonnaise and horseradish in a small bowl, if used.
5. Set up a wood pellet smoker grill for direct cooking to use griddle accessories. Contact the manufacturer to see if there is a griddle accessory that works with the wooden pellet smoker grill.
6. Spray a cooking spray on the griddle cooking surface for best non-stick results.
7. Preheat wood pellet smoker grill to 350 ° F using selected pellets. Griddle surface should be approximately 400 ° F.
8. Grill the putty for 3-4 minutes each until the internal temperature reaches 160 ° F.
9. If necessary, place a sharp cheddar cheese slice on each patty while the patty is on the griddle or after the patty is removed from the griddle. Place a small amount of mayonnaise mixture, a slice of red onion, and a hamburger pate in the lower half of each roll. Pickled slices, bacon, and ketchup.

Nutrition: Calories 77, Total fat 1g, Saturated fat 1g, Total carbs 17g, Net carbs 15g, Protein 3g, Sugars 6g, Fiber 2g, Sodium 14mg, Potassium 243mg

401. Garlic Parmesan Wedge

Preparation Time: 15 minutes
Cooking Time: 30-35 minutes
Servings: 3
Recommended pellet: Optional
- 3 large russet potatoes
- ¼ cup of extra virgin olive oil
- 1 tsp salt
- ¾ teaspoon black hu pepper
- 2 tsp garlic powder
- ¾ cup grated parmesan cheese.
- 3 tablespoons of fresh coriander or flat leaf parsley (optional)
- ½ cup blue cheese or ranch dressing per serving, for soaking (optional)

Directions:
1. Gently rub the potatoes with cold water using a vegetable brush to dry the potatoes.
2. Cut the potatoes in half vertically and cut them in half.
3. Wipe off any water released when cutting potatoes with a paper towel. Moisture prevents wedges from becoming crunchy.
4. Put the potato wedge, olive oil, salt, pepper, and garlic powder in a large bowl and shake lightly by hand to distribute the oil and spices evenly.

5. Place the wedges on a single layer of non-stick grill tray / pan / basket (about 15 x 12 inches).
6. Set the wood pellet r grill for indirect cooking and use all types of wood pellets to preheat to 425 degrees Fahrenheit.
7. Put the grill tray in the preheated smoker grill, roast the potato wedge for 15 minutes, and turn. Roast the potato wedge for an additional 15-20 minutes until the potatoes are soft inside and crispy golden on the outside.
8. Sprinkle potato wedge with parmesan cheese and add coriander or parsley as needed. If necessary, add blue cheese or ranch dressing for the dip.

Nutrition: Calories 87, Total fat 1g, Saturated fat 2g, Total carbs 27g, Net carbs 15g, Protein 3g, Sugars 6g, Fiber 2g, Sodium 14mg, Potassium 143mg

402. Roasted Vegetables

Preparation Time: 20 Minutes
Cooking Time: 20 to 40 Minutes
Servings: 4
Ingredients:
- 1 cup cauliflower floret
- 1 cup small mushroom, half
- One medium zucchini sliced in half.
- One medium yellow squash sliced in half.
- One medium-sized red pepper chopped to 1.5-2 inches.
- One small red onion chopped to 1½-2 inch.
- 6 ounces small baby carrot
- Six mid-stem asparagus spears cut into 1-inch pieces.
- 1 cup cherry or grape tomato
- ¼ Extra virgin olive oil with cup roasted garlic flavor.
- 2 tbsp. of balsamic vinegar
- Three garlic, chopped.
- 1 tsp. dry time
- 1 tsp. dried oregano
- One teaspoon of garlic salt
- ½ teaspoon black pepper

Directions:
1. Put cauliflower florets, mushrooms, zucchini, yellow pumpkin, red peppers, red onions, carrots, asparagus, and tomatoes in a large bowl.
2. Add olive oil, balsamic vinegar, garlic, thyme, oregano, garlic salt, and black hu to add to the vegetables.
3. Gently throw the vegetables by hand until completely covered with olive oil, herbs, and spices.
4. Spread the seasoned vegetables evenly on a non-stick grill tray/bread/basket (about 15 x 12 inches).
5. Set the wood pellet smoker and grill for indirect cooking and preheat to 425 degrees Fahrenheit using all wood pellets.

6. Transfer the grill tray to a preheated smoker and grill and roast the vegetables for 20-40 minutes or until the vegetables are perfectly cooked. Please put it out immediately.

Nutrition: Calories: 114 Carbs: 17g Fat: 4g Protein: 3g

403. Smoked Cashews

Preparation Time: 5 minutes
Cooking Time: 1 hour
Servings: 4 to 6
Ingredients:
- 1 pound (454 g) roasted, salted cashews.

Directions:
1. Supply your smoker with wood pellets and follow the manufacturer's specific start-up procedure. Preheat the grill, with the lid closed to 120°F (49°C).
2. Pour the cashews onto a rimmed baking sheet and smoke for 1 hour, stirring once about halfway through the smoking time.
3. Remove the cashews from the grill, let cool, and store in an airtight container for as long as you can resist.

Nutrition: Calories: 57 Total Fat: 3 g Saturated Fat: 1 g Total Carbs: 6 g Net Carbs: 4 g Protein: 4 g Sugars: 2 g Fiber: 2 g Sodium: 484 mg

404. Easy Eggs

Preparation Time: 10 minutes
Cooking Time: 30 minutes
Servings: 12
Ingredients
- 12 hardboiled eggs peeled and rinsed.

Directions:
1. Supply your smoker with wood pellets and follow the manufacturer's specific start-up procedure. Preheat the grill, with the lid closed to 120°F (49°C).
2. Place the eggs directly on the grill grate and smoke for 30 minutes. They will begin to take on a slight brown sheen.
3. Remove the eggs and refrigerate for at least 30 minutes before serving. Refrigerate any leftovers in an airtight container for 1 or 2 weeks.

Nutrition: Calories: 57 Total Fat: 3 g Saturated Fat: 1 g Total Carbs: 6 g Net Carbs: 4 g Protein: 4 g Sugars: 2 g Fiber: 2 g Sodium: 484 mg

405. Cheese with Crackers

Preparation Time: 5 minutes
Cooking Time: 2½ hours
Servings: 4
Ingredients:
- 1 (2-pounds / 907-g) block medium Cheddar cheese, or your favorite cheese, quartered lengthwise.

Directions:

1. Supply your smoker with wood pellets and follow the manufacturer's specific start-up procedure. Preheat the grill, with the lid closed to 90°F (32°C).
2. Place the cheese directly on the grill grate and smoke for 2 hours, 30 minutes, checking frequently to be sure it is not melting. If the cheese begins to melt, try flipping it. If that does not help, remove it from the grill and refrigerate for about 1 hour and then return it to the cold smoker.
3. Remove the cheese, place it in a zip-top bag, and refrigerate overnight.
4. Slice the cheese and serve with crackers or grate it and use for making a smoked mac and cheese.

Nutrition: Calories: 57 Total Fat: 3 g Saturated Fat: 1 g Total Carbs: 6 g Net Carbs: 4 g Protein: 4 g Sugars: 2 g Fiber: 2 g Sodium: 484 mg

406. Bacon and Crab Cheese Poppers

Preparation Time: 20 minutes
Cooking Time: 30 to 40 minutes
Servings: 6 to 8
Ingredients:

- 12 large jalapeño peppers
- 8 ounces (227 g) cream cheese, at room temperature
- Finely grated zest of 1 lemon
- 1 teaspoon Old Bay seasoning, or to taste.
- 8 ounces (227 g) crab meat, drained, picked over, and finely shredded or chopped.
- Sweet or smoked paprika, for sprinkling.
- 12 strips artisanal bacon cut crosswise in half.

Directions:

- Set up your smoker following the manufacturer's instructions and preheat to 350°F (177°C). (Yes, I know this is hotter than the conventional low and slow method—it gives you crisper bacon.) Add the wood as specified by the manufacturer.
- Cut each jalapeño in half lengthwise, cutting through the stem and leaving it in place. Scrape out the seeds and veins; a grapefruit spoon or melon baller works well for this. Arrange the jalapeño halves on a wire rack, cut side up.
- Place the cream cheese in a mixing bowl. Add the lemon zest and Old Bay seasoning and beat with a wooden spoon until light. Gently fold in the crab. Spoon a heaping tablespoon of crab mixture into each jalapeño half, mounding it toward the center. Sprinkle with paprika.
- Wrap each jalapeño half with a strip of bacon (you want the filling exposed at each end). Secure the bacon with a toothpick and arrange the poppers in a single layer on the wire rack.

- Place the wire rack in the smoker. Smoke the poppers until the bacon and filling are browned and the peppers are tender (squeeze them between your thumb and forefinger), 30 to 40 minutes.
- Transfer the poppers to a platter. Let cool slightly before serving.

Nutrition: Calories: 57 Total Fat: 3 g Saturated Fat: 1 g Total Carbs: 6 g Net Carbs: 4 g Protein: 4 g Sugars: 2 g Fiber: 2 g Sodium: 484 mg

407. Honey Bread

Preparation Time: 10 minutes
Cooking Time: 1½ to 2 hours
Servings: 1 loaf
Ingredients:

- 2 cups unbleached all-purpose white flour or as needed.
- 1 cup whole wheat flour or 1 additional cup white flour
- 1 teaspoon coarse salt (sea or kosher), plus extra for sprinkling
- 1¼ cups water, plus extra as needed.
- 1 envelope (2½ teaspoons) dry yeast
- 2 tablespoons honey
- 1 tablespoon extra-virgin olive oil, plus oil for the bowl, loaf pan, and top of the bread

Directions:

1. Set up your smoker following the manufacturer's instructions and preheat it as low as it will go (200°F (93°C) or below). Spread out the flours and salt in a thin layer (not more than ¼ inch thick) in an aluminum foil pan or on a rimmed baking sheet. Place the water in another foil pan.
2. Place the pans in the smoker and smoke until the white flour is lightly browned on the surface and tastes smoky and the water tastes smoky. Total smoking time is 15 to 20 minutes for hot-smoking or 1 to 1½ hours for cold-smoking.
3. Let the flours cool to room temperature. The water should only cool to warm 105°F (41°C).
4. Place the smoked flours, smoked salt, and yeast in a food processor and process to mix. Add the honey, olive oil, and the smoked warm water. Process in short bursts to obtain a soft, pliable dough. If the dough is too stiff, add a little warmer tap water; if too soft, add a little more flour. Alternatively, you can mix and knead the dough by hand or in a stand mixer fitted with a dough hook. Turn the dough onto a lightly floured cutting board and knead by hand into a smooth ball.
5. Place the dough in a large lightly oiled bowl, turning it to oil both sides. Cover with plastic wrap and let the dough rise in a warm spot until doubled in bulk, 1 to 1½ hours.

6. Punch down the dough, knead it into an oblong shape, and place it in an oiled loaf pan. Cover with plastic wrap. Let the dough rise again until doubled in bulk, 30 minutes to 1 hour.

7. Meanwhile, set up a grill for indirect grilling and preheat to 400°F (204°C) or preheat your oven to 400°F (204°C). If your smoker goes up to 400°F (204°C), you can bake the bread in it. No need to add wood—you have already smoked the flour.

8. Brush the top of the loaf with a little more olive oil and sprinkle with a little salt. Bake the loaf until the top is browned and firm and the bottom sounds hollow when tapped, 30 to 40 minutes. Transfer the loaf pan to a wire rack and let cool for 10 minutes. Remove the bread from the pan, cool for 10 minutes more, slice crosswise and serve warm. Serve with the smoked butter and smoked honey.

Nutrition:
Calories: 20
Carbs: 5g
Protein: 1g

408. Tomato and Cucumber Gazpacho

Preparation Time: 30 minutes
Cooking Time: 1 hour
Servings: 4
Ingredients:
- 4 luscious red ripe tomatoes (about 2 pounds / 907 g) cut in half widthwise.
- 1 medium-size cucumber, peeled, cut in half lengthwise, seeds scraped out.
- ½ green or yellow bell pepper, stemmed, seeded, and cut into 2 pieces.
- ½ red bell pepper, stemmed, seeded, and cut into 2 pieces.
- 1 small, sweet onion peeled and cut lengthwise in quarters.
- 1 clove garlic, peeled.
- 3 tablespoons good extra virgin olive oil, plus extra for drizzling
- About 2 tablespoons red wine or Spanish sherry vinegar
- ½ cup water, plus extra as needed.
- Coarse salt (sea or kosher) and freshly ground black pepper, to taste.
- 1 tablespoon chopped fresh chives or scallion greens.

Directions:
1. Arrange the tomatoes, cucumber, peppers, and onion, cut side up, in an aluminum foil pan. Add the garlic.
2. Set up your smoker for cold smoking, following the manufacturer's instructions. Add the wood as specified by the manufacturer.

3. Place the vegetables in the smoker. Smoke until bronzed with smoke (dip your finger in one cut tomato—the juices should taste smoky), 1 hour, or as needed. The vegetables should remain raw.

4. Cut the vegetables into 1-inch pieces, reserving the juices. Place in a food processor and process to a coarse or smooth puree (your choice). Gradually add the reserved juices, oil, vinegar, and enough water (about ½ cup) to make a pourable soup. Work in salt and pepper to taste, plus a few more drops of vinegar if needed to balance the sweetness of the vegetables. Alternatively, place the vegetables and their juices, oil, vinegar, and water in a blender and blend to your preferred consistency. Season with salt, pepper, and more vinegar. The gazpacho can be made several hours ahead to this stage, covered, and refrigerated, but taste and re-season it before serving.

5. Ladle the gazpacho into serving bowls. Drizzle additional olive oil on top and sprinkle with the chopped chives.

Nutrition: Calories: 57 Total Fat: 3 g Saturated Fat: 1 g Total Carbs: 6 g Net Carbs: 4 g Protein: 4 g Sugars: 2 g Fiber: 2 g Sodium: 484 mg

409. Chicken Livers with White Wine

Preparation Time: 15 minutes
Cooking Time: 30 to 40 minutes
Servings: 4
Ingredients:
- 1 pound (454 g) chicken or turkey livers
- 1 cup hot water
- 1½ tablespoons coarse salt (sea or kosher)
- 1 teaspoon black peppercorns
- ½ teaspoon fresh or dried thyme leaves
- 1 cup ice water
- ½ cup dry white wine
- Vegetable oil, for oiling the rack.
- About 1 tablespoon extra-virgin olive oil
- 1 tablespoon butter or bacon fat, for pan-frying (optional)

Directions:
1. Trim any green or bloody spots off the livers.
2. Make the brine: Place the hot water, salt, peppercorns, and thyme in a deep bowl and whisk until the salt dissolves. Whisk in the ice water and wine. When the mixture is cold, stir in the chicken livers. Brine, covered, in the refrigerator for 3 hours.
3. Drain the livers in a colander and blot dry with paper towels. Oil a wire rack and arrange the livers on it. Let dry in the refrigerator for 30 minutes. Lightly brush the livers with olive oil on both sides.
4. Meanwhile, set up your smoker following the manufacturer's instructions and preheat to

300°F (149°C). Add the wood as specified by the manufacturer.

5. Place the rack in the smoker and smoke the livers until cooked to taste, 30 to 40 minutes for pink in the center. (Make a slit in one of the livers to check for doneness.) Do not overcook.

6. You can serve the livers hot from the smoker. To add a little crunch to the exterior, melt the butter in a large skillet over high heat. Pan-fry the livers until seared and crusty, 1 to 2 minutes per side.

Nutrition: Calories: 57 Total Fat: 3 g Saturated Fat: 1 g Total Carbs: 6 g Net Carbs: 4 g Protein: 4 g Sugars: 2 g Fiber: 2 g Sodium: 484 mg

410. Chicken and Bean Cheese Nachos

Preparation Time: 20 minutes
Cooking Time: 12 to 15 minutes
Servings: 6 to 8
Ingredients:

- 8 cups tortilla chips
- 2 cups shredded smoked brisket or chicken.
- 1 can (15 ounces / 425 g) black beans (preferably organic and low sodium), drained well in a colander, rinsed, and drained again.
- 12 ounces (340 g) finely grated mixed cheeses (like Cheddar, smoked Cheddar, Jack, and/or pepper Jack; about 3 cups)
- 4 fresh jalapeño peppers stemmed and thinly sliced crosswise, or 1/3 cup drained pickled jalapeño slices.
- 4 scallions, trimmed, white and green parts thinly sliced crosswise.
- 2 to 4 tablespoons of your favorite hot sauce (I like Cholula) or barbecue sauce.
- ¼ cup coarsely chopped fresh cilantro (optional)

Directions:

1. Set up your smoker following the manufacturer's instructions and preheat to 275°F (135°C). Add the wood as specified by the manufacturer.

2. Loosely arrange one third of the tortilla chips in the grill skillet. Sprinkle one third of the shredded brisket, beans, cheese, jalapeños, and scallions on top. Shake on hot sauce. Add a second layer of these ingredients, followed by a third.

3. Place the skillet with the nachos in your smoker and smoke until the cheese is melted and bubbling, 12 to 15 minutes.

4. Sprinkle the cilantro on top, if using, and dig in. Yes—you eat the nachos right out of the skillet, so be careful not to burn your fingers on the rim.

5. Smoked Nachos on the Grill

6. Set up the grill for indirect grilling and preheat to medium-high 400°F (204°C).

Place the nachos pan on the grate away from the heat and toss the wood chips on the coals. Indirect grill until the cheese is melted and bubbling, 5 minutes.

Nutrition: Calories: 57 Total Fat: 3 g Saturated Fat: 1 g Total Carbs: 6 g Net Carbs: 4 g Protein: 4 g Sugars: 2 g Fiber: 2 g Sodium: 484 mg

411. Butter Chicken Wings with Peanuts

Preparation Time: 15 minutes
Cooking Time: ½ to 2 hours
Servings: 4 to 6
Ingredients:

- 3 pounds (1.4 kg) chicken wings (about 24 pieces)
- ½ cup finely chopped fresh cilantro.
- 2 teaspoons coarse salt (sea or kosher)
- 2 teaspoons cracked black peppercorns.
- 2 teaspoons ground coriander (optional)
- 2 tablespoons Asian (dark) sesame oil
- Vegetable oil, for oiling the rack.
- 6 tablespoons (¾ stick) butter
- 4 jalapeño peppers, thinly sliced crosswise (leave the seeds in)
- 6 tablespoons sriracha (or other favorite hot sauce)
- ¼ cup chopped dry-roasted peanuts.

Directions:

1. Place the chicken wings in a large bowl. Sprinkle in ¼ cup of the cilantro, the salt, pepper, and coriander, if using, and stir to mix. Stir in the sesame oil. Cover the bowl and marinate, refrigerated, for 15 to 60 minutes (the longer they marinate, the richer the flavor).

2. Meanwhile, set up your smoker following the manufacturer's instructions and preheat to 375°F (191°C). (If your smoker's incapable of reaching that temperature, preheat as hot as the smoker will go.) Add the wood as specified by the manufacturer.

3. Oil the smoker rack and arrange the drumettes on it. Smoke the wings until sizzling, brown with smoke, and cooked through, 30 to 50 minutes. At lower temperatures, for example, at 250°F (121°C), you will need 1½ to 2 hours. In some smokers, the piece's closest to the fire will cook faster; if this is the case, rotate the pieces so all cook evenly. To check for doneness, make a tiny cut in the thickest part of a few of the wings. The meat at the bone should be white, with no traces of red. Do not overcook. Arrange the wings on a heatproof platter.

4. Just before serving, melt the butter in a cast-iron skillet on the stove over high heat. Add the jalapeños and cook until they sizzle and start to brown, 3 minutes. Stir in the sriracha and bring to a boil. Pour over the chicken.

5. Sprinkle the chicken with the peanuts and the remaining ¼ cup cilantro and serve at once with plenty of napkins.

Nutrition: Calories: 57 Total Fat: 3 g Saturated Fat: 1 g Total Carbs: 6 g Net Carbs: 4 g Protein: 4 g Sugars: 2 g Fiber: 2 g Sodium: 484 mg

412. Tomato and Corn Salsa with Lime

Preparation Time: 15 minutes
Cooking Time: 15 to 20 minutes
Servings: 6 to 8
Ingredients.

- 4 luscious ripe red tomatoes (about 2 pounds / 907 g) cut in half widthwise.
- 4 jalapeño peppers, stemmed and cut in half lengthwise (seeded for a milder salsa; seeds left in for hotter)
- 2 ears sweet corn, shucked.
- 1 small, sweet onion peeled and quartered.
- ½ cup chopped fresh cilantro.
- ¼ cup fresh lime juice (2 to 3 limes), or to taste.
- Coarse salt (sea or kosher), to taste
- Tortilla chips, for serving.

Directions:
1. Set up your smoker following the manufacturer's instructions and preheat to 225°F (107°C). Add the wood as specified by the manufacturer.
2. Place the tomatoes and jalapeños (both cut side up), corn, and onion in the smoker. Smoke the vegetables long enough to impart a smoke flavor (but not so long that you cook them), 15 to 20 minutes. Transfer the vegetables to a platter and let cool to room temperature.
3. Lay the corn flat on a cutting board and slice the kernels off the cob using broad strokes of a chef's knife. Transfer the corn kernels to a large bowl.
4. Coarsely chop the tomatoes, jalapeños, and onion by hand or in a food processor. Add to the corn and stir in the cilantro, lime juice, and salt to taste. The salsa should be highly seasoned. Transfer the salsa to a serving bowl. Serve with chips alongside.

Nutrition: Calories: 57 Total Fat: 3 g Saturated Fat: 1 g Total Carbs: 6 g Net Carbs: 4 g Protein: 4 g Sugars: 2 g Fiber: 2 g Sodium: 484 mg

413. Camembert with Pepper Jelly

Preparation Time: 10 minutes
Cooking Time: 10 minutes
Servings: 4
Ingredients.

- 1 Camembert or small Brie cheese (8 ounces / 227 g)
- 3 tablespoons pepper jelly, tomato jam, or apricot jam

- 1 large jalapeño pepper stemmed and thinly sliced crosswise.
- Grilled or toasted baguette slices or favorite crackers, for serving.

Directions:
1. Set up your grill for smoke-roasting and preheat to medium-high 400°F (204°C).
2. If you are charring the plank (this step is optional, but it gives you a lot more flavor), place it directly over the fire and grill until singed on both sides, 1 to 2 minutes per side. Set aside and let cool.
3. Place the cheese in the center of the plank. Spread the top with pepper jelly using the back of a spoon. Shingle the jalapeño slices on top so they overlap in a decorative pattern.
4. Place the plank on the grill away from the heat and toss the wood chips or chunks on the coals. Smoke-roast the cheese until the sides are soft and beginning to bulge, 6 to 10 minutes.
5. Serve the cheese on the plank, hot off the grill, with a basket of grilled baguette slices or your favorite crackers.

Nutrition: Calories: 57 Total Fat: 3 g Saturated Fat: 1 g Total Carbs: 6 g Net Carbs: 4 g Protein: 4 g Sugars: 2 g Fiber: 2 g Sodium: 484 mg

414. Homemade Cheese

Preparation Time: 5 minutes
Cooking Time: 2 to 4 minutes
Servings: 2 to 3
Ingredients:

- Vegetable oil, for oiling the grate.
- 1 ball (8 to 12 ounces / 227 to 340 g) fresh Mozzarella patted dry.
- Extra virgin olive oil (optional)
- Coarse salt (sea or kosher) or fleur de sell, to taste (optional)

Directions:
1. Place a small mound of charcoal in the smoker firebox or to one side of a kettle grill and light it. Brush and oil the grate. When the coals glow red, place the cheese in the smoke chamber (or on the side of the kettle grill opposite the embers), as far away as possible from the fire. Toss the hay on the coals and close the smoker or cover the grill. Smoke the cheese until it is colored with smoke (but not long enough to melt it), 2 to 4 minutes.
2. Slide a spatula under the cheese and transfer it to a plate to cool. Do not grab it when hot, or the deposit of smoke will come off on your fingers. Serve once it has cooled to room temperature or refrigerate until serving. (For maximum flavor, let the cheese warm to room temperature before serving.) Drizzle with olive oil and/or salt, if desired, and serve.

Nutrition: Calories: 57 Total Fat: 3 g Saturated Fat: 1 g Total Carbs: 6 g Net Carbs: 4 g Protein: 4 g Sugars: 2 g Fiber: 2 g Sodium: 484 mg

415. Syrupy Bacon Pig Pops

Preparation Time: 15 minutes
Cooking Time: 25 to 30 minutes
Servings: 24
Ingredients:

- Nonstick cooking spray, oil, or butter, for greasing
- 2 pounds (907 g) thick-cut bacon (24 slices)
- 24 metal skewers
- 1 cup packed light brown sugar.
- 2 to 3 teaspoons cayenne pepper
- ½ cup maple syrup, divided.

Directions:

1. Supply your smoker with wood pellets and follow the manufacturer's specific start-up procedure. Preheat, with the lid closed to 350°F (177°C).
2. Coat a disposable aluminum foil baking sheet with cooking spray, oil, or butter.
3. Thread each bacon slice onto a metal skewer and place on the prepared baking sheet.
4. In a medium bowl, stir together the brown sugar and cayenne.
5. Baste the top sides of the bacon with ¼ cup of maple syrup.
6. Sprinkle half of the brown sugar mixture over the bacon.
7. Place the baking sheet on the grill, close the lid, and smoke for 15 to 30 minutes.
8. Using tongs, flip the bacon skewers. Baste with the remaining ¼ cup of maple syrup and top with the remaining brown sugar mixture.
9. Continue smoking with the lid closed for 10 to 15 minutes, or until crispy. You can eyeball the bacon and smoke to your desired doneness, but the actual ideal internal temperature for bacon is 155°F (68°C) (if you want to try to get a thermometer into it—ha!).
10. Using tongs, carefully remove the bacon skewers from the grill. Let cool completely before handling.

Nutrition: Calories: 57 Total Fat: 3 g Saturated Fat: 1 g Total Carbs: 6 g Net Carbs: 4 g Protein: 4 g Sugars: 2 g Fiber: 2 g Sodium: 484 mg

416. Cheesy Sausage Balls

Preparation Time: 15 minutes
Cooking Time: 30 minutes
Servings: 4 to 5
Ingredients:

- 1 pound (454 g) ground hot sausage, uncooked
- 8 ounces (227 g) cream cheese, softened.
- 1 package mini filo dough shells

Directions:

1. Supply your smoker with wood pellets and follow the manufacturer's specific start-up procedure. Preheat, with the lid closed to 350°F (177°C).
2. In a large bowl, using your hands, thoroughly mix the sausage and cream cheese until well blended.

3. Place the filo dough shells on a rimmed perforated pizza pan or into a mini muffin tin.
4. Roll the sausage and cheese mixture into 1-inch balls and place into the filo shells.
5. Place the pizza pan or mini muffin tin on the grill, close the lid, and smoke the sausage balls for 30 minutes, or until cooked through and the sausage is no longer pink.
6. Plate and serve warm.

Nutrition: Calories: 57 Total Fat: 3 g Saturated Fat: 1 g Total Carbs: 6 g Net Carbs: 4 g Protein: 4 g Sugars: 2 g Fiber: 2 g Sodium: 484 mg

417. Corn and Crab Cakes

Preparation Time: 25 minutes
Cooking Time: 10 minutes
Servings: 30 mini crab cakes
Ingredients

- Nonstick cooking spray, oil, or butter, for greasing
- 1 cup panko breadcrumbs, divided.
- 1 cup canned corn, drained
- ½ cup chopped scallions, divided.
- ½ red bell pepper, finely chopped.
- 16 ounces (454 g) jumbo lump crab meat
- ¾ cup mayonnaise, divided.
- 1 egg, beaten.
- 1 teaspoon salt
- 1 teaspoon freshly ground black pepper.
- 2 teaspoons cayenne pepper, divided.
- Juice of 1 lemon

Directions:

1. Supply your smoker with wood pellets and follow the manufacturer's specific start-up procedure. Preheat, with the lid closed to 425°F (218°C).
2. Spray three 12-cup mini muffin pans with cooking spray and divide ½ cup of the panko between 30 of the muffin cups, pressing into the bottoms and up the sides. (Work in batches, if necessary, depending on the number of pans you have.)
3. In a medium bowl, combine the corn, ¼ cup of scallions, the bell pepper, crab meat, half of the mayonnaise, the egg, salt, pepper, and 1 teaspoon of cayenne pepper.
4. Gently fold in the remaining ½ cup of breadcrumbs and divide the mixture between the prepared mini muffin cups.
5. Place the pans on the grill grate, close the lid, and smoke for 10 minutes, or until golden brown.
6. In a small bowl, combine the lemon juice and the remaining mayonnaise, scallions, and cayenne pepper to make a sauce.
7. Brush the tops of the mini crab cakes with the sauce and serve hot.

Nutrition: Calories: 57 Total Fat: 3 g Saturated Fat: 1 g Total Carbs: 6 g Net Carbs: 4 g Protein: 4 g Sugars: 2 g Fiber: 2 g Sodium: 484 mg

Chapter 13. <u>Snacks</u>

418. Corn Salsa

Preparation Time: 10 Minutes
Cooking Time: 15 Minutes
Servings: 4
Ingredients:

- 4 Ears Corn, large with the husk on
- 4 Tomatoes (Roma) diced and seeded.
- 1 tsp. of Onion powder
- 1 tsp. of Garlic powder
- 1 Onion, diced.
- ½ cup chopped Cilantro.
- Black pepper and salt to taste
- 1 lime, the juice
- 1 grille jalapeno, diced.

Directions:
1. Preheat the grill to 450F.
2. Place the ears corn on the grate and cook until charred. Remove husk. Cut into kernels.
3. Combine all ingredients, plus the corn and mix well. Refrigerate before serving.
4. Enjoy!
Nutrition: Calories: 120 Protein: 2f Carbs: 4g Fat: 1g

419. Nut Mix on the Grill.

Preparation Time: 15 Minutes
Cooking Time: 20 Minutes
Servings: 8
Ingredients:

- 3 cups Mixed Nuts, salted
- 1 tsp. Thyme, dried
- 1 ½ tbsp. brown sugar, packed.
- 1 tbsp. Olive oil
- ¼ tsp. of Mustard powder
- ¼ tsp. Cayenne pepper

Directions:
1. Preheat the grill to 250F with closed lid.
2. In a bowl combine the ingredients and place the nuts on a baking tray lined with parchment paper. Place the try on the grill. Cook 20 minutes.
3. Serve and enjoy!
Nutrition: Calories: 65 Protein: 23g Carbs 4g: Fat: 52g

420. Grilled French Dip

Preparation Time: 15 Minutes
Cooking Time: 35 Minutes
Servings: 8 to 12
Ingredients:

- 3 lbs. onions, thinly sliced (yellow)
- 2 tbsp. oil
- 2 tbsp. of Butter
- Salt to taste
- Black pepper to taste
- 1 tsp. Thyme, chopped.
- 2 tsp. of Lemon juice
- 1 cup Mayo
- 1 cup of Sour cream

Directions:
1. Preheat the grill to high with closed lid.
2. In a pan combine the oil and butter. Place on the grill to melt. Add 2 tsp. salt and add the onions.
3. Stir well and close the lid of the grill. Cook 30 minutes stirring often.
4. Add the thyme. Cook for an additional 3 minutes. Set aside and add black pepper.
5. Once cooled add lemon juice, mayo, and sour cream. Stir to combine. Taste and add more black pepper and salt if needed.
6. Serve with veggies or chips. Enjoy!
Nutrition: Calories: 60 Protein: 4g Carbs: 5g Fat: 6g

421. Roasted Cashews

Preparation Time: 15 Minutes
Cooking Time: 12 Minutes
Servings: 6
Ingredients:

- ¼ cup Rosemary, chopped.
- 2 ½ tbsp. Butter, melted.
- 2 cups Cashews, raw
- ½ tsp. of Cayenne pepper
- 1 tsp. of salt

Directions:
1. Preheat the grill to 350F with closed lid.
2. In a baking dish layer the nuts. Combine the cayenne, salt rosemary, and butter. Add on top. Toss to combine.
3. Grill for 12 minutes.
4. Serve and enjoy!
Nutrition: Calories: 150 Proteins: 5g Carbs: 7g Fat: 15g

422. Smoked Jerky

Preparation Time: 20 Minutes
Cooking Time: 6 Hours
Servings: 6 to 8
Ingredients:

- 1 Flank Steak (3lb.)
- ½ cup of Brown Sugar
- 1 cup of Bourbon
- ¼ cup Jerky rub
- 2 tbsp. of Worcestershire sauce
- 1 can of Chipotle
- ½ cup Cider Vinegar

Directions:
1. Slice the steak into ¼ inch slices.
2. Combine the remaining ingredients in a bowl. Stir well.
3. Place the steak in a plastic bag and add the marinade sauce. Marinade in the fridge overnight.
4. Preheat the grill to 180F with closed lid.
5. Remove the flank from marinade. Place directly on a rack and on the grill.

6. Smoke for 6 hours.

7. Cover them lightly for 1 hour before serving. Store leftovers in the fridge.

Nutrition: Calories: 105 Protein: 14g Carbs 4g: Fat: 3g

423. Bacon BBQ Bites

Preparation Time: 10 Minutes
Cooking Time: 30 Minutes
Servings: 4
Ingredients:

- 1 tbsp. Fennel, ground
- ½ cup of Brown Sugar
- 1 lb. Slab Bacon, cut into cubes (1 inch)
- 1 tsp. Black pepper
- Salt

Directions:

1. Take an aluminum foil and then fold in half. Once you do that, then turn the edges so that a rim is made. With a fork make small holes on the bottom. In this way, the excess fat will escape and will make the bites crispy.

2. Preheat the grill to 350F with closed lid.

3. In a bowl combine the black pepper, salt, fennel, and sugar. Stir.

4. Place the pork in the seasoning mixture. Toss to coat. Transfer on the foil.

5. Place the foil on the grill. Bake for 25 minutes, or until crispy and bubbly.

6. Serve and enjoy!

Nutrition: Calories: 300 Protein: 27g Carbs: 4g Fat: 36g

424. Smoked Guacamole

Preparation Time: 25 Minutes
Cooking Time: 30 Minutes
Servings: 6 to 8
Ingredients:

- ¼ cup chopped Cilantro.
- 7 Avocados peeled and seeded.
- ¼ cup chopped Onion, red.
- ¼ cup chopped tomato.
- 3 ears corn
- 1 tsp. of Chile Powder
- 1 tsp. of Cumin
- 2 tbsp. of Lime juice
- 1 tbsp. minced Garlic
- 1 Chile, poblano
- Black pepper and salt to taste

Directions:

1. Preheat the grill to 180F with closed lid.

2. Smoke the avocado for 10 min.

3. Set the avocados aside and increase the temperature of the girl to high.

4. Once heated grill the corn and chili. Roast for 20 minutes.

5. Cut the corn. Set aside. Place the chili in a bowl. Cover with a plastic wrap and let it sit for about 10 minutes. Peel the chili and dice. Add it to the kernels.

6. In a bowl mash the avocados, leave few chunks. Add the remaining ingredients and mix.

7. Serve right away because it is best eaten fresh. Enjoy!

Nutrition: Calories: 51 Protein: 1g Carbs: 3g Fat: 4.5g

425. Jalapeno Poppers

Preparation Time: 15 Minutes
Cooking Time: 60 Minutes
Servings: 4 to 6
Ingredients:

- 6 Bacon slices halved.
- 12 Jalapenos, medium
- 1 cup grated Cheese.
- 8 oz. softened Cream cheese.
- 2 tbsp. Poultry seasoning

Directions:

1. Preheat the grill to 180F with closed lid.

2. Cut the jalapenos lengthwise. Clean them from the ribs and seeds.

3. Mix the poultry seasoning, grated cheese, and cream cheese.

4. Fill each jalapeno with the mixture and wrap with 1 half bacon. Place a toothpick to secure it. Place them on a baking sheet and smoke and grill 20 minutes.

5. Increase the temperature of the grill to 375F. Cook for 30 minutes more.

6. Serve and enjoy!

Nutrition: Calories: 60 Protein: 4g Carbs: 2g Fat: 8g Pellet: Mesquite

426. Shrimp Cocktail

Preparation Time: 10 Minutes
Cooking Time: 20 Minutes
Servings: 2-4
Ingredients:

- 2 lbs. of Shrimp with tails, deveined.
- Black pepper and salt
- 1 tsp. of Old Bay
- 2 tbsp. Oil
- ½ cup of Ketchup
- 1 tbsp. of Lemon Juice
- 2 tbsp. Horseradish, Prepared.
- 1 tbsp. of Lemon juice
- For garnish: chopped parsley
- Optional: Hot sauce

Directions:

1. Preheat the grill to 350F with closed lid.

2. Clean the shrimp. Pat dry using paper towels.

3. In a bowl add the shrimp, Old Bay, and oil. Toss to coat. Spread on a baking tray. Place the tray on the grill and let it cook for 7 minutes.

4. In the meantime make the sauce: Combine the lemon juice, horseradish, and ketchup. Season with black pepper and sauce and if you like add hot sauce. Stir.

5. Serve the shrimp with the sauce and enjoy!

Nutrition: Calories: 80 Protein: 8g Carbs: 5g Fat: 1g Pellet: Mesquite

427. Deviled Eggs

Preparation Time: 15 Minutes
Cooking Time: 30 Minutes
Servings: 4 to 6
Ingredients:

- 3 tsp. diced chives
- 3 tbsp. Mayo
- 7 Eggs, hard - boiled, peeled.
- 1 tsp. Cider vinegar
- 1 tsp. Mustard, brown
- 1/8 tsp. Hot sauce
- 2 tbsp. crumbled Bacon
- Black pepper and salt to taste
- For dusting: Paprika

Directions:

1. Preheat the grill to 180F with closed lid.
2. Place the cooked eggs on the grate. Smoke 30 minutes. Set aside and let them cool.
3. Slice the eggs in half lengthwise. Scoop the yolks and transfer into a zip lock bag. Now add the black pepper, salt, hot sauce, vinegar, mustard, chives, and mayo. Close the bag and knead the ingredients until smooth.
4. Cut one corner and squeeze the mixture into the egg whites.
5. Top with bacon and dust with paprika.
6. Serve and enjoy! Or chill in the fridge until serving.

Nutrition: Calories: 140 Protein: 6g Carbs: 2g Fat: 6g
Pellet: Hickory

428. Smoked Summer Sausage

Preparation Time: 15 Minutes
Cooking Time: 4 Hours and 15 Minutes
Servings: 4 to 6
Ingredients:

- 1 ½ tsp. of Morton Salt
- ½ lb. Ground venison
- ½ lb. of ground Boar
- 1 tbsp. Salt
- ½ tsp. of mustard seeds
- ½ tsp. of Garlic powder
- ½ tsp. of Black pepper

Directions:

1. Add all ingredients into a bowl and mix until combined. Cover the bowl with a plastic bag and let it rest in the fridge overnight.
2. Form a log from the mixture and wrap with a plastic wrap. Twist the log's end tightly. Now unwrap carefully.
3. Preheat the grill to 225F with closed lit.
4. Grill the meat for 4 hours. Set aside and let it cool for 1 hour.
5. Once cooled wrap and store in the fridge.
6. Serve and enjoy!

Nutrition: Calories: 170 Protein: 8g Carbs: 0 Fat: 14g
Pellet: Apple

429. Roasted Tomatoes

Preparation Time: 10 Minutes
Cooking Time: 3 Hours
Servings: 2-4
Ingredients:

- 3 ripe Tomatoes, large
- 1 tbsp. black pepper
- 2 tbsp. Salt
- 2 tsp. Basil
- 2 tsp. of Sugar
- Oil

Directions:

1. Place a parchment paper on a baking sheet. Preheat the grill to 225F with closed lid.
2. Remove the stems from the tomatoes. Cut them into slices (1/2 inch).
3. In a bowl combine the basil, sugar, pepper, and salt. Mix well.
4. Pour oil on a plate. Dip the tomatoes (just one side) in the oil. Transfer on the Prepared baking sheet.
5. Dust each slice with the mixture.
6. Grill the tomatoes for 3 hours.
7. Serve and enjoy! (You can serve it with mozzarella pieces).

Nutrition: Calories: 40 Protein: 1g Carbs: 2g Fat: 3g
Pellet: Alder

430. Turkey Jerky

Preparation Time: 30 mins.
Cooking Time: 2 hrs. 30 mins.
Servings: 8
Ingredients:

- One T. Asian chili-garlic paste.
- One T. curing salt
- ½ c. soy sauce
- ¼ c. water
- Two T. honey
- Two T. lime juice
- Two pounds boneless, skinless turkey breast

Directions:

1. Mix the salt, water, lime juice, chili-garlic paste, honey, and soy sauce.
2. Slice the turkey into thin strips. Lay the slices into a large zip-top baggie. If there is more meat that can fit into one bag, use as many as you need. Pour marinade over the turkey.
3. Seal the bag and shake it around so that each slice gets coated with the marinade. Place the bag into the refrigerator overnight.
4. Add wood pellets to your smoker and follow your cooker's startup procedure. Preheat your smoker, with your lid closed, until it reaches 350.
5. Take the sliced turkey out of the bags. Use paper towels to pat them dry. Place them evenly over the grill into one layer. Smoke the turkey for two hours. The jerky should feel dry but still chewable when done.

6. Place into the zip-top bag to keep fresh until ready to eat.
Nutrition: Calories: 80 Protein: 13g   Carbs: 5.1g Fat: 0.8g

431. Smoked Veggie Medley

Preparation Time: 30 mins.
Cooking Time: 1 hr.
Servings: 4
Ingredients:
- 1 Spanish red onion peeled and cut into quarters.
- 1 red pepper seeded and sliced.
- 2 zucchinis, sliced.
- 1 yellow summer squash, sliced.
- Olive oil – 2 tablespoons
- Balsamic vinegar – 2 tablespoons
- 6 garlic cloves, peeled, minced.
- Sea salt – 1 teaspoon
- Black pepper – ½ teaspoon

Directions:
1. Preheat the pellet grill to 350°F.
2. In a large bowl, combine the red onion, red pepper, zucchinis, summer squash, olive oil, balsamic vinegar, garlic, sea salt, and black pepper. Toss to combine.
3. Transfer the veggies to the smoker and with the lid closed cook for between 30-45 minutes, until cooked through and caramelized.
4. Serve and enjoy.
Nutrition: Calories: 63 Protein: 3g   Carbs: 9g Fat: 3g

432. Feta Cheese Stuffed Meatballs

Preparation Time: 30 mins.
Cooking Time: 35 mins.
Servings: 6
Ingredients:
- Pepper
- Salt
- ¾ c. Feta cheese
- ½ t. thyme
- Two t. chopped oregano.
- Zest of one lemon
- One-pound ground pork
- One-pound ground beef
- One T. olive oil

Directions:
1. Place the pepper, salt, thyme, oregano, olive oil, lemon zest, and ground meats into a large bowl.
2. Combine thoroughly the ingredients using your hands.
3. Cut the Feta into little cubes and begin making the meatballs. Take a half tablespoon of the meat mixture and roll it around a piece of cheese. Continue until all meat has been used.
4. Add wood pellets to your smoker and follow your cooker's startup procedure. Preheat your smoker, with your lid closed, until it reaches 350.

5. Brush the meatballs with more olive oil and put onto the grill. Grill for ten minutes until browned.
Nutrition: Calories: 294.5 Protein: 28.4g   Carbs: 15.2g   Fat: 12.8g

433. Butternut Squash

Preparation Time: 30 mins.
Cooking Time: 2 hrs.
Servings: 4-6
Ingredients:
- Brown sugar
- Maple syrup
- 6 T. butter
- Butternut squash

Directions:
1. Add wood pellets to your smoker and follow your cooker's startup procedure. Preheat your smoke, with your lid closed, until it reaches 300.
2. Slice the squash in half, lengthwise. Clean out all the seeds and membrane.
3. Place this cut-side down on the grill and smoke for 30 minutes. Flip the squash over and cook for another 30 minutes.
4. Place each half of the squash onto aluminum foil. Sprinkle each half with brown sugar and maple syrup and put 3 T. of butter onto each. Wrap foil around to create a tight seal.
5. Increase temperature to 400 and place onto the grill for another 35 minutes.
6. Carefully unwrap each half making sure to reserve juices in the bottom. Place onto serving platter and drizzle juices over each half. Use a spoon to scoop out and enjoy.
Nutrition: Calories: 82 Protein: 1.8g   Carbs: 21.5g Fat: 0.18g

434. Cajun Artichokes

Preparation Time: 30 mins.
Cooking Time: 2 hrs.
Servings: 4
Ingredients:
- 1 2-16 canned, whole artichoke hearts
- Cajun seasoning – 2 tablespoons
- Hickory wood pellets

Directions:
1. Preheat the smoker, for cold smoking
2. Slice the artichoke hearts in half.
3. Toss the artichoke halves in the Cajun seasoning.
4. Spread the hearts in a single layer on the smoker rack and cold smoke for 2 hours.
5. Serve and enjoy.
Nutrition: Calories: 25 Protein: 3g   Carbs: 9g Fat: 0g

435. For Maggi Macaroni and Cheese

Preparation Time: 30 mins.
Cooking Time: 1 hr. 30 mins.
Servings: 8
Ingredients:

- ¼ c. all-purpose flour
- ½ stick butter.
- Butter, for greasing
- One-pound cooked elbow macaroni
- One c. grated Parmesan
- 8 ounces cream cheese
- Two c. shredded Monterey Jack
- 3 t. garlic powder
- Two t. salt
- One t. pepper
- Two c. shredded Cheddar, divided.
- 3 c. milk

Directions:

1. Put the butter into the pot and melt. Mix in the flour. Stir constantly for a minute. Mix in the pepper, salt, garlic powder, and milk. Let it boil.
2. After lowering the heat, let it simmer for about 5 mins, or until it has thickened. Remove from the heat.
3. Mix in the cream cheese, parmesan, Monterey jack, and 1 ½ c. of cheddar. Stir everything until melted. Fold in the pasta.
4. Add wood pellets to your smoker and follow your cooker's startup procedure. Preheat your smoker, with your lid closed, until it reaches 225.
5. Butter a 9" x 13" baking pan. Pour the macaroni mixture to the pan and lay on the grill. Cover and allow it to smoke for an hour, or until it has become bubbly. Top the macaroni with rest of the cheddar during the last
6. Serve.

Nutrition: Calories: 493 Protein: 19.29g   Carbs: 52.15g Fat: 22.84g

Chapter 14. __Dessert recipe__

436. Grilled Pineapple with Chocolate Sauce

Preparation Time: 10 Minutes
Cooking Time: 25 Minutes
Servings: 8
Ingredients:

- 1pineapple
- 8 oz bittersweet chocolate chips
- 1/2 cup spiced rum
- 1/2 cup whipping cream
- 2tbsp light brown sugar

Directions:

1. Preheat pellet grill to 400°F.
2. De-skin, the pineapple, then slice the pineapple into 1 in cubes.
3. In a saucepan, combine chocolate chips. When chips begin to melt, add rum to the saucepan. Continue to stir until combined, then add a splash of the pineapple's juice.
4. Add in whipping cream and continue to stir the mixture. Once the sauce is smooth and thickening, lower heat to simmer to keep warm.
5. Thread pineapple cubes onto skewers. Sprinkle skewers with brown sugar.
6. Place skewers on the grill grate. Grill for about 5 minutes per side, or until grill marks begin to develop.
7. Remove skewers from grill and allow to rest on a plate for about 5 minutes. Serve alongside warm chocolate sauce for dipping.

Nutrition:
Calories: 112.6
Fat: 0.5 g
Cholesterol: 0
Carbohydrate: 28.8 g
Fiber: 1.6 g
Sugar: 0.1 g
Protein: 0.4 g

437. Nectarine and Nutella Sundae

Preparation Time: 10 Minutes
Cooking Time: 25 Minutes
Servings: 4
Ingredients:

- 2nectarines halved and pitted.
- 2tsp honey
- 4tbsp Nutella
- 4scoops vanilla ice cream
- 1/4 cup pecans, chopped.
- Whipped cream, to top
- 4cherries, to top

Directions:

1. Preheat pellet grill to 400°F.
2. Slice nectarines in half and remove the pits.
3. Brush the inside (cut side) of each nectarine half with honey.
4. Place nectarines directly on the grill grate, cut side down—Cook for 5-6 minutes, or until grill marks develop.
5. Flip nectarines and cook on the other side for about 2 minutes.
6. Remove nectarines from the grill and allow it to cool.
7. Fill the pit cavity on each nectarine half with 1 tbsp Nutella.
8. Place one scoop of ice cream on top of Nutella. Top with whipped cream, cherries, and sprinkle chopped pecans. Serve and enjoy!

Nutrition:
Calories: 90
Fat: 3 g
Carbohydrate: 15g
Sugar: 13 g
Protein: 2 g

438. Cinnamon Sugar Donut Holes

Preparation Time: 10 Minutes
Cooking Time: 35 Minutes
Servings: 4
Ingredients:

- 1/2 cup flour
- 1tbsp cornstarch
- 1/2 tsp baking powder
- 1/8 tsp baking soda
- 1/8 tsp ground cinnamon
- 1/2 tsp kosher salt
- 1/4 cup buttermilk
- 1/4 cup sugar
- 11/2 tbsp butter, melted.
- 1egg
- 1/2 tsp vanilla
- Topping
- 2tbsp sugar
- 1tbsp sugar
- 1tsp ground cinnamon

Directions:

1. Preheat pellet grill to 350°F.
2. In a medium bowl, combine flour, cornstarch, baking powder, baking soda, ground cinnamon, and kosher salt. Whisk to combine.
3. In a separate bowl, combine buttermilk, sugar, melted butter, egg, and vanilla. Whisk until the egg is thoroughly combined.
4. Pour wet mixture into the flour mixture and stir. Stir just until combined, careful not to overwork the mixture.
5. Spray mini muffin tin with cooking spray.
6. Spoon 1 tbsp of donut mixture into each mini muffin hole.
7. Place the tin on the pellet grill grate and bake for about 18 minutes, or until a toothpick can come out clean.

8. Remove muffin tin from the grill and let rest for about 5 minutes.
9. In a small bowl, combine 1 tbsp sugar and 1 tsp ground cinnamon.
10. Melt 2 tbsp of butter in a glass dish. Dip each donut hole in the melted butter, then mix and toss with cinnamon sugar. Place completed donut holes on a plate to serve.

Nutrition:
Calories: 190
Fat: 17 g
Carbohydrate: 21 g
Fiber: 1 g
Sugar: 8 g
Protein: 3 g

439. Pellet Grill Chocolate Chip Cookies

Preparation Time: 20 Minutes
Cooking Time: 45 Minutes
Servings: 12
Ingredients:
- 1cup salted butter softened.
- 1cup of sugar
- 1cup light brown sugar
- 2tsp vanilla extract
- 2large eggs
- 3cups all-purpose flour
- 1tsp baking soda.
- 1/2 tsp baking powder
- 1tsp natural sea salt
- 2cups semi-sweet chocolate chips or chunks

Directions:
1. Preheat pellet grill to 375°F.
2. Line a large baking sheet with parchment paper and set aside.
3. In a medium bowl, mix flour, baking soda, salt, and baking powder. Once combined, set aside.
4. In stand mixer bowl, combine butter, white sugar, and brown sugar until combined. Beat in eggs and vanilla. Beat until fluffy.
5. Mix in dry ingredients, continue to stir until combined.
6. Add chocolate chips and mix thoroughly.
7. Roll 3 tbsp of dough at a time into balls and place them on your cookie sheet. Evenly space them apart, with about 2-3 inches in between each ball.
8. Place cookie sheet directly on the grill grate and bake for 20-25 minutes until the cookies' outside is slightly browned.
9. Remove from grill and allow to rest for 10 minutes. Serve and enjoy!

Nutrition:
Calories: 120
Fat: 4
Cholesterol: 7.8 mg
Carbohydrate: 22.8 g
Fiber: 0.3 g

Sugar: 14.4 g
Protein: 1.4 g

440. Delicious Donuts on a Grill

Preparation Time: 5 Minutes
Cooking Time: 10 Minutes
Servings: 6
Ingredients:
- 1-1/2 cups sugar, powdered.
- 1/3 cup whole milk
- 1/2 teaspoon vanilla extract
- 16 ounces of biscuit dough, prepared.
- Oil spray, for greasing
- 1cup chocolate sprinkles, for sprinkling

Directions:
1. Take a medium bowl and mix sugar, milk, and vanilla extract.
2. Combine well to create a glaze.
3. Set the glaze aside for further use.
4. Place the dough onto the flat, clean surface.
5. Flat the dough with a rolling pin.
6. Use a ring mold, about an inch, and cut the hole in each round dough's center.
7. Place the dough on a plate and refrigerate for 10 minutes.
8. Open the grill and install the grill grate inside it.
9. Close the hood.
10. Now, select the grill from the menu, and set the temperature to medium.
11. Set the time to 6 minutes.
12. Select start and begin preheating.
13. Remove the dough from the refrigerator and coat it with cooking spray from both sides.
14. When the unit beeps, the grill is preheated; place the adjustable amount of dough on the grill grate.
15. Close the hood and cook for 3 minutes.
16. After 3 minutes, remove donuts and place the remaining dough inside.
17. Cook for 3 minutes.
18. Once all the donuts are ready, sprinkle chocolate sprinkles on top.
19. Enjoy.

Nutrition:
Calories: 400
Total Fat: 11g
Cholesterol: 1mg
Sodium: 787mg
Total Carbohydrate: 71.3g
Dietary Fiber 0.9g
Total Sugars: 45.3g
Protein: 5.7g

441. Smoked Pumpkin Pie

Preparation Time: 10 Minutes
Cooking Time: 50 Minutes
Servings: 8
Ingredients:

- 1tbsp cinnamon
- 1-1/2 tbsp pumpkin pie spice
- 15oz can pumpkin
- 14oz can sweetened condensed milk.
- 2beaten eggs
- 1unbaked pie shell
- Topping: whipped cream

Directions:
1. Preheat your smoker to 3250F.
2. Place a baking sheet, rimmed, on the smoker upside down, or use a cake pan.
3. Combine all your ingredients in a bowl, large, except the pie shell, then pour the mixture into a pie crust.
4. Place the pie on the baking sheet and smoke for about 50-60 minutes until a knife comes out clean when inserted. Make sure the center is set.
5. Remove and cool for about 2 hours or refrigerate overnight.
6. Serve with a whipped cream dollop and enjoy it!

Nutrition:
Calories: 292
Total Fat: 11g
Total Carbs: 42g
Protein: 7g
Sugars: 29g
Fiber: 5g
Sodium: 168mg

442. Wood Pellet Smoked Nut Mix

Preparation Time: 15 Minutes
Cooking Time: 20 Minutes
Servings: 12
Ingredients:
- 3cups mixed nuts (pecans, peanuts, almonds, etc.)
- 1/2 tbsp brown sugar
- 1tbsp thyme, dried
- 1/4 tbsp mustard powder
- 1tbsp olive oil, extra-virgin

Directions:
1. Preheat your pellet grill to 2500F with the lid closed for about 15 minutes.
2. Combine all ingredients in a bowl, large, then transfer into a cookie sheet lined with parchment paper.
3. Place the cookie sheet on a grill and grill for about 20 minutes.
4. Remove the nuts from the grill and let cool.
5. Serve and enjoy.

Nutrition:
Calories: 249
Total Fat: 21.5g
Saturated Fat: 3.5g
Total Carbs: 12.3g
Net Carbs: 10.1g
Protein: 5.7g

Sugars: 5.6g
Fiber: 2.1g
Sodium: 111mg

443. Grilled Peaches and Cream

Preparation Time: 15 Minutes
Cooking Time: 8 Minutes
Servings: 8
Ingredients:
- 4halved and pitted peaches
- 1tbsp vegetable oil
- 2tbsp clover honey
- 1cup cream cheese, soft with honey and nuts

Directions:
1. Preheat your pellet grill to medium-high heat.
2. Coat the peaches lightly with oil and place on the grill pit side down.
3. Grill for about 5 minutes until nice grill marks on the surfaces.
4. Turn over the peaches, then drizzle with honey.
5. Spread and cream cheese dollop where the pit was and grill for additional 2-3 minutes until the filling becomes warm.
6. Serve immediately.

Nutrition:
Calories: 139
Total Fat: 10.2g
Total Carbs: 11.6g
Protein: 1.1g
Sugars: 12g
Sodium: 135mg

444. Berry Cobbler on a Pellet Grill

Preparation Time: 15 Minutes
Cooking Time: 35 Minutes
Servings: 8
Ingredients:
For fruit filling
- 3cups frozen mixed berries
- 1lemon juice
- 1cup brown sugar
- 1tbsp vanilla extract
- 1bsp lemon zest, finely grated.
- A pinch of salt

For cobbler topping
- 1-1/2 cups all-purpose flour
- 1-1/2 tbsp baking powder
- 3tbsp sugar, granulated.
- 1/2 tbsp salt
- 8tbsp cold butter
- 1/2 cup sour cream
- 2tbsp raw sugar

Directions:
1. Set your pellet grill on "smoke" for about 4-5 minutes with the lid open until fire establishes, and your grill starts smoking.
2. Preheat your grill to 350 for about 10-15 minutes with the grill lid closed.

3. Meanwhile, combine frozen mixed berries, Lemon juice, brown sugar, vanilla, lemon zest, and salt pinch. Transfer into a skillet and let the fruit sit and thaw.

4. Mix flour, baking powder, sugar, and salt in a bowl, medium. Cut cold butter into peas sizes using a pastry blender, then add to the mixture. Stir to mix everything.

5. Stir in sour cream until dough starts coming together.

6. Pinch small pieces of dough and place over the fruit until fully covered. Splash the top with raw sugar.

7. Now place the skillet directly on the grill grate, close the lid, cook for about 35 minutes until juices bubble, and a golden-brown dough topping.

8. Remove the skillet from the pellet grill and cool for several minutes.

9. Scoop and serve warm.

Nutrition:
Calories: 371
Total Fat: 13g
Total Carbs: 60g
Protein: 3g
Sugars: 39g
Fiber: 2g
Sodium: 269mg

445. Pellet Grill Apple Crisp

Preparation Time: 20 Minutes
Cooking Time: 60 Minutes
Servings: 15
Ingredients:
- Apples
- Ten large apples
- 1/2 cup flour
- 1cup sugar, dark brown
- 1/2 tbsp cinnamon
- 1/2 cup butter slices
- Crisp
- 3cups oatmeal, old-fashioned
- 1-1/2 cups softened butter, salted.
- 1-1/2 tbsp cinnamon
- 2cups brown sugar

Directions:
1. Preheat your grill to 350.
2. Wash, peel, core, and dice the apples into cubes, medium size.
3. Mix flour, dark brown sugar, and cinnamon, then toss with your apple cubes.
4. Spray a baking pan, 10x13", with cooking spray, then place apples inside. Top with butter slices.
5. Mix all crisp ingredients in a medium bowl until well combined. Place the mixture over the apples.
6. Place on the grill and cook for about 1-hour checking after every 15-20 minutes to ensure

cooking is even. Do not place it on the hottest grill part.

7. Remove and let sit for about 20-25 minutes.

8. It is very warm.

Nutrition:
Calories: 528
Total Fat: 26g
Total Carbs: 75g
Protein: 4g
Sugars: 51g
Fiber: 5g
Sodium: 209mg

446. Fromage Macaroni and Cheese

Preparation Time: 30 Minutes
Cooking Time: 1 Hour
Servings: 8
Ingredients:
- ¼ c. all-purpose flour
- ½ stick butter.
- Butter, for greasing
- One-pound cooked elbow macaroni
- One c. grated Parmesan
- 8 ounces cream cheese
- Two c. shredded Monterey Jack
- 3 t. garlic powder
- Two t. salt
- One t. pepper
- Two c. shredded Cheddar, divided.
- Three c. milk

Directions:
1. Add the butter to a pot and melt. Mix in the flour. Stir constantly for a minute. Mix in the pepper, salt, garlic powder, and milk. Let it boil.
2. After lowering the heat, let it simmer for about 5 mins, or until it has thickened. Remove from the heat.
3. Mix in the cream cheese, parmesan, Monterey Jack, and 1 ½ c. of cheddar. Stir everything until melted. Fold in the pasta.
4. Add wood pellets to your smoker and keep your cooker's startup procedure. Preheat your smoker, with your lid closed, until it reaches 225.
5. Butter a 9" x 13" baking pan. Pour the macaroni mixture into the pan and lay on the grill. Cover and allow it to smoke for an hour, or until it has become bubbly. Top the macaroni with the rest of the cheddar during the last
6. Serve.

Nutrition:
Calories: 180
Carbs: 19g
Fat: 8g
Protein: 8g

447. Spicy Barbecue Pecans

Preparation Time: 15 Minutes
Cooking Time: 1 Hour
Servings: 2
Ingredients:
- 2 ½ t. garlic powder
- 16 ounces raw pecan halves
- One t. onion powder
- One t. pepper
- Two t. salt
- One t. dried thyme
- Butter, for greasing
- 3 T. melted butter.

Directions:
1. Add wood pellets to your smoker and follow your cooker's startup method.
2. Preheat your smoker, with your lid closed, until it reaches 225.
3. Cover and smoke for an hour, flipping the nuts one. Make sure the nuts are toasted and heated. They should be removed from the grill.
4. Set aside to cool and dry.

Nutrition:
Calories: 150
Carbs: 16g
Fat: 9g
Protein: 1g

448. Pit boss Blackberry Pie

Preparation Time: 10 Minutes
Cooking Time: 40 Minutes
Servings: 8
Ingredients:
- Butter, for greasing
- ½ c. all-purpose flour
- ½ c. milk
- Two pints blackberries
- Two c. sugar, divided.
- One box of refrigerated piecrusts
- One stick melted butter.
- One stick of butter
- Vanilla ice cream

Directions:
1. Add wood pellets to your smoker and follow your cooker's startup method.
2. Preheat your smoker, with your lid closed, until it reaches 375.
3. Unroll the second pie crust and lay it over the skillet.
4. Lower the lid, then smoke for 15 to 20 minutes or until it is browned and bubbly.
5. Serve the hot pie with some vanilla ice cream.

Nutrition:
Calories: 100
Carbs: 10g
Fat: 0g
Protein: 15g

449. S'mores Dip

Preparation Time: 0 Minutes
Cooking Time: 15 Minutes
Servings: 6-8
Ingredients:
- 12 ounces semisweet chocolate chips
- ¼ c. milk
- Two T. melted salted butter.
- 16 ounces marshmallows
- Apple wedges
- Graham crackers

Directions:
1. Add wood pellets to your smoker and get your cooker's startup procedure. Preheat your smoker, with your lid closed, until it reaches 450.
2. Put a cast-iron skillet on your grill and add in the milk and melted butter. Stir together for a minute.
3. Cover, and let it smoke for five to seven minutes. The marshmallows should be toasted lightly.
4. Take the skillet off the heat and serve with apple wedges and graham crackers.

Nutrition:
Calories: 90
Carbs: 15g
Fat: 3g
Protein: 1g

450. Bacon Chocolate Chip Cookies

Preparation Time: 10 Minutes
Cooking Time: 30 Minutes
Servings: 24
Ingredients:
- Eight slices of cooked and crumbled bacon
- 2 ½ t. apple cider vinegar
- One t. vanilla
- Two c. semisweet chocolate chips
- Two-room temp eggs
- 1 ½ t. baking soda
- One c. granulated sugar
- ½ t. salt
- Two ¾ c. all-purpose flour
- One c. light brown sugar
- 1 ½ stick softened butter.

Directions:
1. Mix the flour, baking soda, and salt.
2. Cream the sugar and the butter together. Then lower the speed. Add in the eggs, vinegar, and vanilla.
3. Still on low, slowly add in the flour mixture, bacon pieces, and chocolate chips.
4. Add wood pellets to your smoker and follow your cooker's startup method.
5. Preheat your smoker, with your lid closed, until it reaches 375.

6. Place some parchment on a baking sheet and drop a teaspoonful of cookie batter on the baking sheet. Let them cook on the grill,
7. covered, for approximately 12 minutes or until they are browned. Enjoy.

Nutrition:
Calories: 167
Carbs: 21g
Fat: 9g
Protein: 2g

451. Cinnamon Sugar Pumpkin Seeds

Preparation Time: 12 Minutes
Cooking Time: 30 Minutes
Servings: 8-12
Ingredients:
- Two T. sugar
- seeds from a pumpkin
- One t. cinnamon
- Two T. melted butter.

Directions:
1. Add wood pellets to your smoker and follow your cooker's startup operation. Preheat your smoker, with your lid closed, until it reaches 350.
2. Clean the seeds and toss them in the melted butter. Add them to the sugar and cinnamon. Spread them out on a baking sheet, place on the grill, and smoke for 25 minutes.
3. Serve.

Nutrition:
Calories: 160
Carbs: 5g
Fat: 12g
Protein: 7g

452. Apple Cobbler

Preparation Time: 20 Minutes
Cooking Time: 1 Hour and 30 Minutes
Servings: 8
Ingredients:
- 8 Granny Smith apples
- One c. sugar
- Two eggs
- Two t. baking powder
- Two c. plain flour
- 1 ½ c. sugar

Directions:
1. Peel and quarter apples, place into a bowl. Add in the cinnamon and one c. sugar. Stir well to coat and let it sit for one hour.
2. Add wood pellets to your smoker and follow your cooker's startup form. Preheat your smoker, with your lid closed, until it reaches 350.
3. Place apples into a Dutch oven. Add the crumble mixture on top and drizzle with melted butter.

4. Place on the grill and cook for 50 minutes.

Nutrition:
Calories: 152
Carbs: 26g
Fat: 5g
Protein: 1g

453. Pineapple Cake

Preparation Time: 20 Minutes
Cooking Time: 60 Minutes
Servings: 8
Ingredients:
- One c. sugar
- One T. baking powder
- One c. buttermilk
- Two eggs
- ½ t. salt
- One jar maraschino cherry
- One stick butter, divided.
- ¾ c. brown sugar
- One can pineapple slice
- 1 ½ c. flour

Directions:
1. Add wood pellets to your smoker and observe your cooker's startup procedure. Preheat your smoker, with your lid closed, until it reaches 350.
2. Take a medium-sized cast-iron skillet and melt one half stick butter. Be sure to coat the entire skillet. Sprinkle brown sugar into a cast-iron skillet.
3. Lay the sliced pineapple on top of the brown sugar. Place a cherry into the middle of each pineapple ring.
4. Mix the salt, baking powder, flour, and sugar. Add in the eggs; one-half stick melted butter and buttermilk. Whisk to combine.
5. Put the cake on the grill and cook for an hour.
6. Take off from the grill and let it sit for ten minutes. Flip onto a serving platter.

Nutrition:
Calories: 165
Carbs: 40g
Fat: 0g
Protein: 1g

454. Ice Cream Bread

Preparation Time: 10 Minutes
Cooking Time: 1 Hour
Servings: 12-16
Ingredients:
- 1 ½ quart full-fat butter pecan ice cream, softened.
- One t. salt
- Two c. semisweet chocolate chips
- One c. sugar
- One stick melted butter.
- Butter, for greasing
- 4 c. self-rising flour

Directions:

1. Add wood pellets to your smoker and follow your cooker's startup program. Preheat your smoker, with your lid closed, until it reaches 350.
2. Set the cake on the grill, cover, and smoke for 50 minutes to an hour. A toothpick should come out clean.
3. Take the pan off the grill. For 10 mins., cool the bread.

Nutrition:
Calories: 135
Carbs: 0g
Fat: 0g
Protein: 0g

455. Mediterranean Meatballs

Preparation Time: 15 Minutes
Cooking Time: 35 Minutes
Servings: 8
Ingredients:

- Pepper
- Salt
- One t. vinegar
- Two T. olive oil
- Two eggs
- One chopped onion
- One soaked slice of bread
- ½ t. cumin
- One T. chopped basil.
- 1 ½ T. chopped parsley.
- 2 ½ pounds ground beef

Directions:

1. Use your hands to combine everything until thoroughly combined. If needed, when forming meatballs, dip your hands into some water. Shape into 12 meatballs.
2. Add wood pellets to your smoker.
3. Preheat your smoker, with your lid closed, until it reaches 380.
4. Place the meatballs onto the grill and cook on all sides for eight minutes. Take off the grill and let sit for five minutes.
5. Serve with favorite condiments or a salad.

Nutrition:
Calories: 33
Carbs: 6g
Fat: 0g
Protein: 1g

456. Greek Meatballs

Preparation Time: 10 Minutes
Cooking Time: 40 Minutes
Servings: 6
Ingredients:

- Pepper
- Salt
- Two chopped green onions
- One T. almond flour

- Two eggs
- ½ pound ground pork
- 2 ½ pound ground beef

Directions:

1. Mix all the ingredients using your hands until everything is incorporated evenly. Form mixture into meatballs until all meat is used.
2. Add wood pellets to your smoker and follow your cooker's startup procedure. Preheat your smoker, with your lid closed, until it reaches 380.
3. Brush the meatballs with olive oil and place onto the grill—Cook for ten minutes on all sides.

Nutrition:
Calories: 161
Carbs: 10g
Fat: 6g
Protein: 17g

457. Banana Boats

Preparation Time: 30 minutes
Cooking Time: 10 minutes
Servings: 4
Ingredients:

- Four green bananas
- Chocolate chips
- Miniature marshmallows
- Peanut butter chips
- Crushed cookies

Directions:

1. Split a banana lengthwise from end to end, leaving the peel intact on the opposite side.
2. Top with desired toppings.
3. Wrap the banana in heavy-duty aluminum foil.
4. Grilling:
5. Place the bananas on a 400F grill and close the dome for 10 minutes.
6. Unwrap and serve topped with vanilla ice cream, whipped cream, or by them.

Nutrition:
Calories: 310
Fat: 17 g
Carbohydrates: 40 g
Protein: 4 g

458. Grilled Pineapple Sundaes

Preparation Time: 30 minutes
Cooking Time: 5 minutes
Servings: 4
Ingredients:

- 4 fresh pineapple spears
- Vanilla Ice Cream
- Jarred Caramel Sauce
- Toasted Coconut

Directions:

1. Place pineapple spears on a 400F grill and close the dome for 2 minutes.

2. Turn the pineapple and close the dome for another 2 minutes.
3. Turn the pineapple once more and close the dome for another minute.
4. Serve pineapple topped with ice cream, caramel sauce, and toasted coconut.

Nutrition:
Calories: 112
Fat: 1 g
Carbohydrates: 29 g
Protein: 0.4g

459. Blueberry Cobbler

Preparation Time: 15 minutes
Cooking Time: 30 minutes
Servings: 6
Ingredients:
- 4 cups fresh blueberries
- 1 tsp. grated lemon zest
- 1 cup sugar, plus 2 tbsp.
- 1 cup all-purpose flour, plus 2 tbsp.
- Juice of 1 lemon
- 2 tsp. baking powder
- ¼ teaspoon salt
- Six tablespoons unsalted butter
- ¾ cup whole milk
- 1/8 teaspoon ground cinnamon

Directions:
1. In a prepared medium bowl, combine the blueberries, lemon zest, two tablespoons of sugar, two tablespoons of flour, and lemon juice.
2. In a prepared medium bowl, combine the remaining 1 cup of flour and 1 cup of sugar, baking powder, and salt. Cut the butter into the flour mixture until it forms an even crumb texture. Stir in the milk until a dough form.
3. Select BAKE, set the temperature to 350degrees F, and set the time to 30 minutes. Select START/STOP to begin preheating.
4. Meanwhile, pour the blueberry mixture into the Multi-Purpose Pan, spreading it evenly across the pan. Gently pour the batter over the blueberry mixture, and then sprinkle the cinnamon over the top.
5. If the unit beeps to signify it has preheated, place the pan directly in the pot. Close the hood and cook for 30 minutes, until lightly golden.
6. When cooking is complete, serve warm.

Nutrition:
Calories: 408
Saturated fat: 8g
Carbohydrates: 72g
Protein: 5g

460. Rum-Soaked Grilled Pineapple Sundaes

Preparation Time: 15 minutes
Cooking Time: 8 minutes
Servings: 6
Ingredients:
- ½ cup dark rum
- ½ cup packed brown sugar.
- One teaspoon ground cinnamon, plus more for garnish
- One pineapple cored and sliced.
- Vanilla ice cream, for serving.

Directions:
1. In a large shallow bowl or storage container, combine the rum, sugar, and cinnamon. Add the pineapple slices and arrange them in a single layer. Coat with the mixture, then let soak for at least 5 minutes per side.
2. Insert the Grill Grate and cover the hood. Select GRILL, then set the temperature to MAX, and set the time to 8 minutes. Select START/STOP to begin preheating.
3. While the unit is preheating, strain the extra rum sauce from the pineapple.
4. When the unit beeps to it is a sign that it has preheated, place the fruit on the Grill Grate in a single layer (you may need to do this in multiple batches). Gently press the fruit down to maximize grill marks. Close the hood and grill for about 6 to 8 minutes without flipping. If working in batches, remove the pineapple, and repeat this step for the remaining pineapple slices.
5. When cooking is complete, remove, and top each pineapple ring with a scoop of ice cream. Sprinkle with cinnamon and serve immediately.

Nutrition:
Calories: 240
Saturated fat: 2g
Carbohydrates: 43g
Protein: 2g

461. Charred Peaches with Bourbon Butter Sauce

Preparation Time: 10 minutes
Cooking Time: 12 minutes
Servings: 4
Ingredients:
- Four tablespoons salted butter
- ¼ cup bourbon
- ½ cup brown sugar
- Four ripe peaches halved and pitted.
- ¼ cup candied pecans

Directions

1. Insert the Grill Grate and cover the hood. Select GRILL, then set the temperature to MAX, and set the time to 12 minutes. Select START/STOP to begin preheating.
2. While the unit is preheating, in a saucepan over medium heat, melt the butter for about 5 minutes. Once the butter is browned, remove the pan from the heat and carefully add the bourbon.
3. Return the saucepan into medium-high heat and add the brown sugar. Bring to a boil and let the sugar dissolve for 5 minutes, stirring occasionally.
4. Pour the bourbon butter sauce into a medium shallow bowl and arrange the peaches cut side down to coat in the sauce.
5. When the unit beeps a sign that it has preheated, place the fruit on the Grill Grate in a single layer (you may need to do this in multiple batches). Gently press the fruit down to maximize grill marks. Close the hood and grill for 10 to 12 minutes without flipping. If working in batches, repeat this step for all the peaches.
6. When cooking is complete, remove the peaches and top each with the pecans. Drizzle with the remaining bourbon butter sauce and serve immediately.

Nutrition:
Calories: 309
Saturated fat: 8g
Carbohydrates: 34g
Protein: 2g

462. Chocolate-Hazelnut and Strawberry Grilled Dessert Pizza

Preparation Time: 10 minutes
Total **Cooking Time:** 6 minutes
Servings: 4
Ingredients:
- 2 tbsp. all-purpose flour, plus more as needed.
- ½ store-bought pizza dough (about 8 ounces)
- 1 tbsp. canola oil
- 1 cup sliced fresh strawberries.
- 1 tbsp. sugar
- ½ cup chocolate-hazelnut spread.

Directions:
1. Insert the Grill Grate and cover the hood. Select GRILL, then set the temperature to MAX, and set the time to 6 minutes. Select START/STOP to begin preheating.
2. While the unit is preheating, dust a clean work surface with the flour, place the dough on the floured surface and roll it out to a 9-inch round of even thickness. Sprinkle the roller and work surface with additional flour, as needed, to ensure the dough does not stick.
3. Brush the surface of the rolled-out dough evenly with half the oil. Flip the dough over, and brush with the remaining oil. Poke the dough with a fork 5 or 6 times across its surface to prevent air pockets from forming during cooking.
4. When the unit beeps to signify it has preheated, place the dough on the Grill Grate. Close the hood and cook for 3 minutes.
5. After 3 minutes, flip the dough. Close the hood and continue cooking for the remaining 3 minutes.
6. Meanwhile, in a medium mixing bowl, combine the strawberries and sugar.
7. Move the pizza to a cutting board and let cool. Top with the chocolate-hazelnut spread and strawberries. Cut into pieces and serve.

Nutrition:
Calories: 377
Saturated fat: 4g
Sodium: 258mg
Carbohydrates: 53g
Protein: 7g

Chapter 15. Traditional Recipes

463. Sweet & Spicy Chicken Thighs

Preparation Time: 15 minutes
Cooking Time: 15 minutes
Servings: 4
Ingredients:

- 2 garlic cloves, minced.
- ¼ cup honey
- 2 tablespoons soy sauce
- ¼ teaspoon red pepper flakes, crushed.
- 4 (5-ounce) skinless, boneless chicken thighs
- 2 tablespoons olive oil
- 2 teaspoons sweet rub
- ¼ teaspoon red chili powder
- Ground black pepper, as required.

Directions

1. Preheat the Pit boss grill & Smoker on grill setting to 400 degrees F.
2. In a small bowl, add garlic, honey, soy sauce and red pepper flakes and with a wire whisk, beat until well combined.
3. Coat chicken thighs with oil and season with sweet rub, chili powder and black pepper generously.
4. Arrange the chicken drumsticks onto the grill and cook for about 15 minutes per
5. In the last 4-5 minutes of cooking, coat drumsticks with garlic mixture.
6. Serve immediately.

Nutrition:
> Calories 309
> Total Fat 12.1 g
> Saturated Fat 2.9 g
> Cholesterol 82 mg
> Sodium 504 mg
> Total Carbs 18.7 g
> Fiber 0.2 g
> Sugar 17.6 g
> Protein 32.3 g

464. Bacon Wrapped Chicken Breasts

Preparation Time: 0 minute
Cooking Time: 3 hours
Servings: 6
Ingredients:
For Brine:

- ¼ cup brown sugar
- ¼ cup kosher salt
- 4 cups water
  For Chicken:
- 6 skinless, boneless chicken breasts
- ¼ cup chicken rub
- 18 bacon slices
- 1½ cups BBQ sauce

Directions:

1. For brine: in a large pitcher, dissolve sugar and salt in water.

2. Place the chicken breasts in brine and refrigerate for about 2 hours, flipping once in the middle way.
3. Preheat the Pit boss grill & Smoker on grill setting to 230 degrees F.
4. Remove chicken breasts from brine and rinse under cold running water.
5. Season chicken breasts with rub generously.
6. Arrange 3 bacon strips of bacon onto a cutting board, against each other.
7. Place 1 chicken breast across the bacon, leaving enough bacon on the left side to wrap it over just a little.
8. Wrap the bacon strips around chicken breast and secure with toothpicks.
9. Repeat with remaining breasts and bacon slices.
10. Arrange the chicken breasts into Pit boss grill and cook for about 2½ hours.
11. Coat the breasts with BBQ sauce and cook for about 30 minutes more.
12. Serve immediately.

Nutrition:
> Calories 481
> Total Fat 12.3 g
> Saturated Fat 4.2 g
> Cholesterol 41 mg
> Sodium 3000 mg
> Total Carbs 32 g
> Fiber 0.4g
> Sugar 22.2 g
> Protein 55.9 g

465. Glazed Chicken Wings

Preparation Time: 15 minutes
Cooking Time: 2 hours
Servings: 6
Ingredients:

- 2 pounds' chicken wings
- 2 garlic cloves, crushed.
- 3 tablespoons hoisin sauce
- 2 tablespoons soy sauce
- 1 teaspoon dark sesame oil
- 1 tablespoon honey
- ½ teaspoon ginger powder
- 1 tablespoon sesame seeds toasted lightly.

Directions:

1. Preheat the Pit boss grill & Smoker on grill setting to 225 degrees F.
2. Arrange the wings onto the lower rack of grill and cook for about 1½ hours.
3. Meanwhile, in a large bowl, mix remaining all ingredients.
4. Remove wings from grill and place in the bowl of garlic mixture.
5. Coat wings with garlic mixture generously.
6. Now, set the grill to 375 degrees F.

7. Arrange the coated wings onto a foil-lined baking sheet and sprinkle with sesame seeds.
8. Place the pan onto the lower rack of Pit boss grill and cook for about 25-30 minutes.
9. Serve immediately.

Nutrition:

Calories 336
Total Fat 13 g
Saturated Fat 3.3 g
Cholesterol 135 mg
Sodium 560 mg
Total Carbs 7.6 g
Fiber 0.5 g
Sugar 5.2 g
Protein 44.7 g

466. Chicken Casserole

Preparation Time: 15 minutes
Cooking Time: 55 minutes
Servings: 8
Ingredients:

- 2 (15-ounce) cans cream of chicken soup
- 2 cups milk
- 2 tablespoons unsalted butter
- ¼ cup all-purpose flour
- 1-pound skinless, boneless chicken thighs, chopped.
- ½ cup hatch chiles, chopped.
- 2 medium onions, chopped.
- 1 tablespoon fresh thyme, chopped.
- Salt and ground black pepper, as required.
- 1 cup cooked bacon, chopped.
- 1 cup tater tots

Directions:

1. Preheat the Pit boss grill & Smoker on grill setting to 400 degrees F.
2. In a large bowl, mix chicken soup and milk.
3. In a skillet, melt butter over medium heat.
4. Slowly, add flour and cook for about 1-2 minutes or until smooth, stirring continuously.
5. Slowly, add soup mixture, beating continuously until smooth.
6. Cook until mixture starts to thicken, stirring continuously.
7. Stir in remaining ingredients except bacon and simmer for about 10-15 minutes.
8. Stir in bacon and transfer mixture into a 2½-quart casserole dish.
9. Place tater tots on top of casserole evenly.
10. Arrange the pan onto the grill and cook for about 30-35 minutes.
11. Serve hot.

Nutrition:

Calories 440
Total Fat 25.8 g
Saturated Fat 9.3 g
Cholesterol 86 mg
Sodium 1565 mg

Total Carbs 22.2 g
Fiber 1.5 g
Sugar 4.6 g
Protein 28.9 g

467. Buttered Turkey

Preparation Time: 15 minutes
Cooking Time: 4 hours
Servings: 16
Ingredients:

- ½ pound butter, softened.
- 2 tablespoons fresh thyme, chopped.
- 2 fresh rosemary, chopped.
- 6 garlic cloves, crushed.
- 1 (20-pound) whole turkey, neck and giblets removed.
- Salt and ground black pepper, as required.

Directions:

1. Preheat the Pit boss grill & Smoker on smoke setting to 300 degrees F, using charcoal.
2. In a bowl, place butter, fresh herbs, garlic, salt, and black pepper and mix well.
3. With your fingers, separate the turkey skin from breast to create a pocket.
4. Stuff the breast pocket with ¼-inch thick layer of butter mixture.
5. Season the turkey with salt and black pepper evenly.
6. Arrange the turkey onto the grill and cook for 3-4 hours.
7. Remove turkey from pallet grill and place onto a cutting board for about 15-20 minutes before carving.
8. With a sharp knife, cut the turkey into desired-sized pieces and serve.

Nutrition:

Calories 965
Total Fat 52 g
Saturated Fat 19.9 g
Cholesterol 385 mg
Sodium 1916 mg
Total Carbs 0.6 g
Fiber 0.2 g
Sugar 0 g
Protein 106.5 g

468. Glazed Turkey Breast

Preparation Time: 15 minutes
Cooking Time: 4 hours
Servings: 6
Ingredients:

- ½ cup honey
- ¼ cup dry sherry
- 1 tablespoon butter
- 2 tablespoons fresh lemon juice
- Salt, as required.
- 1 (3-3½-pound) skinless, boneless turkey breast

Directions:

1. In a small pan, place honey, sherry and butter over low heat and cook until the mixture becomes smooth, stirring continuously.
2. Remove from heat and stir in lemon juice and salt. Set aside to cool.
3. Transfer the honey mixture and turkey breast in a sealable bag.
4. Seal the bag and shake to coat well.
5. Refrigerate for about 6-10 hours.
6. Preheat the Pit boss grill & Smoker on grill setting to 225-250 degrees F.
7. Place the turkey breast onto the grill and cook for about 2½-4 hours or until desired doneness.
8. Remove turkey breast from pallet grill and place onto a cutting board for about 15-20 minutes before slicing.
9. With a sharp knife, cut the turkey breast into desired-sized slices and serve.

Nutrition:

Calories 443
Total Fat 11.4 g
Saturated Fat 4.8 g
Cholesterol 159 mg
Sodium 138 mg
Total Carbs 23.7 g
Fiber 0.1 g
Sugar 23.4 g
Protein 59.2 g

469. Crispy Duck

Preparation Time: 15 minutes
Cooking Time: 4 hours 5 minutes
Servings: 6
Ingredients:

- ¾ cup honey
- ¾ cup soy sauce
- ¾ cup red wine
- 1 teaspoon paprika
- 1½ tablespoons garlic salt
- Ground black pepper, as required
- 1 (5-pound) whole duck, giblets removed and trimmed

Directions:

1. Preheat the Pit boss grill & Smoker on grill setting to 225-250 degrees F.
2. In a bowl, add all ingredients except for duck and mix until well combined.
3. With a fork, poke holes in the skin of the duck.
4. Coat the duck with honey mixture generously.
5. Arrange duck in Pit boss gill, breast side down and cook for about 4 hours, coating with honey mixture one after 2 hours.
6. Remove the duck from grill and place onto a cutting board for about 15 minutes before carving.
7. With a sharp knife, cut the duck into desired-sized pieces and serve.

Nutrition:

Calories 878
Total Fat 52.1 g
Saturated Fat 13.9 g
Cholesterol 3341 mg
Sodium 2300 mg
Total Carbs 45.4 g
Fiber 0.7 g
Sugar 39.6 g
Protein 51 g

470. Jerked Up Tilapia

Preparation Time: 20 minutes
Cooking Time: 45 minutes
Servings: 8
Ingredients:

- 5 cloves of garlic
- 1 small sized onion
- 3 Jalapeno Chiles
- 3 teaspoon of ground ginger
- 3 tablespoons of light brown sugar
- 3 teaspoons of dried thyme
- 2 teaspoons of salt
- 2 teaspoons of ground cinnamon
- 1 teaspoon of black pepper
- 1 teaspoon of ground allspice
- ¼ teaspoon of cayenne pepper
- 4 -6 ounce of tilapia fillets
- ¼ cup of olive oil
- 1 cup of sliced up carrots.
- 1 bunch of whole green onions
- 2 tablespoons of whole allspice

Directions:

1. Take a blending bowl and combine the first 11 of the listed ingredients and puree them nicely using your blender or food processor.
2. Add the fish pieces in a large-sized zip bag and toss in the pureed mixture alongside olive oil.
3. Seal it up and press to make sure that the fish is coated well.
4. Let it marinate in your fridge for at least 30 minutes to 1 hour.
5. Take your drip pan and add water, cover with aluminum foil. Pre-heat your smoker to 225 degrees F
6. Use water fill water pan halfway through and place it over drip pan. Add wood chips to the side tray.
7. Take a medium-sized bowl and toss in some pecan wood chips and soak them underwater alongside whole allspice.
8. Prepare an excellent 9x 13-inch foil pan by poking a dozen holes and spraying it with non-stick cooking spray.
9. Spread out the carrots, green onions across the bottom of the pan.
10. Arrange the fishes on top of them.
11. Place the container in your smoker.

12. Smoke for about 45 minutes making sure to add more chips after every 15 minutes until the internal temperature of the fish rises to 145 degrees Fahrenheit.
13. Serve hot.

Nutrition:
- Calories: 347
- Fats: 19g
- Carbs: 18g
- Fiber: 1g

471. Premium Salmon Nuggets

Preparation Time: 20 minutes +marinate time.
Cooking Time: 1-2 hours
Servings: 8
Ingredients:
- 3 cups of packed brown sugar
- 1 cup of salt
- 1 tablespoon of onion, minced.
- 2 teaspoons of chipotle seasoning
- 2 teaspoons of fresh ground black pepper
- 1 garlic clove, minced.
- 1-2 pound of salmon fillets cut up into bite-sized portions.

Directions:
1. Take a large-sized bowl and stir in brown sugar, salt, chipotle seasoning, onion, garlic, and pepper.
2. Transfer salmon to a large shallow marinating dish
3. Pour dry marinade over fish and cover, refrigerate overnight.
4. Take your drip pan and add water, cover with aluminum foil. Pre-heat your smoker to 180 degrees F
5. Use water fill water pan halfway through and place it over drip pan. Add wood chips to the side tray.
6. Rinse the salmon chunks thoroughly and remove salt.
7. Transfer them to grill rack and smoke for 1-2 hours.
8. Remove the heat and enjoy it!

Nutrition:
- Calories: 120
- Fats: 18g
- Carbs: 3g
- Fiber: 2g

472. Creative Sablefish

Preparation Time: 15 minutes
Cooking Time: 3 hours
Servings: 8
Ingredients:
- 2-3 pounds of sablefish fillets
- 1 cup of kosher salts
- ¼ cup of sugar
- 2 tablespoon of garlic powder

- Honey for glazing
- Sweet paprika for dusting

Directions:
1. Take a bowl and mix salt, garlic powder, and sugar.
2. Pour on a healthy layer of your mix into a lidded plastic tub, large enough to hold the fish.
3. Cut up the fillet into pieces.
4. Gently massage the salt mix into your fish meat and place them with the skin side down on to the salt mix in the plastic tub.
5. Cover up the container and keep it in your fridge for as many hours as the fish weighs.
6. Remove the sablefish from the tub and place it under cold water for a while.
7. Pat, it dries using a kitchen towel and puts it back to the fridge, keep it uncovered overnight.
8. Take your drip pan and add water, cover with aluminum foil. Pre-heat your smoker to 225 degrees F
9. Use water fill water pan halfway through and place it over drip pan. Add wood chips to the side tray.
10. Smoke for 2-3 hours
11. After the first hour of smoking, make sure to baste the fish with honey and keep repeating this after every hour.
12. One done, move the fish to a cooling rack and baste it with honey one last time.
13. Let it cool for about an hour.
14. Use tweezers to pull out the bone pins.
15. Dust the top with some paprika and wait for 30 minutes to let the paprika sink in
16. Put the fish in your fridge.
17. Serve hot or chilled!

Nutrition:
- Calories: 171
- Fats: 10g
- Carbs: 13g
- Fiber: 1g

473. Halibut Delight

Preparation Time: 4-6 hours
Cooking Time: 15 minutes
Servings: 4-6
Ingredients:
- ½ a cup of salt
- ½ a cup of brown sugar
- 1 teaspoon of smoked paprika
- 1 teaspoon of ground cumin
- 2 pounds of halibut
- 1/3 cup of mayonnaise

Directions:
1. Take a small bowl and add salt, brown sugar, cumin, and paprika.
2. Coat the halibut well and cover, refrigerate for 4-6 hours.

3. Take your drip pan and add water, cover with aluminum foil. Pre-heat your smoker to 200 degrees F
4. Use water fill water pan halfway through and place it over drip pan. Add wood chips to the side tray.
5. Remove the fish from refrigerator and rinse it well, pat it dry.
6. Rub the mayonnaise on the fish.
7. Transfer the halibut to smoker and smoke for 2 hours until the internal temperature reaches 120 degrees Fahrenheit.

Nutrition:
Calories: 375
Fats: 21g
Carbs: 10g
Fiber: 2g

474. Roast Rack of Lamb

Preparation Time: 10 minutes
Cooking Time: 1 hour
Servings: 6-8
Ingredients:
- Pit boss Flavor: Alder
- 1 (2-pound) rack of lamb
- 1 batch Rosemary-Garlic Lamb Seasoning

Directions:
1. Supply your smoker with Traeger's and follow the manufacturer's specific start-up procedure. Preheat the grill to 450°F.
2. Using a boning knife, score the bottom fat portion of the rib meat.
3. Using your hands, rub the rack of lamb with the lamb seasoning, making sure it penetrates the scored fat.
4. Place the rack directly on the grill grate and smoke until its internal temperature reaches 145F.
5. Take off the rack from the grill and let it rest for 20 to 30 minutes, before slicing into individual ribs to serve.

Nutrition:
- Calories: 50
- Carbs: 4g
- Fiber: 2g
- Fat: 2.5g
- Protein: 2g

475. Ultimate Lamb Burgers

Preparation Time: 20 minutes
Cooking Time: 30 minutes
Servings: 4
Ingredients:
Traeger's: Apple
Burger:
- 2 lbs. ground lamb
- 1 jalapeño
- 6 scallions, diced.
- 2 tablespoons mint

- 2 tablespoons dill, minced.
- 3 cloves garlic, minced.
- Salt and pepper
- 4 brioche buns
- 4 slices mancheron cheese

Sauce:
- 1 cup mayonnaise
- 2 teaspoons lemon juice
- 2 cloves garlic
- 1 bell pepper, diced.
- salt and pepper

Directions
1. When ready to cook, turn your smoker to 400F and preheat.
2. Add the mint, scallions, salt, garlic, dill, jalapeño, lamb, and pepper to the mixing bowl.
3. Form the lamb mixture into eight patties.
4. Lay the pepper on the grill and cook for 20 minutes.
5. Take the pepper from the grill and place it in a bag, and seal. After ten minutes, remove pepper from the bag, remove seeds and peel the skin.
6. Add the garlic, lemon juice, mayo, roasted red pepper, salt, and pepper and process until smooth. Serve alongside the burger.
7. Lay the lamb burgers on the grill, and cook for five minutes per side, then place in the buns with a slice of cheese and serve with the homemade sauce.

Nutrition:
- Calories: 50
- Carbs: 4g
- Fiber: 2g
- Fat: 2.5g
- Protein: 2g

476. Citrus- Smoked Trout

Preparation Time: 10 minutes
Cooking Time: 1 to 2 hours
Servings: 6 to 8
Ingredients:
- 6 to 8 skin-on rainbow trout cleaned and scaled.
- 1-gallon orange juice
- ½ cup packed light brown sugar.
- ¼ cup salt
- 1 tablespoon freshly ground black pepper.
- Nonstick spray, oil, or butter, for greasing
- 1 tablespoon chopped fresh parsley.
- 1 lemon, sliced.

Directions:
1. Fillet the fish and pat dry with paper towels.
2. Pour the orange juice into a large container with a lid and stir in the brown sugar, salt, and pepper.

3. Place the trout in the brine, cover, and refrigerate for 1 hour.
4. Cover the grill grate with heavy-duty aluminum foil. Poke holes in the foil and spray with cooking spray
5. Supply your smoker with Traeger's and follow the manufacturer's specific start-up procedure. Preheat, with the lid closed to 225°F.
6. Remove the trout from the brine and pat dry. Arrange the fish on the foil-covered grill grate, close the lid, and smoke for 1 hour 30 minutes to 2 hours, or until flaky.
7. Remove the fish from the heat. Serve garnished with the fresh parsley and lemon slices.

Nutrition:
- Calories: 220,
- Protein: 33 g
- Fat: 4 g,
- Carbohydrates: 17 g,

477. Sunday Supper Salmon with Olive Tapenade

Preparation Time: 1 hour and 20 minutes
Cooking Time: 1 to 2 hours
Servings: 10 to 12
Ingredients:
- 2 cups packed light brown sugar.
- ½ cup salt
- ¼ cup maple syrup
- ⅓ cup crab boil seasoning
- 1 (3- to 5-pound) whole salmon fillet, skin removed.
- ¼ cup extra-virgin olive oil
- 1 (15-ounce) can pitted green olives, drained.
- 1 (15-ounce) can pitted black olives, drained.
- 3 tablespoons jarred sun-dried tomatoes, drained.
- 3 tablespoons chopped fresh basil.
- 1 tablespoon dried oregano
- 2 tablespoons freshly squeezed lemon juice
- 2 tablespoons jarred capers, drained
- 2 tablespoons chopped fresh parsley, plus more for sprinkling.

Directions:
1. In a medium bowl, combine the brown sugar, salt, maple syrup, and crab boil seasoning.
2. Rub the paste all over the salmon and place the fish in a shallow dish. Cover and marinate in the refrigerator for at least 8 hours or overnight.
3. Remove the salmon from dish, rinse, and pat dry, and let stand for 1 hour to take off the chill.
4. Meanwhile, in a food processor, pulse the olive oil, green olives, black olives, sun-dried tomatoes, basil, oregano, lemon juice, capers,

and parsley to a chunky consistency. Refrigerate the tapenade until ready to serve.
5. Supply your smoker with Traeger's and follow the manufacturer's specific start-up procedure. Preheat, with the lid closed to 250°F.
6. Place the salmon on the grill grate (or on a cedar plank on the grill grate), close the lid, and smoke for 1 to 2 hours, or until the internal temperature reaches 140°F to 145°F. When the fish flakes easily with a fork, it has done.
7. Remove the salmon from the heat and sprinkle with parsley. Serve with the olive tapenade.

Nutrition:
- Calories: 240.
- Proteins: 23g.
- Carbs: 3g.
- Fat: 16g

478. Grilled Tuna

Preparation Time: 20 minutes
Cooking Time: 4 hours
Servings: 6
Ingredients:
- Albacore tuna fillets – 6, each about 8 ounces
- Salt – 1 cup
- Brown sugar – 1 cup
- Orange zested – 1.
- Lemon zested – 1.

Directions:
1. Before preheating the grill, brine the tuna, and for this, prepare brine stirring together all its ingredients until mixed.
2. Take a large container, layer tuna fillets in it, covering each fillet with it, and then let them sit in the refrigerator for 6 hours.
3. Then remove tuna fillets from the brine, rinse well, pat dry and cool in the refrigerator for 30 minutes.
4. When the grill has preheated, place tuna fillets on the grilling rack and let smoke for 3 hours, turning halfway.
5. Check the fire after one hour of smoking and add more wood pallets if required.
6. Then switch temperature of the grill to 225 degrees F and continue grilling for another 1 hour until tuna has turned nicely golden and fork tender.
7. Serve immediately.

Nutrition:
- Calories: 311.
- Fiber: 3 g.
- Saturated Fat: 1.2 g.
- Protein: 45 g.
- Carbs: 11 g.
- Total Fat: 8.8 g.
- Sugar: 1.3 g

479. Grilled Swordfish

Preparation Time: 10 minutes
Cooking Time: 18 minutes
Servings: 4
Ingredients:

- Swordfish fillets – 4
- Salt – 1 tablespoon
- Ground black pepper – ¾ tablespoon
- Olive oil – 2 tablespoons
- Ears of corn – 4
- Cherry tomatoes – 1 pint
- Cilantro chopped – 1/3 cup.
- Medium red onion, peeled, diced – 1.
- Serrano pepper minced – 1.
- Lime juiced – 1.
- Salt – ½ teaspoon
- Ground black pepper – ¼ teaspoon

Directions:

1. In the meantime, prepare fillets and for this, brush them with oil and then season with salt and black pepper.
2. Prepare the corn, and for this, brush with olive oil and season with ¼ teaspoon each of salt and black pepper.
3. When the grill has preheated, place fillets on the grilling rack along with corns and grill corn for 15 minutes until light brown and fillets for 18 minutes until fork tender.
4. When corn has grilled, cut kernels from it, place them into a medium bowl, add remaining ingredients for the salsa and stir until mixed.
5. When fillets have grilled, divide them evenly among plates, top with corn salsa and then serve.

Nutrition:

- Calories: 311.
- Total Fat: 8.8 g.
- Saturated Fat: 1.2 g.
- Fiber: 3 g.
- Protein: 45 g.
- Sugar: 1.3 g
- Carbs: 11 g.

480. Lamb Kebabs

Preparation Time: 15 minutes
Cooking Time: 10 minutes
Servings: 4
Ingredients:
Traeger's: Mesquite

- 1/2 tablespoon salt
- 2 tablespoons fresh mint
- 3 lbs. leg of lamb
- 1/2 cup lemon juice
- 1 tablespoon lemon zest
- 15 apricots, pitted.
- 1/2 tablespoon cilantro
- 2 teaspoons black pepper
- 1/2 cup olive oil
- 1 teaspoon cumin
- 2 red onion

Directions:

1. Combine the olive oil, pepper, lemon juice, mint, salt, lemon zest, cumin, and cilantro. Add lamb leg, then place in the refrigerator overnight.
2. Remove the lamb from the marinade, cube them, and then thread onto the skewer with the apricots and onions.
3. When ready to cook, turn your smoker to 400F and preheat.
4. Lay the skewers on the grill and cook for ten minutes.
5. Remove from the grill and serve.

Nutrition:

- Calories: 50
- Carbs: 4g
- Fiber: 2g
- Fat: 2.5g
- Protein: 2g

Chapter 16. Sauces and Rubs

481. Heavenly Rabbit Smoke

Preparation Time: 10 minutes
Cooking Time: Nil
Servings: 5
Ingredients

- 1 teaspoon dried thyme
- 1 teaspoon dried parsley
- 2 teaspoons dried oregano
- ½ teaspoon dried marjoram
- ½ teaspoon ground nutmeg
- ½ teaspoon ground cinnamon
- 1 teaspoon chicken bouillon granules
- 1 and ½ teaspoons garlic powder
- 1 teaspoon cracked pepper
- ½ teaspoon salt
- 1 and ½ teaspoon onion powder

Directions:

1. Mix the ingredients mentioned above to prepare the seasoning and use it as needed.
   Nutrition:
   Calories: 20
   Carbs: 5g
   Protein: 1g

482. Uncle Johnny's Rub

Preparation Time: 10 minutes
Cooking Time: Nil
Servings: 4
Ingredients

- ½ teaspoon oregano
- 4 tablespoons ground paprika
- 1 tablespoon brown sugar
- 1 tablespoon ground cumin
- 1 tablespoon chili powder
- 1 tablespoon mustard powder
- 1 tablespoon salt
- 2 tablespoons pepper
- 1 tablespoon garlic powder

Directions:

1. Mix the ingredients mentioned above to prepare the seasoning and use it as needed.
   Nutrition:
   Calories: 20
   Carbs: 5g
   Protein: 1g

483. Fajita Seasoning

Preparation Time: 10 minutes
Cooking Time: Nil
Servings: 4
Ingredients

- ¼ cup of chili powder
- 2 tablespoon of ground cumin
- 1 tablespoon of salt
- 4 teaspoons of black pepper
- 3 teaspoons of dried oregano
- 2 teaspoons of paprika
- 1 teaspoon of onion powder
- 1 teaspoon of parsley

Directions:

1. Mix the ingredients mentioned above to prepare the seasoning and use it as needed.
   Nutrition:
   Calories: 20
   Carbs: 5g
   Protein: 1g

484. Herbed Mixed Salt

Preparation Time: 10 minutes
Cooking Time: Nil
Servings: 4
Ingredients

- ½ cup coarse salt
- ¼ cup packed fresh rosemary leaves.
- ¼ cup packed fresh lemon thyme.
- 1 cup of salt

Directions:

1. Mix the ingredients mentioned above.
2. Let it sit and Air Dry for 2 hours
3. Use as needed.
   Nutrition:
   Calories: 20
   Carbs: 5g
   Protein: 1g

485. Classic BBQ Rub

Preparation Time: 10 minutes
Cooking Time: Nil
Servings: 4
Ingredients

- 1 teaspoon salt
- 1/8 teaspoon ground cumin
- ¾ teaspoon ground white pepper
- ¾ teaspoon ground black pepper
- ¾ teaspoon dried thyme
- ¾ teaspoon ground savory
- ¾ teaspoon ground coriander seeds
- 1 teaspoon ground bay leaves
- 1 and ½ teaspoon dried basil
- 2 teaspoons garlic powder

Directions:

1. Mix the ingredients mentioned above to prepare the seasoning and use it as needed.
   Nutrition:
   Calories: 20
   Carbs: 5g
   Protein: 1g

486. Garlic and Rosemary Meat Rub

Preparation Time: 10 minutes
Cooking Time: Nil
Servings: 4
Ingredients

- 1 tablespoon pepper
- 1 tablespoon salt
- 3 tablespoons fresh rosemary, chopped.
- 1 tablespoon dried rosemary
- 8 garlic cloves, diced.
- ½ cup olive oil

Directions:

1. Mix the ingredients mentioned above to prepare the seasoning and use it as needed.

Nutrition:
Calories: 20
Carbs: 5g
Protein: 1g

487. A Viking Mix

Preparation Time: 10 minutes
Cooking Time: Nil
Servings: 4
Ingredients

- 5 teaspoons paprika
- 2 teaspoons salt
- 2 teaspoons onion powder
- 1 teaspoon cayenne
- 2 teaspoons ground pepper
- 1 teaspoon dry mustard

Directions:

1. Mix the ingredients mentioned above to prepare the seasoning and use it as needed.

Nutrition:
Calories: 20
Carbs: 5g
Protein: 1g

488. Fancy Taco Seasoning

Preparation Time: 10 minutes
Cooking Time: Nil
Servings: 4
Ingredients

- 1 tablespoon of Chili powder
- ½ a teaspoon of Garlic powder
- ½ a teaspoon of Onion powder
- 1 and a ½ teaspoon of ground cumin
- 1 teaspoon of salt
- 1 teaspoon of pepper
- ¼ teaspoon of crushed red pepper flakes
- ¼ teaspoon of dried oregano
- ½ a teaspoon of paprika

Directions:

1. Mix the ingredients mentioned above to prepare the Taco seasoning and use it as needed.

Nutrition:
Calories: 10
Carbs: 7g
Protein: 2g

489. Special BBQ Sauce

Preparation Time: 10 minutes
Cooking Time: Nil
Servings: 4
Ingredients

- ½ a cup of apple cider vinegar
- 2 tablespoons of water
- 2 tablespoon of coconut aminos
- ¼ teaspoon of mustard seeds
- ¼ teaspoon of onion powder
- ¼ teaspoon of garlic powder
- 1/8 teaspoon of cinnamon
- 1/8 teaspoon of black pepper

Directions:

1. Add all the listed ingredients to your saucepan.
2. Bring it to a boil and stir well.
3. Simmer for a few minutes
4. Remove the heat and allow it to cool.
5. Use as needed!

Nutrition:
Calories: 10
Carbs: 7g
Protein: 2g

490. Classic Home-Made Worcestershire Sauce

Preparation Time: 10 minutes
Cooking Time: 15 minutes
Servings: 4
Ingredients

- ½ a cup of apple cider vinegar
- 2 tablespoons of water
- 2 tablespoon of coconut aminos
- ¼ teaspoon of mustard seeds
- ¼ teaspoon of onion powder
- ¼ teaspoon of garlic powder
- 1/8 teaspoon of cinnamon
- 1/8 teaspoon of black pepper

Directions:

1. Add all the listed ingredients to your saucepan.
2. Bring it to a boil and stir well.
3. Simmer for a few minutes
4. Remove the heat and allow it to cool.
5. Use as needed!

Nutrition:
Calories: 10
Carbs: 7g
Protein: 2g

491. Original Ketchup

Preparation Time: 10 minutes
Cooking Time: 20 minutes
Servings: 4
Ingredients

- ½ a cup of chopped pitted dates.
- 1 can of 6-ounce tomato paste
- 1 can of 14-ounce diced tomatoes
- 2 tablespoon of coconut vinegar
- ½ a cup of bone broth
- 1 teaspoon of garlic powder
- 1 teaspoon of onion powder
- 1 teaspoon of salt
- ½ a teaspoon of cayenne pepper

Directions:

1. Add the ingredients to a small-sized saucepan.
2. Cook on medium-low for 20 minutes.
3. Remove the heat.
4. Take an immersion blender and blend the mixture until smooth.
5. Remove the mixer and simmer on low for 10 minutes.
6. Use as needed.

Nutrition:
Calories: 10
Carbs: 7g
Protein: 2g

492. Lovely Mayonnaise

Preparation Time: 10 minutes
Cooking Time: Nil
Servings: 4
Ingredients

- 1 whole egg
- ½ a teaspoon of sea salt
- ½ a teaspoon of ground mustard
- 1 and a ¼ cup of extra light olive oil
- 1 tablespoon of lemon juice

Directions:

1. Place the egg, ground mustard, salt and ¼ cup of olive oil into a food processor.
2. Whirl on low until mixed
3. While the processor is running, drizzle remaining olive oil and keep whirling for 3 minutes.
4. Add lemon juice and pulse on low until thoroughly mixed.
5. Chill for 30 minutes
6. Use as needed.

Nutrition:
Calories: 10
Carbs: 7g
Protein: 2g

493. Mouthwatering Sour Cream

Preparation Time: 10 minutes
Cooking Time: Nil
Servings: 4
Ingredients

- 1 can of thick unsweetened coconut milk
- 1 and a ½ tablespoon of lemon juice
- ½ a tablespoon of apple cider vinegar
- 1/8 teaspoon of salt

Directions:

1. Chill the coconut milk in the can overnight.
2. Flip the can upside and open, pour off the liquid.
3. Scrape out the thick cream and add lemon juice, salt, and vinegar.
4. Whisk until smooth.
5. Use it when needed!

Nutrition:
Calories: 10
Carbs: 7g
Protein: 2g

494. Regular Everyday Breadcrumbs

Preparation Time: 10 minutes
Cooking Time: Nil
Servings: 4
Ingredients

- 1 cup of almond flour/meal
- ½ a teaspoon of sea salt
- ½ a teaspoon of black pepper
- ½ a teaspoon of garlic powder
- ½ a teaspoon of dried parsley
- ¼ teaspoon of onion powder
- ¼ teaspoon of dried oregano

Directions:

1. Take a small-sized bowl and add all the listed ingredients and whisk them well.
2. Use as needed.

Nutrition:
Calories: 10
Carbs: 7g
Protein: 2g

495. Salted Raw Caramel Dip

Preparation Time: 5 minutes
Cooking Time: 0 minute
Servings: 2
Ingredients

- 1 cup soft Medjool date, pitted.
- 1 teaspoon vanilla extract
- ¼ cup almond milk
- 1 teaspoon fresh lemon juice
- 1 tablespoon coconut oil
- ¼ teaspoon salt

Directions:

1. Add all ingredients in your blender.
2. Pulse until you get a smooth mixture.

3. Serve chilled and enjoy!
   Nutrition:
   Calories: 10
   Carbs: 5g
   Protein: 2g

496. Hot Sauce with Cilantro

Preparation Time: 10 Minutes
Cooking Time: 30 Minutes
Servings: 4
Ingredients:
- ½ tsp coriander
- ½ tsp cumin seeds
- ¼ tsp black pepper
- 2 green cardamom pods
- 2 garlic cloves
- 1 tsp salt
- 1 oz. parsley
- 2 tablespoons olive oil

Directions:
1. In a blender place all ingredients and blend until smooth
2. Pour smoothie in a glass and serve.

Nutrition:
Calories: 60
Carbs: 13g
Fat: 1g
Protein: 0g

497. Pit boss Chimichurri Sauce

Preparation Time: 10 Minutes
Cooking Time: 30 Minutes
Servings: 4
Ingredients:
- 1 cup parsley
- 2 garlic cloves
- 1 tablespoon oregano leaves
- ¼ cup olive oil
- ¼ cup red wine vinegar
- ½ tsp red pepper flakes

Directions:
1. In a blender place all ingredients and blend until smooth
2. Pour smoothie in a glass and serve.

Nutrition:
Calories: 60
Carbs: 13g
Fat: 1g
Protein: 0g

498. Basil Pesto Sauce

Preparation Time: 10 Minutes
Cooking Time: 30 Minutes
Servings: 4
Ingredients:
- 2 cloves garlic
- 2 oz. basil leaves
- 1 tablespoon pine nuts

- 1 oz. parmesan cheese
- ½ cup olive oil

Directions:
1. In a blender place all ingredients and blend until smooth
2. Pour smoothie in a glass and serve.

Nutrition:
Calories: 60
Carbs: 13g
Fat: 1g
Protein: 0g

499. Vegan Pesto

Preparation Time: 10 Minutes
Cooking Time: 30 Minutes
Servings: 4
Ingredients:
- 1 cup cilantro leaves
- 1 cup basil leaves
- 1 cup parsley leaves
- ½ cup mint leaves
- ½ cup walnuts
- 1 tsp miso
- 1 tsp lemon juice
- ¼ cup olive oil

Directions:
1. In a blender place all ingredients and blend until smooth
2. Pour smoothie in a glass and serve.

Nutrition:
Calories: 60
Carbs: 13g
Fat: 1g
Protein: 0g

500. Fennel and Almonds Sauce

Preparation Time: 10 Minutes
Cooking Time: 30 Minutes
Servings: 4
Ingredients:
- 1 cup fennel bulb
- 1 cup olive oil
- 1 cup almonds
- 1 cup fennel fronds

Directions:
1. In a blender place all ingredients and blend until smooth
2. Pour smoothie in a glass and serve.

Nutrition:
Calories: 60
Carbs: 13g
Fat: 1g
Protein: 0g

501. Honey Dipping Sauce

Preparation Time: 10 Minutes
Cooking Time: 30 Minutes
Servings: 4
Ingredients:
- 5 tablespoons unsalted butter
- 8 tablespoons kimchi paste
- 2 tablespoons honey
- 1 tsp sesame seeds

Directions:
1. In a blender place all ingredients and blend until smooth
2. Pour smoothie in a glass and serve.

Nutrition:
Calories: 60
Carbs: 13g
Fat: 1g
Protein: 0g

502. Ginger Dipping Sauce

Preparation Time: 10 Minutes
Cooking Time: 30 Minutes
Servings: 4
Ingredients:
- 6 tablespoons ponzu sauce
- 2 tablespoons scallions
- 2 tsp ginger
- 2 tsp mirin
- 1 tsp sesame oil
- ¼ tsp salt

Directions:
1. In a blender place all ingredients and blend until smooth
2. Pour smoothie in a glass and serve.

Nutrition:
Calories: 60
Carbs: 13g
Fat: 1g
Protein: 0g

Conclusion

To summarize, the Pit boss pellet grill has made grilling simpler and safer for humanity, and grilling, which is part of "dietetic" cooking, has been made easier by the Pit boss grill. Providing us with the delicious meal we have been missing and thereby enhancing our quality of life. This book contains a variety of recipes that you can cook at home using your new Pit boss Pellet grill. The tenderness and tasty BBQ in the recipes can provide a lot of satisfaction.

The Pit boss barbecues are electric, and they are regulated by a standard 3-position mechanism. A cylindrical unit, like a pellet stove, transports pellets from the storage to the fireplace. The Pit boss Grill smoker ensures that your meat and other recipes work out perfectly. This smoker creates a wonderful atmosphere for your food. To achieve such a genuine flavor, high-quality materials and precise smoking are needed. It is best if you can reach the highest degree of smoking accuracy possible so that your meat and other recipes work out perfectly. Furthermore, if you want to add more spice to your recipes, use the best wood pellet for cooking.

Many people ask me why I choose Pit boss pellet grills, and you would think, well, the answer is easy and straightforward, and yes! It is right in front of us. What is the explanation for this?

It cooks over a wood fire, resulting in exceptional flavor because nothing compares real wood, real smoking, and natural aroma. The cooking method has evolved significantly. Expert chefs are known for experimenting with different flavors and ingredients to produce a delectable and tasty dish.

Grilling is one of the most common cooking methods for achieving a perfect flavor in your dishes. Grilling is a better cooking method than others because it benefits the food, retains flavor, and preserves nutrients. A Pit boss grill smoker's wood pellet grill, on the other hand, helps you to grill your food easily and with less effort and smoke. The benefit of having a Pit boss grill smoker in your home is that it is flexible, helps you cook food faster, offers a temperature control scale, and is one of the most critical aspects of cooking.

It is a flexible grill. In fact, the Pit boss grill smoker can be used to grill, smoke, bake, roast, and stew everything you can think of. This Pit boss grill smoker is a powerful tool that offers excellent service.

As we can all attest, Pit boss has made using the pellet grill simple: its intuitive control panel has a power button and a knob that allows you to easily change the temperature.

Finally, we should add that we can always find new flavors in our dishes through grilling: you can smoke your dishes with Pit boss pellets, giving them a constantly new and different taste. The Pit boss Grill smoker is the answer to your taste buds' prayers. Do not waste any more time; get your own smoker and begin cooking your favorite recipes with this book.

CPSIA information can be obtained
at www.ICGtesting.com
Printed in the USA
BVHW051005180621
609824BV00007B/1540